THE
BIG
BASICS
BOOK OF

EXCEL FOR
WINDOWS® 95

by Elaine Marmel, Lisa Bucki,
and Ed Guilford

A Division of Macmillan Computer Publishing
201 West 103rd Street, Indianapolis, Indiana 46290 USA

International Standard Book Number: 0-7897-0459-5
Library of Congress Catalog Card Number: 95-72555

97 96 95   8 7 6 5 4 3 2 1

Interpretation of the printing code: the rightmost number of the first series of numbers is the year of the book's printing; the rightmost number of the second series of numbers is the number of the book's printing. For example, a printing code of 95-1 shows that the first printing of the book occurred in 1995.

Screen reproductions in this book were created by means of the program Collage Complete from Inner Media, Inc., Hollis, NH.

Printed in the United States of America

President
Roland Elgey

Vice President and Publisher
Marie Butler-Knight

Editorial Services Director
Elizabeth Keaffaber

Publishing Manager
Barry Pruett

Managing Editor
Michael Cunningham

Development Editor
Melanie Palaisa

Production Editor
Mark Enochs

Copy Editor
Rebecca Mayfield

Cover Designer
Jay Corpus

Book Designer
Barbara Kordesh

Indexer
Mary Jane Frisby

Production Team
Brian Buschkill
Anne Dickerson
Bryan Flores
Jason Hand
Bob LaRoche
Bobbi Satterfield
Craig Small
Mike Thomas
Scott Tullis
Kelly Warner
Todd Wente
Jody York

➤ *Special thanks to C. Herbert Feltner for ensuring the technical accuracy of this book.*

Contents

Part 1 How To...

Manage Workbooks and Worksheets   81

Format Worksheets   99

Print Worksheets   125

"Do" Math   147

Part 2   Do-It-Yourself

Part 3   Quick Fixes

Part 4   Handy References

Introduction

Computers supposedly make your life easier, and Windows 95 in particular presumes to make using a computer easier. Make the computer easy to use! Windows 95's developers also designed their operating system to let your computer work faster.

With this end in mind, Microsoft released its suite of Office products, including Excel for Windows 95. You also can purchase Excel for Windows 95 as a stand-alone product. Excel for Windows 95 was specifically designed to work in the Windows 95 environment, so it works faster than previous versions of Excel. It also contains some enhancements you don't find in earlier versions of Excel.

Why This Book?

When you do start using your computer, you may wish you had a book that just shows you what to do, a visual book like those hardware store books that show you how to build a deck or landscape your house. Well, here's the book for you. *The Big Basics Book of Excel for Windows 95* provides Guided Tours that show you which keys to press and which commands to select. By following the step-by-step, picture-by-picture presentation, you learn all the basics you need to run Excel for Windows 95.

Where's the Information I Need?

How you use this book is pretty much up to you. You can read the book from cover to cover to move through the tasks in a logical progression, or you may prefer to use the book as a reference, jumping around and using the table of contents and the index to quickly find specific information. Running heads at the top of each page show you which chapter you're in and which task you're on. You can simply flip through the book to quickly scan for a topic.

We've divided this book into four distinct parts, so you can jump to the specific information you need:

Part 1: How To... covers all the skills that a new or casual Excel for Windows 95 user needs. You master the basics of how to operate in the Windows 95 environment, install Excel, and start and exit the program. You learn how to navigate in an Excel workbook, edit and format worksheets, manage your workbooks and worksheets, perform mathematical functions, print worksheets, and use Excel to create databases, charts, and maps. Each task in this section leads you step-by-step through the basics. To find out more about each task, read the accompanying explanation.

Part 2: Do It Yourself shows you how to apply the skills you learned in Part 1 to create real projects. You'll learn how to use Excel to track personal information, manage your finances, and use spreadsheet information with other applications.

Part 3: Quick Fixes provides quick answers to your questions and quick solutions to your problems. When an error message pops up in Excel for Windows 95, you can stare the problem down and get up and running in a snap. A Quick Finder table helps you zero in on the solution that's right for you.

Part 4: Handy Reference is a handy collection of reference information: parts of the Excel screen, keyboard and mouse shortcuts, and examples of common functions you can use in Excel.

Conventions, Conventions, Conventions

This book is designed to be easy to use. Each task has a title that shows you what you're doing. Immediately following the title is background or additional explanatory information to help you understand the feature as well as a Guided Tour that shows you step-by-step how to perform the task. The figure below each step tells you how the Guided Tour works.

The following special conventions make this book even easier to use:

Text you are instructed to type appears bold. For example, if the step says, type **Sales** and press **Enter**, you type the word "Sales" and press the Enter key on your keyboard.

Keys you press are bold, too, to make them easier to spot.

The key+key combinations you use when you have to press two or more keys to enter a command are bold as well. When you encounter one of these combinations, hold down the first key while typing the second key.

Menu names and commands are also bold. When you're told to open a menu and select a command, move the mouse pointer over it, and press and release the left mouse button.

Look for these notes for tips, hints, and shortcuts.

Running heads help you find what you want to learn.

Additional information answers all your questions.

Tips provide shortcuts or reference other useful information.

The Guided Tour shows you how to complete a computer task step-by-step.

Trademarks

Terms suspected of being trademarks or service marks have been appropriately capitalized. Que Corporation cannot attest to the accuracy of this information. Use of a term in this book should not be regarded as affecting the validity of any trademark or service mark.

PART 1
How To...

The headings in Part 1 will make more sense to you if you precede them with the words "how to" as you read. There's a reason for that—this part of the book teaches you how to use the most common Excel features. You learn such things as "how to" use the mouse; install Excel; use Excel's menus, dialog boxes, and toolbars; and get help. You learn to navigate in a workbook—Excel's name for a document— so you can create, edit, print, save, close, and open workbooks.

You also learn to apply formatting, such as shading, borders, colors, and font styles, to a worksheet. Then, you learn to use Excel to perform mathematical operations, manage lists of information with databases, and even create charts and maps. Last, you learn about some of the common housekeeping tasks you can perform in Excel.

What You Will Find in This Part

HOW TO...

Master the Basics

Before you can begin using Excel, you need to cover some introductory ground. To break the ice, I'll introduce you to Windows 95 and teach you a few basic Windows skills. Excel is easier to use if you know how to use a mouse, so we'll cover some mouse techniques.

We'll show you how to install Excel, and start it up. While we're in Excel, we cover how to get help—knowledge you'll use frequently as you use Excel more and more. Finally, we'll show you how to exit Excel.

What You Will Find in This Section

Understand the Windows 95 Screen

The Windows 95 screen is quite different from the Windows 3.x screen with which you may be familiar. It's quite a bit less cluttered.

This book is not going to cover the technical background of Windows 95—there are lots of books and articles available on that subject. This book provides you with an introduction to Windows 95, answers some questions, and shows you some basic operations.

What is Windows 95? Windows 95 is Microsoft's new operating system. Basically, operating systems are programs that act as traffic cops and control what goes on in your PC while you work. Operating systems perform basic functions like accepting keystrokes, redrawing your screen, and retrieving and storing data. Just like traffic cops, operating systems make sure that all the components on your PC—including software, like your word processor and Excel, and hardware, such as your hard drive and CD-ROM drive—all work together in a cooperative fashion. In all probability, your previous operating system was DOS (or, possibly, OS/2 or UNIX). Whichever operating system you used before Windows 95, the basic purpose of all operating systems is to serve as a traffic cop.

> Windows 3.x is not really an operating system; it is more like an operating environment. While Windows 3.x handles some traffic cop functions, it still requires DOS to perform basic functions such as starting the computer.

What makes Windows 95 different? Well, that's a question that could fill a book—in fact, it fills several books! Basically, think of it this way: Windows 95 handles applications that run faster than those to which you are accustomed. Why? Because Windows 95 is a 32-bit operating system, and DOS is a 16-bit operating system. DOS's developers designed the operating system to run on 8086 machines (the old PC XT and 286 processors) which were 16-bit microprocessors. Starting with the 386 machines, computers had the capability to run applications in 32-bit protected mode, which is a much more efficient (and faster) way for a computer to use memory. Unfortunately, although computers could run applications operating in 32-bit protected mode, the operating system—DOS—couldn't. Windows 95 can.

If you've ever used a Mac, you will be very much at home with what you see on the opening screen, or the Desktop, of Windows 95. On the Desktop, you see *icons*. Icons are images (just like you thought); on computers, icons represent programs, documents, or commands. On the Desktop, the icons represent programs. The actual icons that appear on the Desktop depend on the installation options you choose when you install Windows 95 and the shortcuts you create for your favorite programs.

When you open a document, Windows 95 opens the program in which you created the document. Windows 95 also borrows the *folder* analogy from the Mac. For long-time DOS and Windows 3.x users, folders are the equivalent of directories. Folders contain *documents*, which is the generic term for files you create, regardless of whether you created the documents on a word processor or a spreadsheet. Folders also contain *objects* such as programs and program files.

Begin Guided Tour   Use Windows 95's Opening Screen

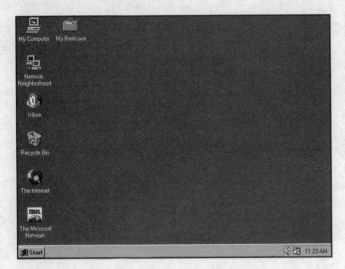

1 Because Windows 95 is an operating system, it starts immediately when you turn on your computer. The opening screen of Windows 95 is called the Desktop.

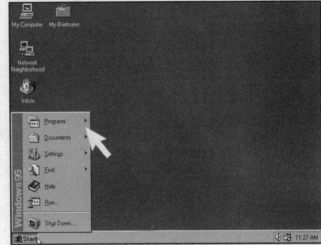

3 When you click the Start button, Windows 95 displays the Start menu. Notice both the Documents folder and the Programs folder on this menu.

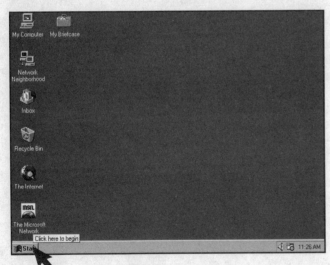

2 When you position the mouse pointer over the Start button, you see a message that says "Click here to begin."

4 If you highlight an option on the Start menu that has a right-pointing caret next to it, Windows 95 opens the folder to display a menu.

If you upgrade your existing version of Windows 3.x when you install Windows 95, you see something different here: the Program menu shows folders for each of your Windows 3.x program groups, listed in alphabetical order.

(continues)

Guided Tour   Use Windows 95's Opening Screen

(continued)

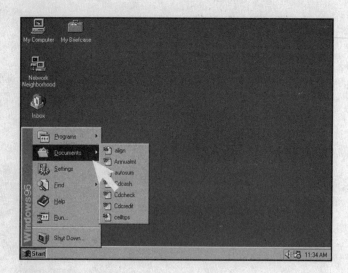

You can reorganize the entries on the Program menu. This is especially helpful if you have lots of Windows 3.x program groups. Try reorganizing by subject.

5 You can work the way you worked in Windows 3.x. Start the program and then open the document from inside the program. Or, use the Documents menu to reopen a document you recently opened. Windows 95 starts the program and opens the document.

Rule the Rodent (or "Master the Mouse")

I learned a new "clinical" term recently while reading a Windows 95 book—*rodentophobia*. The book defines it as "fear of using the mouse." I like the expression; I think it describes the problem well.

Often, new users find that controlling the mouse is the hardest part of using a graphical environment like Windows 95 and Excel for Windows 95. Many tasks in this environment are ultimately easier if you use the mouse, so learning to "master the mouse" is important.

When you work with the mouse, you perform four actions:

- **Point**　To point, slide the mouse on your desktop, or roll the trackball. On-screen, the mouse pointer moves in a way that corresponds with the movements you make on your desk.

- **Click**　To click, press and release the left mouse button. Sometimes in this book, there is a step that specifically tells you to press and release the right mouse button. Unless specifically instructed otherwise, click the left mouse button.

- **Double-click**　To double-click, press and release the left mouse button twice rapidly.

- **Drag**　You drag the mouse to move on-screen objects. To drag, place the mouse pointer over the item you want to move and then press the left mouse button once, but do not release it. Then, while holding down the mouse button, slide the mouse on your desktop, or rotate the trackball. Release the mouse button when the mouse pointer on-screen appears in the location you want.

Dragging is probably the trickiest of these actions.

Most people use one of two varieties of mice (if you're following along on the rodent analogy, maybe these are species?). The typical mouse is one you slide on your desktop or on a mouse pad. With this type of mouse, you physically move the mouse; this movement causes a ball located on the bottom of the mouse to roll. The other popular type of mouse is the trackball. This mouse remains stationary on your desktop, and you roll its ball with your fingers instead of moving the entire mouse with your hand. Both of these mice contain buttons you click, or push. Clicking usually causes an action to take place. For example, in Solitaire, when you click on the pile of cards in the upper left corner, a new card turns over.

In order to "rule the rodent," you must understand the difference between the mouse and the mouse *pointer*. The mouse sits on your desk. It's the physical hardware you move.

The mouse pointer is the on-screen representation of the mouse. Think of the mouse pointer as the icon that represents the mouse. The mouse pointer on-screen changes shapes, depending on where it is and what you're trying to do with it. The most common mouse pointer shape is the arrow, which points up and to the left. Another common shape is the hourglass, which means "please wait" while your computer does something. In Excel, the most common mouse pointer shape is the plus sign—some people think it looks like a white version of the Red Cross symbol. See the table "Common Mouse Pointer Shapes," in Part 4, p. 519, for a listing of mouse pointer shapes you see while working in Excel.

One of the most effective ways to learn to use the mouse is to play Solitaire. Playing Solitaire helps you learn all basic mouse movements—pointing, clicking, double-clicking, and dragging. The game comes with Windows 95, and you can find it if you open the Accessories folder and then the Games folder.

Begin Guided Tour   Use the Mouse

1 Point at the **Start** button. To point, slide the mouse on your desktop, or roll the trackball. On-screen, the mouse pointer moves in a way that corresponds with the movements you make on your desk.

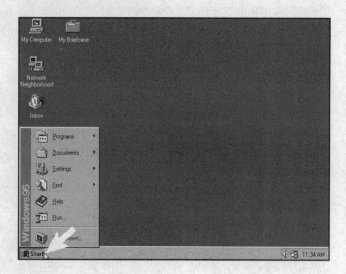

2 Click the **Start** button. To click, press and release the left mouse button.

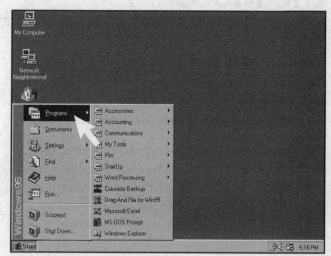

3 Point at the **Programs** folder. Windows 95 displays the Programs menu.

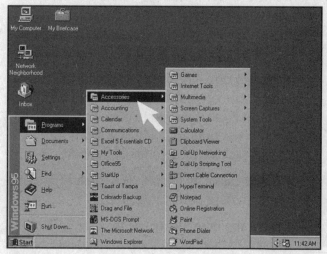

4 Point at the **Accessories** folder. Windows 95 displays the Accessories menu.

Guided Tour   Use the Mouse   *(continued)*

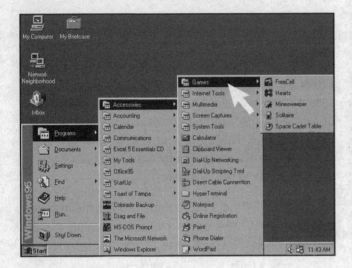

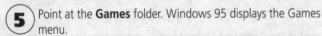

5 Point at the **Games** folder. Windows 95 displays the Games menu.

7 To place a card from the playing area onto the ace pile, you double-click on the card. To double-click, press and release the left mouse button twice rapidly.

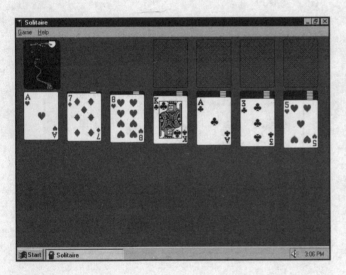

6 Point at **Solitaire** and click the left mouse button. Solitaire starts, and the computer screen displays the Solitaire cards.

Clicking the **X** in the upper right corner of the screen of any program closes that program. If you've changed the information in the file you're working in, you get a chance to save before the program closes.

8 Place the mouse pointer over the card you want to move and then drag it to its new location. To drag, press once, but do not release the left mouse button. Then, while holding down the mouse button, slide the mouse on your desktop, or rotate the trackball. Release the mouse button when the mouse pointer on-screen appears in the location you want. In Solitaire, you drag cards to move them in the playing area.

Install Excel 7

Installing programs is not difficult. Nowadays, most software vendors automate the process so that you just follow the instructions you see on-screen. Here you're going to take a walk through installing Excel on a single computer using the Windows 95 installation wizard. *Wizards* are tools supplied with Windows 95 that walk you through procedures such as installing software or setting up a new piece of hardware.

We're going to walk through installing Excel from floppy disks using Drive A. If you are using a CD-ROM, you should follow these steps but make sure, in Step 5, that the command line shows the drive of your CD-ROM drive. If you need to install Excel on a

network, please see Microsoft's installation instructions.

When the installation program starts to run, you see a screen from which you can choose a Typical, Custom, or Compact installation. In most cases, a Typical install works just fine. The Custom option enables you to select files to install, and Compact is the option you use when disk space is limited.

You also see a product ID number during the installation process. Write it down and put it in a safe place. You may need it if you ever call Microsoft for support.

Begin Guided Tour   Install Excel 7

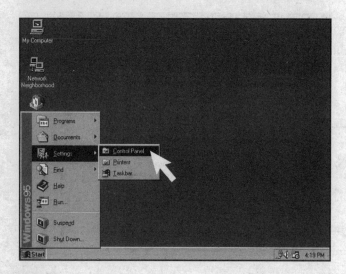

1 Click the **Start** button. Then select **Settings** and click **Control Panel**.

2 Windows 95 opens the Control Panel window. Double-click the **Add/Remove Programs** icon.

Guided Tour Install Excel 7   *(continued)*

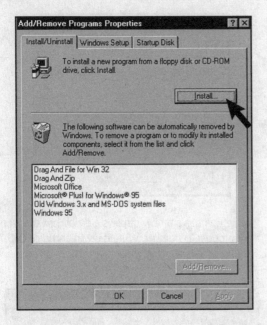

3 Windows 95 displays the Add/Remove Programs Properties dialog box. Click the **Install** button.

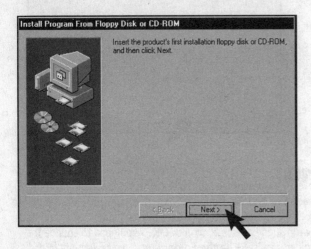

4 You see a dialog box that tells you to insert a disk into either your floppy drive or, if you are using one, your CD-ROM drive. After you place the disk in the disk drive, click the **Next** button.

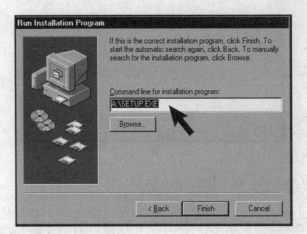

5 You see the Run Installation Program, which has searched the disk and found the program that installs Excel. The command line should read A:\SETUP.EXE. Click the **Finish** button.

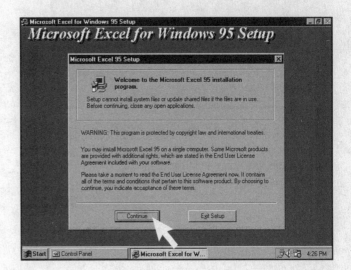

6 The Setup program starts. As the Setup program begins, you see a message telling you that the Excel for Windows 95 setup program is starting and that you should wait. Then, you see the licensing screen. After you read it, click **Continue**.

(continues)

Guided Tour   Install Excel 7   *(continued)*

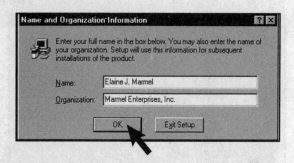

7 You next see the Name and Organization Information dialog box—it may already contain information about you. If not, fill in your name in the Name text box, press the **Tab** key or click in the Organization text box, and type the name of your company. Then, click **OK**.

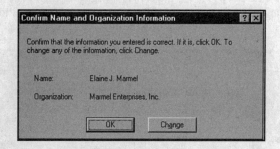

8 Setup asks you to confirm that you typed your name and company name correctly. If you did, click **OK**. If you didn't, click **Change**. The Name and Organization Information dialog box appears again, and you can correct your mistake.

9 The Setup program now displays a dialog box that contains your product ID number. Write it down and click **OK**. The Setup program searches for earlier versions of Excel.

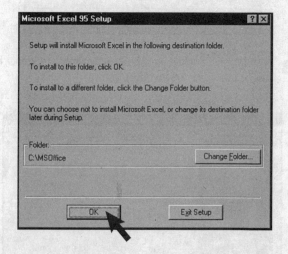

10 If you have an earlier version of Excel, the Setup program suggests that you replace it, using the folder from the earlier version. Or, from the Setup program, you can change the folder into which you place Excel. In most cases, what the folder Setup suggests is fine, so click **OK**. If you need to change the folder, click the **Change Folder** button and select the folder. Regardless of the folder into which you install Excel, you see an icon for Excel right on your Program list after installation is complete.

Guided Tour   Install Excel 7

To quit the Excel installation at any time, click on the **Exit Setup** button. If you quit installation and later restart it, you may not see all these screens.

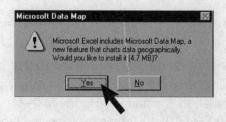

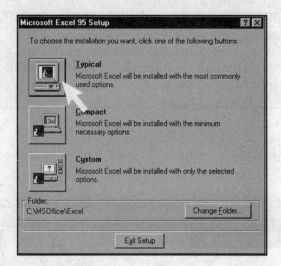

12 During the installation process, the Setup program asks you if you want to install Excel's Data Map. If you plan to create maps, click **Yes**.

11 You next see a screen from which you can choose a Typical, Custom, or Compact installation. Click the **Typical** button. Setup starts copying files, and you see a progress bar on the bottom of your screen that tells you how far along the installation is.

13 As the Setup program works, it prompts you to insert disks as needed. You may not use all the disks, depending on the options you chose to install. When the Setup program finishes, you see a dialog box like this one. If you have a modem, click the **Online Registration** button to automatically register Excel. Otherwise, click **OK**.

Start and Exit Excel

Starting Excel is not difficult. After you finish installing, you see that Windows 95 places an entry for Excel on the Programs menu so that you can start it. Entries on the Programs menu are in alphabetical order, so you find Excel in the M's—for Microsoft Excel. The first time you start the program, you use the Programs menu method. However, after you create and save a workbook in Excel, you can open the Documents menu from the Start menu and select the workbook. When you use this method, Windows 95 starts Excel and opens the selected workbook.

You can close Excel, and any other program, by clicking the X in the upper right corner of the screen. If you edit any information in your workbook, Excel prompts you to save before closing the program (see "Save a Workbook," p. 82).

> You can also close any program by using the Exit command for that program. You learn more about the Exit command after you work with menus in Excel.

Begin Guided Tour   Start Excel for the First Time

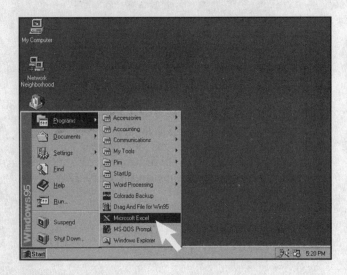

1 Click the **Start** button and highlight **Programs**. You see the list of programs installed on your computer; some programs are in folders. Click the **Excel** icon.

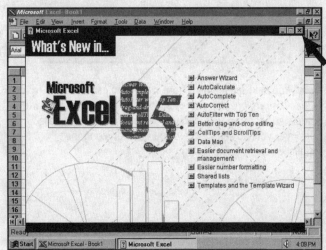

2 The first time you start Excel, you see some Help information that describes new features in Excel 7. Close this window by clicking on the **X** in the upper right corner.

Guided Tour Start Excel for the First Time

(continued)

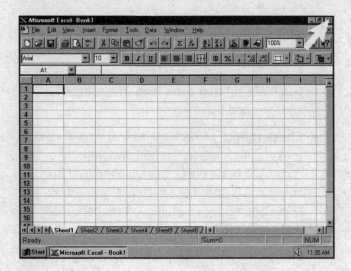

3 After you close the Help screen, you see the Excel screen. To close Excel, click on the **X** in the upper right corner of the screen.

Get Your Ideas (& Wishes) Across to Excel

As you work in Excel, you find that you need to "communicate" with the program. For example, you may need to tell Excel to open a file. Or, you may need to answer Excel's questions about a particular task you are performing, such as changing fonts.

To tell Excel what to do, you use either *menus* that contain *commands* or *tools* on *toolbars*. When you need to answer questions about a task, Excel typically presents you with a *dialog box* in which you select options or supply information.

See "Parts of the Excel Screen," p. 519, for a picture that identifies all the parts of the Excel Screen.

Open and Close Menus

To use menus, you must open them. You can open a menu with either the mouse or the keyboard. The guided tour for this task focuses on using the mouse to open menus and choose commands. Here are two alternate ways to open menus using the keyboard:

1. Press the **Alt** key to activate Excel's menu bar. Then, highlight the menu you want to open using the right or left arrow key and press **Enter**. The menu opens.

2. Or, press the **Alt** key to activate the menu bar and use the *hot key* (the underscored letter) for the menu you want to open. For example, press the Alt key and "F" to open the File menu.

Once you open a menu, choose a command. To select a command, highlight the command by pressing the up or down arrow keys and then pressing the Enter key, or, type the command's hot key letter.

Commands operate in one of four ways, and you can tell what's going to happen by looking at the way the command appears on the menu.

- **Right-pointing arrow carets**   Right-pointing arrow carets (pointing to the right of the command) indicate that a submenu appears when you highlight that command. The submenu contains additional commands.

- **Check marks**   Check marks that appear next to commands signify "on/off switches." If a command has a check mark next to it, the command is "on," or selected. If you choose the command again, you remove the check mark and "turn off," or deselect, the command.

- **Ellipsis**   If an ellipsis (...) follows a command, a dialog box appears when you choose the command. You use the dialog box to supply additional information to Excel about executing the command.

- **Plain**   If you see a command with no marks next to it, Excel executes the command as soon as you choose it.

Use the Toolbars

The tools on the toolbars are shortcuts for selecting commands from menus; therefore, tools save you time. You must, however, use a mouse to choose a tool from a toolbar.

Excel contains different toolbars for different circumstances, and the appropriate toolbar usually appears for each task you attempt. For example, when you create a map, Excel automatically displays the Mapping toolbar.

Certain toolbars are on-screen all the time by default. For instance, when you start Excel, you automatically see the Standard toolbar and the Formatting toolbar. If you move the mouse pointer over an individual tool on a toolbar, you see a "ToolTip," a short description of the tool's function. That way, you don't have to memorize the purpose of every tool.

Understand Dialog Boxes

Excel presents dialog boxes whenever it cannot complete a task without further information from you. Dialog boxes just appear; you don't have to do anything special to make them appear. However, you can predict if a dialog box is going to appear by noting the way the command appears on the menu. If you see an ellipsis (...) next to a command, you see a dialog box when you choose that command.

Within a dialog box there are a variety of ways you can answer Excel's questions:

- **List Boxes** Some are already open, and others drop down when you click on the arrow that appears to the right of the list box.

- **Option Buttons** You can't select more than one option button in a group of option buttons.

- **Check Boxes** If a dialog box contains more than one check box in a group of check boxes, you can select more than one.

- **Text Boxes** Like list boxes, text boxes come in two varieties: with and without spinner buttons. In a text box without spinner buttons, you type an answer. Usually, text boxes with spinner buttons are text boxes where the answer is a number, and the spinner buttons increment or decrement the number by one. You can type in a text box with spinner buttons, or you can use the spinner buttons to increase or decrease the number.

- **Command Buttons** Like list boxes and text boxes, command buttons come in two varieties. Plain command buttons have no markings other than a name. Clicking any plain command button makes Excel take the action written on the button. Tunnel-through command buttons have an ellipsis after the name. When you choose a tunnel-through command button, Excel displays a dialog box (just as you would expect from your experiences with the ellipsis in menu commands).

Begin Guided Tour   Use the Mouse to Open Menus and Choose Commands

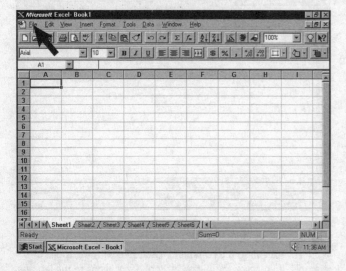

1 Slide the mouse until the mouse pointer points at the menu you want to open.

2 Click on the menu; Excel opens the menu. Notice the Exit command on the File menu. Choosing this command also closes Excel.

(continues)

Guided Tour　Use the Mouse to Open Menus and Choose Commands
(continued)

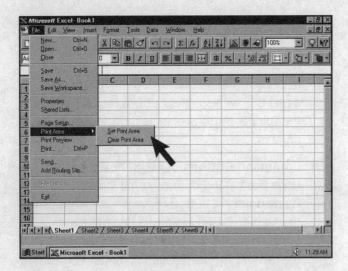

In many instances, you can open a shortcut menu to accomplish a task. For example, slide the mouse so that the pointer appears in the grid area of the worksheet and click the right mouse button to open a shortcut menu.

3 Slide the mouse until the mouse pointer highlights the command you want and click the left mouse button to choose the command. If you highlight a command that has a caret next to it, Excel displays a submenu. If you choose a command that has an ellipsis following it, Excel displays a dialog box.

Begin Guided Tour　Choose a Tool from a Toolbar

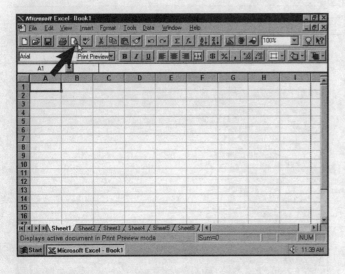

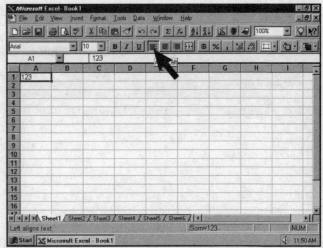

1 Slide the mouse until the mouse pointer highlights a tool on a toolbar. You see a ToolTip (I think of them as sticky notes) that defines the tool's function.

2 When you find the tool you want, click. Excel responds by executing the command associated with the tool. For example, if you click the Align Left tool, Excel aligns to the left any information in the selected area. The Align Left button on the Toolbar appears "depressed."

Begin Guided Tour Provide Answers in Dialog Boxes

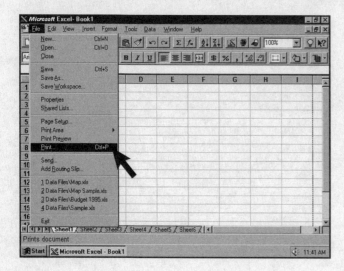

1 Open the **File** menu and choose the **Print** command. Notice that the Print command has an ellipsis following it, so when you choose it, the Print dialog box now appears.

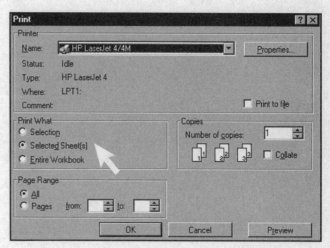

3 In the Print What section, you see options buttons. Click the option you want.

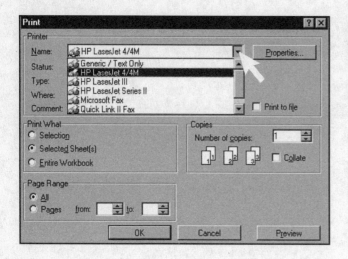

2 The Name box is a drop-down list box. If you click the arrow to the right of the box, Excel opens the list box to display a list of the available printers you can use.

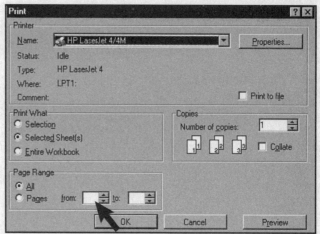

4 The Page Range box contains option buttons and spinner text boxes (to the right of the Pages option button). You use the spinner text boxes to specify which pages to print.

(continues)

Guided Tour   Provide Answers in Dialog Boxes   *(continued)*

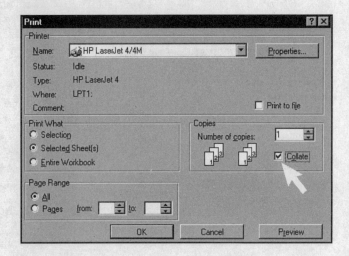

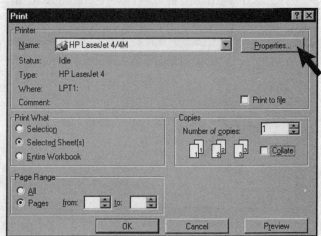

5 Both Print to file (in the Printer area) and Collate (in the Copies area) are check boxes. Click a check box to select it. Clicking a check box a second time deselects the choice and removes the check mark.

6 OK, Cancel, and Preview are command buttons. Properties is a tunnel-through command button. (Note the ellipsis on the Properties button.)

Learn Windows Skills

Why did they name this operating system "Windows"? Primarily because you work in screens that look like *windows*. Unlike the DOS environment, in Windows you can have several screens open at one time. This is beneficial because you may open two different programs, such as Excel and Word; or, you may need to open two different Excel workbooks. If you open two different programs or workbooks, each appears in its own window. To arrange the appearance of the windows on your screen, you can resize and move windows.

Minimize, Maximize, Restore

When you first start Excel, both the program and the default workbook, Book 1, appear *maximized*. That means that both windows fill the entire screen; so, if you have another program open, you can't see it.

The first thing you should understand about these windows is that you're looking at two of them—one is the *program window* and the other is the *document window*. Every window has three buttons in its upper right corner; these buttons help control the window's size. When you look at the upper right corner of Excel, you see two sets of three buttons each. The top set controls the Excel program window, and the bottom set controls the workbook, or document window. Regardless of the set of buttons, the X remains constant. The middle two buttons change appearance depending on the window's current size so you always see one of three icons that you can click to achieve a particular size:

- You already learned about the X. It closes a window. The X is always on the button on the right.

- The button containing the flat line is the Minimize button. When you click it, you make the

window "disappear." Well, not really disappear, but shrink in size. If you minimize the program's window, an icon appears on the Windows taskbar. If you minimize a document window, you see only a *title bar* for the document. Every window has a title bar at the top that contains the name of the window. And, on the right edge of the document title bar, you see three size control buttons.

- The button containing a single square is the Maximize button. When you click it, the window increases to its maximum size. In the case of a maximized program window, the program fills your entire screen. In the case of a maximized document window, the document fills all the space available in the program window, and you don't see a separate window title bar.

- The button containing a pair of squares, one slightly behind the other, is the Restore button. When you click this button, the window changes to a size between its largest and smallest sizes. When you click a program's Restore button, the program fills most but not all of the screen. When you click a document's Restore button, the document fills a part of the program window and has its own title.

Resize Windows

So far, you've learned about the three automatic sizes for a window. In reality, there are an infinite number of sizes for windows because you can adjust a window's "restored" size.

You can change the "restored" size of a window by dragging any border of the window. If you drag the top or bottom of a window, you adjust its height. If you drag either side of a window, you adjust its width. And, if you drag a corner, you simultaneously adjust both the height and width of a window. After adjusting a window's "restored" size, you can maximize and minimize as you please, but each time you click the Restore button, the window appears in its new adjusted size.

Begin Guided Tour   Automatically Change a Window's Size

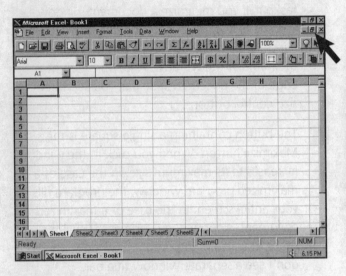

1 If Excel isn't already open, start it using the **Start** button and the **Programs** menu. Excel appears in its maximized state, filling your screen. Note that both windows have Restore buttons. (The lower Restore button belongs to the workbook.) Click the workbook's **Restore** button.

3 The entire workbook window shrinks down in size to a title bar with Restore, Maximize, and Close buttons. Click the **Maximize** button on the workbook's title bar.

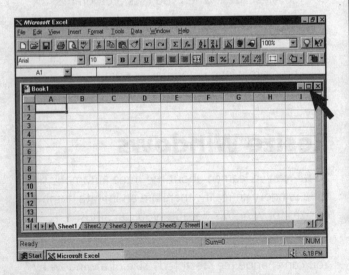

2 The workbook appears in its own window with a title bar. Notice that the Maximize button now replaces the Restore button in the workbook's window. Now click the workbook's **Minimize** button.

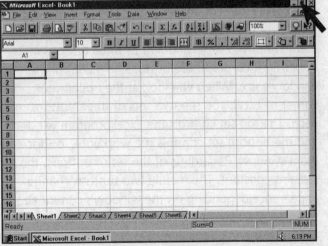

4 The workbook's window returns to full size. Notice that the Restore button replaces the Maximize button. Click Excel's **Restore** button.

Guided Tour Automatically Change a Window's Size

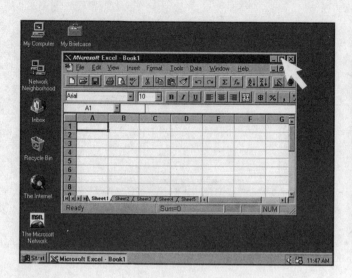

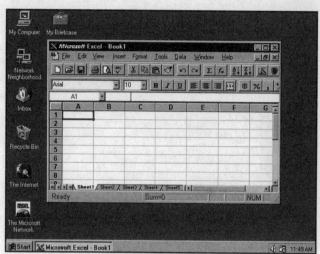

5 This reduces both the Excel window and the workbook window in size so neither window fills the screen. Notice that the Maximize button replaces the Restore button in the Excel window.

7 Click Excel's icon on the taskbar, and Excel returns to its "restored" size.

You can move any window that appears on-screen in its "restored" state. Simply drag its title bar.

6 If you click Excel's **Minimize** button (the button to the left of the program's Maximize button), you see the entire Windows 95 Desktop, and Excel's icon appears as a button on the taskbar at the bottom edge of your screen.

Begin Guided Tour   Adjust a Window's Size

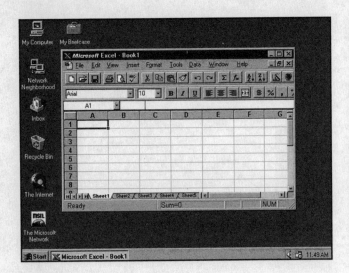

1 If your Excel window fills the entire screen, click the **Restore** button so that it fills only a portion of the screen.

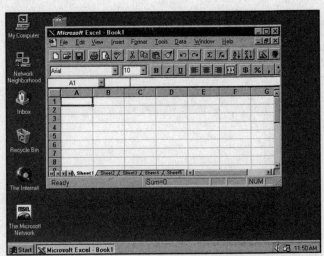

3 To increase the height of the window, drag the edge of the Excel window toward the top of the screen. When you release the mouse button, the window fills a larger portion of the screen from top to bottom.

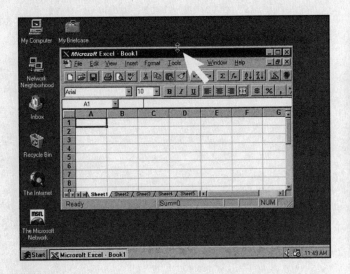

2 Place the mouse pointer on the top edge of the window. The mouse pointer changes to a two-headed arrow pointing up and down.

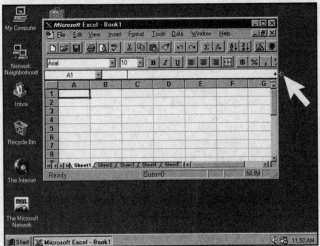

4 Place the mouse pointer on the right edge of the Excel window. The mouse pointer changes to a two-headed arrow pointing right and left.

Guided Tour   Adjust a Window's Size

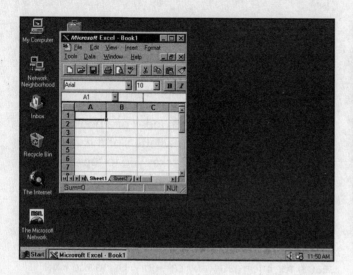

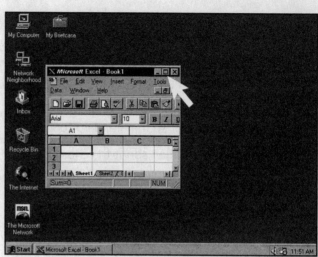

5 Drag the edge of the Excel window to the left. When you release the mouse button, the Excel window fills a smaller area of the screen from side to side.

7 Drag the edge of the Excel window down and to the left. When you release the mouse pointer, the Excel window fills a smaller area of the screen from top to bottom and side to side. To fill the screen with the window, click Excel's **Maximize** button.

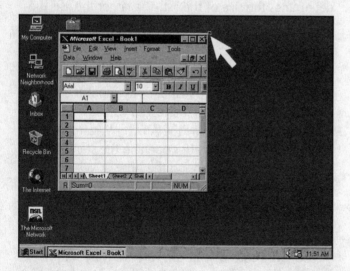

6 Place the mouse pointer in the upper right corner of the Excel window. The mouse pointer changes to a two-headed arrow pointing diagonally.

Get Help

Excel offers several ways for you to get help:

- For help performing any task, you can use the standard Help system.

- To get help using menu commands, you can access the Help tool on the Standard toolbar.

- For specific information about the choices you find in a dialog box, you can select the question mark button in the upper right corner of every dialog box to receive help.

Using the standard Help system gives you your first introduction to *wizards*. Wizards are automated tools that Excel provides to help you with your work. For example, when you're stuck and can't figure out how to perform a task, you can ask the Answer Wizard for guidance. You formulate a question and type it into the Answer Wizard's text box. The Answer Wizard tries to answer your question by displaying a series of help topics you might want to browse. The TipWizard feature monitors your work and informs you if there is a quicker or better way to perform the task on which you're working.

Get Help Performing a Task

When you use the standard Help system, you see a dialog box with four different tabs: the Contents tab, the Index tab, the Find tab, and the Answer Wizard tab.

Think of the Contents tab as a table of contents in a book. When you click the Contents tab, you see an icon that looks like a book to the left of each help category for which additional information is available.

When you open the book, you see either additional books or topics represented by icons of pages containing a question mark. When you display a help topic, you see the actual help information.

Think of the Index tab as the index of a book. On the Index tab, you type a few letters of the word you want to look up, and Help takes you to topics that begin with those letters. When you find a topic close to the one you want, you can display additional topics or the help information.

Using either the Contents tab or the Index tab, you search for information by category. Using the Find tab, you search for information by words or phrases. To be able to make this kind of search, the Help system builds a list of phrases with the Find Setup Wizard. The first time you click on the Find tab, you start the Find Setup Wizard, which automatically determines the size of the list. The larger the list, the longer it takes Help to build the list, but you only go through this process once.

Using the Answer Wizard tab, you input a question, and the Answer Wizard responds by supplying a list of topics that may be of interest to you based on your question. You can display the Answer Wizard tab either by clicking on it after opening the standard Help system, or by choosing the Answer Wizard directly from the Help menu.

> You can leave the Help window open while you work so that you can refer to it by simply clicking anywhere in the workbook window. The Help window disappears from your screen, but you still see Help for Microsoft Excel on the taskbar. If you finish using Help, close it by clicking the X in the Help window.

Get Help for Menu Commands and Dialog Box Choices

While you work, you may stumble upon a command on a menu you don't recognize. Without interrupting your work, you'd like to know what that command does. Or, you may see options in dialog boxes and wonder what those options do, but again, you don't want to interrupt your work. So, instead, you can use Excel's screen tips.

The last tool on the Standard toolbar, the Help tool, enables you to display screen tips for menu commands. After clicking on this tool, Excel displays help about the menu command you click on.

When you work inside dialog boxes, you may notice a button containing a question mark in the upper right corner of the dialog box. Clicking that button in a dialog box is the equivalent of clicking the Help tool on the Standard toolbar. After you click the button,

Excel displays help about the next option you click on in the dialog box.

Use the Tip Wizard

The TipWizard button is the button with the light bulb on it near the right end of the Standard toolbar. The TipWizard helps you learn to use Excel in a more efficient way. If the TipWizard has a tip for the action you are performing, the TipWizard button "lights up," appearing in bright yellow, after you perform the action. A white TipWizard button means the TipWizard has no tip for the action you just performed. When you click the TipWizard button, the TipWizard toolbar appears. If the tip concerns a tool on one of the toolbars, you see that tool to the right of the TipWizard toolbar. When the TipWizard toolbar displays, you can click the up- and down-arrow buttons on the TipWizard toolbar to scroll through the list of tips from the current session.

Begin Guided Tour   Get Help with a Task

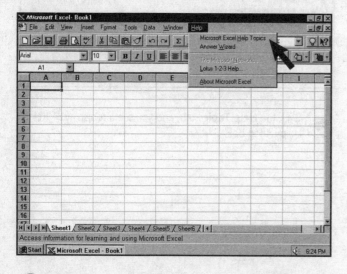

1 If the Excel window doesn't fill the entire screen, click the **Maximize** button. Then, click **Help** in the menu bar to open the Help menu. Click **Microsoft Excel Help Topics**.

2 Excel opens the Help window. If this is the first time you have opened Help, you see the Contents tab. Otherwise, you see the last tab you used. If you don't see the Contents tab, click it.

(continues)

Guided Tour   Get Help with a Task   (continued)

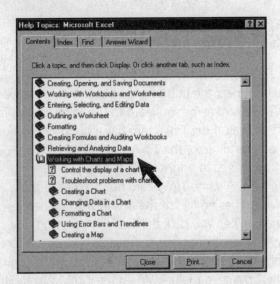

3 Double-click any book icon or highlight any book icon and click the **Open** button (which changes to the Close button) to display additional help categories and topics.

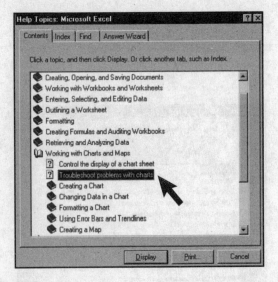

4 Highlight a topic. (The icon for a topic is a piece of paper with a question mark on it.) Click the **Display** button.

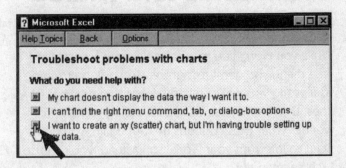

5 After you click the **Display** button, you see a help topic on-screen. On some topics, you may see markers you can click on to jump to related help topics. Or, you may see underlined phrases you can click on for definitions.

When the mouse pointer is on an underlined phrase or a topic to which you can jump to get help, the pointer changes to a hand with a pointing finger.

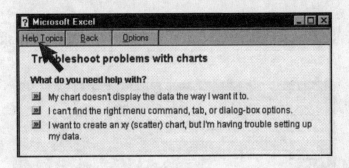

6 Click the **Help Topics** tab, and you see a redisplay of the Help dialog box.

Guided Tour Get Help with a Task

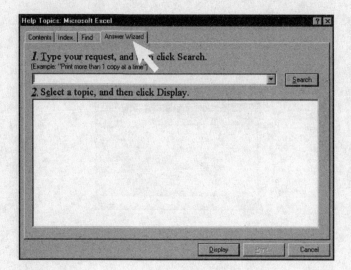

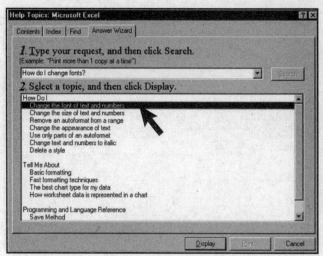

7 Now, try using the Answer Wizard. Click the **Answer Wizard** tab.

9 Highlight one of the indented topics. When you click **Display**, the Answer Wizard displays the corresponding help topic. When you finish, click the **X** in the upper right corner of the box to close it.

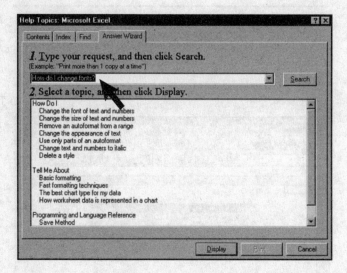

8 Type in a question and click the **Display** button. Excel displays a series of topics related to your question.

Begin Guided Tour   Use Screen Tips for Help with Menus and Dialog Boxes

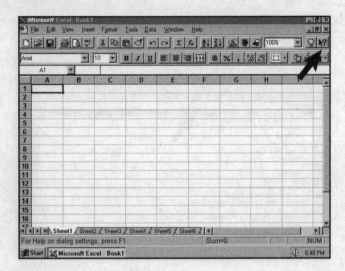

1 Click on the **Help** tool on the Standard toolbar. When you move the mouse, you notice that the mouse pointer shape changes; it now looks like the icon that appears on the Help tool.

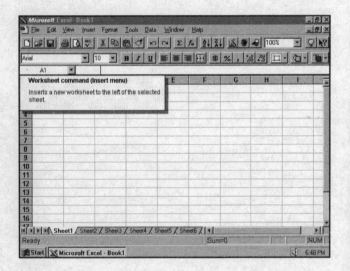

2 Open the **Insert** menu and choose the **Worksheet** command. Instead of executing the command, Excel displays a screen tip. Click anywhere in the worksheet to remove the help message that appears in the screen tip.

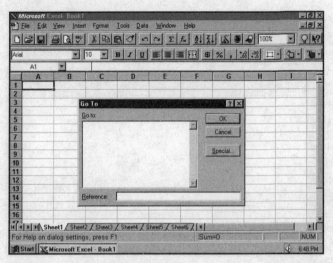

3 Open the **Edit** menu and choose the **Go To** command. Excel opens the Go To dialog box.

You can also display the Go To dialog box if you press **F5**. F5 is the Go To key. Pressing F5 selects the Go To command.

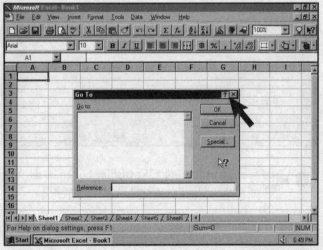

4 Click the question mark button that appears in the upper right corner of the dialog box. Again, the mouse pointer changes shape to look like the Help tool on the Standard toolbar.

Guided Tour Use Screen Tips for Help with Menus and Dialog Boxes

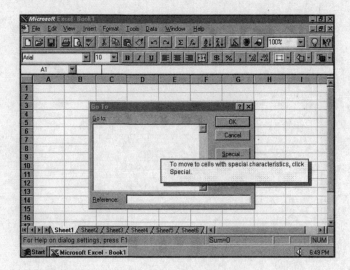

5 Click on the item in the dialog box about which you want information. For example, in the Go To dialog box, click the **Special** button. Excel displays a help message that explains the item.

6 To close the screen tip, click anywhere outside the dialog box. To close the dialog box, click the **X** in its upper right corner.

Begin Guided Tour Get Help from the TipWizard

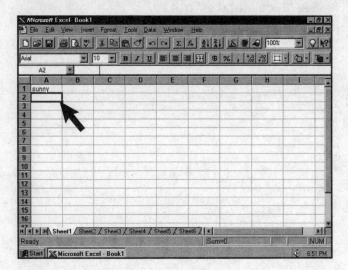

1 Type **sunny** and press **Enter**. After you press Enter, the cell pointer moves down.

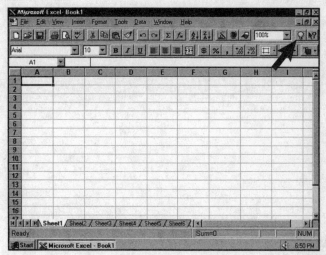

2 Open the **Edit** menu and select **Undo Entry**. Sunny disappears, and the TipWizard button appears "lit up" in bright yellow.

(continues)

Guided Tour   Get Help from the TipWizard   *(continued)*

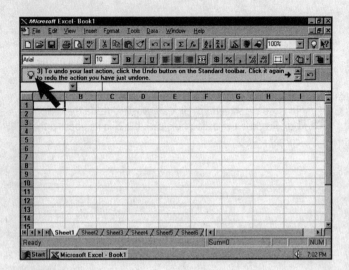

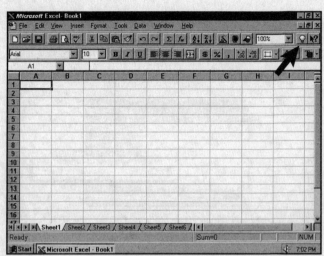

3 Click the **TipWizard** button. Excel displays the TipWizard toolbar; the toolbar contains a tip on how to undo actions more quickly and efficiently.

4 Click the **TipWizard** button to close the TipWizard toolbar.

See "Fix a Mistake," p. 45.

Navigate in a Workbook

Before you learn how to enter information in Excel workbooks, you need to learn how to move around in Excel. This is a good time to define some terms.

When you first start Excel, you see the first worksheet in a workbook. You can think of the workbook as a three-ring binder that contains information about a project. Each workbook initially contains 16 worksheets (notice, toward the bottom of the screen, the tabs labeled Sheet1, Sheet2, Sheet3, and so on). You can use the sheets within a workbook to store and organize different kinds of information about a project. Sheet1, for example, may show a company budget, and subsequent worksheets might show the individual departmental budgets that make up the company budget. When you save your work in Excel, you save the entire workbook and all of the worksheets in it.

A worksheet is a grid of rows and columns. There are 16,384 rows and 256 columns in each worksheet. A number marks each row, and a letter marks each column. Reading from left to right, the first column is A, the second is B, and so on through column Z. The next column after Z is AA, the next AB, and so on. This progression continues through column IV.

A *cell* is the intersection of a row and a column in a worksheet. To refer to a cell, you use an address that consists of its column letter and its row number. The address of the first cell in the worksheet is A1. Sometimes, you need to refer to more than one cell at a time. When you refer to a group of cells, you call the group a *range*; as you may expect, the range of cells has an address too. The *address* for a range is a combination of the address of the upper left cell and the lower right cell in the range.

What You Will Find in This Section

Select Cells

The intersection of a row and a column is a cell. And, each cell has a unique address, also called a *cell reference*. A cell's address is its column letter and its row number. The first cell in the worksheet is cell A1; the last cell in the worksheet is cell IV16384. You use cell addresses to refer to cells in formulas. The *active cell* (also called the selected cell) is the cell into which you enter data. A heavy rectangle, or cell pointer, outlines the active cell. When you first start Excel, cell A1 is the active cell. The address of the active cell always appears in the Name box at the left edge of the Formula bar.

Sometimes, you need to refer to more than one cell at a time. A group of cells is a range. Ranges, like cells, have addresses. You refer to a range by the addresses of the upper left and lower right cells that comprise the range. A colon (:) separates the two addresses. For example, the range A1:C3 includes the cells A1, A2, A3, B1, B2, B3, C1, C2, and C3.

You can select cells using either the keyboard or the mouse, but in most cases, you probably find that selecting cells with the mouse is easier.

To select a single cell using the mouse, move the mouse pointer over the cell and click on the cell. However, if the cell you want to select is not within view on your screen, the easiest selection method is to select that cell using the keyboard and the Go To dialog box. You can select a range of cells using either the mouse or the arrow keys on your keyboard. With the mouse, you drag to select cells. You use the Shift key and the arrow keys to select cells with the keyboard.

In Part 4, you'll find a list of shortcuts you can use when you want to select various combinations of cells.

Begin Guided Tour Select a Single Cell

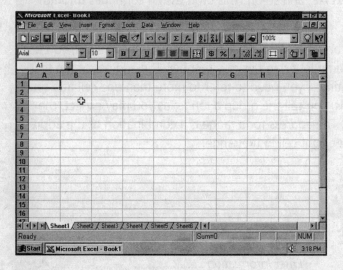

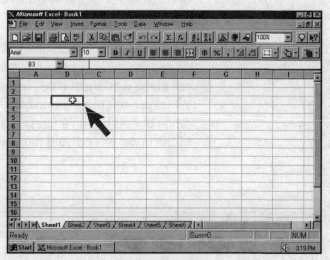

1 Slide the mouse on your desk until the mouse pointer (in a Red Cross-type shape) appears over the cell you want to select.

2 Click on the cell you want to select using the left mouse button.

Guided Tour   Select a Single Cell

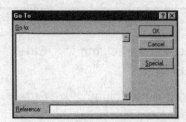

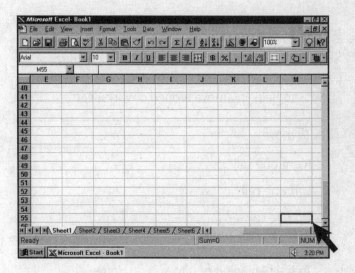

3 If you can't see the cell you want to select, press **F5** to display the Go To dialog box.

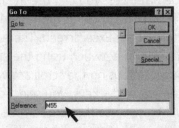

5 After you click **OK** the dialog box disappears, and Excel selects the cell with the address you typed.

4 Type the address of the cell you want to select in the **Reference** text box. Click **OK**.

Begin Guided Tour   Select a Range of Cells

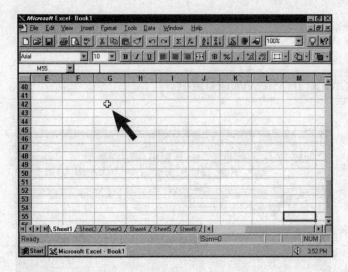

1 Position the cell pointer over the first cell in the range you want to select. If you can't see the cell on-screen, press **F5** to use the Go To dialog box.

2 Click on the first cell and hold the left mouse button down while you drag the mouse pointer over the cells you want to select. As you drag, Excel selects cells. Release the mouse button when the range you want to select is highlighted.

Move Around in a Worksheet

Moving around in a worksheet actually means changing the active cell. Most of the time, you use the arrow keys to move around in a worksheet. Try using the following arrow keys and key combinations to help you move around a worksheet:

To move	Press
Right one cell	→
Left one cell	←
Up one cell	↑
Down one cell	↓
To the beginning of a row	Home
To the end of a row	End+→
To the first cell (A1)	Ctrl+Home
The first cell in the row containing data	Ctrl+¨
The last cell in the row containing data	Ctrl+→

To move	Press
The first cell in the column containing data	Ctrl+↑
The last cell in the column containing data	Ctrl+↓
The last cell containing data	Ctrl+End

To move large distances, you can use the mouse and the scroll arrows that appear at both the right side and the bottom of the Excel screen. There is one important distinction between using the arrow keys on the keyboard and using the scroll arrows to move. When you use the arrow keys, you select cells while you move. When you use the scroll arrows, Excel shifts the screen so that you can see different portions of the worksheet, but you do not actually select any cells. It's important to remember that you must either click in a visible cell or use the Go To box to select a cell.

Begin Guided Tour   Move to a New Location in the Worksheet

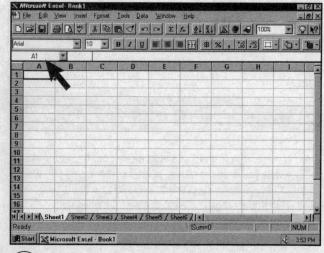

1 Press **Ctrl+Home**. Excel selects cell A1.

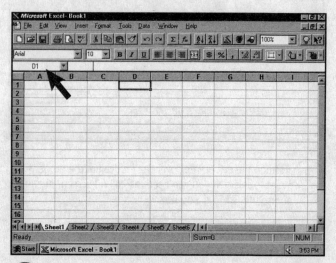

2 Press the right arrow key three times. Excel selects cell D1.

Guided Tour Move to a New Location in the Worksheet

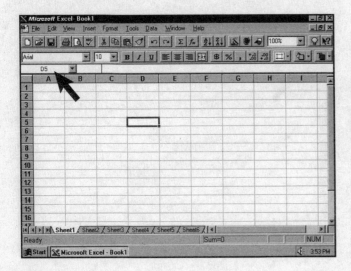

3 Press the down arrow key four times. Excel selects cell D5.

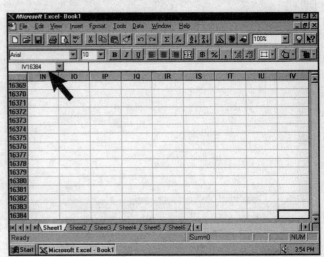

5 Press **End+right arrow** key. Excel selects cell IV16384.

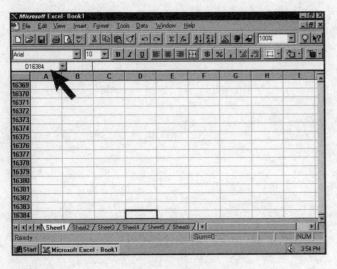

4 Press **End+down arrow** key. Excel selects cell D16384.

You'll find additional shortcuts you can use to move around the worksheet in Part 4.

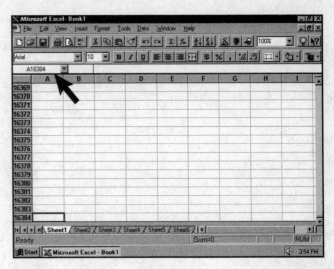

6 Press **Home**. Excel selects cell A16384.

(continues)

Guided Tour   Move to a New Location in the Worksheet

(continued)

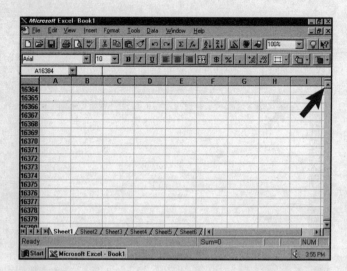

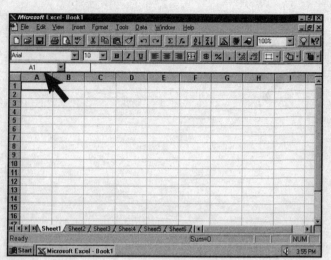

7 Click on the up scroll arrow five times. Excel shifts the screen so that you can no longer see the active cell (A16384). Instead, you see rows 16364-16379.

8 Press **Ctrl+Home**. Excel selects cell A1.

Move to Another Worksheet

ach Excel workbook contains, initially, 16 worksheets. Notice, toward the bottom of the screen, the tabs labeled Sheet1, Sheet2, Sheet3, and so on. You can use these worksheets to store and organize different kinds of information about the same project. Sheet1, for example, might show a department budget, and subsequent worksheets might show the details that comprise each line of the department budget. You may even want to store a chart depicting various budget expenses on a separate sheet in the workbook.

To use the different worksheets, you must be able to move between them. You may notice, as you move between sheets, that each worksheet has its own active cell, depending on where you have placed the cell pointer. You can place the cell pointer in different cells on different sheets. On Sheet1, for example, the active cell may be cell D5, while on Sheet2, the active cell is C8.

Begin Guided Tour   Switch to a Different Worksheet

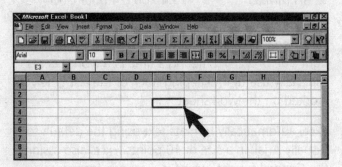

1 Click cell **E3** to select it.

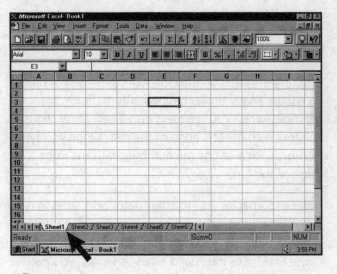

3 Click on the **Sheet1** tab. Excel returns you to Sheet1, where the active cell is E3.

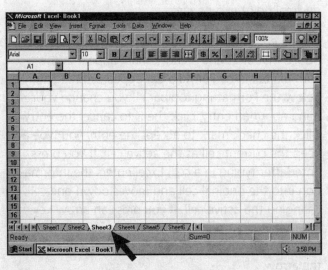

2 Click on the **Sheet3** tab. Notice the active cell in this sheet is A1.

Enter Information

Most people use worksheets primarily to track or calculate numbers. However, to give meaning to the columns and rows of numbers that make up a worksheet, you can supply names for the columns and rows to describe what the numbers represent; in Excel, these names are *labels*. While you can enter information in any order, you may find it most useful to enter labels before you enter numbers. That way, you can ensure that you enter the numbers into the appropriate cells.

Number entries are also called *values*. Values contain numbers and other symbols. Values must begin with a numeral or one of the following symbols: +,–, (, ., or $. You use the period as a decimal point in decimal values. You may find it is quicker to enter numbers using the numbers and the Enter key on your numeric keypad.

Entering information into the worksheet is as simple as typing. Many things happen automatically. For example, when you type text into a cell, Excel aligns the text with the left edge of the cell. When you type numbers, Excel aligns the numbers with the right edge of the cell.

Excel also enables you to enter dates and times in a worksheet and treat them as values. You can format dates and times to appear any way you want. Because Excel sees dates and times as values, you can use date and time information in calculations. For example, you can type a date in one cell and, in another cell, add 45 days to it. The answer Excel displays (in date format) equals the original date plus 45 days.

If you use the following formats, you can expect the corresponding results:

Format	Example
MM/DD/YY	9/12/94
DD-MMM-YY	12-Sep-94
DD-MMM	12-Sep (assumes the current year)
MMM-YY	Sep-94 (assumes the first day of the month)
HH:MM AM/PM	2:45 AM (12-hour clock)
HH:MM	13:45 (24-hour clock)
HH:MM:SS AM/PM	2:45:06 PM (12-hour clock)
HH:MM:SS	13:45:06 (24-hour clock)

Date and time entries are values and align with the right side of a cell. Entering a time in a worksheet is especially useful for keeping track of the last time you worked on the worksheet.

Excel automatically formats text using the default font (usually Arial) in a size of 10 points. Excel also assigns the General format, which is a generic format, to numbers. If you include a decimal point in the number, Excel includes all numbers that appear after the decimal point except zero.

As you enter numbers into the worksheet, you may notice that an X and a check mark appear in the Formula bar. (The Formula bar appears immediately below the Formatting toolbar.) If you change your mind about an entry, click the X to cancel the entry. Click the check mark to accept the entry you type and keep the current cell as the active cell. If you press Enter after typing in a cell, Excel enters the information into the original cell and moves down one cell, changing the active cell. If you press an arrow key after typing in a cell, Excel enters the information into the original cell and moves one cell in the direction of the arrow.

Talk about getting smarter: Excel comes with a feature that completes cells in a column based on the column's *labels*—the words you type in a column. Excel analyzes the information you type in the cells in a column and creates a list. If you start to type an entry, Excel suggests an entry to you, using the words you have already typed in the column. Or, you can choose an entry from a list. This feature is AutoComplete. (You can turn it on and off.)

The Guided Tour shows you how to enter text and numbers and how to use AutoComplete.

Begin Guided Tour   Type Text and Numbers

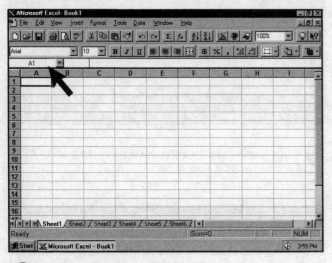

1 Press **Ctrl+Home** to select cell A1.

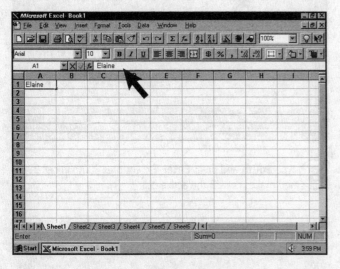

2 Type your first name. As you type, your first name appears in cell A1 and in the Formula bar.

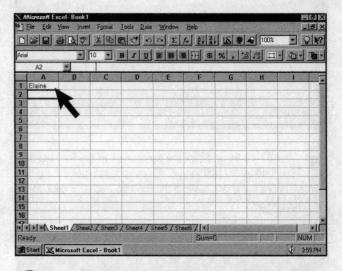

3 Press **Enter**. Excel stores your name (aligned to the left) in cell A1 and moves the cell pointer to cell A2.

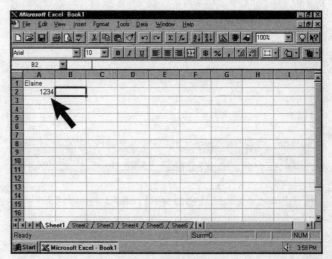

4 Type **1234** and press the right arrow key. Excel stores 1234 (aligned to the right) in cell A2 and moves the cell pointer to cell B2.

(continues)

Guided Tour   Type Text and Numbers

(continued)

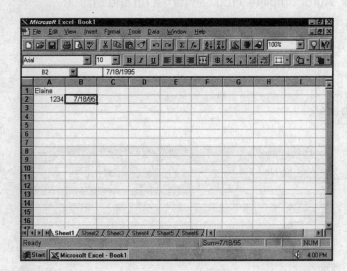

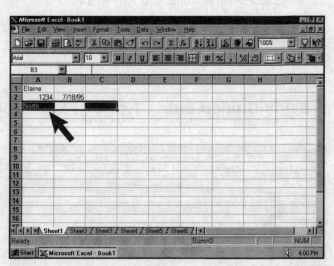

5 Type **07-18-95** and click the check mark in the Formula bar. Excel stores 07/18/95 in cell B2 and doesn't move the cell pointer. To see the check mark in the Formula bar, refer back to the figure for step 2.

7 Type **North** and press **Enter**. Excel stores North in cell A3 and makes B3 the active cell.

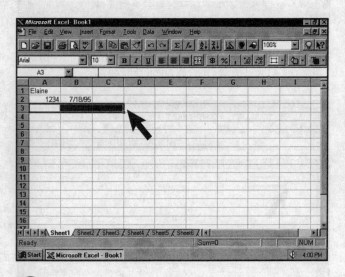

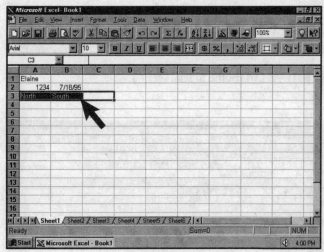

6 Using the mouse, drag to select cells **A3** through **C3**.

8 Type **South** and press **Enter**. Excel stores South in cell B3 and makes cell C3 the active cell.

Guided Tour   Type Text and Numbers

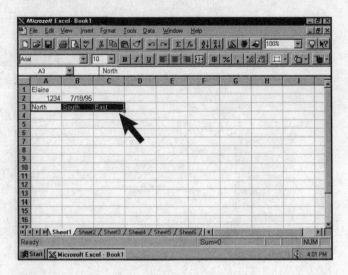

Here's a shortcut to enter information across a row: select the cells in the row into which you want to enter the information, type the first entry, and press Enter. Excel stores the first entry in the first selected cell and moves one cell to the right (instead of down).

9 Type **East** and press **Enter**. Excel stores East in cell C3 and leaves C3 as the active cell.

Begin Guided Tour   Take Advantage of AutoComplete

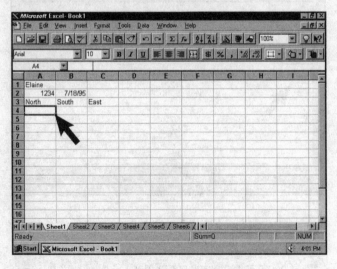

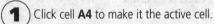

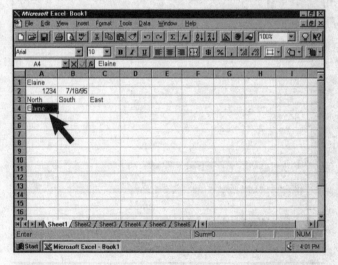

1 Click cell **A4** to make it the active cell.

2 Begin to type your name. After you type enough characters for Excel to distinguish your name from other possible entries in column A, Excel suggests your name to you.

(continues)

Guided Tour Take Advantage of AutoComplete

(continued)

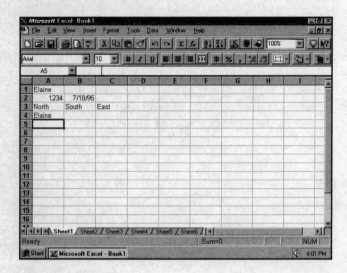

3 Press **Enter**. Your name appears again in cell A4 and the cell pointer moves to cell A5.

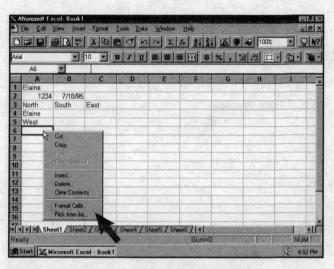

5 In cell A6, click the right mouse button. A shortcut menu appears. Choose **Pick from list**.

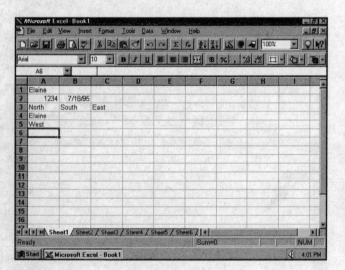

4 Type **West** and press **Enter**.

Excel only includes labels in the list it creates. If you type numeric entries, Excel does not include the numbers in the AutoComplete list.

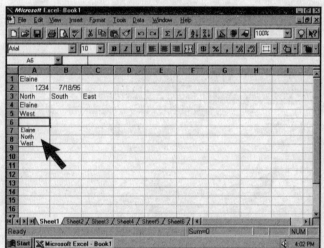

6 After you choose **Pick from list**, Excel displays a list of the text entries that appear in column A.

7 Choose any entry and press **Enter**.

Fix a Mistake

Mistakes are a fact of life. Unless you're perfect. In Excel, there are several ways to fix a mistake. You can:

- Use the Undo feature.
- Overwrite information in a cell.
- Erase the information in a cell.
- Clear the information in a cell.
- Edit the cell to change its contents.

You can use any of these methods when you need to correct a mistake. Choosing the "right" method isn't an issue most of the time, but the following guidelines tell you the best way to quickly fix common mistakes.

- Use the Undo feature if you just made the mistake, and you've already pressed Enter. Undo

puts things back to the way they were just before you completed your last action.

- Overwrite the information in the cell if the information is completely wrong, and you want to replace it with other information.
- Erase a cell if the information in it is completely wrong, and you want the cell to be blank.
- Clear a cell if both the information and the formatting in the cell are wrong and you intend to put other information in the cell that you want to format differently than the original information.
- Edit a cell if the cell contains a lot of information and only a small portion of the information is incorrect.

Begin Guided Tour Undo a Mistake

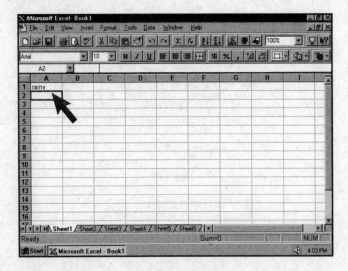

1 Type **rainy** into cell A1 and press **Enter**. The word rainy appears aligned to the left edge of cell A1, and Excel moves the cell pointer to cell A2.

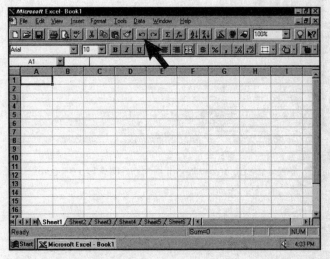

2 Click the **Undo** tool on the Standard toolbar. The word rainy disappears from cell A1, and Excel moves the cell pointer back to cell A1.

Begin Guided Tour Overwriting Information

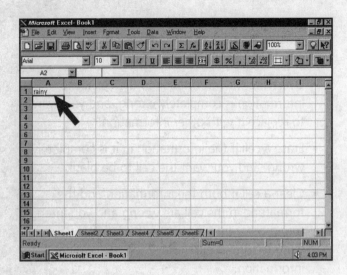

1 Type **rainy** into cell A1 and press **Enter**. The word rainy appears aligned to the left edge of cell A1, and Excel moves the cell pointer to cell A2.

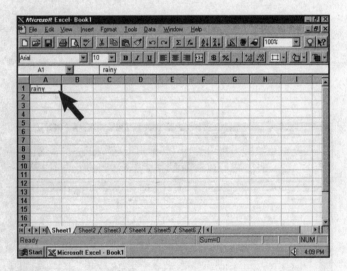

2 Press the **up arrow** key, or click on cell **A1** to select it.

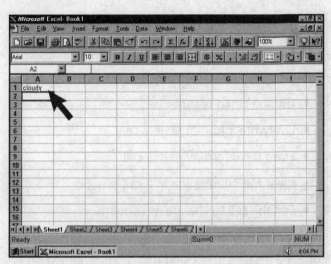

3 Type **cloudy** and press **Enter**. Excel replaces the word rainy with the word cloudy.

Begin Guided Tour Erase a Cell

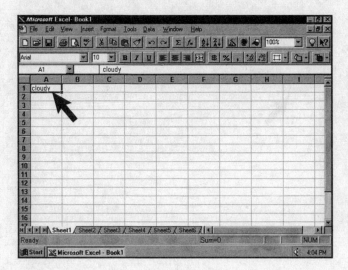

1 Click on cell **A1,** which contains the word cloudy. If it doesn't contain the word cloudy, type the word **cloudy** into cell A1 and click the **check mark** in the Formula bar.

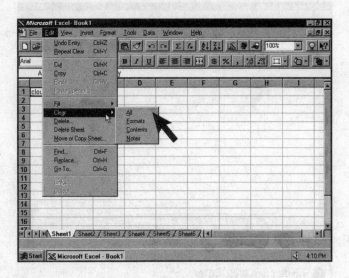

2 Open the **Edit** menu and select the **Clear** command. Choose **All** from the submenu Excel displays.

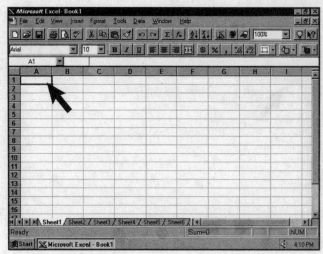

3 After choosing **All** from the submenu, Excel removes cloudy from cell A1.

You can press the **Delete** key to remove the contents of a cell, but any formatting you applied to the cell (bold, italics, and so on) appears on any entry you subsequently make in the cell.

Begin Guided Tour Edit a Cell

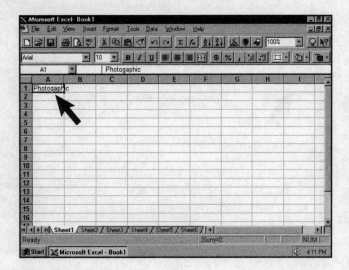

1 In cell A1, type **Photogaphic**. Be sure to spell it wrong by leaving out the r. When you finish, click the **check mark** in the Formula bar.

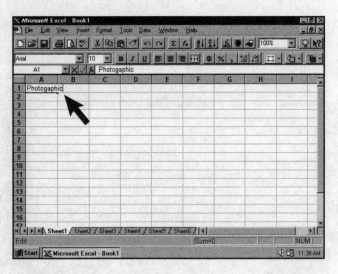

2 With cell A1 selected, press **F2** on the keyboard or double-click. An insertion point appears in the cell.

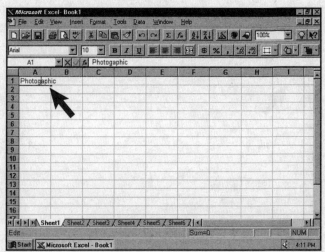

3 Use the left and right arrow keys to move the insertion point so that it appears between the g and the a.

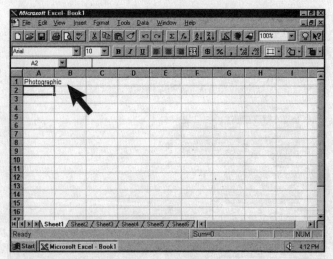

4 Type **r** and press **Enter**.

To remove characters, use the **Backspace** key to remove the characters immediately to the left of the insertion point, and the **Delete** key to remove the characters immediately to the right of the insertion point.

HOW TO...

Edit a Worksheet

Now that you know how to enter information into a worksheet, move around, and select cells and ranges, you need to know how to modify the information in the worksheet and the structure of the worksheet. After you enter data, you can copy and move information to other locations in the worksheet. You also can insert and delete cells, rows, and columns; sort and find information; and check spelling in your worksheet.

Most of these actions require working with ranges, so you need to start by expanding your knowledge of ranges.

What You Will Find in This Section

Work with Ranges

Earlier, you learned that ranges are groups of cells. Like single cells, we refer to a range by its address. The address for a range of cells consists of the addresses of the upper left and lower right cells that comprise the range, separated by a colon (:). For example, the range A1:C3 includes the cells A1, A2, A3, B1, B2, B3, C1, C2, and C3.

You don't need to use cell addresses to refer to a range; sometimes, it's much more meaningful and easier to name a range. That is, you identify a range and supply an English language name for it. For example, you can identify the range that contains the numbers for the first quarter of the year and call that range Quarter1. When you create formulas (you'll learn how later) that include the cells in the Quarter1 range, you'll be able to type the range name, not the cell addresses that comprise it.

In addition to naming a range, you can, of course, delete any range name you create. Deleting a range name has no effect on the data in the range.

Automatically Filling a Range

Often, you find that you need to fill a range with text you use frequently, such as the days of the week or the months of the year. Excel fills that range for you by simply providing an example of what you want.

The same holds true for numbers. Suppose you want column headings that represent years, but you only want every fifth year. Again, by providing Excel with an example, Excel fills the range for you.

When you use Excel to fill a range (whether with text or numbers), you use the *fill handle* on the cell pointer. The fill handle is the small black square in the lower right corner of the cell pointer.

Begin Guided Tour   Name a Range

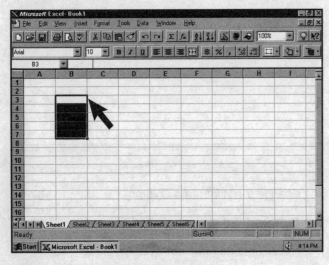

1 Select cells **B3:B7**.

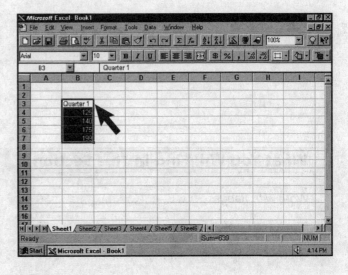

2 Type the column heading **Quarter 1**, press **Enter**, and type values until you fill the cells in the selected range.

Guided Tour Name a Range

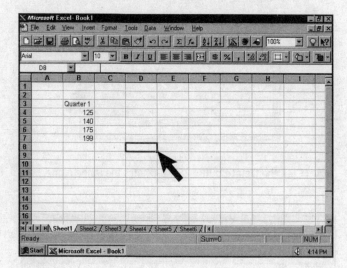

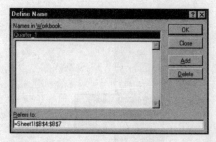

6 Excel displays the Define Name dialog box and suggests that you name the range Quarter_1.

3 Click anywhere outside the selection to deselect the range.

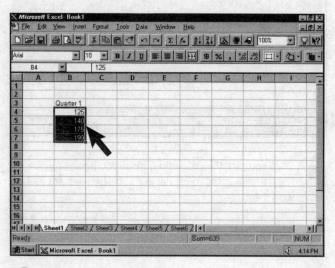

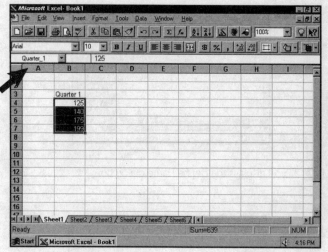

7 Once you choose **OK** in the Define Names dialog box, Excel displays the range name for the selection instead of a cell address.

4 Select cells **B4:B7**.

If you do not type a column label in Step 2, Excel does not suggest a name. You then have to type a range name in Step 6.

5 Open the **Insert** menu, select the **Name** command, and choose **Define** from the Name submenu.

Begin Guided Tour   Delete a Range Name

1 Open the **Insert** menu and select the **Name** command. From the Name submenu, choose the **Define** command.

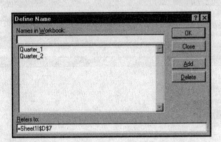

2 Excel displays the Define Name dialog box.

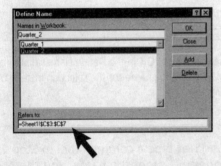

3 Highlight the range name in the **Names in Workbook** list box that you want to delete. Notice the cell address of the range appears at the bottom of the dialog box. (In the Refers to text box, the range name contains dollar signs ($). You'll learn more in "Use Cell Addresses Correctly," p. 160.)

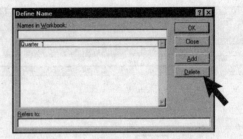

4 Click the **Delete** button. Excel deletes the range name.

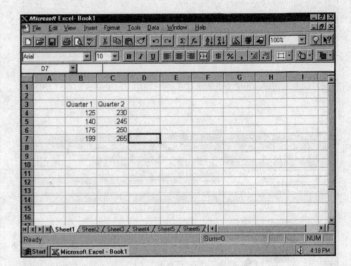

5 Once you click the **OK** button, the dialog box disappears, but the data in the range name you deleted remains in the worksheet.

Begin Guided Tour   Fill a Range with Text

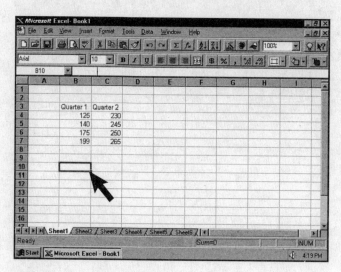

1 Click cell **B10** to select it.

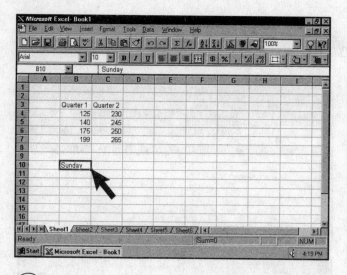

2 Type **Sunday** and click the **check mark** in the Formula bar.

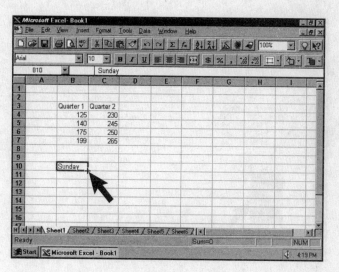

3 Place the mouse pointer over the fill handle of the cell pointer. The mouse pointer changes from a white cross to a black plus sign.

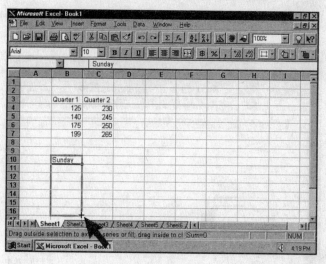

4 Press and hold the left mouse button and drag the mouse down to highlight cells **B10:B16**.

(continues)

Guided Tour   Fill a Range with Text   *(continued)*

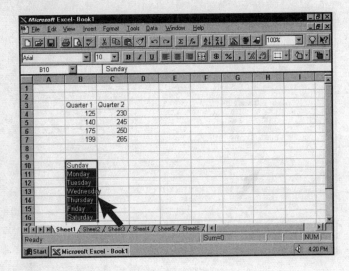

You can format a range of data using Excel's automatic formatting feature. See "Automatically Format a Range," p. 100 for more information.

5 Release the mouse button. Excel fills B10:B16 with the days of the week.

Begin Guided Tour   Fill a Range with Numbers

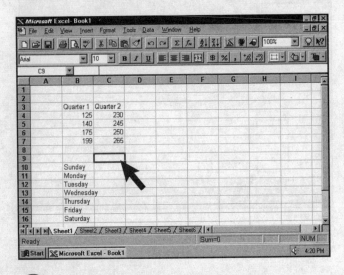

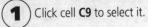

1 Click cell **C9** to select it.

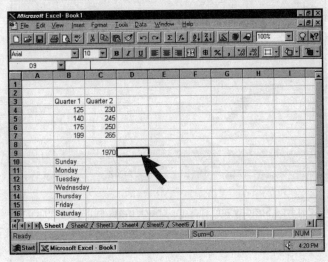

2 Type **1970** and press the **right arrow** key to move the cell pointer to D9.

Guided Tour   Fill a Range with Numbers

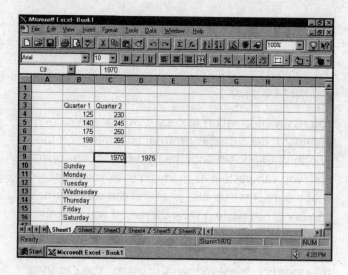

3 Type **1975** and press the **left arrow** key to move the cell pointer back to cell C9.

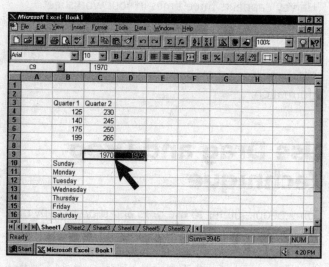

4 Select **C9:D9**.

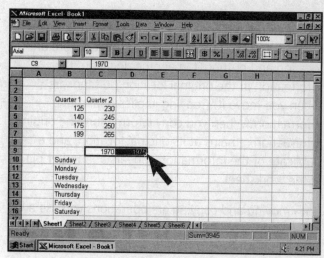

5 Move the mouse pointer onto the fill handle so that the pointer shape changes from a white cross to a black plus sign.

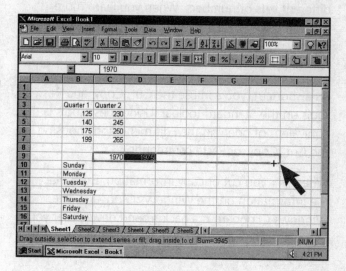

6 Drag the mouse (hold down the left mouse button and slide the mouse) to highlight **C9:H9**.

7 Release the mouse button. Excel fills the highlighted range with the years 1970, 1975, 1980, 1985, 1990, and 1995.

Move and Copy Information

Moving and copying are very similar operations. Moving implies taking information from one location and putting it in another location; the information in the original location "disappears" when you move it. Copying implies duplicating information. When you copy information, the original information remains at its original location, and a duplicate of the information appears at another place in the worksheet.

Both moving and copying are operations you use a lot when you set up a worksheet. Why? You can save a lot of time copying or moving information instead of retyping it. For example, you may want to move a title that is in the wrong cell. Or, when you create a formula, you may want to copy it to another location so that Excel performs the same calculation on two different sets of numbers. When you learn more about math and Excel, you'll begin to see the value of copying formulas. (See "Copy a Formula or Function," p. 160.)

As a shortcut, you can use the Cut, Copy, and Paste tools on the Standard toolbar. Using these tools is the equivalent of opening the Edit menu and choosing the Cut, Copy, or Paste commands.

Whenever you cut or copy information, Excel places the information on the Windows *Clipboard*. The Windows Clipboard is a background device that you don't actually "see," but you can think of as a "holding tank."

In Windows 95, you may have installed an accessory called the Clipboard Viewer. This accessory program opens a window that displays the information you stored on the Clipboard. If you installed it and want to open it, click the **Start** button, and highlight **Programs**. Then, select **Accessories** and click on **Clipboard Viewer**.

Information remains on the Windows Clipboard until you cut or copy again. Then, Windows 95 replaces the original information with the new information you cut or copied.

You paste information to copy it from the Windows Clipboard. Because the information remains on the Windows Clipboard until the next cut or copy operation, you can paste it as many times as you want. That means, for example, that you can cut information once, but paste it several times. If you type the word "Harvey" in a cell and then cut the information from the cell, "Harvey" disappears from the cell but is still stored on the Windows Clipboard. You can then move the cell pointer around the worksheet and paste the contents of the Windows Clipboard as many times as you want. If you paste three times, "Harvey" appears three times in your worksheet.

When you move or copy using the Edit menu, you can move or copy information from one cell to many cells. Simply select multiple cells before you paste the information.

Use Drag and Drop Technique

Some people prefer to use *drag and drop* to copy or move information. When you drag and drop, you use the mouse to drag information from one cell and drop it in another cell. This technique is quick, but not as quick as cut, copy, and paste. The drag and drop technique does not place information on the Windows Clipboard. Therefore, the information isn't readily available for multiple operations. So, if you need to paste several times, use traditional methods. For quick and dirty fixes, use drag and drop. Also, you may find it more practical to use traditional copying and moving techniques if you need to copy or move information to a location you can't see on the worksheet.

Begin Guided Tour   Move Information Using the Cut Button on the Standard Toolbar

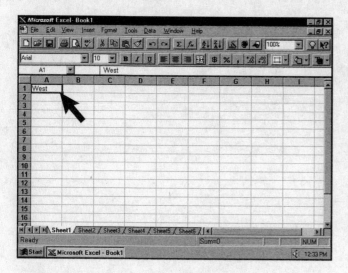

1 Type **West** in cell A1 and click the **check mark** in the Formula bar so that cell A1 remains selected.

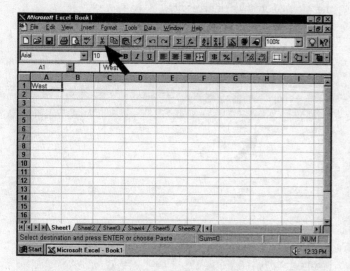

2 Click the **Cut** tool. Excel displays a flashing marquee around cell A1 to indicate that Excel placed the information in cell A1 on the Windows Clipboard.

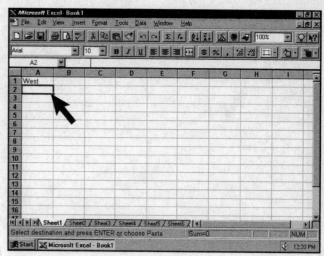

3 Move the cell pointer to the cell where you want to place information. For example, move the cell pointer to cell A2 to place information in cell A2.

If you want to move the information to A2:A6, for example, you select those cells and click the Paste button.

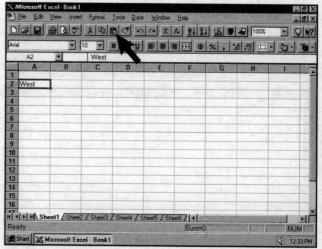

4 Click the **Paste** tool. Excel pastes the information from cell A1 into cell A2 and removes the information from cell A1.

Begin Guided Tour   Copy Information Using the Copy Button on the Standard Toolbar

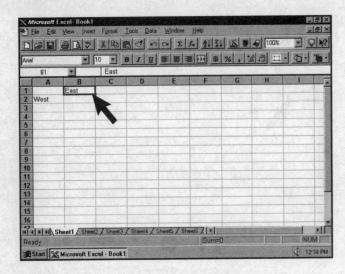

1 Type **East** in cell B1 and click the **check mark** in the Formula bar so that cell B1 remains selected.

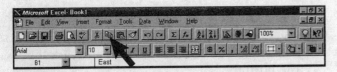

2 Click the **Copy** tool. Excel displays a flashing marquee around cell B1 to indicate that it placed the information in cell B1 on the Windows Clipboard.

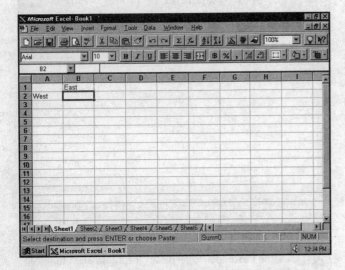

3 Move the cell pointer to the cell where you want to copy information. For example, move the cell pointer to cell B2 to copy information to cell B2.

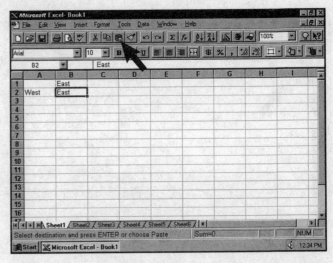

4 Click the **Paste** tool. Excel pastes the information you copied to the Windows Clipboard into cell B2. The flashing marquee continues to surround cell B1, indicating you can paste the information again, if necessary.

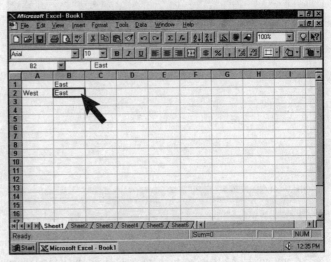

5 Press the **Esc** key to make the flashing marquee disappear and indicate to Excel that you are finished copying.

Begin Guided Tour   Move Using Drag and Drop

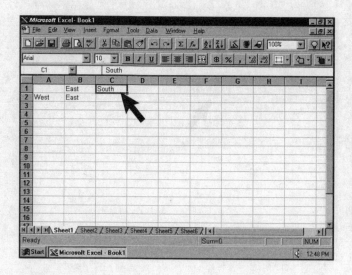

1 Click cell **C1**, type **South**, and click the **check mark** in the Formula bar so that C1 remains selected.

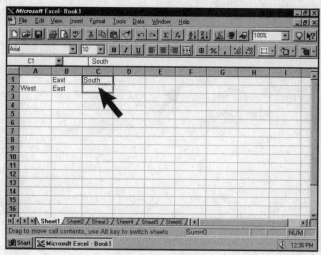

3 Drag the mouse (press and hold the left mouse button and then move the mouse) until the pointer appears over cell C2.

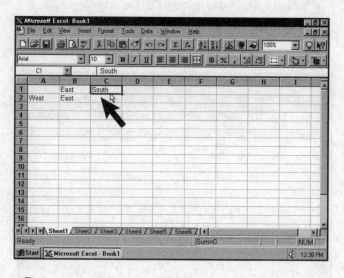

2 Slide the mouse pointer over the edge of the cell pointer until it changes to the shape of an arrow pointing up and to the left.

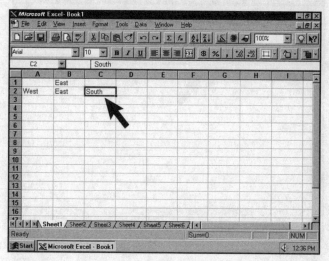

4 Release the mouse button. Excel moves the information from cell C1 to cell C2.

Begin Guided Tour   Copy Using Drag and Drop

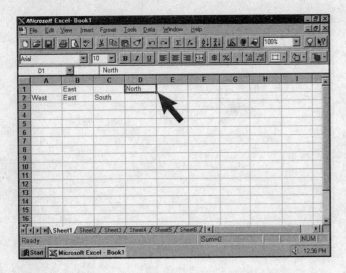

1 Click cell **D1**, type **North**, and click the **check mark** in the Formula bar so that D1 remains selected.

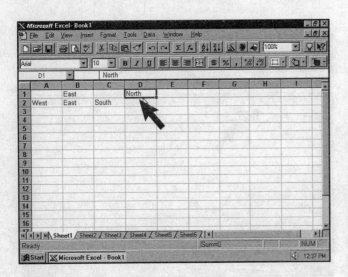

2 Slide the mouse pointer over the edge of the cell pointer until it changes to the shape of an arrow pointing up and to the left.

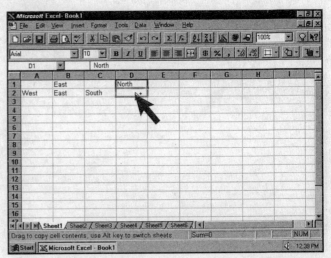

3 Press and hold the **Ctrl** key. The mouse pointer shape changes to an arrow with a small plus sign attached to it.

4 While continuing to hold the **Ctrl** key, drag the mouse (press and hold the left mouse button and then move the mouse) until the pointer appears over cell D2.

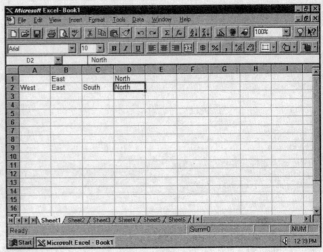

5 Release both the mouse button and the Ctrl key. Excel copies the information from cell D1 to cell D2. Both cells now contain North.

Check Your Spelling

Excel comes with a spell checker so you don't need to worry if you make typing or spelling mistakes when you type labels in your worksheet. The spell checker is easy to use. Once you start it, Excel starts in cell A1 and checks the spelling of words in all cells. If Excel finds mistakes while checking spelling, it attempts to suggest the correct spelling to you. It is possible that you may use words that are technical terms and aren't in Excel's dictionary. In these cases, you can add the word to the dictionary so that Excel doesn't consider these terms misspellings.

Use Excel's AutoCorrect Feature

All of us have words we type all the time that we invariably mistype. You can use Excel's AutoCorrect feature to store your own common typing mistakes so Excel corrects them immediately as you type. Excel already contains common typing mistakes such as "teh" for "the." You can add your own to the AutoCorrect list. Then, when you type your mistake, Excel simply corrects it for you.

Begin Guided Tour   Run the Spelling Checker

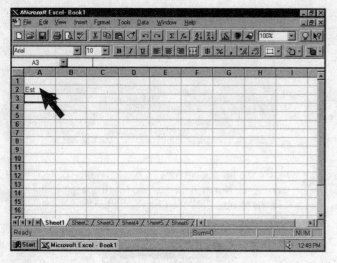

1 Click cell **A2**, type **Est** (for East), and press **Enter**.

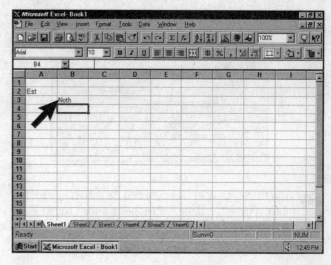

2 In cell B3, type **Noth** (for North) and press **Ctrl+Home**.

(continues)

Guided Tour Run the Spelling Checker *(continued)*

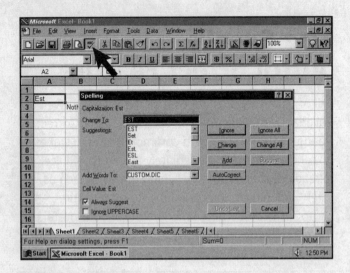

3 Start the Spelling Checker by clicking the **Spelling** tool. Excel starts in cell A1, checking for misspellings. It stops in cell A2 at the word Est and displays the Spelling dialog box.

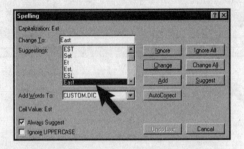

4 Use the Suggestions list box to find the correct word. Click **East** in the list, and the word appears in the Change To box.

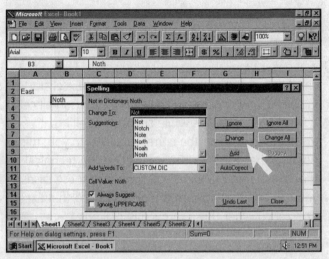

5 Click the **Change** button. Excel changes Est to East in cell A2 and looks for the next misspelling. It finds Noth.

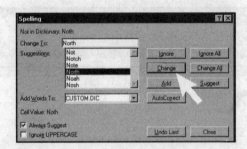

6 Again, use the Suggestions list box to find the correct word. Click **North** in the list, and North appears in the Change to box. Click the **Change** button.

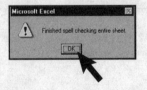

7 Excel changes Noth to North in cell B3 and continues spell checking. Excel finds no additional misspellings and displays a dialog box telling you that spell checking is complete. Click **OK**.

Begin Guided Tour Take Advantage of AutoCorrect

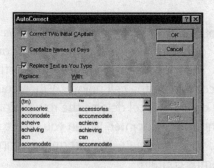

1 Open the **Tools** menu and choose the **AutoCorrect** command. Excel displays the AutoCorrect dialog box.

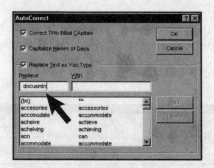

2 In the Replace text box, type the incorrect spelling of the word you want Excel to change. For example, type **docuemtn**.

Press the **Tab** key to move the insertion point to the With text box.

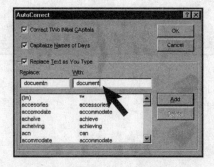

3 Type the correct spelling of the word you want Excel to change. For example, type **document**.

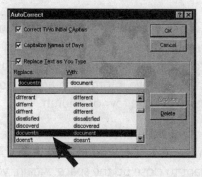

4 After you click the **Add** button, Excel adds the item to the list of corrections to make. If you want to add typing mistakes for Excel to correct, repeat steps 2 through 5.

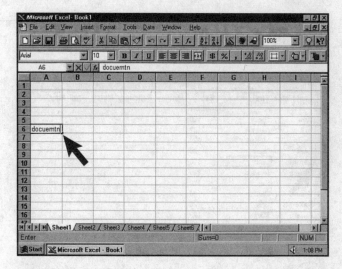

5 After you click the **OK** button, Excel closes the AutoCorrect dialog box. Click cell **A6** and type **docuemtn**.

6 After you press **Enter** or an **arrow** key, or click the **check mark**, Excel changes the spelling to document.

Removing the check marks from the check boxes tells Excel not to perform the actions next to the check boxes. In most cases, you should leave the check marks in the boxes.

Insert and Delete Rows and Columns

Often, when you set up a worksheet, you place information in the worksheet and then discover you need to add information in between two columns or rows. You can move information around, but it is much easier to insert a row or column.

Similarly, at times you find you included spare rows or columns in the middle of information in a worksheet, and you want to close up the space. Again, you can move information, but that is a lot more work than simply deleting the spare rows or columns.

When you insert rows, Excel inserts the rows above the row containing the cell pointer. When you insert columns, Excel inserts the columns to the left of the column containing the cell pointer. When you delete a row or column, Excel deletes the row or column containing the cell pointer. When you delete rows or columns, you also delete any information those rows and columns contain.

Begin Guided Tour   Insert a Row

	A	B	C	D	E	F	G	H	I
1	Last Name	First Name	Est.	January	February	March	April	May	
2			Donation						
3	Drew	Nancy	120	5	9	8	7	2	
4	Jackson	Andrew	120	10	3	7	8	6	
5	Hardy	Michael	120	7	8	3	9	4	
6	Jones	Janice	120	8	7	10	3	2	
7	Lilliputian	Linda	120	3	10	9	5	6	
8	son	Jonathan	120	9	5	5	9	4	
9	A	Sam	120	2	9	1	8	10	
10	Tipton	Charles	120	4	4	7	7	8	
11	Burke	Greg	120	7	6	2	3	9	
12	Poole	Margo	120	9	2	8	1	3	
13									

Sheet1 / Sheet2 / Sheet3 / Sheet4 / Sheet5 / Sheet6 /

1 Click any cell in the row above which you want to add a new row. For example, click a cell in row 7 to add a row above row 7.

2 Open the **Insert** menu and choose the **Rows** command.

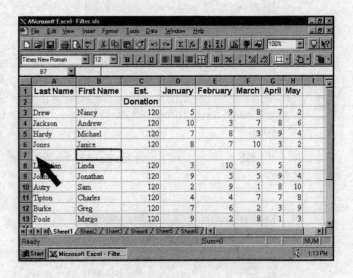

3 Excel inserts a row above the row containing the cell pointer.

Begin Guided Tour Insert a Column

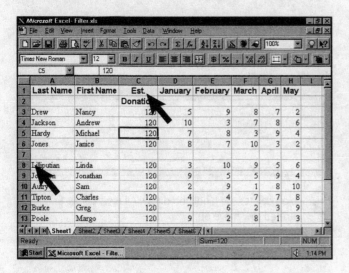

1 Click any cell in the column to the right of which you want to add a column. For example, click in column C to add a column between columns B and C.

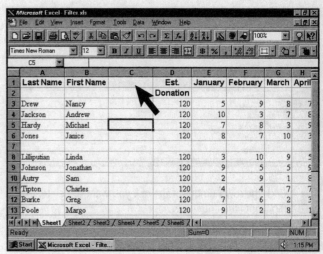

3 Excel inserts a column to the left of the column containing the cell pointer.

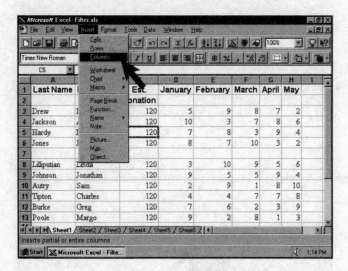

2 Open the **Insert** menu and choose the **Columns** command.

Begin Guided Tour   Delete a Row

	A	B	C	D	E	F	G	H
1	Last Name	First Name		Est.	January	February	March	April
2				Donation				
3	Drew	Nancy		120	5	9	8	7
4	Jackson	Andrew		120	10	3	7	8
5	Hardy	Michael		120	7	8	3	9
6	Jones	Janice		120	8	7	10	
7								
8	...utian	Linda		120	3	10	9	5
9	Joh..n	Jonathan		120	9	5	5	9
10	Autry	Sam		120	2	9	1	8
11	Tipton	Charles		120	4	4	7	
12	Burke	Greg		120	7	6	2	
13	Poole	Margo		120	9	2	8	1

Sheet1 / Sheet2 / Sheet3 / Sheet4 / Sheet5 / Sheet6 /

1 Click the row number of the row you want to delete. Excel highlights the entire row.

	A	B	C	D	E	F	G	H
1	Last Name	First Name		Est.	January	February	March	April
2				Donation				
3	Drew	Nancy		120	5	9	8	7
4	Jackson	Andrew		120	10	3	7	8
5	Hardy	Michael		120	7	8	3	9
6	Jones	Janice		120	8	7	10	9
7	Lilliputian	Linda		120	3	10	9	
8	Johnson	Jonathan		120	9	5	5	
9	Autry	Sam		120	2	9	1	8
10	Tipton	Charles		120	4	4	7	7
11	Burke	Greg		120	7	6	2	3
12	Poole	Margo		120	9	2	8	1
13								

Sheet1 / Sheet2 / Sheet3 / Sheet4 / Sheet5 / Sheet6 /

3 Excel deletes the highlighted row. All rows below the deleted row move up.

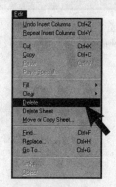

Edit
Undo Insert Columns Ctrl+Z
Repeat Insert Columns Ctrl+Y

Cut Ctrl+X
Copy Ctrl+C
Paste Ctrl+V
Paste Special...

Fill
Clear
Delete
Delete Sheet
Move or Copy Sheet...

Find... Ctrl+F
Replace... Ctrl+H
Go To... Ctrl+G

Links...
Object

2 Open the **Edit** menu and choose the **Delete** command.

Begin Guided Tour   Delete a Column

	A	B	C	D	E	F	G	H
1	Last Name	First Name		Est.	January	February	March	April
2				Donation				
3	Drew	Nancy		120	5	9	8	7
4	Jackson	Andrew		120	10	3	7	8
5	Hardy	Michael		120	7	8	3	9
6	Jones	Janice		120	8	7	10	3
7	Lilliputian	Linda		120	3	10	9	5
8	Johnson	Jonathan		120	9	5	5	9
9	Autry	Sam		120	2	9	1	8
10	Tipton	Charles		120	4	4	7	7
11	Burke	Greg		120	7	6	2	3
12	Poole	Margo		120	9	2	8	1
13								

Sheet1 / Sheet2 / Sheet3 / Sheet4 / Sheet5 / Sheet6 /

1 Click letter of the column you want to delete. Excel highlights the entire column.

	A	B	C	D	E	F	G	H	I
1	Last Name	First Name	Est.	January	February	March	April	May	
2			Donation						
3	Drew	Nancy	120	5	9	8	7	2	
4	Jackson	Andrew	120	10	3	7	8	6	
5	Hardy	Michael	120	7	8	3	9	4	
6	Jones	Janice	120	8	7	10	3	2	
7	Lilliputian	Linda	120	3	10	9	5	6	
8	Johnson	Jonathan	120	9	5	5	9	4	
9	Autry	Sam	120	2	9	1	8	10	
10	Tipton	Charles	120	4	4	7	7	8	
11	Burke	Greg	120	7	6	2	3	9	
12	Poole	Margo	120	9	2	8	1	3	
13									

Sheet1 / Sheet2 / Sheet3 / Sheet4 / Sheet5 / Sheet6 /

2 Open the **Edit** menu and choose the **Delete** command. Excel deletes the highlighted column. All columns to the right of the deleted column move to the left.

Change the Width of a Column

On occasion, you need to make a column wider or narrower than the default column width that Excel provides. For example, if you store a number with a format larger than the column width can handle, Excel displays pound signs (#####) in the cell instead of the value of the cell. Whenever you see this indicator, you simply need to widen the column to view the cell's contents.

You can manually increase or decrease the size of a column, or you can use Excel's AutoFit feature. The AutoFit feature enables you to select a cell in a column and then adjust the column based on the size you need for the selected cell.

Begin Guided Tour   Adjust a Column's Width

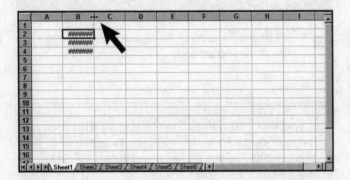

1 Slide the mouse pointer onto the right edge of the letter of the column you want to adjust. The mouse pointer changes shape to a black vertical bar with arrows pointing right and left.

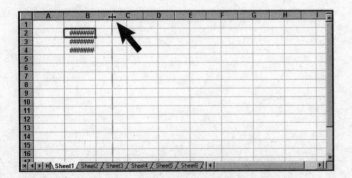

2 Drag the right edge of the column. To make the column larger, drag to the right. To make the column smaller, drag to the left. For example, to make column B wider, drag right.

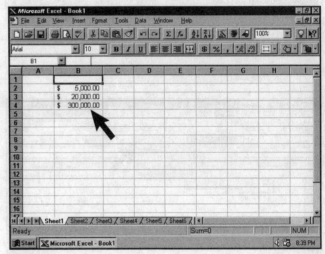

3 When you release the mouse button, Excel modifies the column width. Now that the column is wider, you can see the values in the column.

Although you can manually widen a row, you really don't need to. If you change the point size of the font for a selected cell, Excel widens or narrows the row to accommodate the font.

Begin Guided Tour Automatically Adjusting a Column's Width

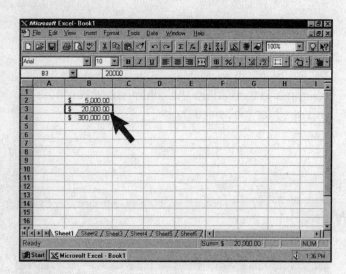

1 In the column you want to adjust, select the cell you want to use as the sample width for the column.

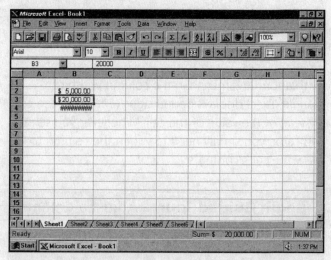

3 Excel adjusts the width of the column to accommodate the width of the selected entry.

If you want to adjust the column so that it is large enough to accommodate all entries in the column, select the entire column by clicking its column letter.

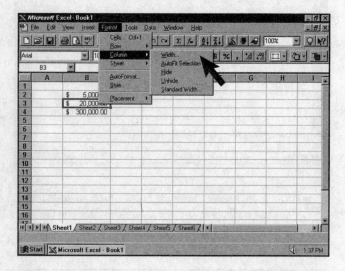

2 Open the **Format** menu and select the **Column** command. Choose the **AutoFit Selection** command from the Column submenu.

Hide (and Redisplay) Rows and Columns

Sometimes, your worksheet gets so large that data in the sheet gets in the way of your viewing the larger picture. For example, suppose you track the monthly dues the members of a club pay. Your worksheet shows monthly information, and, in the column to the right of December, you create a Totals column. To read the information in the Totals column, you need to scroll the worksheet to the right, but then you lose the row labels, so you're not sure whose total you're seeing.

One way to handle this type of problem is to hide some columns on-screen. When you hide columns, you don't see their information, and Excel closes the gap between displayed columns.

Whenever you hide columns or rows, the column or row's corresponding letters and numbers don't appear in the worksheet. You can hide more than one row or column at a time by selecting the rows or columns you want to hide.

Begin Guided Tour   Hide Rows or Columns

1 Place the cell pointer anywhere in the column or row you want to hide. To hide more than one row or column, select the rows or columns you want to hide by pressing the **Shift** key and then clicking each row number or column letter. For example, to hide columns D through O, press **Shift** and click each of those column letters.

2 Open the **Format** menu and highlight the **Column** or **Row** command, depending on what you want to hide. Choose the **Hide** command from the submenu that appears.

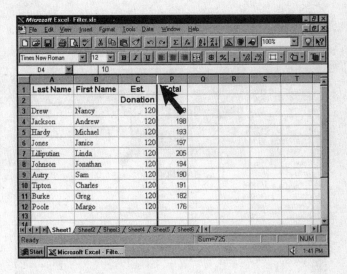

3 Excel hides the selected column(s) or row(s), and the column(s) or row(s)'s letter(s) or number(s) disappear.

You can simultaneously hide groups of rows or groups of columns, but you cannot simultaneously hide rows and columns.

Begin Guided Tour   Redisplay Hidden Rows or Columns

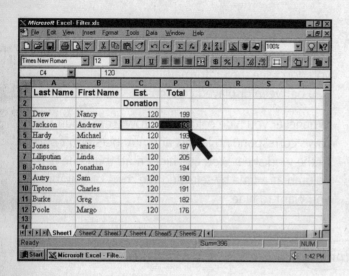

1 Select a cell in each row or column that borders the hidden row or column. You must select at least two cells.

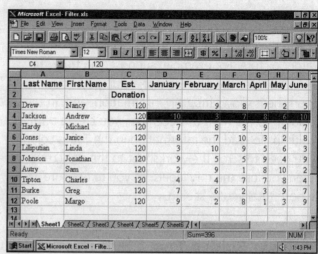

3 Excel redisplays the hidden columns or rows.

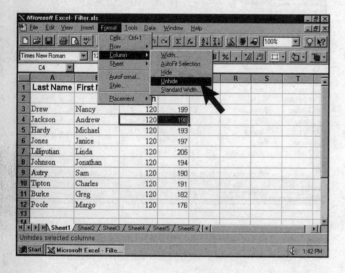

2 Open the **Format** menu and select the **Column** or **Row** command, depending on what you want to redisplay. Choose the **Unhide** command from the submenu.

Freeze Row and Column Titles On-Screen

Freezing row and column titles is another way to deal with large worksheets in which you can't see all of the information on the screen. Again, suppose you track monthly dues paid by the members of a club. Your worksheet shows monthly information, and in the column to the right of December, you create a Totals column. To read the information in the Totals column, you need to scroll the worksheet to the right, but then you lose the row labels, so you're not sure whose total you're seeing.

Another way to handle this problem is to freeze the rows and columns that contain your labels so that they do not scroll off-screen when you scroll the worksheet. When you freeze rows or columns, the rows or columns always appear on-screen. Scrolling does not remove them from your view. Using this method, you can keep the members' names on-screen while you look at the total dues each has paid so far.

When you want to freeze just row headings, click the cell in column A that is below the row(s) you want to freeze. When you want to freeze just column headings, click the cell in row 1 (one) that is to the right of the column(s) you want to freeze. When you want to freeze both row and column headings, select the cell below and to the right of the row(s) and column(s) you want to freeze. Remember, if you freeze both rows and columns, you tell Excel to keep those rows and columns on-screen, regardless of how far you scroll. Suppose, for example, you freeze Column A and Row 1. Column A contains information down to row 20. If you press the Page Down key to display Row 21, Column A is empty.

Begin Guided Tour   Freeze Titles On-Screen

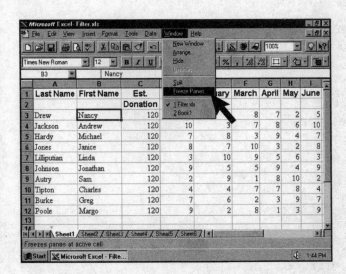

1 Click a cell to mark the row(s) and column(s) you want to freeze. For example, to freeze both column A and rows 1 through 2, select cell **B3**.

2 Open the **Window** menu and choose the **Freeze Panes** command.

(continues)

Guided Tour Freeze Titles On-Screen

(continued)

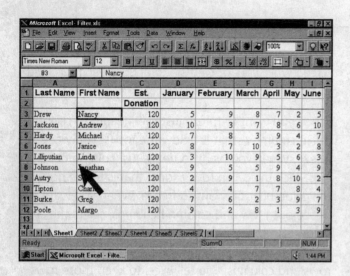

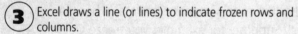

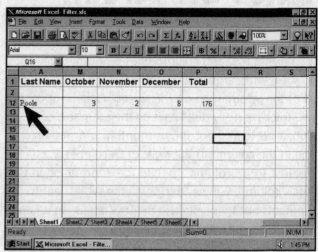

3 Excel draws a line (or lines) to indicate frozen rows and columns.

4 Scroll your worksheet screen. You see both the frozen rows and columns and the rows and columns far below and to the right of the frozen rows and columns. For example, if you scroll to view Columns M through S and Rows 12 through 25, you can still see Column A and Rows 1 and 2 because they are frozen.

To unfreeze rows and columns, re-open the **Window** menu and select the **Unfreeze Panes** command.

Find, Replace, Sort, and Filter Information

There are several ways to find information while working with Excel data. You can find and replace information in Excel in a manner similar to the one you use in a word processor. Or, you can sort a list of information, either from highest to lowest or alphabetically (from A to Z or Z to A). You can even have Excel filter a list of information so that you see items in the list that meet criteria you specify.

Sorting and filtering become quite useful when you set up lists to use in a database environment.

See "Create a Data List," p. 182.

Find Information

Excel contains two commands—the Find command and the Replace command—that you can use to locate information. If you use the Find command, you specify what you want to search for, called *search criteria*. If you use the Replace command, you specify the search criteria and replacement information. For both commands, Excel starts at the cell you select and searches the entire worksheet. Each time Excel finds something that matches the search criteria, Excel stops and highlights the cell. When you use the Replace command, Excel asks if you want to replace what it finds. And, if you know you want to change every occurrence of the search criteria, you can replace all occurrences without viewing individual occurrences.

Suppose, for example that you type the word Total into one cell and then copy it to several cells. Later, you decide that you want every instance of "Total" but one to read "Subtotal." You can find "Total" and replace it with "Subtotal."

Find and replace locates information in one way; when you work with lists of information, two other ways become available:

- Sorting
- Filtering

Sort Lists

When you have a list of items, you can sort the list in ascending or descending order. When the list contains numbers, ascending order means from lowest to highest and descending order means from highest to lowest. If the list contains labels, ascending means alphabetically from A to Z, while descending means alphabetically from Z to A.

Often, the lists you use in Excel contain related information in multiple columns. And, you notice that Excel selects all the columns in your list to be sure that, when you perform the sort, related information doesn't become "disconnected." For example, suppose the list contained a person's last name in column A, the first name in column B, the age in column C, and the height in column D, and you want to sort all the information so that all the information about the tallest person appears first in the list. When you sort, you choose to sort all the information so that it is ordered by Column D (height). When Excel performs the sort, it automatically selects all the columns to ensure that one person's height does not appear to be assigned to another person after you sort the information.

Suppose, in the example above, several people are the same height. You can determine the order they appear in the list by specifying a "tie-breaker" when you set up the sort. You break ties by sorting the list first by one column and then by another. For example, suppose you sorted the list in the example first by Column D (height) in descending order and then by Column A (last name) in ascending order. The tallest person in the list would appear first, followed by the next tallest person, and so on. People who have the same height appear in the list in alphabetical order by last name.

Filter a List

You can have Excel filter a list so that you view only those items in the list that match criteria you establish. Excel calls this the AutoFilter feature.

As a variation on the AutoFilter feature, when you work with lists of values, Excel can show you the top ten items in the list (or even the bottom ten items in the list). You specify whether you want to see top or bottom and how many items (five, ten, and so on).

Begin Guided Tour   Find and Replace Information

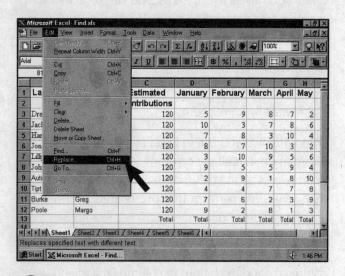

1 Open the **Edit** menu and choose the **Replace** command.

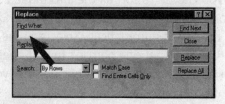

2 Excel displays the Replace dialog box.

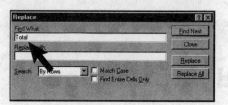

3 Type the information you want to find in the Find What text box. In this example, type **Total**. Press the **Tab** key to move to the Replace with text box.

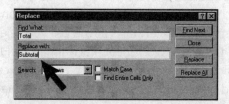

4 In the Replace with text box, type the information you want Excel to use when it replaces the information you just specified in the Find What text box. For example, type **Subtotal**.

Guided Tour Find and Replace Information

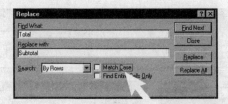

5 Place a check mark in the Match Case check box if you want Excel to find occurrences that match the case (uppercase, lowercase) of your criteria.

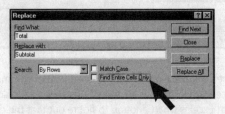

6 Place a check mark in the Find Entire Cells Only check box if you want Excel to make changes to cells that contain only the information you specified in the Find What text box. In this example, if you check this box and a cell in the worksheet contains Total of All instead of just Total, Excel skips that cell. When you're ready to begin, click **Find Next**.

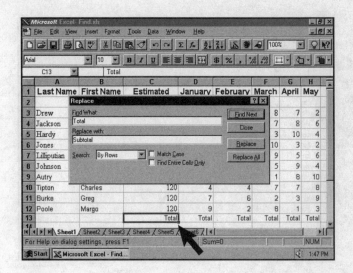

7 Excel highlights the first occurrence of your criteria.

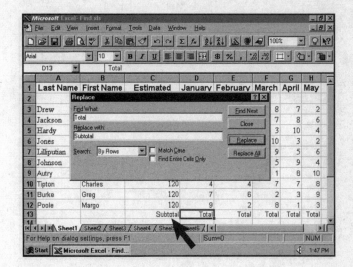

8 Click **Replace** to change the information in the selected cell, or click **Find Next** to leave the cell unchanged and find the next occurrence.

9 Repeat step 8 until you finish. Or, if you know you want to change all occurrences in the worksheet, choose **Replace All**.

Begin Guided Tour   Sort Information

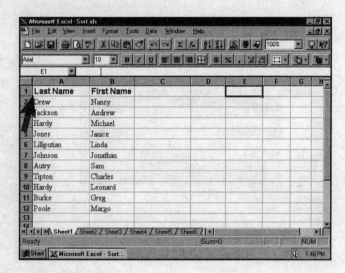

1 Set up your list of information. You don't need a column title, but you can have one if you want.

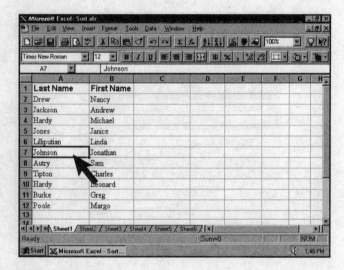

2 Select any cell in the list. You find sorting is easier if you select a cell in the column you want to sort by primarily. In the example, to sort all the information in the list by last name, select any cell in Column A.

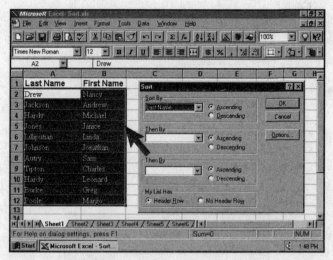

3 Open the **Data** menu and choose the **Sort** command. Excel highlights your list and displays the Sort dialog box. Notice that Excel is smart enough to figure out that the column label is not part of the list you want to sort.

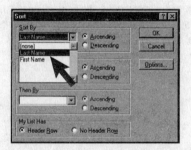

4 The Sort By list box suggests that you sort by the column heading. If you have no column heading, you see the column letter in the list box (for example, column A). If the suggestion is wrong, open the list box and change it.

Guided Tour   Sort Information

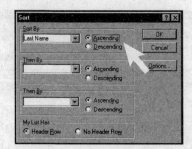

⑤ Decide whether you want to sort in ascending or descending order and click the appropriate option button.

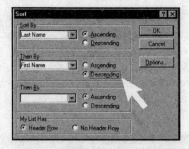

⑥ Use the other two list boxes to choose columns you want Excel to use to "break ties." In this example, you sort first by Last Name in either ascending or descending order. Then, to break ties for those people with the same last name, sort by First Name, again choosing Ascending or Descending. Choose **OK**.

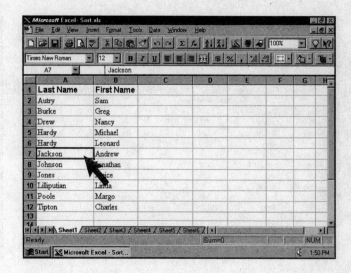

⑦ Excel closes the Sort dialog box and displays your sorted list.

Begin Guided Tour   Filter to Display the Top Ten Items

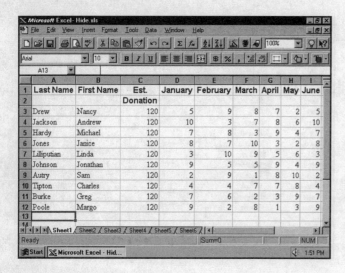

1 Set up your list. To filter for the top items, the list must contain a column of values.

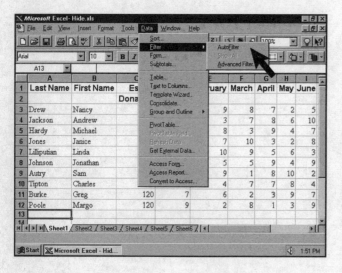

2 Open the **Data** menu and select the **Filter** command. From the Filter submenu, choose **AutoFilter**.

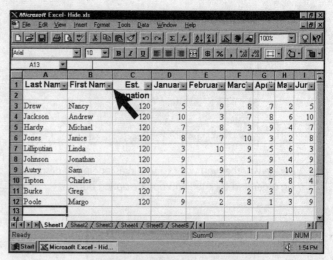

3 Excel places a check mark to the left of the AutoFilter command and displays drop-down list box arrows to the right of each column in your worksheet.

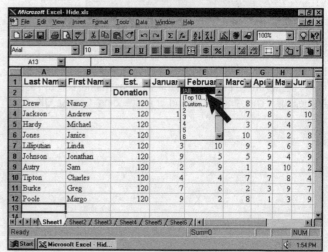

4 Click the list box arrow of the column by which you want to filter the data. If you're filtering for the top ten (or bottom ten), choose a column containing values. Choose **Top 10**.

Guided Tour Filter to Display the Top Ten Items

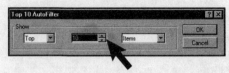

5 Excel displays the Top 10 AutoFilter dialog box.

6 From the first (leftmost) list box, choose to see the top or bottom of the list.

7 From the middle list box, specify the quantity of items you want to see.

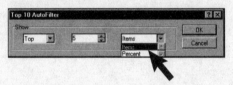

8 From the last rightmost list box, choose whether you want to filter by actual value or by percentage. Choose **OK** when you finish.

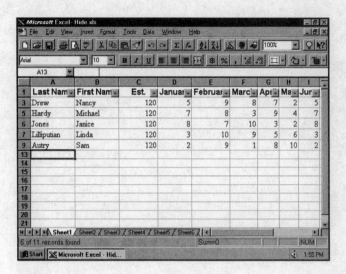

9 Excel displays the results of your filter.

To redisplay all your data and remove the filter, reopen the **Data** menu, highlight the **Filter** command, and choose the **AutoFilter** command to remove the check mark and redisplay all your data.

HOW TO...

Manage Workbooks and Worksheets

You've learned a lot so far about moving around, entering, and editing worksheets and workbooks. Focus now on managing your files.

What You Will Find in This Section

Save a Workbook

S aving your work is obviously important. When you save, you save a workbook and all the worksheets in it. The workbook is your document or file, whichever you prefer to call it.

When you make any changes to a workbook, Excel prompts you to save the workbook when you try to close either the workbook or Excel. If you did not save this workbook previously, Excel behaves differently than if you did save the workbook previously: you see a dialog box in which you can assign the workbook a name plus a drive and folder where you want to store the workbook. The suggested folder appears in the Save in list box. Use the three icons immediately to the right of the Save in list box:

 To choose a folder up one level.

 To look in the "favorites" folder.

 To create a new folder.

Or, double-click one of the folders that appears below the list box to open it.

If you know that you will only use a file in Windows 95, you can name your file anything you want. Be aware, however, if you intend to share your file with someone who doesn't use Windows 95. If you plan to do this, you need to follow standard DOS naming conventions.

When you save a workbook that you saved before, you save the current version on-screen and overwrite the original version on disk. This means you always store the most current version of your file on disk. Because you saved the file before, Excel assumes you want to continue using the original name, so you don't see a dialog box.

If you want to keep both versions—the on-screen version and the original—you can save the on-screen version with a different name. See "Rename a Workbook," p. 90.

Saving a workbook does not remove it from the screen. Saving a workbook copies updates you made on-screen to disk. To remove a workbook from the screen, you must close the workbook. See "Get a Workbook Off the Screen," p. 87.

AutoSave

Originally, Excel did not offer a means for you to automatically save your work. You had to remember to save your work every five or ten minutes to guard against power losses or other disasters beyond your control.

Now, you can take advantage of the AutoSave feature. You use the AutoSave feature to set up a time interval for Excel to save your work automatically. AutoSave doesn't replace the Save command; AutoSave creates a temporary copy of your work that remains out there in cyberland until you save your work. Since the AutoSave version is only temporary, you still need to save your workbooks. AutoSave simply helps you save most of your work if a disaster, such as a power failure, strikes.

The AutoSave feature is an add-in you can choose to install when you install Excel. You may have installed the AutoSave feature, but you don't see any evidence of it in Excel until you activate the AutoSave feature and set it up. Once you activate the AutoSave feature, the AutoSave command appears on the Tools menu, preceded by a check mark.

Begin Guided Tour   Save a New Workbook

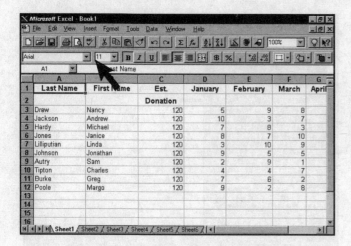

1 Check the title bar to make sure you're working in Book1 or any other workbook that you haven't saved.

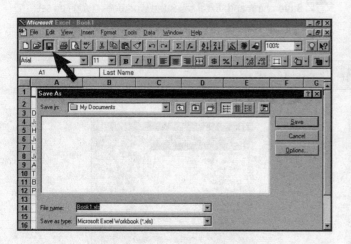

2 Click the **Save** tool, or open the **File** menu and choose the **Save** command. Excel displays the Save As dialog box.

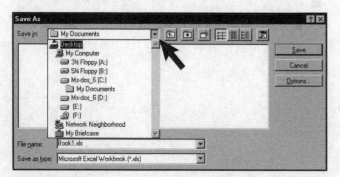

3 Click the down arrow in the Save in drop-down list to store the workbook in an existing folder, or click the **Create a New Folder** button to create a new folder for the workbook.

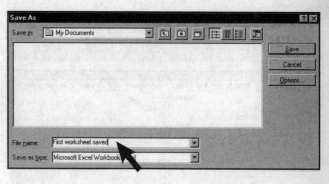

4 Type a name for the workbook in the File Name list box. In Windows 95, you're not bound by DOS naming conventions, so you can name the workbook any name up to 255 characters long (and even include spaces). Choose the **Save** button.

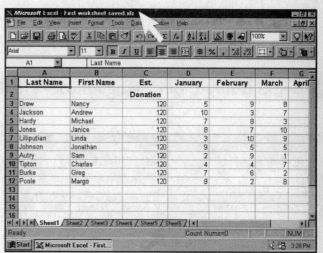

5 Excel saves the workbook, closes the dialog box, and places the new name in the title bar.

Begin Guided Tour   Save an Existing Workbook

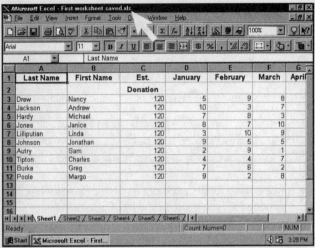

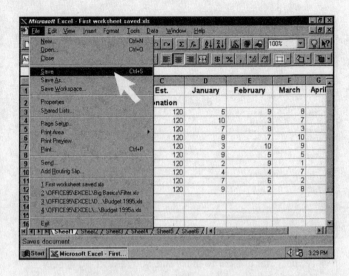

1 Check the title bar to make sure you're not working in Book1 or any other workbook that you have saved.

2 Click the **Save** tool or open the **File** menu and choose the **Save** command. Excel saves the workbook. (You can see Excel saving your workbook if you watch the status bar.)

Begin Guided Tour   Add AutoSave to the Tools Menu

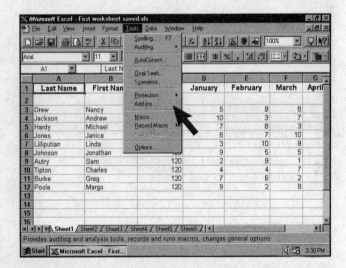

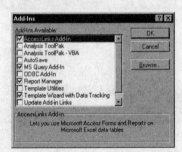

2 Choose the **Add-Ins** command. Excel displays the Add-Ins dialog box.

1 Open the **Tools** menu. If AutoSave isn't activated, you don't see the AutoSave command on the menu.

Guided Tour Add AutoSave to the Tools Menu

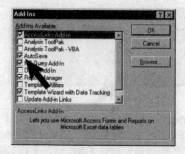

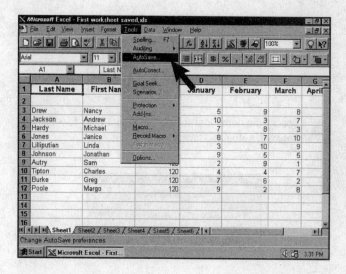

3 Place a check mark in the AutoSave check box and click **OK**.

If you don't see AutoSave in Add-Ins dialog box, you didn't install the feature when you installed Excel. Run the Setup program again and add the AutoSave component to Excel's Add-ins. See "Install Excel 7," page 10.

4 Reopen the **Tools** menu. You now see the **AutoSave** command.

Begin Guided Tour Set AutoSave Settings

1 Open the **Tools** menu and choose the **AutoSave** command. Excel displays the AutoSave dialog box.

2 Place a check mark in the Automatic Save Every check box. Remove the check mark from the Automatic Save Every check box only if you want to disable AutoSave.

(continues)

Guided Tour Set AutoSave Settings *(continued)*

3 Specify the number of minutes you want Excel to wait between automatic saves.

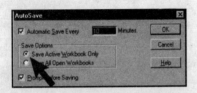

4 Decide whether to save the current workbook only or all open workbooks.

> You can have many workbooks open at the same time. See "Create a New Workbook," p. 88, and "Open an Existing Workbook," p. 89.

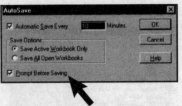

5 If you simply want Excel to save the workbook, you can remove the check mark from the Prompt Before Saving check box. If you leave the check mark, Excel asks you to confirm the save. Click **OK** to save your settings.

Get a Workbook Off the Screen

Eventually, you're going to finish working with a workbook and want to get it off your screen. To do that, you close the workbook. Closing the workbook is not the same as closing the program. When you close a workbook, Excel is still running and ready to start another workbook or open an existing workbook.

If you make any changes to the current workbook and you don't save those changes, Excel asks if you want to save the workbook. Otherwise, Excel simply removes the workbook from your screen.

Begin Guided Tour   Close a Workbook

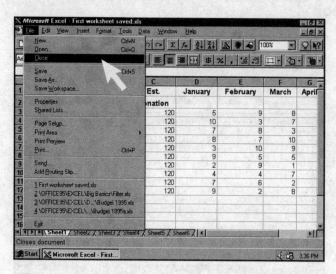

1 With an existing workbook open, open the **File** menu.

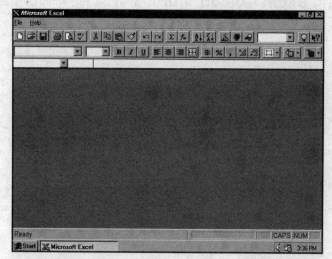

2 Choose the **Close** command. Excel either closes the workbook or asks if you want to save the workbook.

Create a New Workbook

Y ou need, at some point, to begin a new workbook. Each time you start Excel, the program supplies a new workbook, Book1. Suppose you use that workbook, save it, and close it. Now you need to start another new workbook. You don't need to exit from the program and then restart it. You can create your own new workbook—Excel names it Book, followed by a sequential number (Book2, Book3, Book4, and so on).

Book1 has a series of default settings based on a template. You can start new workbooks based on other templates with other settings. See "Use Templates Included with Excel," p. 166.

Begin Guided Tour   Start a New Workbook

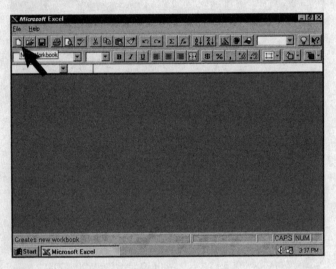

1 Point at the **New Workbook** tool on the Standard toolbar.

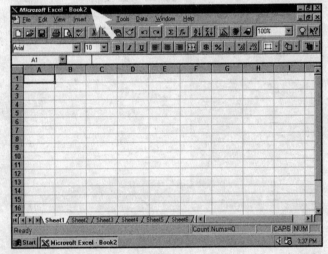

2 Click the **New Workbook** tool. Excel starts a new workbook, in this case, Book2.

Open an Existing Workbook

Suppose you create a workbook, save it, and close it because you finish working with it. Now, you receive some new information that you need to include in that workbook. So, how do you open that workbook to add that information?

Begin Guided Tour   Re-open a Workbook

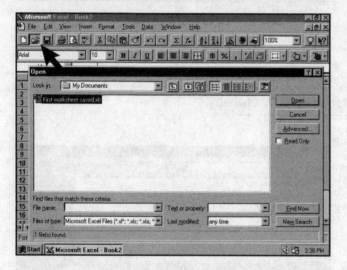

1 Click the **Open** tool on the Standard toolbar. Excel displays the Open dialog box.

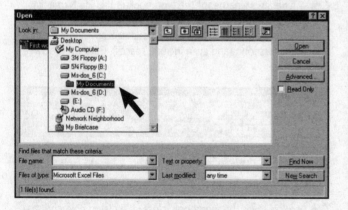

2 Select a folder that contains the workbook you want to open.

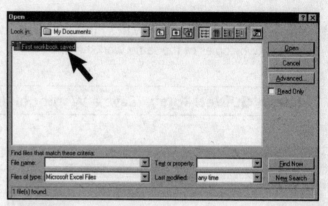

3 Highlight the workbook to select it. Click the **Open** button. Or, just double-click on the workbook file.

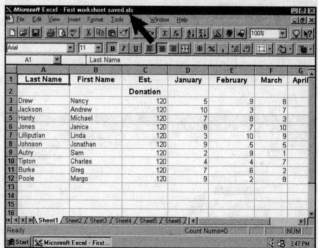

4 Excel opens the workbook, closes the dialog box, and the workbook appears on-screen.

Rename a Workbook

When you save a workbook you saved before, typically you save the current version on-screen and overwrite the original version on disk. This means you always store the most current version of your file on disk. But sometimes, you want to keep both versions—the on-screen version and the original. Rename the workbook using the Save As command on the File menu and save the on-screen version with a different name. Saving a file with a different name gives you two copies of the same worksheet.

It's important to understand that you cannot use the Save tool on the Standard toolbar to rename a file. The Save tool saves the file using its current file name. Only the Save As command gives you the opportunity to supply a different name for the file.

Begin Guided Tour   Save a Workbook Using a New Name

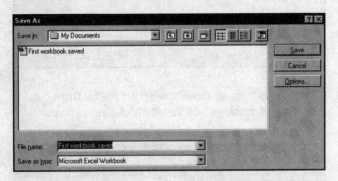

1 Open the **File** menu and choose the **Save As** command. Excel displays the Save As dialog box.

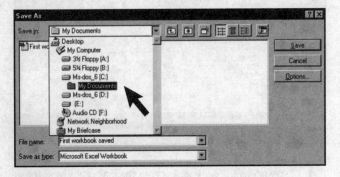

2 Click the down arrow in the Save in list and select a folder in which to store the workbook.

3 Type a new name for the workbook in the File Name list box. In Windows 95, you're not bound by DOS naming conventions, and you can name the workbook any name up to 255 characters long (and even include spaces). Click on the **Save** button.

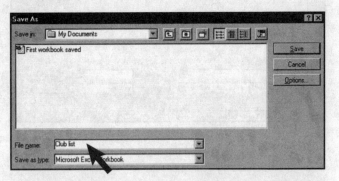

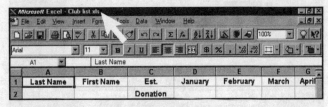

4 Excel saves the workbook, closes the dialog box, and the new name appears in the title bar.

Remember, the original version of your workbook, under the original name, still exists. You can reopen it and make changes to it.

Rename a Worksheet

As you may notice, each workbook has 16 worksheets in it when you first start the workbook. Excel names these sheets, originally enough, Sheet1, Sheet2, Sheet3, and so on. Obviously, these names aren't particularly meaningful, but you can change them so that the names mean something to you.

Suppose, for example, that you create a budget on Sheet1 and use Sheet2 through Sheet7 to calculate details for line items on the budget such as Groceries, Electricity, Water, and Telephone. Your worksheets are more meaningful if they have names such as Household Budget, Groceries, Electricity, Water, and Telephone. You can rename the sheet tabs.

Begin Guided Tour   Rename a Worksheet Tab

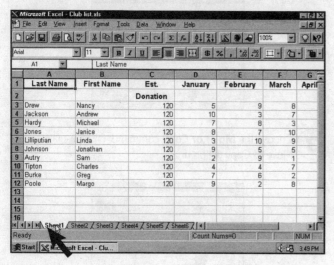

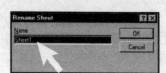

3 Choose the **Rename** command. Excel displays the Rename Sheet dialog box. Type a new name for the worksheet and click **OK**.

1 Move the mouse pointer over the sheet tab you want to rename. The pointer changes to an arrow pointing up and to the left.

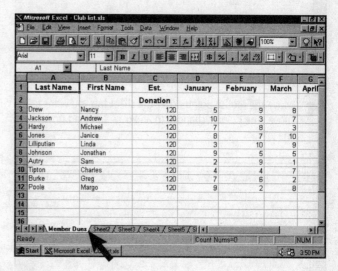

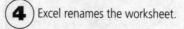

4 Excel renames the worksheet.

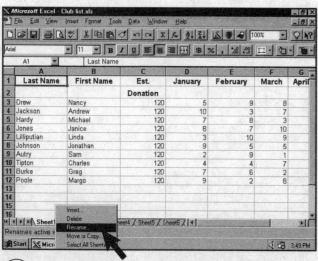

2 Click the right mouse button. A shortcut menu appears.

Move and Copy Worksheets Within a Workbook

Sometimes, you start working in a workbook and you get all the information in it that you want, but then you realize that the sheets aren't in the order you want them to appear. You can move and copy worksheets within a workbook. You also can move or copy a worksheet in one workbook to another workbook.

Begin Guided Tour Move a Worksheet

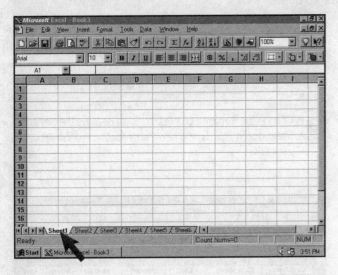

1 Move the mouse pointer over the sheet tab you want to move. The pointer changes to an arrow pointing up and to the left.

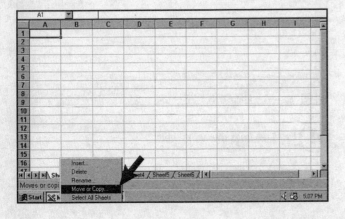

2 Click the right mouse button. A shortcut menu appears.

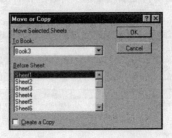

3 Choose the **Move or Copy** command. Excel displays the Move or Copy dialog box.

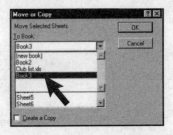

4 Click on the To Book list's arrow to display the drop-down list. Click the workbook to which you want to move the worksheet.

Guided Tour   Move a Worksheet

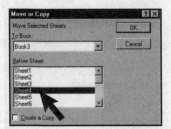

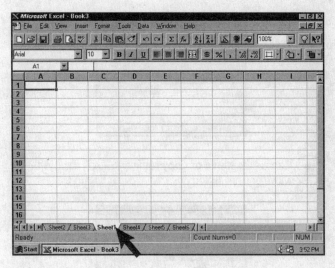

5 In the Before Sheet list box, click the sheet you want to appear *after* the one you're moving. Click **OK**.

If you want to move a sheet within a workbook, you can use the drag-and-drop technique. Point at the sheet tab you want to move and drag it along the sheet tab markers to its new location.

6 Excel moves the worksheet.

Begin Guided Tour   Copy a Worksheet

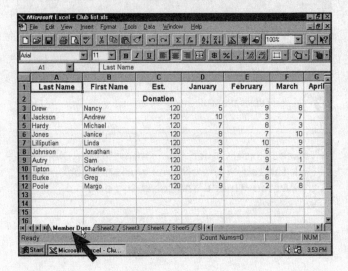

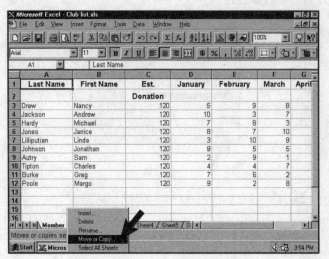

1 Move the mouse pointer over the sheet tab you want to copy. The pointer changes to an arrow pointing up and to the left.

2 Click the right mouse button. A shortcut menu appears.

(continues)

Guided Tour Copy a Worksheet *(continued)*

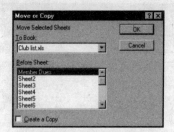

3 Choose the **Move or Copy** command. Excel displays the Move or Copy dialog box.

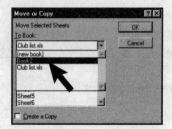

4 Click the arrow on the To Book list to display the drop-down list. Click the workbook to which you want to copy the worksheet.

5 Place a check mark in the Create a Copy check box.

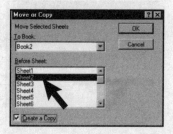

6 In the Before Sheet list box, select the sheet you want to appear *after* the one you're copying. Choose **OK**.

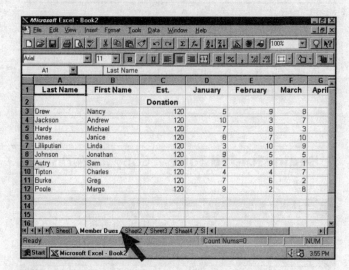

7 Excel copies the worksheet.

To see if Excel copied the information, either click the tab of the original worksheet or open the Window menu and select the original workbook.

Insert and Delete Worksheets

There are times when you store information on a worksheet and then decide you no longer need that worksheet. You can erase the worksheet, but the workbook looks strange if the previous and subsequent sheets contain information. So, you need to delete the worksheet.

At other times, you find you need a new worksheet in between two sheets you already set up. You can

insert a new worksheet in a workbook. When you insert a worksheet, Excel places the sheet to the left of the active worksheet.

> You can ultimately store up to 255 worksheets in a workbook.

Begin Guided Tour　　Insert a Worksheet

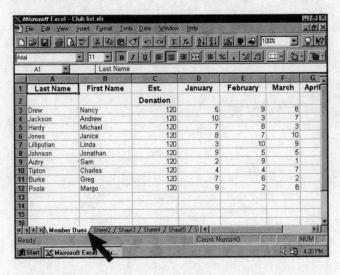

1 Click the worksheet tab of the worksheet you want to appear *behind* the new worksheet.

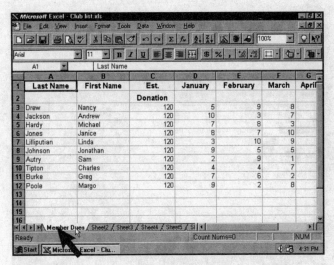

2 Move the mouse pointer over the active worksheet's tab. The pointer changes to an arrow pointing up and to the left.

(continues)

Guided Tour   Insert a Worksheet

(continued)

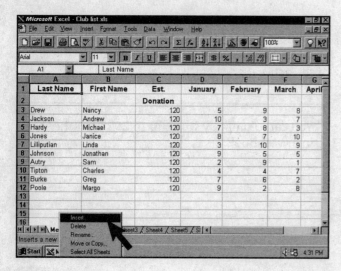

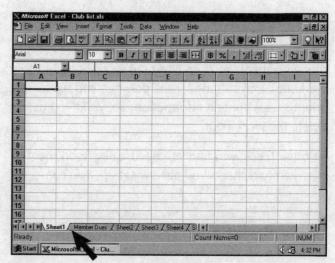

3 Click the right mouse button. A shortcut menu appears.

5 Excel inserts a new worksheet in front of the original worksheet.

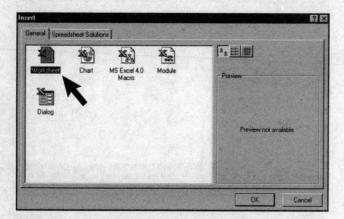

4 Choose the **Insert** command. Excel displays the Insert dialog box. Highlight the **Worksheet** icon and choose **OK**.

Begin Guided Tour   Delete a Worksheet

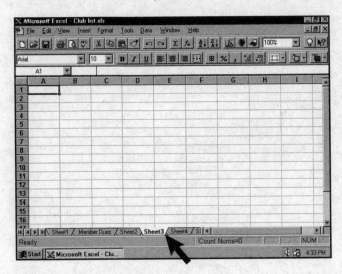

1 Select the sheet you want to delete.

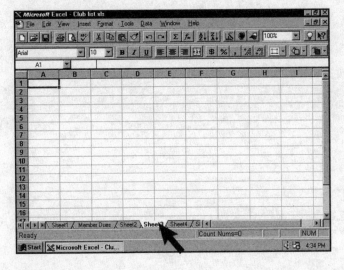

2 Move the mouse pointer over the sheet tab you want to delete. The pointer changes to an arrow pointing up and to the left.

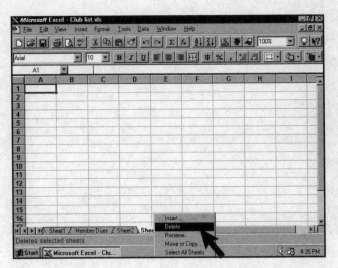

3 Click the right mouse button. A shortcut menu appears.

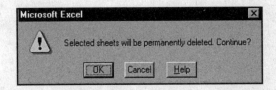

4 Choose the **Delete** command. Excel displays a warning box to tell you Excel is going to delete the active worksheet. Choose **OK**.

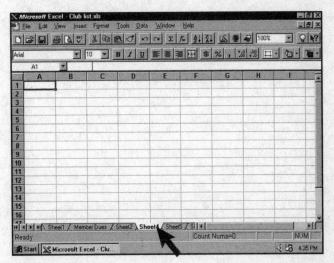

5 Excel deletes the worksheet.

HOW TO...

Format Worksheets

Now that you know how to enter information into a worksheet and save, open, and close worksheets, you're probably wondering how to spiff up the appearance of the worksheet. In this chapter, you'll learn about formatting the worksheet. By formatting the worksheet, you change the appearance of data on your worksheet, making your worksheet more attractive and readable.

What You Will Find in This Section

Automatically Format a Range

Excel's AutoFormat feature is the easiest way to apply formatting to a table-like range in your worksheet. You choose from a group of predefined formatting options, and Excel applies them to the specified range.

The AutoFormat feature works well on table-like ranges in your worksheet and quickly formats data that appears in a table. But, you also need to know how to format individual cells or small groups of cells. The formats from which you choose when using the AutoFormat feature include many of the options you learn about later, so view this task on the AutoFormat feature as a preview to applying individual formatting options as well as instruction on automatically formatting a table-like range.

Begin Guided Tour Use the AutoFormat Feature

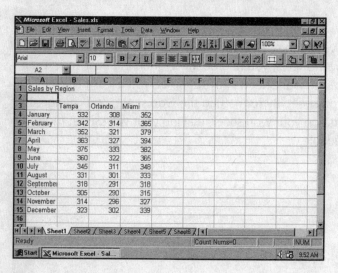

1 In a worksheet, enter the data in a table-like format, similar to the data you see in the figure.

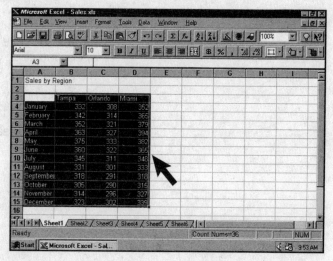

2 Select the range you want to format. In this example, select cells **A3:D15**.

Guided Tour   Use the AutoFormat Feature

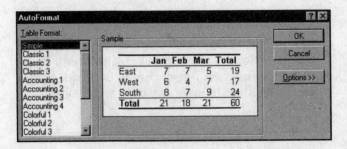

3 Open the **Format** menu and choose the **AutoFormat** command. Excel displays the AutoFormat dialog box.

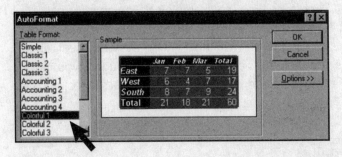

4 To preview the possible formats for your table, click on an option in the Table Format list on the left side of the dialog box. For example, click **Colorful 1**. The Sample box changes to reflect the formatting for that option.

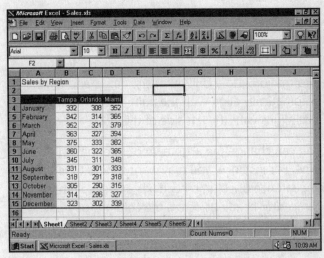

5 To apply formatting, click the option you want to apply and choose **OK**. In this example, you selected Classic 2, and Excel applied it.

If you don't like the results of the AutoFormat feature, click the **Undo** tool on the Standard toolbar. Or, re-open the AutoFormat dialog box and choose **None** from the Table Format list.

Align Information

You can align information in a cell to the left, center, or right. The default alignment is General. With General alignment, when you enter information into a cell, numbers, dates, and times automatically align with the right side of the cell. Text aligns with the left side of the cell.

You can change the alignment of information at any time. For instance, you may want to fine-tune the appearance of column headings across columns. You can center headings across the columns or you can right-align the headings to line them up with the numbers that are right-aligned. You align primarily text entries, but you can align numbers too.

Be sure not to align numbers you want Excel to use to perform a mathematical calculation. If you align numbers left or center, Excel does not recognize the numbers as values and treats them as text.

You can align information within a particular cell, or you can align information over a group of cells. For example, you may want to align a column heading over its column (an example of aligning information within a particular cell). Alternatively, if you create a heading for a small table within the worksheet, and the table runs across columns A through F, you may want to center the title of the table across columns A through F.

Begin Guided Tour   Align Text Within a Cell

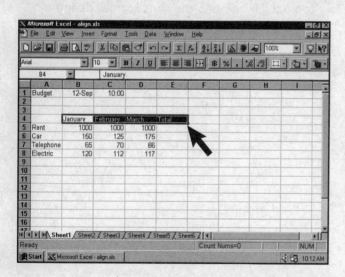

1 Select the cells containing the entries you want to align. In this example, select cells **B4:E4**, which contain column titles that you want to line up with the numbers at the right edge of the column.

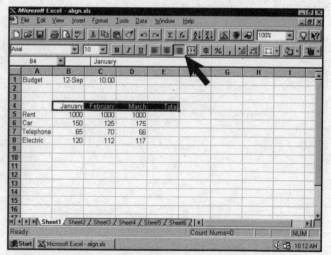

2 Click the **Align Right** button on the Formatting toolbar. Then click any cell to deselect the range. Excel aligns the contents of each cell to the right within the cell.

Begin Guided Tour   Align Text Across a Group of Cells

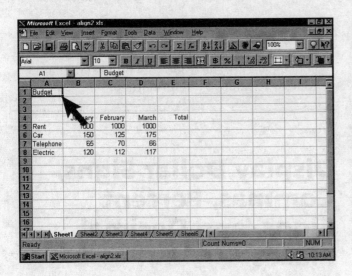

1 Type the title for your table in the upper left corner of the table. In this example, place the title in cell A1.

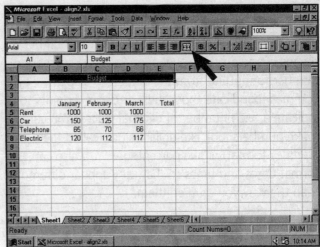

3 Click the **Center Across Columns** tool on the Formatting toolbar. Excel centers the information across the selected cells.

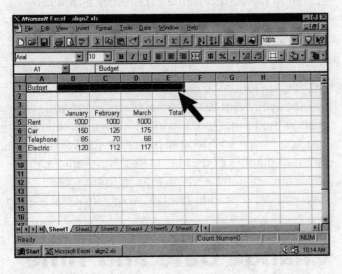

2 Select one cell in each of the columns across which you want to center the title. In this example, select cells **A1:E1**.

Format Numbers

Formatting numbers in Excel makes your worksheet easier to read. Formatting a number means changing the way it appears. You can change number formatting from the default to display commas to indicate thousands, or decimal points to indicate a fixed number of decimal places. You can make numbers look like dollar values (called the currency format) or like percentages. You also can format dates and times so that they appear differently than the way you entered them.

Usually, you format cells after you place information in them, but suppose you know, in advance, that most numbers in your worksheet have commas and two decimal places. You can format all cells in the worksheet before you start working by selecting the entire worksheet and applying the formats you want. When you subsequently enter numbers into those cells, the numbers automatically appear with commas.

> Select the entire worksheet by clicking in the blank box in the upper left corner immediately next to column A and above row 1.

Sometimes, formatting cells adds too many characters to the cell. That is, at the cell's present width, Excel can't display the contents of the cell along with the formatting. Instead you see the cell filled with pound signs (#####). Don't worry—you just need to increase the width of the column to adjust for the formatting. See "Change the Width of a Column," p. 67.

You find tools on the Formatting toolbar for most of the common formatting for numbers. If, however, you need to apply an unusual formatting to selected cells, press **Ctrl+1** or open the **Format** menu and choose the **Cells** command.

> If you change your mind about the formatting you apply, click the **Undo** tool on the Standard toolbar to remove the formatting.

Display Dollar Signs, Commas, Percent Signs, and Decimal Places

You can display numeric values in many ways in Excel. It is important that the numbers in your worksheet appear in the correct format. For instance, you can format the number 400 to look like currency— $400.00 is certainly different than 400%!

You should add decimal places to numbers when you change the format of numbers. For example, Excel assumes you want two decimal places when you change the format to currency. However, sometimes you don't want any decimal places, or you want a different number of decimal places. For example, if your currency numbers aren't going to have cents, then you don't need to display two decimal places.

Change Date and Time Formats

In Excel, you can enter dates in several different ways so that Excel accepts the date and displays it in a particular format. If you like, you can change the way Excel displays the time, too. For instance, you may want to enter your dates in the format 9/12/95, but display them in the format September 12, 1995. Similarly, you may want to enter times using the 24-hour clock but display them using the 12-hour clock.

Begin Guided Tour   Display Commas in Numbers

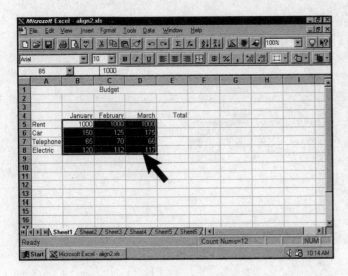

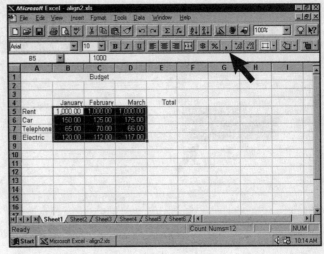

1 In a worksheet containing number values for which you want to display commas, select the range of cells you want to format. In this example, select **B5:D8**.

2 Click the **Comma Style** tool on the Formatting toolbar. Excel adds both commas and decimal places to the values.

Begin Guided Tour   Display (and Hide) Decimal Places in Numbers

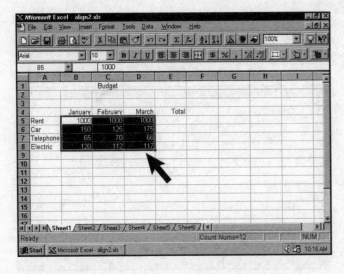

1 In a worksheet containing number values for which you want to hide or display decimal places, select the range of cells you want to format.

2 Click the **Increase Decimal** tool on the Formatting toolbar to increase the number of decimal places Excel displays by one.

3 Click the **Decrease Decimal** tool on the Formatting toolbar to reduce the number of decimal places by one.

If you see pound signs (#####) in cells, you need to widen the cell's column by dragging the right boundary of the column's letter.

Begin Guided Tour   Display Numbers as Dollar Values

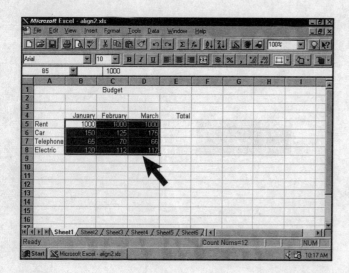

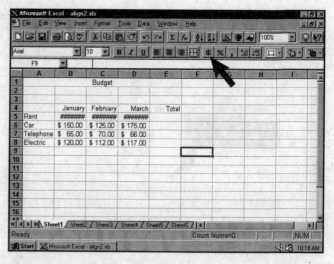

1 In a worksheet containing numbers you want to display as dollar values, select the range of cells you want to format.

2 Click the **Currency Style** tool on the Formatting toolbar. Excel adds dollar signs to the selected numbers. If the selected numbers do not contain commas and two decimal places, Excel adds those as well.

Begin Guided Tour   Display Numbers as Percentages

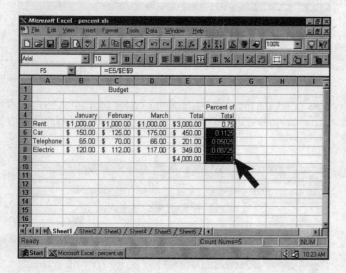

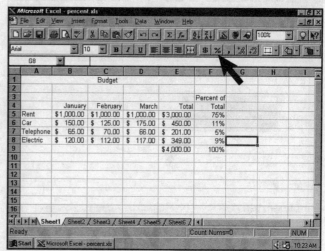

1 In a worksheet containing numbers you want to display as percentages, select the range of cells you want to format.

2 Click the **Percent Style** tool on the Formatting toolbar. Excel reformats the selection as percentages. Notice Excel automatically multiplies the numbers in the selection by 100 to convert them to percentages.

Begin Guided Tour   Change the Appearance of Dates

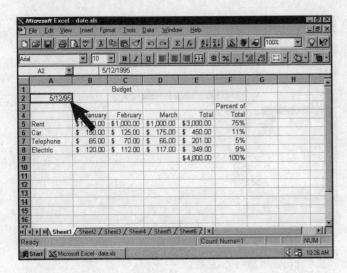

1 In a worksheet containing dates you want to display differently, select the range of cells you want to format.

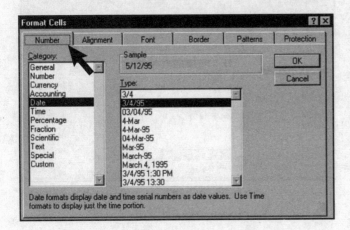

2 Press **Ctrl+1**, or open the **Format** menu and choose the **Cells** command. Excel displays the Format Cells dialog box. If necessary, click on the **Number** tab to bring it to the front.

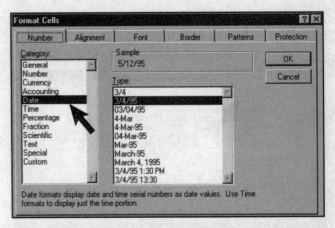

3 Select **Date** from the Category list box. From the Type list box, select the format you want to appear in the worksheet. Watch the Sample box for examples. Click **OK**.

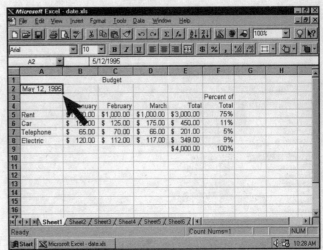

4 After you click OK to close the dialog box, Excel changes the format of the selected cells to the format you selected.

Begin Guided Tour Change the Appearance of Time

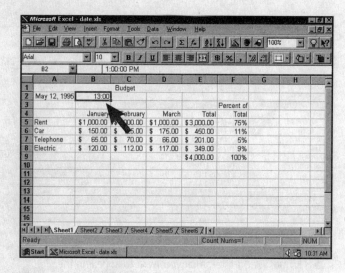

1 In a worksheet containing times you want to display differently, select the range of cells you want to format. Press **Ctrl+1**, or open the **Format** menu and choose the **Cells** command.

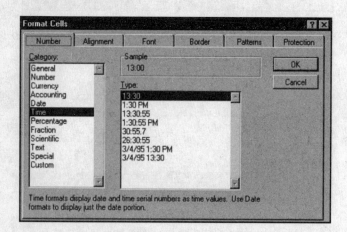

2 Excel displays the Format Cells dialog box. From the Category list box, select **Time**. In the Type list, Excel displays the type of formats available for time.

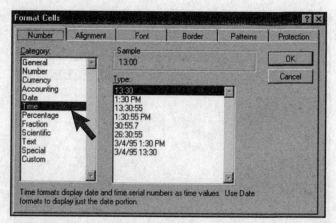

3 From the Type list box, select the format you want to appear in the worksheet.

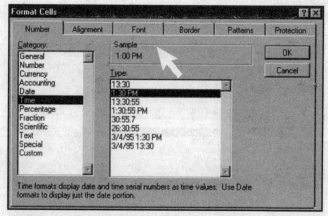

4 Watch the Sample box for examples. Click **OK**.

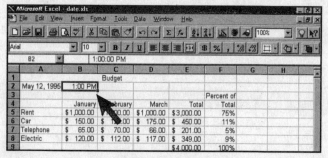

5 Excel closes the dialog box and changes the format of the selected cells to the format you selected.

Change and Enhance Fonts

A font is a particular typeface. Excel displays various fonts and font sizes in the Formatting toolbar. You can change the font for text in the body of your worksheet to Times New Roman, for example, to make reading easier. Desktop publishing guidelines suggest that you use sans serif fonts such as Arial for headlines and titles, while you should use serif fonts such as Times New Roman for text in paragraphs and in the body of the worksheet. Sans serif fonts do not contain tails on the letters, while serif fonts do contain tails.

The text you're reading now appears in a serif font. Note the lines at the bottom of letters such as l, m, n, or f.

You can use the fonts provided by Excel as well as fonts designed especially for your printer. If Excel does not have a screen version of the printer font you select, it substitutes a font. When Excel makes a substitution, the printout of the font looks different than the screen version of the font. In addition to changing the font, you also can change the font size—that is, the size of the letters for the font.

To bring attention to important words and numbers in a worksheet, you can use color or styles such as bold, italic, and underline. To undo any changes, click the **Undo** button on the Standard toolbar.

Begin Guided Tour Change the Font

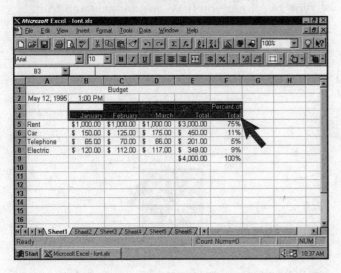

1 In a worksheet containing information for which you want to change font, select the range of cells you want to format.

2 Click the **down arrow** next to the Font box on the Formatting toolbar to display the list of fonts. Click any font in the list.

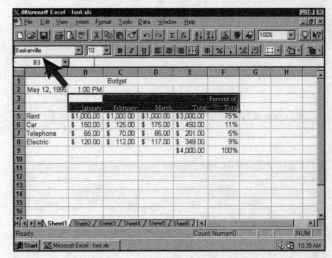

3 In the example, choose **Baskerville**. The text appears in the new font.

The fonts in the list vary depending on the printer you have and the fonts installed.

Begin Guided Tour Change the Font Size

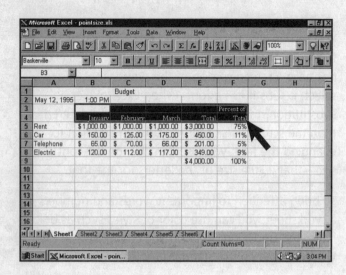

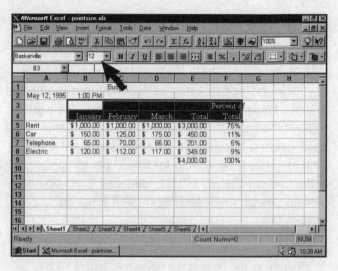

1 In a worksheet containing information you want to make larger or smaller, select the range of cells you want to format.

2 Click the **down arrow** next to the Font Size box on the Formatting toolbar to display the list of font sizes.

3 Click a higher number to change the font size to a larger font. Click a lower number to change the font size to a smaller font.

> The font sizes in the list vary depending on the type of printer you have and the selected font.

Begin Guided Tour Change the Font Color

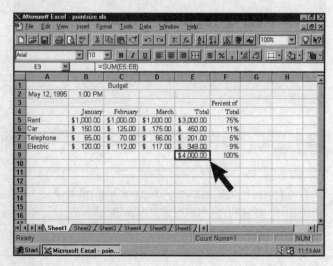

1 In a worksheet containing information whose font color you want to change, select the cell you want to format.

2 Click the **down arrow** next to the Font Color button on the Formatting toolbar. Excel displays a color palette below the Font Color button.

Guided Tour   Change the Font Color

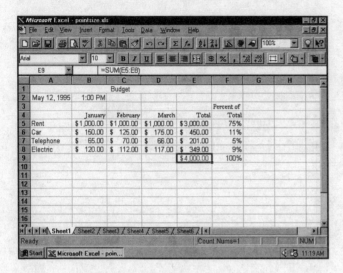

Depending on your printer, changing the font color may result in a printout of font that is different from the font that appears on-screen. The font may not print at all.

3 Click the color in which you want the letters or numbers of the selected cell to appear.

Begin Guided Tour   Add Emphasis

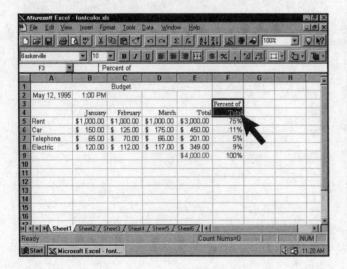

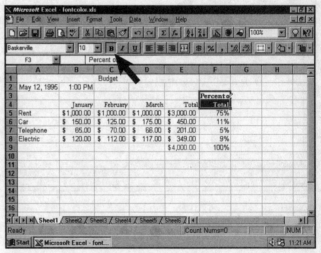

1 In a worksheet containing information you want to emphasize, select the range of cells you want to format.

2 Click the **Bold** button on the Formatting toolbar to apply bold to the selected cells.

(continues)

Guided Tour Add Emphasis *(continued)*

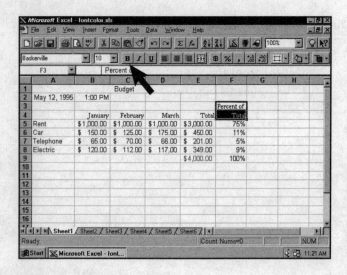

3 Click the **Bold** button again to remove bold from the selected cells.

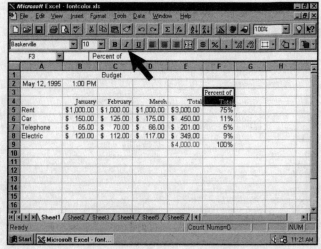

5 Click the **Italic** button again to remove italics from the selected cells.

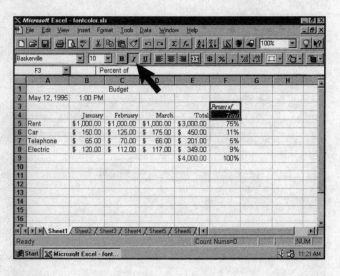

4 Click the **Italic** button on the Formatting toolbar to add italics to the data in the selected cells.

Copy Formatting

Suppose you already formatted some cells in the worksheet, and the cells contain formatting that you want to use again. When the label or the format of a number appears the way you want it, you don't

have to repeat the formatting process for the rest of the labels or numbers you want to change. Use the Format Painter button on the Standard toolbar to copy formats from one cell to another.

Begin Guided Tour Use the Format Painter to Copy Formats

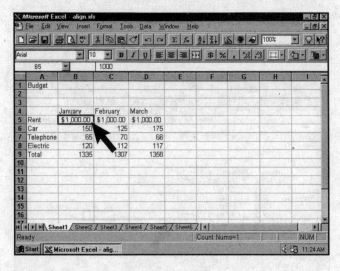

1 In a worksheet where you have already formatted some cells and want to copy the formats to other cells, select a cell containing the formats you want to copy.

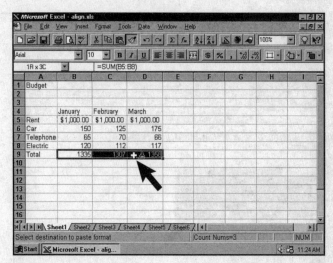

3 Drag to select the cells to which you want to copy formatting.

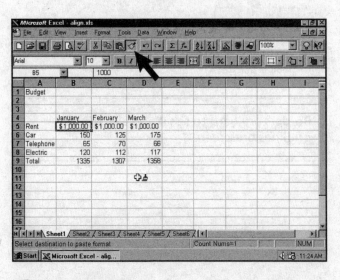

2 Click the **Format Painter** tool on the Standard toolbar. Excel changes the mouse pointer shape so that it appears like the icon on the Format Painter tool.

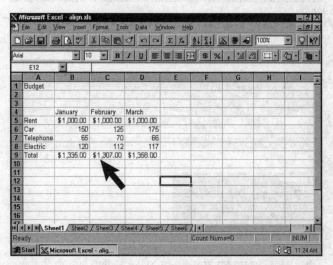

4 Release the mouse button. Excel copies the formats from the first cell to the selected cells.

Add Borders to Cells

Adding borders to cells adds emphasis. Excel's Border button on the Formatting toolbar enables you to add boxes around cells and ranges with either a single or double line. For example, you can have a single thick outline border that creates a box to emphasize the title for the worksheet. Or you can have a double underline on the bottom of cells to bring attention to totals.

> You also can change borders using the Borders tab in the Format Cells dialog box.

Begin Guided Tour   Add Borders

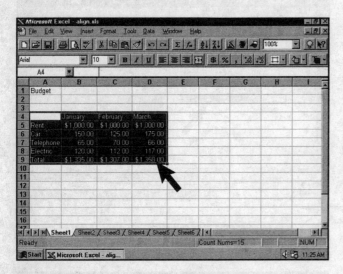

1 Select the cells around which you want to place a border.

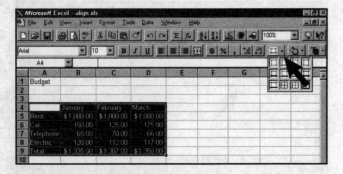

2 Click the **down arrow** next to the Borders button on the Formatting toolbar to display a palette of border samples below the Border button. Select the border sample you want to apply to the selected cells.

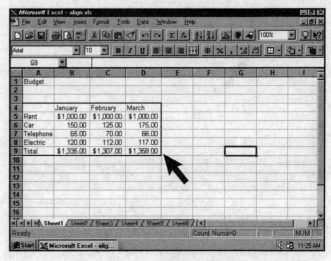

3 Excel applies the border sample you selected. In the example, the edges of the range are outlined with a thick single line. (This is the last border sample in the last column of the Border sample palette.)

> Borders are hard to see if you also display gridlines on-screen.

Shade Cells

An excellent way to draw attention to a cell or group of cells is to shade them. When you shade cells, you add color to the background of the cell.

Make sure you don't choose the same color for font color and shading. If you do, the contents of the cell fade away into the background.

Be aware that if the shading you add to cells is too dark, you may have difficulty reading the information on-screen. In addition, color shading only prints in color if you have a color printer. Black and white printers represent shading as shades of gray. Therefore, if you shade a selection with a dark color and then print the worksheet on a black and white printer, the selection appears black on the printout.

Begin Guided Tour   Add Shading to a Worksheet

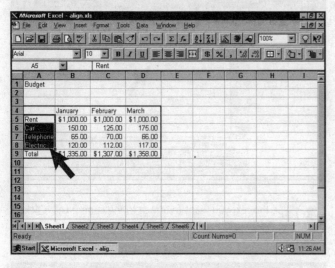

1 Select the range of cells that you want to shade.

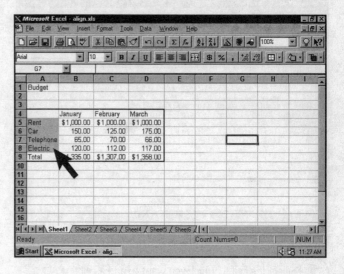

3 Excel adds the shading to the background of the selected cells. To remove shading from a selection, re-open the Color palette by clicking on the **Color** button and choose **None**.

2 Click the **down arrow** next to the Color button on the Formatting toolbar to display a color palette below the Color button. Select the color of shading you want to add to the selected cells.

Add Cell Tips

You're going to find that you wish occasionally that you could add an explanatory note to a cell to describe something about it, like how you got that number. In Excel 7, you can attach notes to cells—called cell tips—that the online user of your worksheet can point at and read. You can identify cells that have cell tips attached by the red dot that appears in the upper right corner of the cell. To view a cell tip on-screen, slide the mouse pointer over any cell containing a red dot in the upper right corner. Excel displays the cell tip.

You also can have Excel print the notes when you print the worksheet.

Begin Guided Tour   Add a Note to a Cell

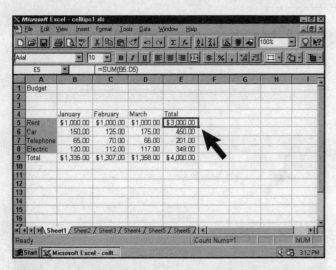

1 Select the cell to which you want to add a cell tip.

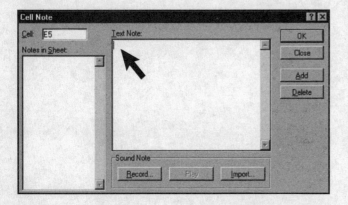

2 Open the **Insert** menu and choose the **Note** command. Excel displays the Cell Note dialog box. An insertion point appears in the Text Note text box.

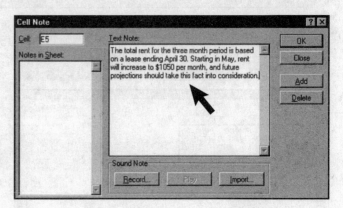

3 Type the text you want to attach to the current cell. Click the **Add** button.

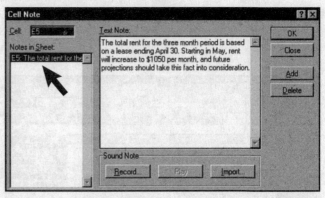

4 Excel adds a reference in the Notes in Sheet list box that identifies the cell to which you attach the note. Click **OK**.

Guided Tour Add a Note to a Cell

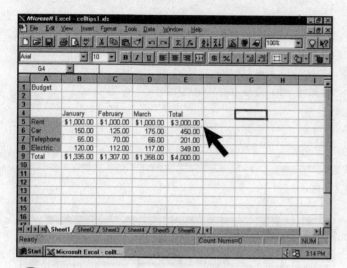

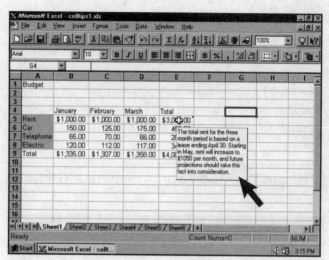

5 Excel closes the dialog box and redisplays the worksheet. Click in any other cell, and you see a red dot in the upper right corner of the cell containing the cell tip.

6 Pass the mouse pointer over the cell to view the cell tip. To remove a note from a worksheet, re-open the **Cell Notes** dialog box and highlight the note you want to remove in the Notes in Sheet list box. Click the **Delete** button.

Begin Guided Tour Print Cell Tips

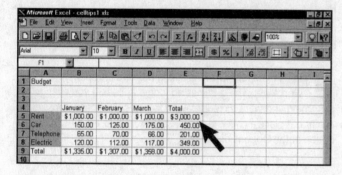

1 Click in the worksheet containing the cell tip. Open the **File** menu and choose the **Page Setup** command.

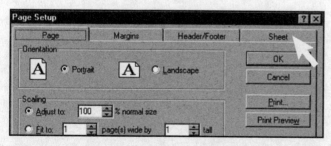

2 Excel displays the Page Setup dialog box with four tabs in it. Click the **Sheet** tab to bring it to the front.

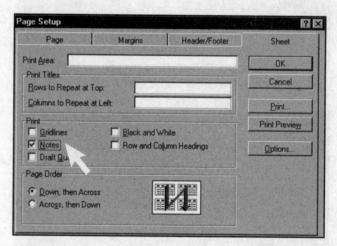

3 Place a check mark in the **Notes** check box. After you save the Page Setup settings, Excel prints the notes on a separate page when you print out the worksheet.

Turn Off Gridlines

Another way to make your worksheet look more attractive is to turn off the gridlines that separate the cells in the worksheet. Your worksheet looks cleaner on the white background without the grids. You may want to turn off gridlines in your worksheets to see how the data looks when printed.

If, after you remove gridlines, you change your mind and you want to turn on the gridlines again, immediately click the **Undo** button in the Standard toolbar before you save the worksheet.

Begin Guided Tour   Eliminate Gridlines

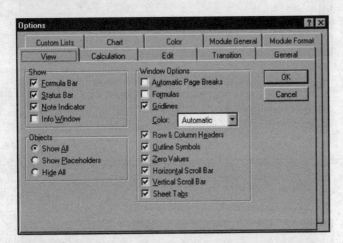

1 Open the **Tools** menu and choose the **Options** command. Excel displays the Options dialog box with its ten tabs. Click the **View** tab to look at the View options.

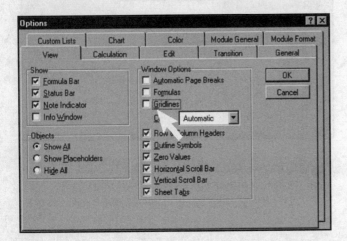

2 Click in the **Gridlines** check box in the Window Options area to remove the check mark from the check box and deselect the Gridlines option. Click **OK** to save your changes.

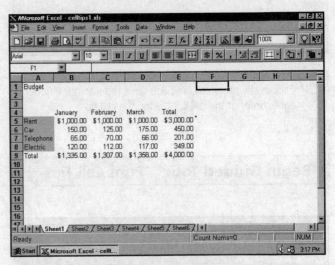

3 Excel closes the Options dialog box and redisplays the worksheet. The gridlines no longer appear. If you change your mind and want to redisplay gridlines, follow these steps again, but place a check in the check box next to the Gridlines option in the Options dialog box.

Use Styles

Often, you find yourself applying more than one format to a particular cell or group of cells. For example, you may always set up a worksheet title in italics in a particular font and font size. To save time, you can create a *style* in Excel that stores all these formats. Then, instead of applying the formats individually, you apply the style that contains all the formats. That way, you accomplish what you want in one step instead of several steps.

Excel comes with some predefined styles, and, of course, you can create your own styles. When you create a style initially, it is available only in the workbook where you create it. However, if you save the

styles in an *autotemplate*, the styles you create are available for each new workbook you create based on the autotemplate.

> Autotemplates are workbooks and worksheets you create that contain settings you want to use for most new workbooks or worksheets.

For more information on using autotemplates, see "Change the Defaults for New Workbooks and Worksheets," p. 168.

Begin Guided Tour   Apply a Style

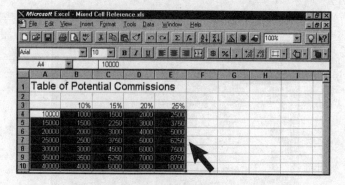

1 Select the cells to which you want to apply a style.

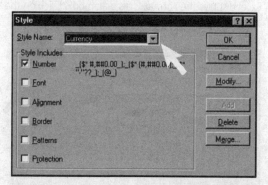

2 Open the **Format** menu and choose the **Style** command. Excel displays the Style dialog box.

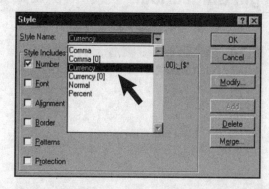

3 Click on the **arrow** on the Style Name list box to open its drop-down list. The available styles appear in the list. Choose one.

> Most of the predefined styles appear as tools on the Formatting toolbar.

(continues)

Guided Tour   Apply a Style   *(continued)*

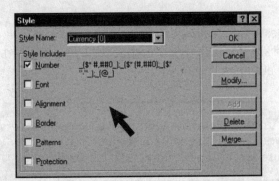

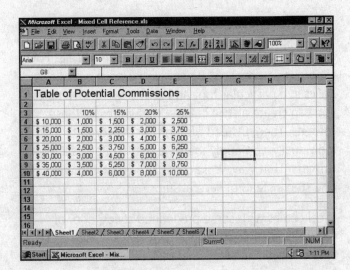

4 Review the attributes of the style you selected. Click **OK**.

To modify the attributes of the style, see "Create a New Style" later in this section.

5 Excel closes the dialog box and applies the new style.

Begin Guided Tour   Create a New Style

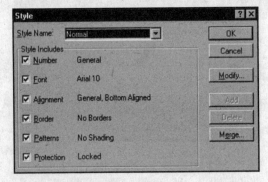

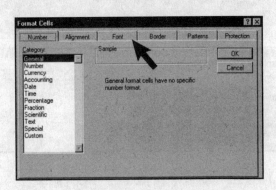

1 Open the **Format** menu and choose the **Style** command. Excel displays the Style dialog box.

3 Excel displays the Format Cells dialog box. Click on the appropriate tab and make your changes.

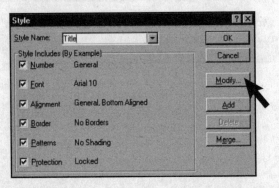

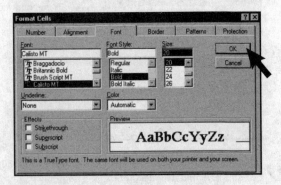

2 In the Style Name text box, type a name for the new style. Click the **Modify** button.

4 Repeat this step until the style has the attributes you want. Choose **OK**.

Guided Tour Create a New Style

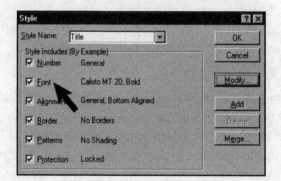

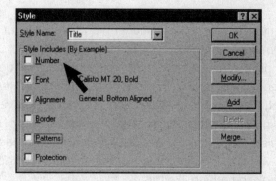

5 The Style dialog box reappears, reflecting the attributes you assigned to the new style.

6 Remove the check mark from any of the attributes you don't want to include in your new style. Click the **Add** button and then the **Close** button to create the new style without applying it. To add the new style and apply it, choose **OK**.

Begin Guided Tour Create a Style by Example

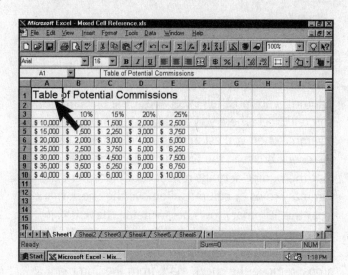

1 In your worksheet, apply the formats you want to store to any cell. You can enter text or numbers into the cell while you apply styles so you can see results. Excel does not store text or numbers in a style, just formats.

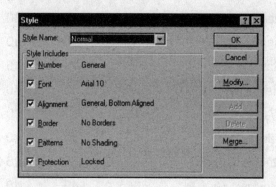

2 Open the **Format** menu and choose the **Style** command. Excel displays the Style dialog box.

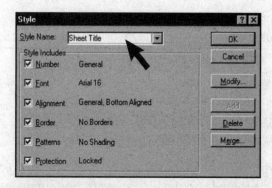

3 In the Style Name box, type a name for the new style. Click **OK**, and Excel saves the style.

Summarize Worksheet Data

Suppose you create a budget worksheet. In your budget worksheet, you create categories that comprise details. For example, you've got a category called Utilities, and in that category, you include Heat, Light, Gas, Electricity, Water, and Telephone. You've also got an Entertainment category that consists of Movies, Video Rentals, and Book Purchases. On paper, you visualize the first three months of your worksheet to look something like this:

Budget Category	January	February	March
Rent	700	700	700
Groceries	75	75	75
Meals Out	50	50	50
Food Subtotal	125	125	125
Heat	50	60	40
Light	30	30	30
Gas	15	15	15
Electricity	30	30	40
Water	10	10	10
Telephone	40	40	40
Utilities Subtotal	425	435	425
Movies	40	40	40
Video Rentals	10	10	10
Book Purchases	25	25	25
Entertainment Subtotal	75	75	75

You want to be able to view the details of the budget or hide the details and view only the summarized budget—the category totals. Use Excel's Outline feature for this purpose.

In Excel, you can manually create an outline, or if you include formulas in the worksheet for the summary rows or columns (in our example, the summary rows are the category totals), Excel can automatically

outline the worksheet for you. In the section called "'Do' Math," p. 147, you'll learn more about formulas.

When your worksheet includes formulas on the lines that you want to summarize, automatically outline your worksheet by selecting the **Auto Outline** command from the Group and Outline submenu on the Data menu.

When you manually outline your worksheet, you identify the rows or columns that you want to summarize. In this example, the categories are the rows Utilities, Food, and Entertainment. Once you make your identifications, your outline looks identical to the same worksheet you outlined using the Auto Outline feature.

You can place summary rows either above or below the details; similarly, you can place summary columns either to the right or left of detail columns. Once you determine where you want to place summary rows or columns, you must tell Excel about the placement. You tell Excel where you are placing summary rows or columns when you establish outline settings. Using the check boxes in the Outline dialog box, make sure that the outline settings reflect your placement of summary rows or columns. Remove the check mark from the Summary rows below detail check box if summary rows appear above detail rows. Similarly, if summary columns appear to the left of detail columns, remove the check mark from the Summary columns to the right of detail check box.

If you no longer want to display outline markers, you can clear outline settings by opening the **Data** menu, highlighting the **Group and Outline** command, and choosing the **Clear Outline** command. Be aware that Excel no longer remembers your outline settings if you do this, and, if you want to view summarized information again, you need to re-establish the outline, either automatically or manually.

Begin Guided Tour   Establish Outline Settings

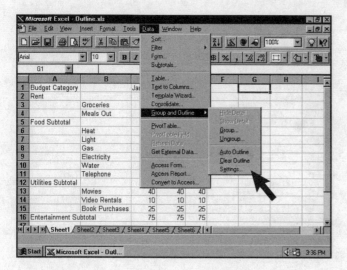

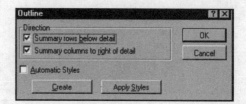

2 Excel displays the Outline dialog box. Select the two check boxes in the Direction box appropriate for the setup of your worksheet and choose **OK**.

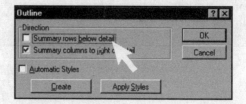

1 Display the worksheet you want to outline. Open the **Data** menu and highlight the **Group and Outline** command. From the submenu, choose the **Settings** command.

3 In the example, remove the check from the Summary rows below detail check box.

Begin Guided Tour   Manually Create an Outline by Rows

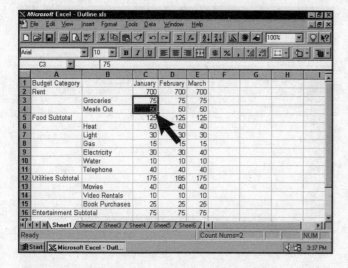

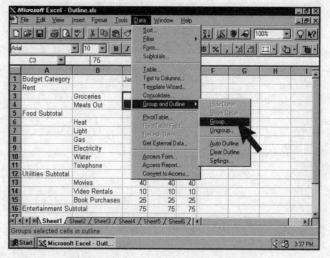

1 For the first group you want to create, select a cell in each of the rows you want to group.

2 Open the **Data** menu and highlight the **Group and Outline** command. Select the **Group** command.

(continues)

Guided Tour Manually Create an Outline by Rows *(continued)*

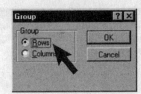

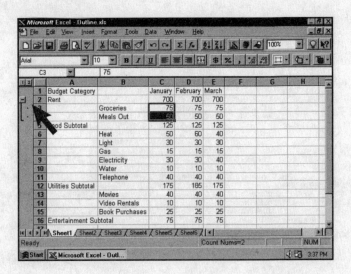

3 Excel displays the Group dialog box. Select **Rows** and click **OK**.

> If you are outlining by columns, choose **Columns** and click **OK**.

4 Excel displays a minus sign to the left of the summary row and dots to the left of the detail rows. Repeat steps 1 through 3 for each set of rows you want to summarize.

Begin Guided Tour Use the Outline to Hide or Display Information

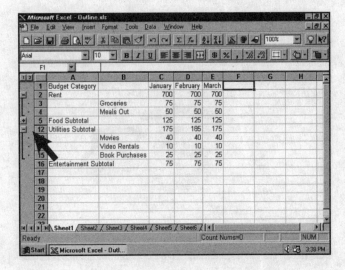

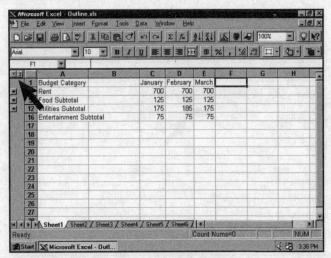

1 In a worksheet you already outlined, click any minus sign. Excel hides the details and shows only the summary line, and the minus sign turns into a plus sign.

2 To quickly display summarized information, click the **1** that appears at the top of the column above the plus. Click the **2** to quickly redisplay all details.

HOW TO...

Print Worksheets

n Excel, you can print your worksheets using a basic printing procedure, or you can enhance the printout using several print options. It is fairly simple to print a worksheet in Excel. Here you learn the basics of printing the worksheet. With some experimentation and practice, you can create some very interesting results.

What You Will Find in This Section

Select a Printer

In Windows 95, like in Windows 3.x, the operating environment controls your printers. You add printers by installing printer drivers in the Windows 95 Control Panel; any printer that you install then becomes available to Excel. It is possible to install several different printer drivers and therefore print from any one of several different printers. You learn how to choose another printer in "Choose Another Printer," p. 320.

The first time you use your printer with Excel, it is a good idea to check the printer setup options. That way, you can verify that Excel is printing to the correct printer, or you can switch to a different printer. Excel uses the options and capabilities available for the printer you select. By checking printer settings in the Print dialog box, you can control paper size and orientation, how much of the workbook to print, and the way your printer handles graphics, fonts, and any special options specific to your printer.

If you want to print only a portion of the workbook, you select that portion before you start to print. For example, to print a range of cells in Sheet1, select those cells before printing. If you want to print only some worksheets in the workbook, select those sheets. If your workbook contains information on several sheets and one sheet contains so much information that it prints on multiple pages, you can print only specified pages of the sheet by clicking in that sheet before you start to print. In the Print dialog box, you can specify the pages of the current sheet you want to print.

To select worksheets, click the sheet tab of the first worksheet and then hold down the **Ctrl** key while clicking the sheet tabs of the other sheets you want to print.

Begin Guided Tour   Check Printer Settings

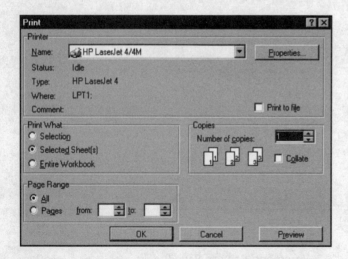

1 Open the **File** menu and choose the **Print** command. Excel displays the Print dialog box.

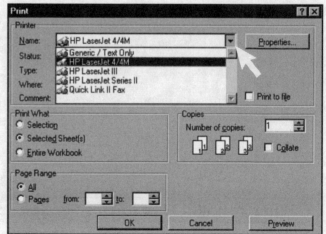

2 Open the **Name** drop-down list box to choose a different printer.

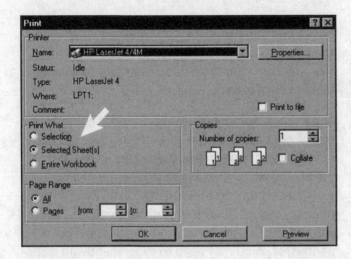

3 Use the **Print What** option buttons to specify how much of the workbook to print.

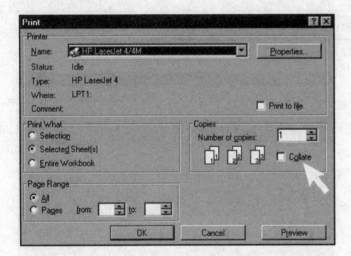

4 Click in the **Copies** box and enter the number of copies you want to print and, if your printer doesn't print pages in ascending order (from first page to last page), click in the **Collate** check box (a check mark appears) to collate the printed copy.

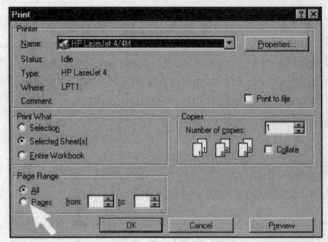

5 Use the Page Range area if you only want to print certain pages of a worksheet. Click the **Pages** option button, then specify the numbers of the pages you want to print in the from and to spinner boxes. Click the **Properties** button to change options for the selected printer.

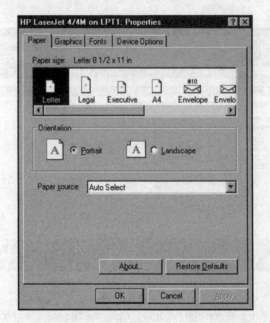

6 You see the Properties dialog box for your printer. This example shows the Properties dialog box for an HP LaserJet 4. The dialog box varies in appearance depending on the printer you select, and you need to consult your printer manual to determine what the options you see control on your printer.

Set Up the Page for Printing

The Page and Margins tabs in the Page Setup dialog box control print settings such as orientation, margins, the size of the paper you use, and whether the information appears centered on the page. The default print orientation is Portrait, which means that the worksheet prints vertically on the paper. If you want to fit a worksheet with many columns or wide columns on one page, use Landscape—Excel then prints the worksheet sideways (horizontally) on the paper.

If the worksheet is still too large to print on one page, you can change the top, bottom, left, and right margins. You also may consider reducing the printout by using the Adjust to option in the Page Setup dialog box. Some printers enable you to reduce or enlarge the printout as it prints. Although 100% is normal size, you can enter the desired reduction or enlargement percentage you want.

The Fit To option prints the entire worksheet to fit the size of the page. You can enter the number of pages in the page(s) wide by and the tall text boxes to specify the document's width and height. If your worksheet is too big to fit on one page, Excel automatically reduces it in size to fit the number of pages you specify. This option may not be available on all printers, and you may need to experiment with all the print options until you get the results you want.

Begin Guided Tour   Choose a Page Orientation and Paper Size

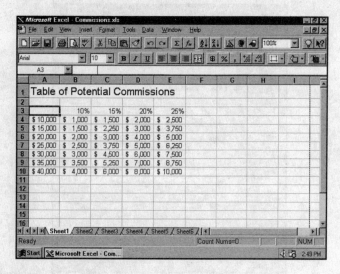

1 Select the worksheet for which you want to set page orientation and paper size. Open the **File** menu and choose the **Page Setup** command.

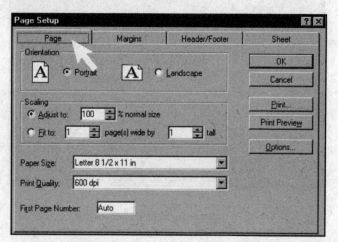

2 Excel displays the Page Setup dialog box. Click the **Page** tab to bring it to the front of the dialog box.

Guided Tour   Choose a Page Orientation and Paper Size

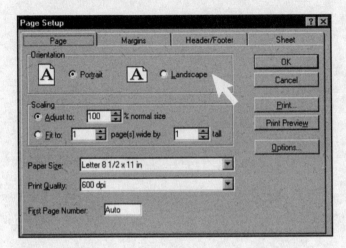

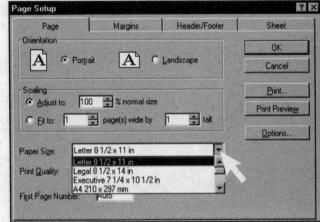

3 In the Orientation area, choose **Portrait** or **Landscape**.

4 Click on the **arrow** on the Paper Size drop-down list box to display a list of paper sizes. Choose a paper size. Choose **OK** to save the settings.

Begin Guided Tour   Scale the Printout to a Percentage of Its Size

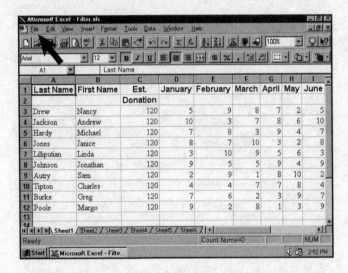

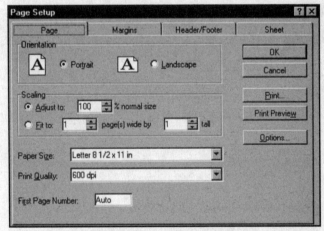

1 Select the worksheet you want to scale. Open the **File** menu and choose the **Page Setup** command.

2 Excel displays the Page Setup dialog box. Click the **Page** tab to bring it to the front of the dialog box.

(continues)

Guided Tour   Scale the Printout to a Percentage of Its Size   *(continued)*

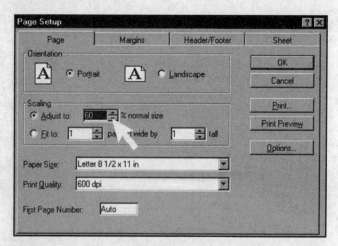

3 Choose the **Adjust to** option button and select a percentage to which you want Excel to scale the worksheet (normal size is 100 percent). Click **OK** for the new scaling to take effect.

Begin Guided Tour   Scale a Printout to Fit on a Specified Number of Pages

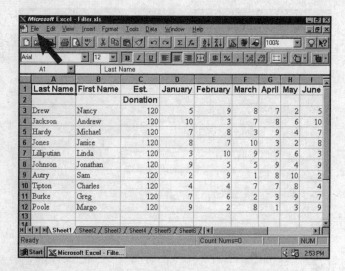

1 Select the worksheet you want to scale. Open the **File** menu and choose the **Page Setup** command.

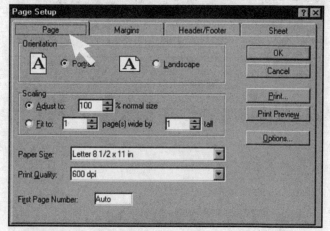

2 Excel displays the Page Setup dialog box. Click the **Page** tab to bring it to the front of the dialog box.

Guided Tour — Scale a Printout to Fit on a Specified Number of Pages

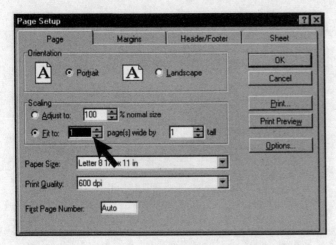

3 Choose the **Fit to** option button and use the spinner boxes to identify the number of pages wide and tall onto which you want to fit the printout. Click **OK** for changes to take effect.

Begin Guided Tour — Change Page Margins

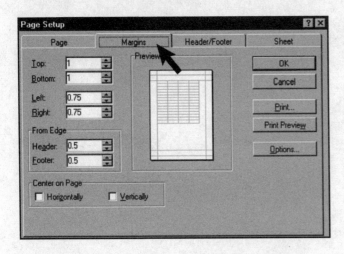

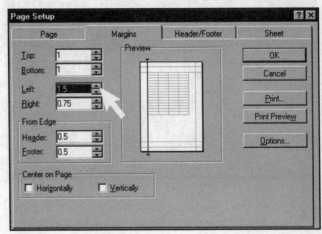

1 In the worksheet for which you want to modify margins, open the **File** menu and choose the **Page Setup** command. Excel displays the Page Setup dialog box. Click the **Margins** tab to bring it to the front.

2 Use the **Top**, **Bottom**, **Left**, and **Right** spinner boxes to increase or decrease the corresponding margins.

3 Review margin changes in the Preview area. Click **OK** for margin changes to take effect.

Begin Guided Tour Center Printed Information on the Page

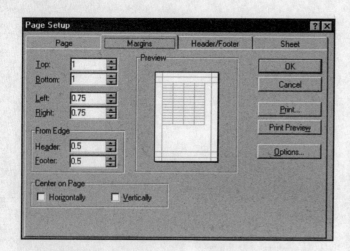

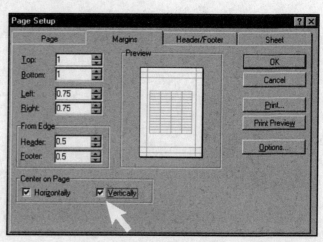

1 In the worksheet that you intend to center on the page, open the **File** menu and choose the **Page Setup** command. Excel displays the Page Setup dialog box. Click the **Margins** tab to bring it to the front.

3 Place a check mark in the Vertically check box to center the printout between the top and bottom margins. Watch the Preview box. Click **OK**.

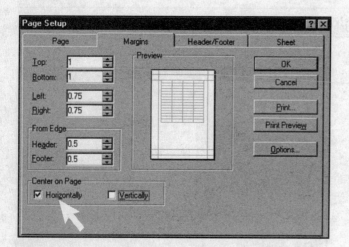

2 Place a check mark in the Horizontally check box to center the printout between the left and right margins. Watch the Preview box.

Enhance the Appearance of a Printout

Using the Sheet tab in the Page Setup dialog box, you can enhance the appearance of your worksheet. The Sheet tab includes some options you may find particularly useful. For example, when you print a large worksheet, the column and row headings appear only on the first page by default. That can make reading subsequent pages difficult. Using options on the Sheet tab, you can print headings for each column at the top of every page, and you can print headings for each row at the left side of every page. Excel refers to these headings as *titles*.

> You should not include any rows or columns you identify as title rows or columns as part of your print range. If you do include them, they print twice on the first page of your printout.

Also from the Sheet tab, you can choose to print the gridlines that appear in your worksheet, and you can choose to print the column letters (A, B, C, and so on) and row numbers (1, 2, 3, and so on). Printing gridlines can make reading the worksheet easier, and printing column letters and row numbers can help you easily identify the location of information in the worksheet. In the examples below, the one on the left shows a printout without gridlines or column letters and row numbers. The one on the right shows the same worksheet with gridlines, column letters and row numbers.

Two other options on the Sheet tab can help speed up printing. When you print in draft quality, Excel doesn't print gridlines and most graphics. Printing in black and white is particularly useful when you format information in color, but you print to a black and white printer. If you format information in color and print to a color printer, choosing this option may speed up the printing time.

You may also find it useful to add headers and footers to your worksheet so that you can print information at the top and bottom of every page of the printout. For example, you may want to include the date and the page number in a header or footer. On the Header/Footer tab of the Page Setup dialog box, Excel suggests headers and footers to you. By default, Excel suggests the sheet name as the header and the page number as the footer.

If you prefer, you can create a custom header or footer and include any text plus special information. When you create a custom header or footer, you

Table of Potential Commissions

	10%	15%	20%	25%
$ 10,000	$ 1,000	$ 1,500	$ 2,000	$ 2,500
$ 15,000	$ 1,500	$ 2,250	$ 3,000	$ 3,750
$ 20,000	$ 2,000	$ 3,000	$ 4,000	$ 5,000
$ 25,000	$ 2,500	$ 3,750	$ 5,000	$ 6,250
$ 30,000	$ 3,000	$ 4,500	$ 6,000	$ 7,500
$ 35,000	$ 3,500	$ 5,250	$ 7,000	$ 8,750
$ 40,000	$ 4,000	$ 6,000	$ 8,000	$ 10,000

	A	B	C	D	E
1	Table of Potential Commissions				
2					
3		10%	15%	20%	25%
4	$ 10,000	$ 1,000	$ 1,500	$ 2,000	$ 2,500
5	$ 15,000	$ 1,500	$ 2,250	$ 3,000	$ 3,750
6	$ 20,000	$ 2,000	$ 3,000	$ 4,000	$ 5,000
7	$ 25,000	$ 2,500	$ 3,750	$ 5,000	$ 6,250
8	$ 30,000	$ 3,000	$ 4,500	$ 6,000	$ 7,500
9	$ 35,000	$ 3,500	$ 5,250	$ 7,000	$ 8,750
10	$ 40,000	$ 4,000	$ 6,000	$ 8,000	$ 10,000

notice that Excel divides the header and footer areas into three sections: left, center, and right. You can type information into any or all of the sections or you can use the buttons in the dialog box to specify special information you want to include in the header or footer. In the following table, you see the buttons that appear in the custom Header or Footer dialog box and the information that you can insert into the left, center, or right sections of the header or footer. You can include one or more items of special information in any or all of the sections of the custom header or footer. If you decide to include more than one item in a particular section, be sure to press the spacebar between the items so that Excel inserts a space between them.

Custom Header and Footer Button Information

Button	Purpose
A	Changes the font and point size of text.
#	Inserts the current page number.
	Inserts the total number of pages in the active worksheet.
	Inserts the current date.
	Inserts the current time.
	Inserts the filename of the workbook.
	Inserts the name of the worksheet tab.

Begin Guided Tour Print Column and Row Titles

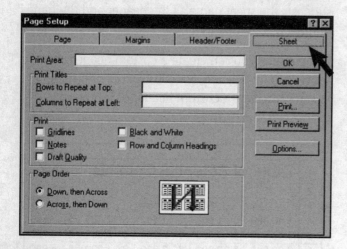

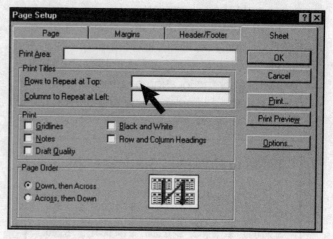

1 Open the **File** menu and choose the **Page Setup** command. Excel displays the Page Setup dialog box. Click the **Sheet** tab.

2 To repeat a row containing headings such as those that you want to appear across the top of the worksheet, place the insertion point in the Rows to Repeat at Top text box in the Print Titles area.

Guided Tour   Print Column and Row Titles

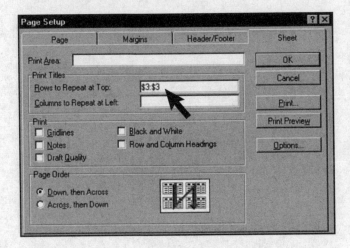

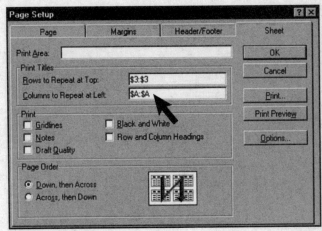

3 In the worksheet, click a cell in the row you want to repeat. Excel displays the row number as an absolute cell reference, using dollar signs ($). For more information on absolute cell references, see "Use Cell Addresses Correctly," Chapter 7.

5 In the worksheet, click a cell in the column you want to repeat. Excel displays the column letter as an absolute cell reference, using dollar signs ($). Click **OK** for print titles to take effect.

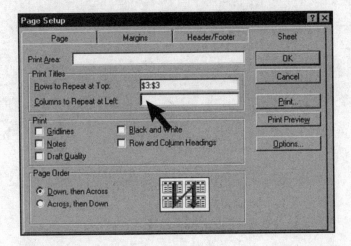

Make sure that rows or columns you select as titles are *not* also part of the print range; if they are, Excel prints the rows and columns twice on the first page of the printout.

4 To repeat a column containing headings such as those that might appear at the left edge of a worksheet, place the insertion point in the Columns to Repeat at Left text box in the Print Titles area.

Begin Guided Tour Print Gridlines and Row Numbers and Column Letters

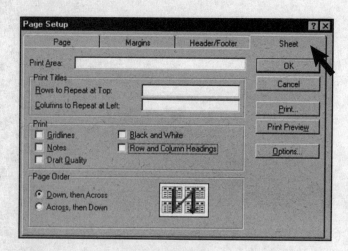

1 Open the **File** menu and choose the **Page Setup** command. Excel displays the Page Setup dialog box. Click the **Sheet** tab.

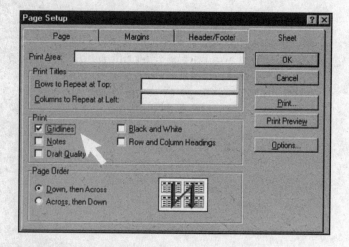

2 In the Print area, place a check mark in the Gridlines check box to produce a printout with gridlines.

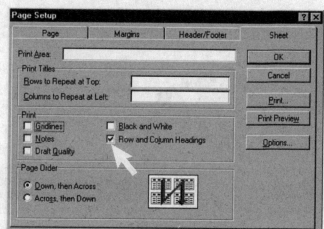

3 To print column letters and row numbers, place a check mark in the Row and Column Headings check box. Click **OK** to close the Page Setup dialog box and for changes to take effect.

Begin Guided Tour Add Page Headers and Footers

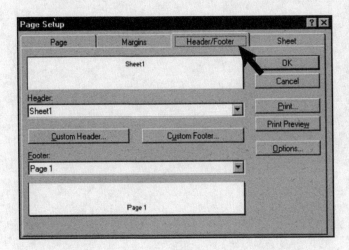

1 While you are viewing the worksheet to which you want to add headers and footers, open the **File** menu and choose the **Page Setup** command. Excel displays the Page Setup dialog box. Click the **Header/Footer** tab.

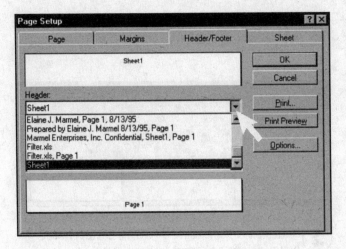

2 Click the **down arrow** next to the Header drop-down list. A list of suggested header information displays. Select the header you want to use.

3 In the example, choose the file's name; the sample header appears centered at the top of the box.

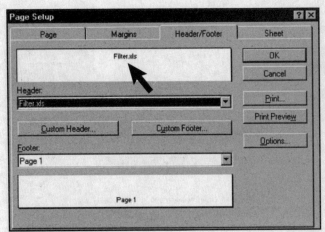

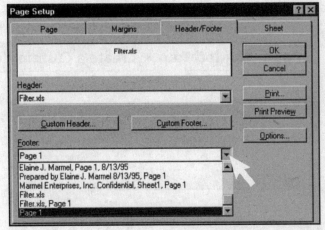

4 Click the **down arrow** next to the Footer drop-down list. A list of suggested footer information displays. Select the footer you want to use.

(continues)

Guided Tour Add Page Headers and Footers

(continued)

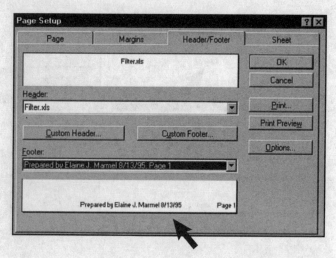

5 In the example, choose the footer that includes the information on who prepared the worksheet; the sample footer appears centered at the bottom of the box. Click **OK** to save changes.

Begin Guided Tour Create a Custom Header or Footer

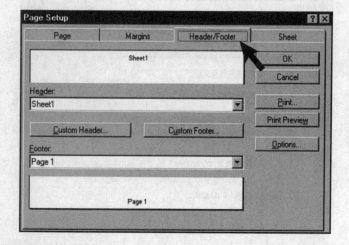

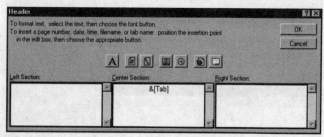

2 To create a custom header, choose the **Custom Header** button. To create a custom footer, choose the **Custom Footer** button. Excel displays the appropriate dialog box.

1 While you are viewing the worksheet to which you want to add headers and footers, open the **File** menu and choose the **Page Setup** command. Excel displays the Page Setup dialog box. Click the **Header/Footer** tab.

Guided Tour   Create a Custom Header or Footer

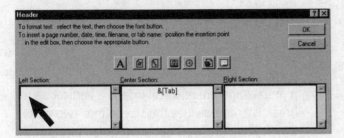

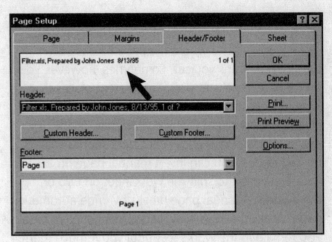

3 Place the insertion point in the section of the header where you want information to appear. In the sample, the insertion point is in the Left Section. Type text in the Left Section text box, or click the appropriate button to insert special information.

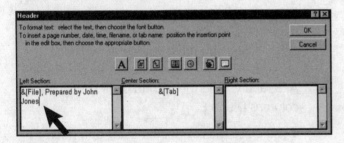

5 Repeat steps 3 and 4 until you complete the customization of your header. Then choose **OK**. Excel redisplays the Header/Footer tab of the Page Setup dialog box with your custom header information in the sample box.

4 If you click a special information button, Excel inserts a code representing the appropriate information. You can choose the font for the text or special information by clicking the **Font** button.

> To determine the purpose of a button, use the mouse to point at it and click the *right* mouse button. Excel displays a screen tip telling you what the button does.

Insert and Remove Page Breaks

On worksheets that span more than one page, Excel decides where the page breaks occur based on margins you set. Sometimes, however, you prefer page breaks to occur in different places than Excel chooses. You can control the page breaks by inserting manual page breaks. You may decide, for example, that a one page worksheet should actually be two pages. You can insert manual page breaks in your worksheet to split the worksheet on two or more pages. Manual page breaks override automatic page breaks that Excel calculates; manual page breaks also remain in the worksheet until you remove them. Inserting a new manual page break simply adds another page break and does not affect any existing manual page breaks.

When you set manual page breaks, you can set horizontal or vertical page breaks by selecting a cell in the row below or the column to the right of where you want the page break to appear. If you select a cell in a column besides column A or any row besides row 1, you are automatically inserting a manual page break that is both horizontal and vertical. Page breaks you insert in columns other than A and rows other than 1 create at least four pages, while page breaks you insert in column A or row 1 create only two pages. Excel prints one page for each of the parts (created by the page break lines) you see on-screen that contains data. Consider these examples while you look at the illustration:

- If you place the cell pointer in A7 and insert a manual page break, Excel inserts a vertical page break line and divides the screen into two parts. When you print, you get a two page printout—the first page contains all the information in row 1 through 6 for all columns, and the second page contains the information in rows 7 through 10 for all columns.

- If you place the cell pointer in D1 and insert a manual page break, Excel inserts a horizontal page break line and divides the screen into two parts. When you print, you get a two page printout—the first page contains all of columns A, B, and C, and the second page contains all of columns D and E.

- If you place the cell pointer in D7 and insert a manual page break, Excel inserts both a horizontal and a vertical page break and divides the screen into four parts. When you print, you get a four page printout—the first page contains the information in rows 1 through 6 for columns A, B, and C. The second page contains the information in rows 7 through 10 for columns A, B, and C. The third page contains the information in rows 1 through 6 for columns D and E. The last page contains the information in rows 7 through 10 for columns D and E.

To remove a manual page break, you must select a cell next to the page break. Removing horizontal or vertical page breaks is easy. If you inserted only a horizontal page break, you can select any cell immediately below the page break. If you inserted only a vertical page break, you can select any cell immediately to the right of the page break.

Removing a combination page break (both horizontal and vertical) is a little trickier. You must start by selecting the same cell you originally selected when you inserted the page break. You can think of this action as selecting the cell immediately below and to the right of the intersection of the page break lines.

But don't worry—you know if you selected the correct cell because you see the Remove Page Break command when you open the Insert menu.

Begin Guided Tour   Insert a Manual Page Break

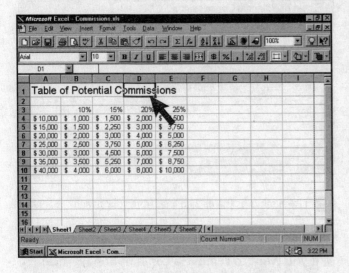

1 Select a cell that is one cell below and to the right of where you want to insert a page break. In the example, select cell **D1**. Open the **Insert** menu and choose the **Page Break** command.

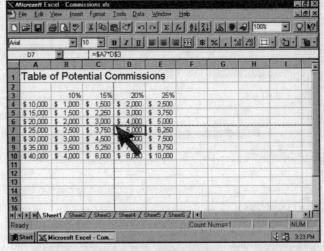

3 If you place the cell pointer in D7 and insert horizontal and vertical page breaks, you see both a horizontal and a vertical dashed line in your worksheet, representing horizontal and vertical page breaks.

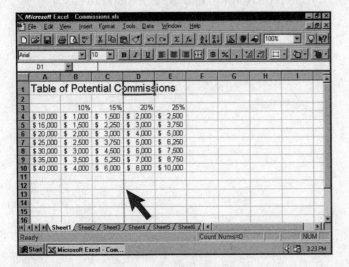

2 Excel inserts a dashed line in your worksheet to represent the page break.

Begin Guided Tour Remove a Manual Page Break

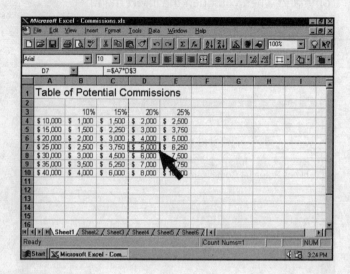

1 Select the cell in the place where you want to remove the page break.

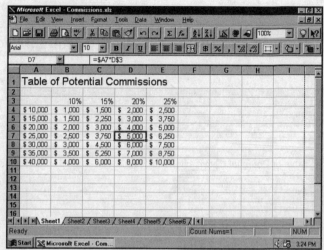

3 Excel removes the dashed lines from your screen.

If you want to remove a combination (vertical and horizontal) page break, select the cell immediately below and to the right of the intersection of the manual page breaks. If you want to remove a horizontal page break, select any cell immediately below the page break. If you want to remove a vertical page break, select any cell immediately to the right of the page break.

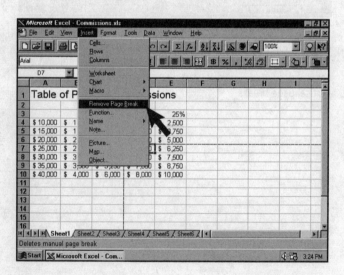

2 Open the **Insert** menu. Select the **Remove Page Break** command.

Preview and Print the Worksheet

By default, Excel prints all of the selected worksheet. However, you can create different print settings for each worksheet in a workbook. For example, you may want to print all of one worksheet, but only part of another worksheet. Printing part of a worksheet is particularly valuable when the worksheet contains both details and summary information. The reader may not need to see the details, so you can choose to print only the summary information.

You also can print the entire workbook. Excel uses the settings for each sheet in the workbook and prints each worksheet on a separate page. If one worksheet doesn't fit on one page, Excel prints that worksheet on as many pages as needed unless you *scale* the sheet to enlarge or reduce the print so that the printout fits on one page.

It is a good idea to save your worksheets before printing, just in case a printer error or other problem occurs. If you do this, you don't lose any work since the last time you saved the worksheet.

It's also a good idea to review the appearance of the worksheet before you print the final product. Use Excel's Print Preview feature to see your worksheet before you print. The first page of the worksheet appears as a reduced image in the Print Preview screen. However, you can use the Zoom feature in Print Preview to magnify the view. This enables you to inspect the printout more closely. Then, when you click the Zoom button again, Excel reduces the view to a smaller image again. If your worksheet is more than one page, you can use the Next and Previous buttons, or press Page Up and Page Down to look at other pages. You can also change the margins and page setup and start printing from the Preview window. To view a different worksheet within the same workbook, click that worksheet's tab before previewing.

Both the Page Setup dialog box and the Print dialog box contain Preview buttons you can click to preview a worksheet. Or, you can choose the Print Preview command from the File menu, or click the Print Preview tool on the Standard toolbar.

You can display the Print dialog box in one of several ways:

- Choose the **Print** button in the Page Setup dialog box.
- Choose the **Print** button on the Print Preview screen.
- Open the **File** menu and choose the **Print** command.

You saw the Print dialog box when you learned how to check printer settings, so you know that you can change printers in this dialog box and also determine which pages and how many copies to print.

Suppose you have already set up your print options, and you're back viewing the worksheet. You really don't need to open the Print dialog box if you want to print one copy of the current worksheet or selected cells in the current worksheet to the default printer. You can bypass the Print dialog box by clicking the Print button on the Standard toolbar to print your worksheet.

> Remember, if you want to print only a portion of the workbook, open the **File** menu and choose the **Print** command to use Excel's Print dialog box.

Begin Guided Tour Print Part of a Worksheet

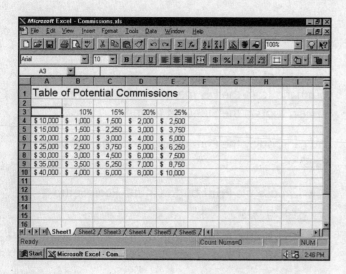

1 Select the worksheet containing the information you want to print.

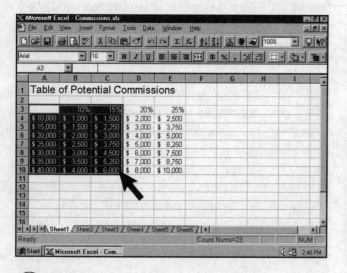

2 Select the area of the sheet that you want to print.

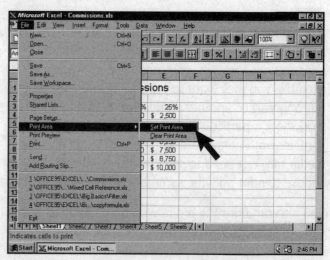

3 Open the **File** menu and highlight the **Print Area** command. Excel displays the Print Area submenu. Choose the **Set Print Area** command.

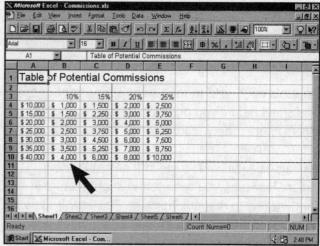

4 Dotted lines surround the area of the worksheet that you selected.

Reset the Print Area by clearing print settings and selecting a new print range. Choose the **Clear Print Area** from the **File, Print Area** submenu.

Begin Guided Tour   Print the Entire Workbook

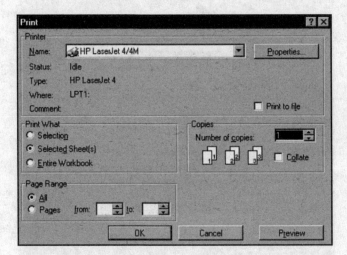

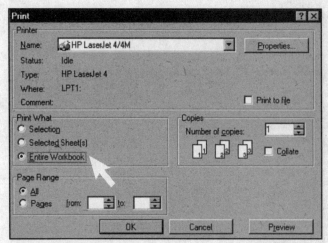

1 Open the **File** menu and choose the **Print** command. Excel displays the Print dialog box.

2 In the Print What area, choose the **Entire Workbook** option button and choose **OK**. Excel prints all worksheets in the workbook using any settings you may have previously specified for those worksheets.

Begin Guided Tour   Preview On-Screen Before Printing

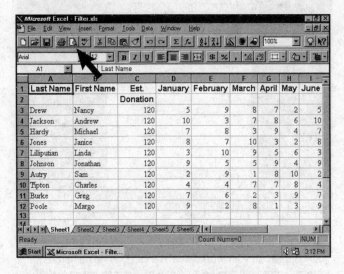

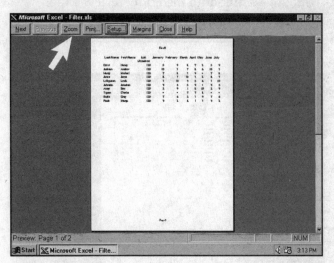

1 Open the worksheet you want to preview before printing. Click the **Print Preview** tool on the Standard toolbar.

2 Excel displays the worksheet in Print Preview mode. Click the **Zoom** button.

(continues)

Guided Tour   Preview On-Screen Before Printing   *(continued)*

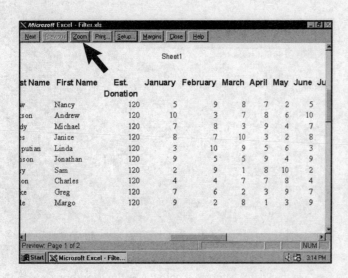

3 A close-up view of your worksheet appears. Click the **Zoom** button again.

> You can move the mouse pointer onto the Print Preview screen and click a particular spot to zoom into that spot. When you move the mouse pointer onto the Print Preview screen, the shape changes to a magnifying glass.

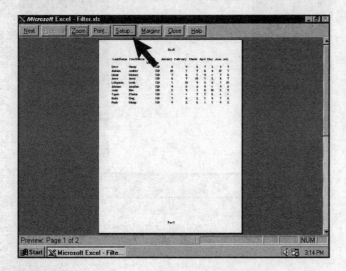

4 Excel returns you to the full-screen Print Preview. Click the **Setup** button.

5 The Page Setup dialog box appears. You can modify any of the settings on any of its tabs (see "Set up the Page for Printing," p. 128). Click **OK** or **Cancel** to return to the Print Preview.

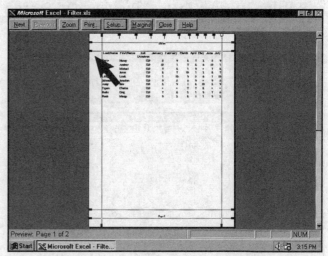

6 Click **Margins**. Margin markers and column width markers appear on your worksheet. You can change margins and column widths by dragging a margin marker or a column width marker. To hide margins, click the **Margins** button a second time.

HOW TO...

"Do" Math

One of the primary reasons people use spreadsheet software is to make mathematical calculations easier. At its simplest, an electronic spreadsheet program like Excel is an expensive, powerful desktop calculator. You can easily perform simple calculations (addition, subtraction, multiplication, and division). What makes an electronic spreadsheet more powerful is the reusability it provides. For example, you can store text and formulas and re-use them. Spreadsheets simplify math so much that it becomes almost a "fill-in-the-blanks" effort.

In Excel, you use formulas to add, subtract, multiply, and divide numbers; you use functions to total cells and calculate averages. In this section, you'll learn how to do all those functions, and you'll also learn about one of the most powerful features available in a worksheet: copying a formula so that you don't have to re-enter it.

Most formulas and functions refer to a range, so this chapter may help you see the value of naming a range, which you learned about in "Work with Ranges," p. 50.

What You Will Find in This Section

Perform Basic Math Calculations

In Excel, you add and subtract using *formulas*—nothing complicated though. Just simple ones, similar to the formulas you use when you add a list of numbers or subtract values in your checkbook.

When you type a formula into a cell in Excel, you see the *result* of the formula in that cell after you press Enter or click the check mark, not the formula itself. If you select the cell containing the formula and look in the Formula bar, you see the formula you typed, but the cell still displays the result of the formula.

Excel knows that you're typing a formula because you start the formula with an equal sign (=). Excel uses the equal sign as a signal that a formula, not text, follows. You also use the following symbols to represent mathematical operators in your formula:

+	Addition
-	Subtraction
*	Multiplication
/	Division

You may think that you add numbers in a worksheet by creating a formula that contains numbers. That is a logical approach, but the beauty of "spreadsheet math" is that your formula can (and does) refer to cell addresses containing numbers instead of actually containing the numbers. Why, and why is this so cool? Suppose you place your formula in D8 and it includes a reference to B3. Further suppose that B3 contains 5. Now suppose that you change the contents of B3 from 5 to 7. That's right, you guessed it. Excel updates the cell containing the formula so that the answer changes, but you don't need to change the formula.

You can include any cells in your formula. The cells do not have to be next to each other. Also, you can combine mathematical operations, for example, C3+C4D5. And that brings up another point, the order of calculations.

The Order of Calculation

Excel follows the natural order of precedence you learned in high school math. (Do you remember your high school math?) It first resolves any exponential expressions in the formula. Then, it solves all multiplication and division. Last, it solves all addition and subtraction.

You can override this natural order of things by using parentheses. If you place parentheses around any of the cell references, Excel performs the calculations within the parentheses first, using the order of precedence rules within the parentheses. After solving the expressions enclosed in parentheses, Excel finishes calculating the rest of the expression using the order of precedence rules.

Look at an example of the effects of parentheses and the order of precedence. Suppose C3 contains the number 8, B6 contains the number 3, A10 contains the number 2, and your formula (in cell D4) initially looks like this:

=C3+4*B6/A10-8

Excel multiplies 4 by B6 and gets 12. Excel divides that result (12) by the 2 in A10 and gets 6. Excel then adds that result (6) to the 8 in C3 and gets 14, and finally Excel subtracts 8 and gets 6. D4 shows this answer.

Now, keeping the same values in place, simply add one set of parentheses to the formula and see how the result changes:

=(C3+4)*B6/A10-8

For this formula, Excel starts by adding the contents of C3 (8) and 4 and gets 12. Then Excel multiplies that result by 3 (the contents of B6) and gets 36. Excel divides that result by 2 (the contents of A10) and gets 18. Last, Excel subtracts 8 from 18 and gets 10.

Begin Guided Tour Write a Formula to Add, Subtract, Multiply, and Divide

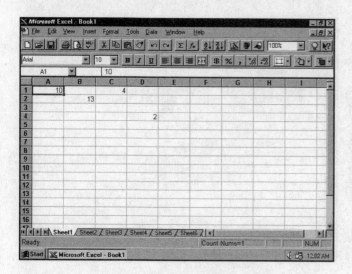

1 Open a worksheet in which you have numbers in cells. In this example, place values in A1, B2, C1, and D4.

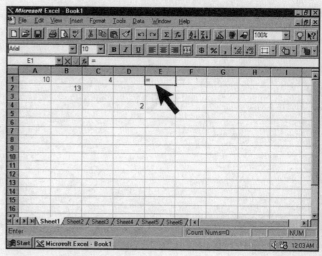

3 Type =.

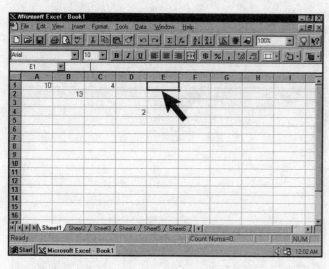

2 Select an empty cell (for example, E1).

4 Click or type the address of the first cell you want to include in the formula. For example, type **B2**.

(continues)

Guided Tour   Write a Formula to Add, Subtract, Multiply, and Divide   *(continued)*

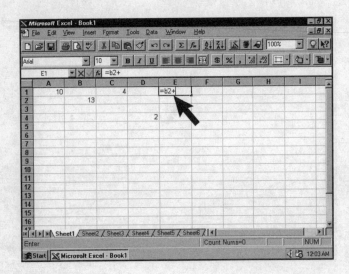

5 Type a mathematical operator: +, -, *, or /. In this example, type **+**.

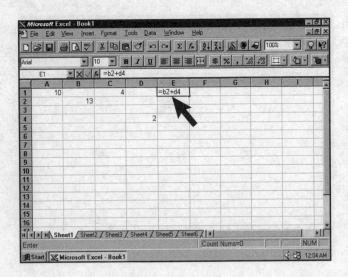

6 Click or type the address of the next cell you want to include in the formula, **D4**.

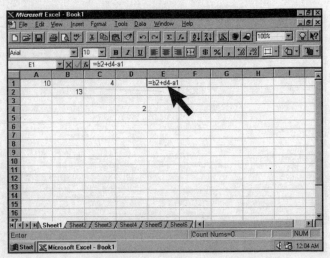

7 Repeat steps 5 and 6 until you finish including all necessary cells in the formula. In this example, include - and A1 in the formula. Click the check mark in the Formula bar.

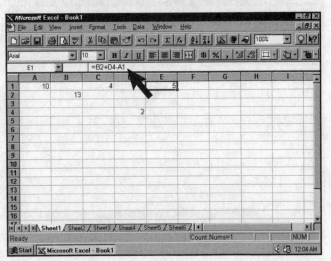

8 Excel displays the results of the formula in the selected cell, and the actual formula appears in the Formula bar.

Calculate Totals and Averages

You need to know how to create formulas, but one of the most common actions you take in a spreadsheet is to calculate a sum for a contiguous group of cells (a column of numbers or a row of numbers). Creating a formula that adds each individual cell is tedious at the very least.

In addition to formulas, Excel contains *functions*, which are abbreviated formulas that perform a specific operation on a group of cells containing values. Excel provides over 250 functions that can help you with tasks ranging from adding a column of numbers to determining loan payments.

The SUM function is a shortcut for entering a formula that automatically calculates a sum for entries in a range. The format for entering any function is basically the same: as with formulas, you start with an equal sign (=) to tell Excel you're entering a function, and then you type the function name and enclose any *arguments* in parentheses. Arguments are *parameters* (such as a range containing values) Excel needs to make the calculation. Think of arguments as the variable part of the function.

The SUM function consists of the function name—SUM—and the range of cells you want to add; you enter the range within parentheses. To enter a SUM function, first you type **=SUM(**. You can type the function in lowercase or uppercase letters. The open parenthesis tells Excel you are going to specify arguments for the function. In the case of the SUM function, you specify a range to add by selecting the range. A dashed border called a marquee surrounds the selected range. Finally, you type a close parenthesis. Typing) tells Excel that you are finished specifying arguments. For the SUM function, Excel inserts the range coordinates in the parentheses.

For a quick and dirty method of placing a SUM function in a worksheet, you can use the AutoSum tool on the Standard toolbar.

Use the AutoCalculate Feature

Suppose you don't really want to place a SUM function in your worksheet, but you want to know the sum of the numbers in a column. The AutoCalculate feature provides you with a quick solution to this problem. In addition to showing you a sum, AutoCalculate can also show you an average, tell you the largest or smallest number in a list, count the number of cells in a list that are not empty, and count the number of cells in a list that contain numbers.

Use the Function Wizard

Excel contains over 250 functions. So what do you do when you want to try a function but you haven't a clue how to set it up? Use the Function Wizard. This helpful wizard prompts you for the information and correctly inserts any syntax information, such as commas. The Function Wizard is particularly helpful when you're trying to enter a function, and you are unsure of the function's correct syntax.

The AVERAGE function is another predefined formula in Excel. The AVERAGE function calculates the average of a list of numbers by adding the values you specify in a range and dividing the sum by the number of values in the range. For example, you can calculate the average expense, income, grade, rating, or salary, and so on.

You don't find a tool on the Standard toolbar to help you enter an AVERAGE function, but you can use Excel's Function Wizard. The Function Wizard walks you through entering any function in Excel. You find a Function Wizard button on the Standard toolbar and also in the Formula bar (after you start typing in a cell).

Suppose, for example, you want to save money for a special Christmas present for your mom. You deposit $50 into a savings account that earns 6 percent annual interest compounded monthly (monthly interest of 6%/12, or 0.5%). You plan to deposit $5 at the beginning of every month for the next 12 months. How much money will you have in the account at the end of 12 months? Use Excel's Future Value function and let the Function Wizard walk you through setting up the function.

When you use the Function Wizard, you see a short definition of the purpose of the function and the structure of the function in the dialog box. This is to help you learn more about what Excel is doing when it sets up the function. The structure for the Future Value function in Excel is FV (rate,nper,pmt,pv,type). This will mean more to you as you go through the Guided Tour.

Be aware that the results of a function may be too large to fit in the column. If you see pound signs (#####) in the cell, make the column wider.

Begin Guided Tour   Calculate a Total with the AutoSum Tool

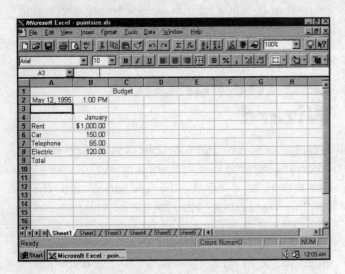

1 In a worksheet, create a list of numbers you want to add. The example shows numbers in cells B5:B8.

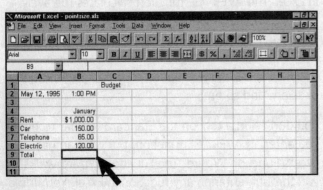

2 Place the insertion point in the cell where you want to store the result of the calculation.

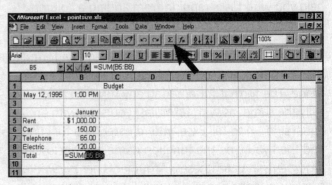

3 Click the **AutoSum** tool on the Standard toolbar. Excel figures out that you want to add the column of numbers above the selected cell and displays the formula in the Formula bar and the selected cell for confirmation (see cell B9).

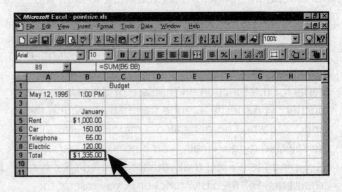

4 Click the **check mark** in the Formula bar. Excel stores the function in the selected cell. You see the result of the formula in the selected cell and in the formula in the Formula bar.

If you double-click the AutoSum tool in step 3, Excel automatically performs both step 3 and step 4.

Begin Guided Tour   Use AutoCalculate to Preview the Largest Number in the List

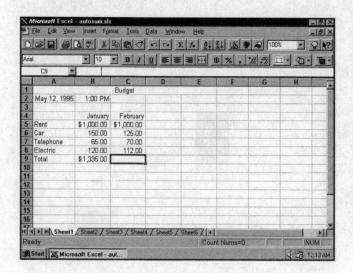

1 In a worksheet, create a list of numbers. Our example shows numbers in cells C5:C8.

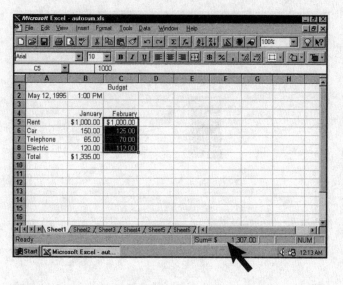

2 Select the cells that contain the numbers. At the right side of the status bar, you see the total of the selected cells.

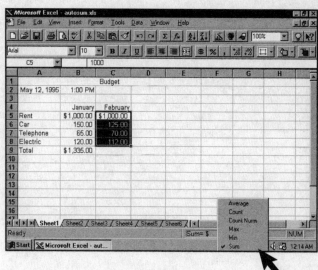

3 Move the mouse pointer into the status bar and press the right mouse button. A shortcut menu appears.

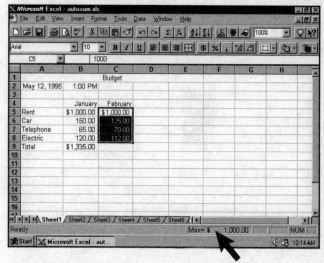

4 Choose **Max**. Excel displays, on the right side of the status bar, the largest number in the selected list.

Begin Guided Tour Use AutoCalculate to See How Many Cells Contain Numbers

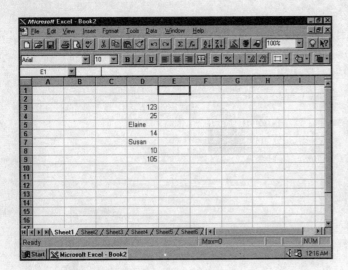

1 In a worksheet, create a list of numbers and labels. Our example shows information in cells D3:D9. Select the list of cells.

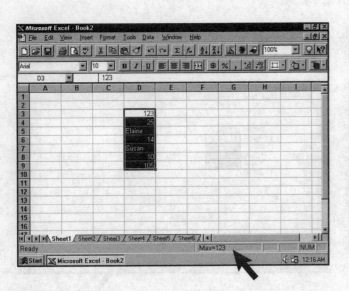

2 At the right side of the status bar, you see the same autocalculation Excel last performed, except for the new list. Move the mouse pointer into the status bar and click the right mouse button.

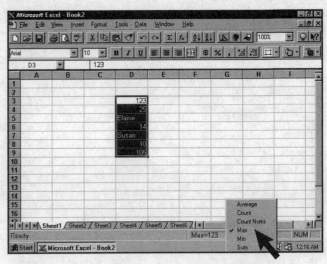

3 A shortcut menu appears. Select **Count Nums**.

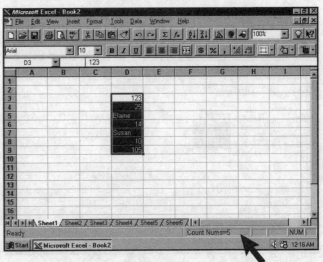

4 Excel displays, on the right side of the status bar, the number of cells in the list that contain numbers.

Begin Guided Tour   Use the Function Wizard to Calculate an Average

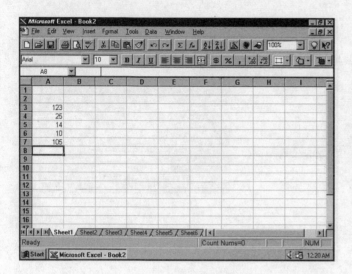

1 Select the cell in which you want to display an average. Type **=**.

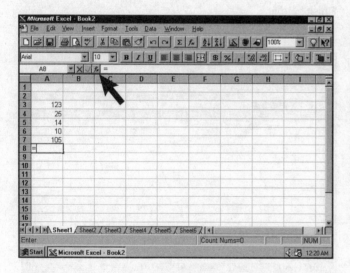

2 You see the Function Wizard button in both the Formula bar and on the Standard toolbar. Click either **Function Wizard** button.

> If you don't type **=**, you can start the Function Wizard from the Standard toolbar.

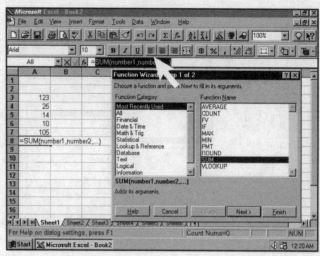

3 Excel starts the Function Wizard and the Function Wizard—Step 1 of 2 dialog box appears.

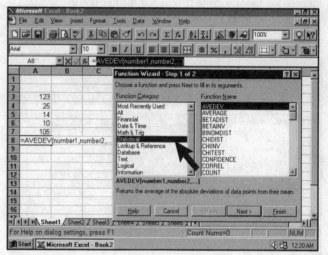

4 From the Function Category list, select the type of function you want to enter. For example, AVERAGE is a statistical function. When you select a Function Category, Excel displays the functions available in that category in the Function Name list.

(continues)

Guided Tour Use the Function Wizard to Calculate an Average *(continued)*

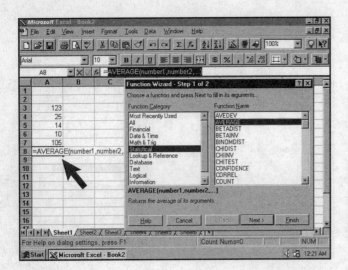

5 In the Function Name list, highlight the function you want to place in the worksheet. Excel displays the function in the selected cell and Formula bar. (Notice the definition of the function's purpose and the structure of the function in the dialog box.) Click the **Next** button.

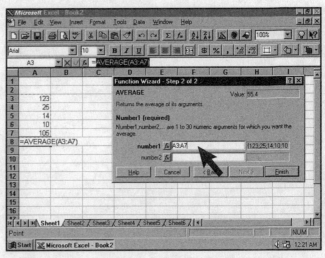

7 Excel places a flashing marquee around the selected cells, adds the range address to the formula you're building in the cell, and displays the address in the dialog box. Click the **Finish** button.

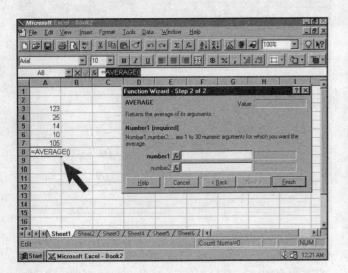

6 Excel displays the Function Wizard—Step 2 of 2 dialog box in which you can define arguments for the function. The argument for an AVERAGE function is the range containing the values you want to average. In the worksheet, select the cells you want to average.

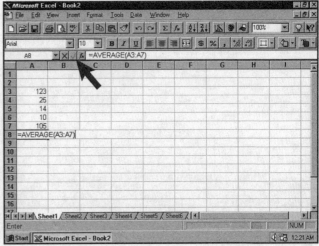

8 Excel closes the Function Wizard dialog box and leaves the formula in the worksheet, waiting for you to confirm. If you didn't type = to start, Excel automatically performs both steps 8 and 9. Click the **check mark** in the Formula bar.

If you can't see the cells you want to select, move the dialog box by dragging its title bar.

Guided Tour   Use the Function Wizard to Calculate an Average

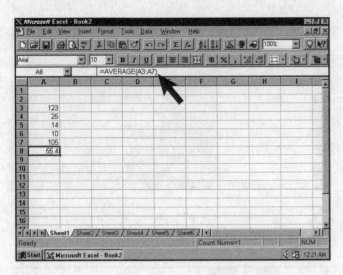

9 Excel stores the formula in the worksheet and displays the results of the formula in the selected cell, and the actual formula in the Formula bar.

Begin Guided Tour   Use the Function Wizard to Calculate a Future Value

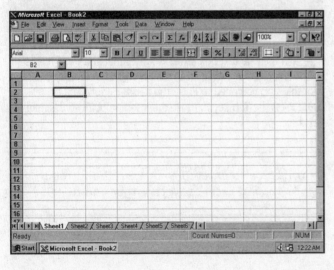

1 Select a cell in the worksheet in which you want to store the Future Value function.

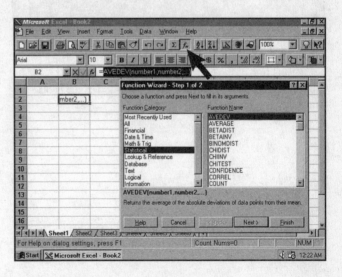

2 Click the **Function Wizard** button on the Standard toolbar. Excel displays the Function Wizard—Step 1 of 2 dialog box.

(continues)

Guided Tour   Use the Function Wizard to Calculate a Future Value

(continued)

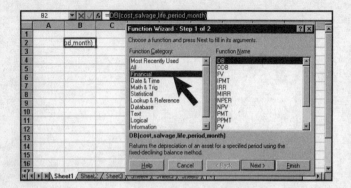

3 Click **Financial** in the Function Category list on the left.

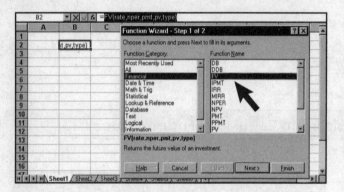

4 Click **FV** in the Function Name list on the right. The structure of the function and its arguments appear immediately below the Function Category list. Click the **Next** button.

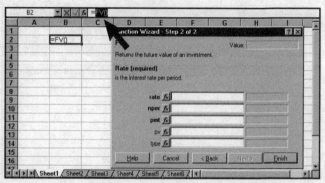

5 Excel displays the second Function Wizard dialog box that prompts to enter values for each argument of the function.

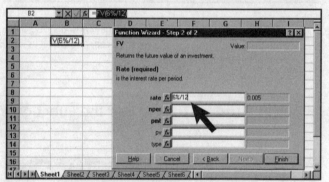

6 In the rate text box, Excel indicates that you need to enter the rate per period. That means that 6% annually is .5% monthly, and you need to enter the decimal equivalent of .5%, **.005**. Press the **Tab** key to move the insertion point to the nper text box.

You can also enter .5%, or even the formula 6%/12, and Excel converts either one to .005.

Guided Tour Use the Function Wizard to Calculate a Future Value

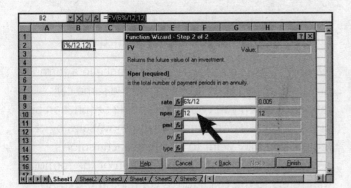

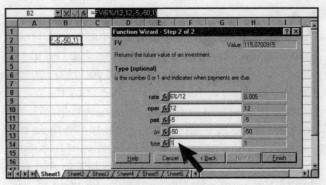

7 Nper represents the total number of payments you intend to make while you save. Since you plan to deposit money monthly for one year, you enter **12**. Press the **Tab** key to move the insertion point to the pmt text box.

10 Use the type text box to tell Excel if you are making payments at the beginning or end of the period. Use 0 for payments you make at the end of the period and 1 for payments you make at the beginning of the period. In this example, type **1**. Click **Finish**.

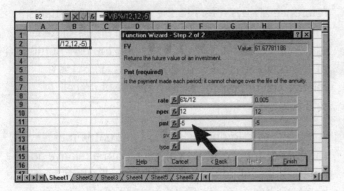

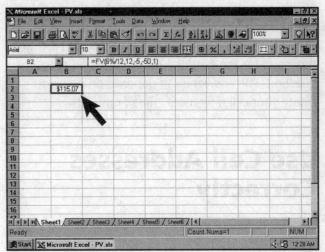

8 For pmt, supply the amount of money you intend to deposit each month. In this example, you type **-5**.

11 Excel displays the results of the function in the selected cell. In this example, you have $115.07 after a year. You see the formula in the formula bar.

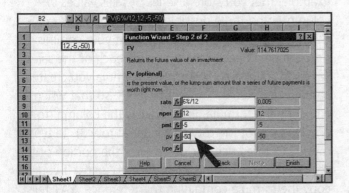

9 Press the **Tab** key to move the insertion point to the pv text box. Pv is optional and represents the amount of money you initially deposit. In this example, you type **-50**. Press **Tab** to move the insertion point to the type text box.

Copy a Formula or Function

When you build your worksheet, you often use the same basic formulas and functions in more than one cell. You already learned that you can use Excel's Copy command to copy data; you also can create a formula or function and then copy the formula or function to other appropriate cells. You do not have to go to each cell and enter the formula or function again. For example, you may want to copy a formula or function across a row of totals so that you don't have to re-enter the formula or function to add up each row of numbers.

This feature is probably one of the most powerful features available in a worksheet, since you do not have to go to each cell and enter the same formula over and over again.

"But," you ask, "suppose I use the AutoSum tool in cell B8 to add cells B3:B7. If I copy that function to cell C8, intending to add cells C3:C7, don't I just get the result for the sum of B3:B7?" What an excellent question. The answer is, "It depends on how you create your cell references." Read on.

Use Cell Addresses Correctly

In Excel, there are three types of cell references:

- Relative
- Absolute
- Mixed

The type of cell reference you use in a formula determines how Excel changes the formula when you copy it into a different cell.

When you use *relative* cell references, the cell references in the formula or function change to reflect the cells at the new location of the formula or function. That means that you can copy to column B a formula or function that adds numbers in column A, and Excel adjusts the formula to add numbers in column B. To

include a relative cell reference, don't do anything different from what you already learned.

When you use an *absolute* cell reference in a formula or function, you force Excel to use the same cell reference when you copy the formula or function as in the original. For example, if you show sales by region, you may want to calculate each region's percentage of total sales. The portion of the formula that refers to the cell address containing the total sales amount should remain unchanged, or absolute. So, in the formula that calculates each region's percentage of total sales, you use an absolute cell reference when you refer to the cell containing total sales. When you copy this formula, the total sales cell reference always refers to the one cell that contains the total sales for all regions. To type an absolute cell entry, precede the column letter and the row number of the cell reference with dollar signs ($). A1 is a relative cell reference; $A$1 is an absolute cell reference.

A *mixed* cell reference is a single cell entry in a formula or function that contains both a relative and an absolute cell reference. A mixed cell reference is helpful when you need a formula that always refers to the values in a specific column, but the values in the rows must change, and vice versa. Suppose, for example, that you store a series of sales values in column A and three possible commission rates in B3, C3, and D3. You want to know what your commission will be, at each rate, if you sell each of the sales values in column A. The original formula you create contains a mixed cell reference to B3, so that when you copy the formula, Excel adjusts the column (to C and D), but not the row (leaving it at row 3). To type a mixed cell reference, include a $ for the portion of the cell reference you don't want Excel to adjust if you copy the formula containing this reference. $A1 tells Excel to change the row numbers, but always use column A, if you copy the formula containing this reference. A$1 tells Excel to change the column letters, but always use row 1, if you copy the formula containing this reference.

Begin Guided Tour Copy a Formula Containing a Relative Cell Reference

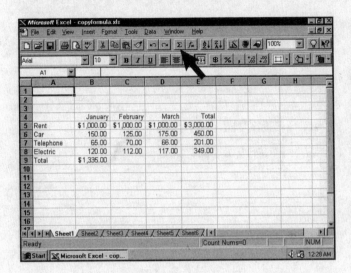

1 Create a worksheet containing four columns of numbers you want to add. Use the AutoSum tool to calculate the sum of the first column of numbers (see "Calculate Totals and Averages," page 151).

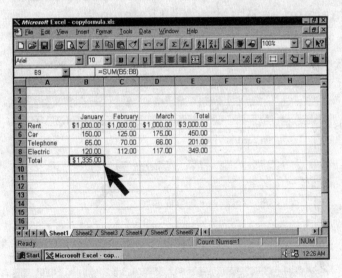

2 Highlight the cell containing the SUM function you just created.

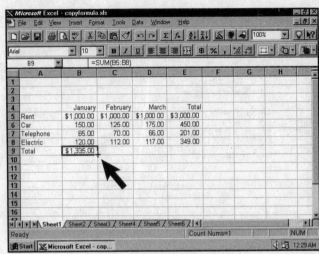

3 Slide the mouse pointer over the fill handle. It turns to a black plus sign.

4 Drag to copy the formula to adjacent cells.

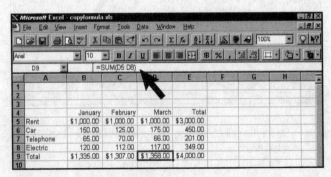

5 Click on any of the newly filled cells to view the formula in the Formula bar. Note that Excel adjusts the original formula to account for location.

Begin Guided Tour   Create a Formula Containing an Absolute Cell Reference

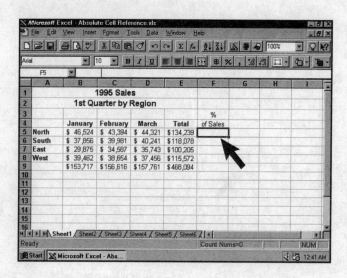

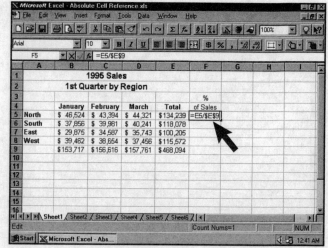

1 Select the cell you want to contain the absolute cell reference.

2 Type the formula you want to use, including dollar signs before the column letter and row number for the cell you want to remain constant when you copy the formula.

Begin Guided Tour   Copy a Formula Containing an Absolute Cell Reference

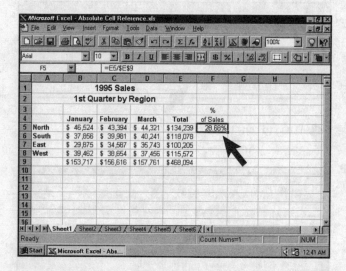

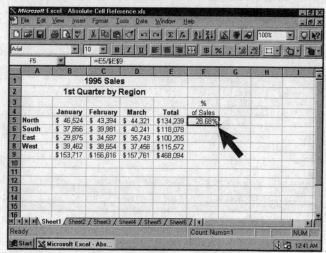

1 Select the cell containing the formula with the absolute cell reference.

2 Slide the mouse pointer over the fill handle. The pointer becomes a black plus sign.

Guided Tour   Copy a Formula Containing an Absolute Cell Reference

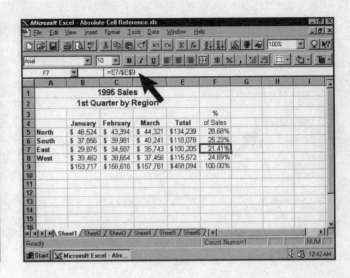

3 Drag to copy the formula to adjacent cells.

4 Click on each of the newly filled cells to view the formula in the Formula bar. Note that Excel adjusts only the first portion of the original formula to account for location, using the absolute cell reference in each formula.

Begin Guided Tour   Create a Formula Containing a Mixed Cell Reference

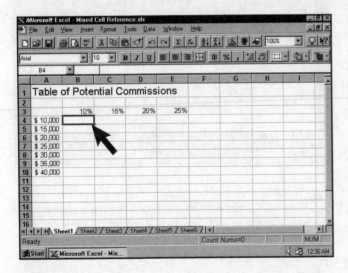

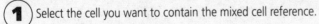

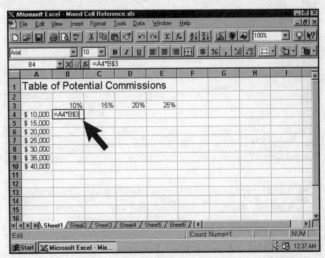

1 Select the cell you want to contain the mixed cell reference.

2 Type the formula you want to use, including a dollar sign before either the column letter or the row number of the cell you want to remain constant when you copy the formula.

Begin Guided Tour   Copy a Formula Containing a Mixed Cell Reference

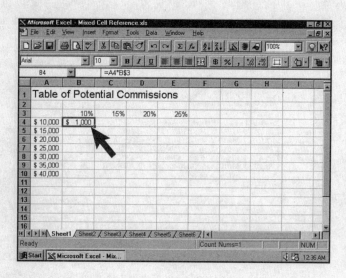

1 Select the cell containing the formula with the mixed cell reference.

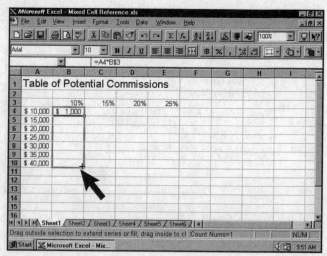

3 Drag to copy the formula to adjacent cells.

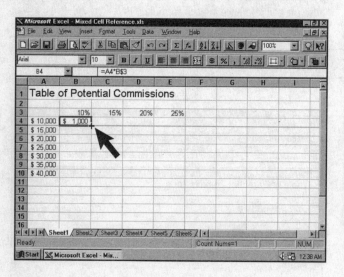

2 Slide the mouse pointer over the fill handle. The mouse pointer changes to the black plus sign.

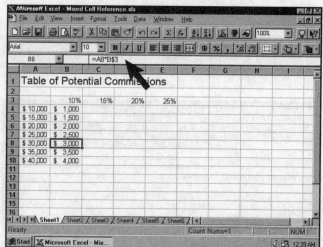

4 Click on several of the newly filled cells to view the formulas in the Formula bar. Note that Excel adjusts only the portion of the original formula that did not contain a dollar sign.

HOW TO...
Use Templates

Whenever you start a new workbook, you may notice that Excel doesn't require you to make any decisions about the layout of the workbook. Instead, Excel creates the workbook for you with its default settings; for example, Excel initially starts using the same font and font size for each workbook and on each sheet in each workbook. These defaults are stored in *templates*, which are special workbooks. Templates store information and formats that you use on a regular basis, so that you don't have to set things up over and over again. You can think of templates as falling into two groups. In one group, you have templates that you create for specific purposes that contain settings you need for particular projects. In the other group, you have *autotemplates*, which are special workbooks or worksheets you create that contain the settings you want to use on a regular, ongoing basis as default settings. Settings in autotemplates are those that you use most of the time.

In the first group of templates, Microsoft has created some templates for you that contain settings designed at performing some very specific tasks. While you'll learn how to open a worksheet based on one of these pre-built templates in this section, Part II of this book focuses more on working with these pre-built templates. In this part of the book, you focus more on working with autotemplates.

Unless you choose a different template, Excel bases new workbooks on a template called Book. If you start a new workbook by clicking the New tool on the Standard toolbar, Excel uses the Book template.

What You Will Find in This Section

Use Templates Included with Excel

Each time you choose the New tool from the Standard toolbar, you are creating a new workbook based on the autotemplate for workbooks. Excel ships with some other pre-built templates that you may find useful. These templates enable you to carry out common tasks and include:

- Business Planner
- Car Lease Manager
- Change Request
- Expense Statement
- Invoice
- Loan Manager
- Personal Budgeter
- Purchase Order

- Sales Quote
- Timecard
- Village Software

The best way to find out more about these templates and what they can help you do is to open a new workbook based on each one. To learn more about using these pre-built templates check out "Use Excel's Pre-Built Templates," which starts on page 391.

As with the default Book template, each workbook you base on one of these templates starts out with a name that includes the template name and a sequential number. Again, when you save the new workbook, give it a new name that is more meaningful to you.

Begin Guided Tour   Open a New Workbook Based on an Excel Template

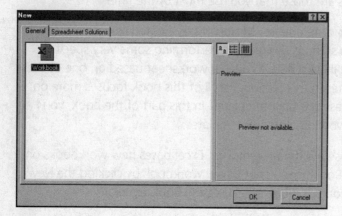

1 Open the **File** menu and choose the **New** command. Excel displays the New dialog box.

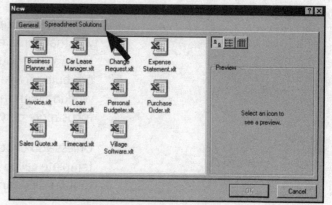

2 Click the **Spreadsheet Solutions** tab. The Spreadsheet Solutions tab appears.

The Workbook template you see on the General tab is associated with the default template Excel uses to create workbooks initially named Book.

Guided Tour   Open a New Workbook Based on an Excel Template

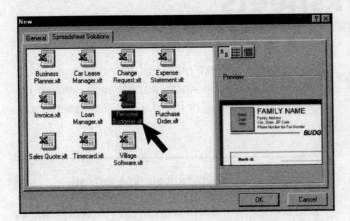

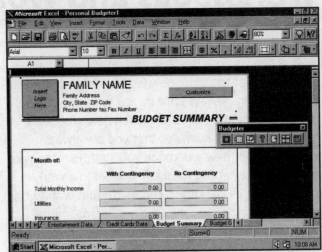

3 Click the template you want to use. Excel displays a sample of the template in the Preview box. Click **OK**.

4 Excel opens a new workbook based on the template you selected. In the figure, the Personal Budgeter template is open.

If you chose the Typical button when you installed Excel, you installed only four of these templates. To install the rest of these templates, run Setup again and choose **Add/ Remove**. Make sure you select all options for Spreadsheet Templates.

Change the Defaults for New Workbooks and Worksheets

When you use the New tool on the Standard toolbar to start a new workbook, you find that certain settings always appear; you see, for example, the same font and font size in each new workbook. Suppose you find, however, that you are always changing each new workbook you start. Perhaps you set up the formatting for the first sheet in a workbook so that its cells are in comma format with two decimal places; or you may use a different font or font size than the one Excel uses; or, you always print the first sheet in the workbook in landscape mode and all subsequent sheets in portrait mode.

You can save time and effort by making these changes once and storing them in an *autotemplate*. An autotemplate is a workbook or worksheet you create that contains the settings you want to use on a regular basis as default settings. You use the workbook and worksheet autotemplates as the basis for new workbooks or worksheets that you create. When you save an autotemplate, you store it in your XLStart folder using a special filename that Excel recognizes as an autotemplate. You'll learn the special file names to use for a workbook autotemplate and a worksheet autotemplate as you work through the Guided Tours.

What kind of changes can you make when you create autotemplates? You can change:

- The number and type of sheets that appear in the workbook.

- The cell formatting in worksheets that you set up in the Cell Format dialog box.

- The page formatting in worksheets that you set up in the Page Setup dialog box.

- Row and column styles.

- Macros, custom menus, or toolbars.

You also can store text, numbers, dates, or any other information that you want to appear every time you start a new workbook or insert a new worksheet into a workbook.

> Be aware that anything you type into an autotemplate appears in every new workbook you create or in every worksheet you insert. In fact, if you move the cell pointer and save the autotemplate, the cell pointer always appears in the new location, not in A1.

To change the default settings that appear each time you create a new workbook, you set up a new workbook that has all the settings you want. Remember, page formatting applies only to the active worksheet, and cell formatting applies only to the selected cells. So, if you want page settings on all worksheets to be the same, you must select all worksheets and then change settings from the Page Setup dialog box. You can select all worksheets by pointing at a worksheet tab, clicking the right mouse button, and, from the shortcut menu that appears, choosing Select All Sheets. If you want to change, for example, the default font for the entire workbook, select all worksheets and then select all cells. Use the technique just described to select all worksheets; you can select all cells by clicking in the blank space of the worksheet above row numbers and to the left of column letters.

After you set up the workbook with the settings you want to use as defaults, you save that workbook as an autotemplate. After that, each time you start a new workbook by clicking the New tool on the Standard toolbar, you see your settings.

If you start a new workbook by opening the **File** menu and choosing the **New** command, you can base the new workbook on the default template by selecting the Workbook template in the New dialog box.

The same basic principles apply to the default worksheet; however, to create a default worksheet, you create a workbook that contains only one

worksheet. You set up that worksheet so that it contains the settings you want. Then, you save that worksheet as an autotemplate. Each new sheet you insert based on the autotemplate has the same characteristics as the autotemplate.

Suppose you previously created some styles that you really wish were in an autotemplate so that you could make them available to all new workbooks or worksheets. Must you recreate those styles? No, just copy them to an autotemplate.

Begin Guided Tour   Change the Default Workbook

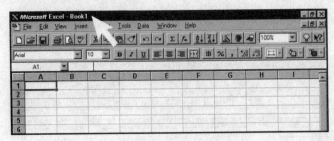

1 Start Excel so that you are viewing Book1. Make any changes to the workbook that you want to be permanent.

To select all worksheets, point at a worksheet tab and click the right mouse button. From the shortcut menu that appears, choose **Select All Sheets**. To select all cells, click in the blank space of the worksheet above row numbers and to the left of column letters.

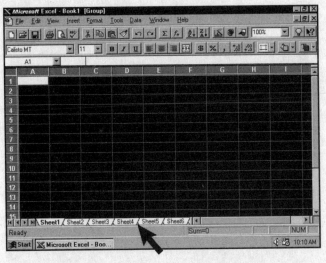

2 In this example, change the font to 11 point Calisto MT. To change the font in the entire workbook, select all worksheets and all cells.

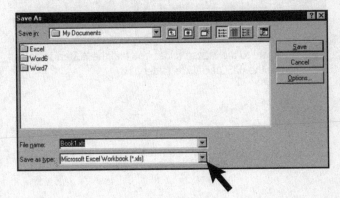

3 Open the **File** menu and choose the **Save As** command. Excel displays the Save As dialog box. Click the arrow on the Save as type drop-down list.

(continues)

Guided Tour   Change the Default Workbook   *(continued)*

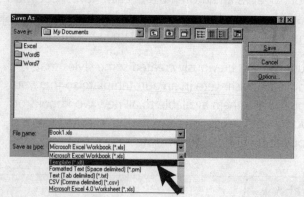

4 Choose **Template (*.xlt)**.

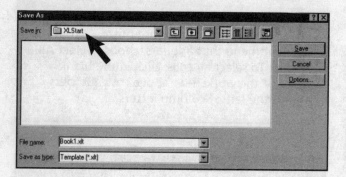

5 Navigate to the XLStart folder. You find the XLStart folder inside the \MSOffice\Excel folder.

6 In the File name list box, type the new name of your template. Name the file BOOK.XLT. (Excel suggests the name Book1.xlt. Be sure to remove the 1 from the suggested name or retype the name completely.) Choose **Save**.

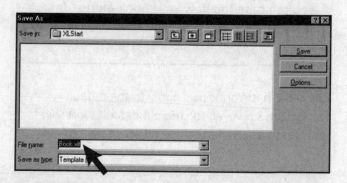

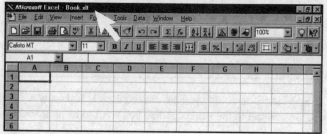

7 Excel saves your settings in the default workbook.

8 To test the changes, close Excel and reopen it. In the new Book1, look for your settings. When you create Book2, you also see your settings.

Begin Guided Tour   Change the Default Worksheet

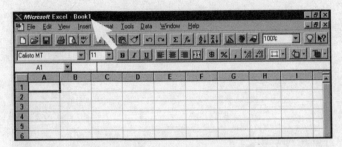

1 Start Excel so that you are viewing Book1.

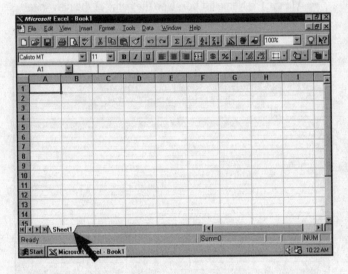

2 Delete all sheets in the workbook except one. To delete multiple sheets simultaneously, click **Sheet2**, hold down the **Shift** key, and click each subsequent sheet in the workbook (use the sheet tab scroll arrows to see each sheet tab). Point at any sheet tab, click the right mouse button, and select **Delete** from the shortcut menu.

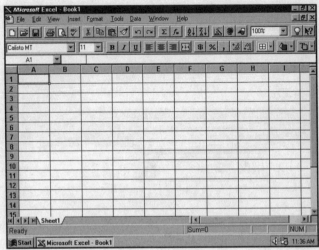

3 Make any changes to the worksheet that you want to be permanent. In the example, select all cells in the sheet and add a black border around each cell to enhance the gridlines.

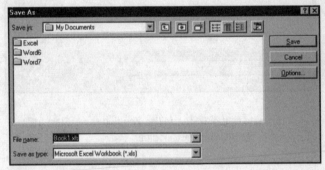

4 Open the **File** menu and choose the **Save As** command. Excel displays the Save As dialog box.

(continues)

Guided Tour Change the Default Worksheet *(continued)*

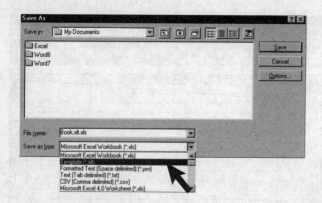

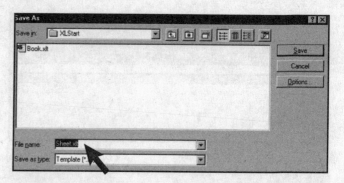

5 Click on the arrow on the Save as type drop-down list. Choose **Template (*.xlt)**.

7 In the File Name list box, type the name of the new sheet autotemplate. Name the file SHEET.XLT. Choose **Save**.

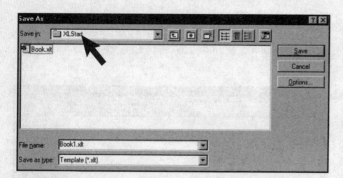

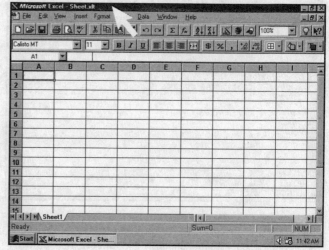

6 Navigate to the XLStart folder. You find the XLStart folder inside the \MSOffice\Excel folder.

8 Excel saves your settings in the default worksheet.

9 To test the changes, close the Sheet template and insert a new worksheet (point at a sheet tab, click the right mouse button, and choose **Insert**). When Excel displays the Insert dialog box, highlight **Sheet** and click **OK**. The new sheet should contain your settings.

Begin Guided Tour   Copy Styles to an Autotemplate

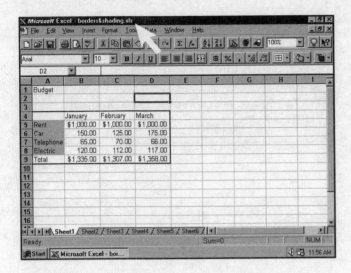

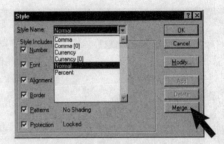

3 Open the **Format** menu and choose the **Style** command. Excel displays the Style dialog box. Open the **Style Name** list box; notice that the autotemplate contains only the default styles. Click the **Merge** button.

1 Open the workbook that contains the styles you want to copy. In the example, the open worksheet contains two styles—Borders and Shading—that you need to copy to an autotemplate.

For information on creating styles, see "Use Styles," p. 119.

4 Excel displays the Merge Styles dialog box.

5 Highlight the workbook containing the styles you want to copy and click **OK**.

(continues)

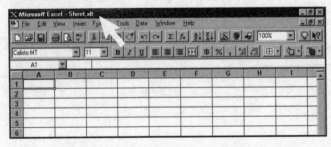

2 Open the autotemplate to which you want to copy the styles. Open **Sheet.xlt**, which you created in the previous Guided Tour.

Guided Tour   Copy Styles to an Autotemplate   *(continued)*

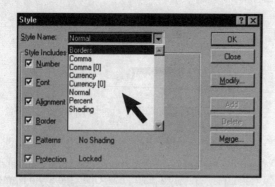

If the autotemplate contains styles with the same names as the styles you are copying, Excel asks (only once) if you want to replace the existing styles with the copied styles. Choose **Yes** to replace all, or choose **No** to keep all existing styles.

6 When you reopen the Style Name list box, you see the styles from the workbook. Be sure to save the autotemplate in your XLStart folder.

Work with Your Own Templates

In addition to using the autotemplates and the templates that come with Excel, you can also create your own templates for workbooks and worksheets. When you create templates, you can control and store the same kinds of information that you find stored in the templates that ship with Excel and the auto-templates:

- The number and type of sheets that appear in the workbook.
- The cell formatting in worksheets that you set up in the Format Cells dialog box.
- The page formatting in worksheets that you set up in the Page Setup dialog box.
- Row and column styles.
- Macros, custom menus, or toolbars.
- Text, numbers, dates, or any other information that you want to appear every time you start a new workbook based on the workbook template or insert a new worksheet based on the worksheet template.

Why not just use an autotemplate? Because you may need a template for some occasions but not all occasions. You use autotemplates for your most common tasks. However, you may find that you need to create workbooks that are similar to each other and even contain complex settings. You don't create these workbooks every day, so using an autotemplate is inappropriate. However, setting up the defaults for these workbooks over and over is tedious to say the least, and certainly time-consuming. So, you create a template that contains the settings for the more unusual task—that way, creating the "unusual" workbook is easier and faster.

The process for creating your own template is very similar to modifying an autotemplate. You open a new workbook, set it up so that it looks that way you want, and then save the workbook as a template. What distinguishes an autotemplate from any other type of template are two things: the template's name and the folder in which you store it.

Using a template you create is also very similar to using one of the templates supplied with Excel. If you want to use a workbook template you created, select it from the New dialog box. If you want to use a worksheet template you created, select it from the Insert dialog box as you insert the sheet.

Begin Guided Tour   Create a Template for a Workbook

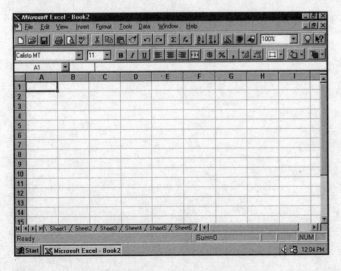

 1 Open a new workbook and create the settings you want to store in the template.

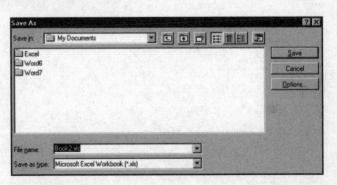

2 Open the **File** menu and select the **Save As** command. Excel displays the Save As dialog box.

(continues)

Guided Tour Create a Template for a Workbook *(continued)*

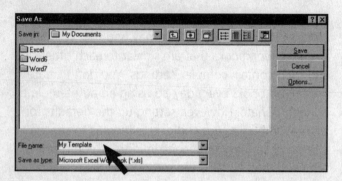

3 In the File Name box, type a name for the template. Don't include an extension.

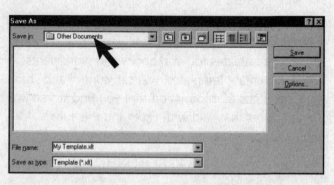

5 Open a folder appropriate for the type of template you are creating and then click the **Save** button.

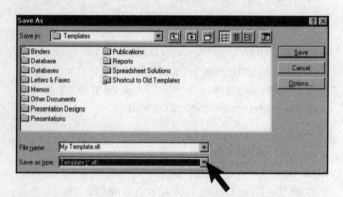

4 Open the **Save as type** list box and choose **Template (*.xlt)**. The Save in list box should change to show the folders inside the Templates folder.

Begin Guided Tour   Create a Custom Sheet Template

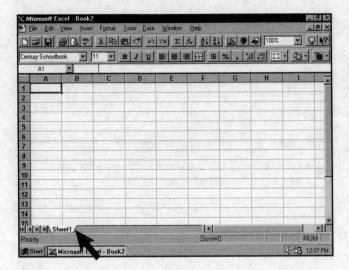

1 Create a one-sheet workbook that contains all the settings you want to appear in each new sheet you base on this sheet template.

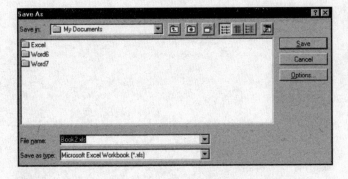

2 Open the **File** menu and select the **Save As** command. Excel displays the Save As dialog box.

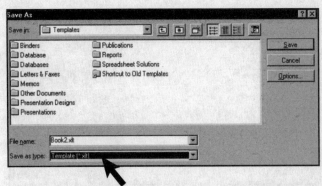

3 Open the **Save as type** list box and choose **Template**. Excel should automatically display the Templates folder. If not, navigate to the Templates folder.

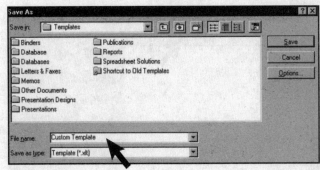

4 In the File Name box, type a name for the custom sheet template. Use any name you want. Click the **Save** button.

Begin Guided Tour   Use a Workbook Template

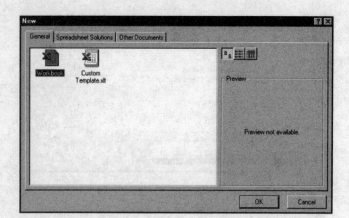

3 Excel displays a new workbook with the title of your template followed by the number 1.

1 Open the **File** menu and select the **New** command.

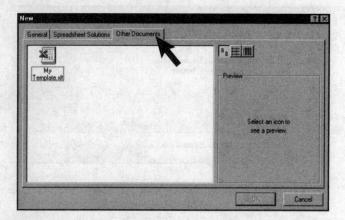

2 Click the tab that represents the folder in which you stored your template. You see your template. Click your template to select it and then click **OK**.

Begin Guided Tour   Use a Custom Sheet Template

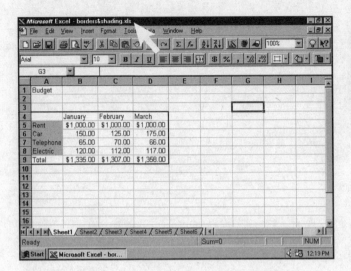

1 Open the workbook into which you want to insert a worksheet based on a custom sheet template you created.

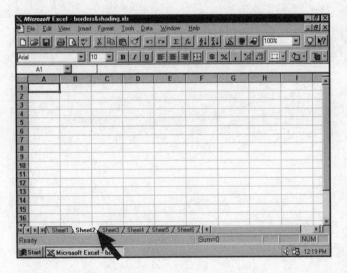

2 Select the sheet tab you want to appear immediately behind the new sheet you will insert.

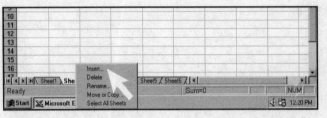

3 Point at the sheet tab and click the right mouse button. From the shortcut menu that appears, choose the **Insert** command.

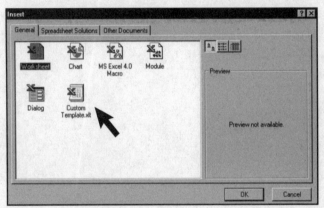

4 Excel displays the Insert dialog box. On the General tab of the Insert dialog box, you see the custom worksheet templates available. Highlight a custom template and click **OK**.

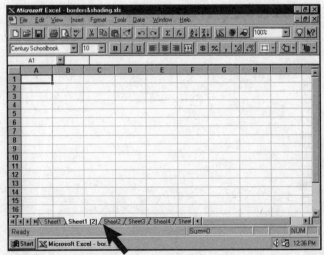

5 Excel inserts a worksheet based on the selected custom template.

HOW TO...

Build a Database

What is a database? It's a collection of related information that you need to track or analyze. Databases can be simple lists comprised of the information in your Rolodex, the telephone book, or your customer or employee list. Or, databases can include mathematical information you want to analyze; for example, you may want to build a database of classes you taught and then use it to analyze how much money you made by teaching each class.

Why build an electronic database? Because the information you're tracking and the analysis you want to perform become so large and complex that finding and using the information becomes a challenge best met by a computer.

Not all computer programs are suited to performing database activities. One of the questions you need to answer is, "Which program can best do what I need to do?" For example, while Excel can perform some complex database functions, it is not suited to handling large volumes of information. If you know, in advance, that your database will include thousands of records, you should probably consider using a program specifically designed for supporting database activities—like Microsoft Access, Lotus Approach, dBASE, or FoxPro.

What database-related actions can you perform in Excel? Too many for us to cover in this book. In this chapter, you'll get an introduction to database activities in Excel. But be aware that Excel's capabilities exceed those about which you'll be reading. For example, suppose you know your database is too large for Excel, so you choose to store it in Access. You can link Excel to your Access database and update the database or perform analysis on it from Excel.

What You Will Find in This Section

Create a Data List

A data list in Excel is synonymous with a database. You don't need to do anything particularly special to create a database in Excel. In fact, you already created some simple data lists in the previous tasks in the book. You can, however, set up a data list using a data form, which makes data entry easier. In this section, we're going to show you two sample data lists and then enter the data from one of these data lists into Excel using a data form. If you want to follow the examples we cover in this section, you'll need to enter the information in the second data list in Excel also. We'll use the information in the second data list to learn to use some of Excel's more common database features.

Data lists look the way you are already accustomed to seeing them: information in rows and columns. Each row in a data list contains all the information about one entry. In database terminology, a row in a data list is a *record*. Each column in the data list contains one type of information. In database terminology, a column in a data list is a *field*. You're going to work with two data lists throughout this section—you find them in the two tables on the following page. The first table is a Student Roster—each record, or row, contains information about a student who attended a class. The fields, or columns, are Last, First, Address, Address2, Class, and Date.

Using the first data list, we count the number of students who took a particular class on a particular date. Then we enter the number of students per class into the second data list. The second data list, which is the Classes Taught list, contains the class titles, the number of students in the class, the price per student, the total amount of money collected for the class, the cost per student, the total expended for the class, the profit per student, and the profit of the class.

In our second data list, several of the columns contain calculated information, which are simple math formulas. The total collected for the class is calculated as the number of students in the class times the money collected. Similarly, the total cost of the class is calculated as the number of students in the class multiplied by a fixed cost per student. The profit per student is calculated as the total paid minus the total cost. And last, total profit is calculated as the number of students in the class multiplied by the profit per student.

Using the second data list, we will look at which class was the largest, which was the smallest, which class was the most profitable, and which class was the least profitable. Then, we will figure out how many students attended a particular type of class and the total profit of each type of class.

Whether you set up a data list using a data form or using methods you learned in earlier tasks, follow some general rules to work with your data as a data list.

- Insert column headings in each data list you create. Make sure the column headings appear in the first row of your data and don't leave any blank rows between the column headings and the first row of data. If you want to distinguish your column labels from your data, use cell borders, or make your column labels different from the data you place in the data list by changing the font, font size, alignment, format, pattern, or capitalization style of the column labels.

- Make sure that each record, or row, of data contains similar information in the same column. Don't insert extra spaces at the beginning of a cell, and use the same format for all cells in a column except, possibly, the column heading.

- Try to set up only one data list per worksheet. If you need two data lists, use separate sheets. If other data also appears on the worksheet, make sure you leave at least one blank row and one blank column between the data list and the other data.

Class Rosters

Last	First	Address	Address2	Class	Date
Drew	Nancy	123 Market St.	Eventon, KS	WP	8/1/95
Jackson	Andrew	456 Charge St.	Midland, KS	Spreadsheet	8/15/95
Hardy	Michael	854 Main St.	Isle Royal, KS	Desktop	8/10/95
Jones	Janice	982 Crest Ave.	Midland, KS	Network	8/3/95
Lilliputian	Linda	654 Little St.	Isle Royal, KS	Network	8/3/95
Johnson	Jonathan	374 Wagon Rd.	Eventon, KS	WP	8/1/95
Autry	Sam	711 Easy St.	Isle Royal, KS	WP	8/1/95
Tipton	Charles	1440 Wavy Rd.	Midland, KS	Spreadsheet	8/15/95
Burke	Greg	126 Forest Ave.	Eventon, KS	WP	8/8/95
Poole	Margo	594 Doctor's Way	Isle Royal, KS	Desktop	8/10/95

Classes Taught

Class	Students	Price/Student	Paid	Cost/Student	Cost	Profit/Student	Profit
WP	3	100	300	25	75	75	225
Spreadsheet	3	100	300	30	90	70	210
Desktop	2	150	300	60	120	90	180
Network	2	200	400	125	250	71	50
Network	3	200	600	125	375	75	225
WP	4	100	400	25	100	75	300
WP	3	100	300	25	75	75	225
Spreadsheet	5	100	500	30	150	70	350
Spreadsheet	4	100	400	30	120	70	280
WP	3	100	300	25	75	75	225
Desktop	3	150	450	60	180	90	270

In the Guided Tour, we'll set up the first data list using a data form. If you want to follow along and try these examples, you need to set up the second data list. Place the second data list on Sheet 2; because of the formulas, you may find it easier to type the information directly into the data list instead of using a data form. Place the class in column A, and you need formulas for columns D, F, and H. In cell D2, type **=C2*B2** and copy the formula down column D. In cell F2, type **=E2*B2** and copy the formula down column F. In cell H2, type **=D2-F2** and copy the formula down column H.

Set Up a Data List for Analysis

Once you decide what kind of information (records) you want to track and the names of the fields (columns) you want in your data list, you can enter your data into your data list directly in the worksheet as you've learned. Or, you can create a data form, which may make it easier for others to enter data into the data list. A data form is a dialog box you use to enter data into a list. Excel uses your data list to automatically set up the form.

To analyze data in a data list, you also need to set up a *criteria range*. A criteria range is a location in the worksheet—usually a couple of rows—where you store the criteria you want Excel to use during a particular analysis. Excel evaluates the information in your data list based on the information in the criteria range. The criteria range must consist of the exact same column headings you use for your data list, along with at least one blank row. Be sure to set up the criteria range so that at least one blank row or one blank column separates it from the data list. And, you find it easier to copy the column headings from your data list when you create the column headings for the criteria range. That way, you can be sure that they match exactly.

Begin Guided Tour   Use a Data Form to Add Records to a Data List

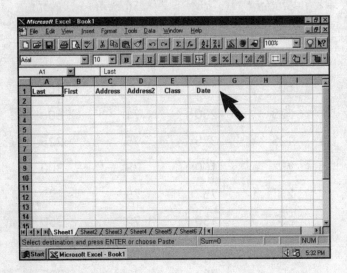

1 Create and format the column headings for your data list.

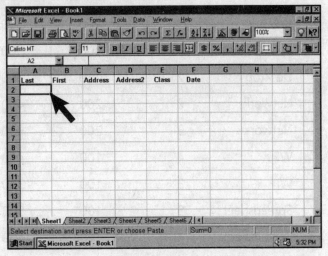

2 Select a blank cell below the column headings. Open the **Data** menu and choose the **Form** command.

Guided Tour Use a Data Form to Add Records to a Data List

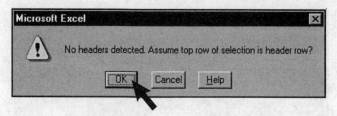

3 Excel displays a dialog box telling you it detected no headings. Click **OK** to let Excel assume that the row above the cell pointer is the header row.

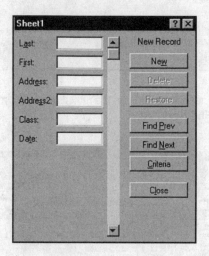

4 Excel displays a dialog box containing the column headings you just created and a blank text box next to each heading.

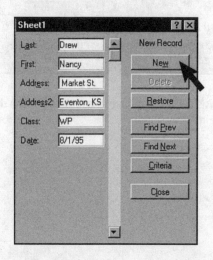

5 Fill in the data form by typing in the appropriate information and pressing the **Tab** key to move from text box to text box. When you finish the record, click the **New** button.

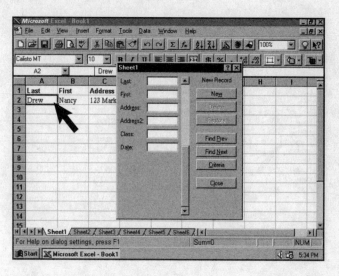

6 Excel places the information you typed into the worksheet and presents you with a new blank data form to complete.

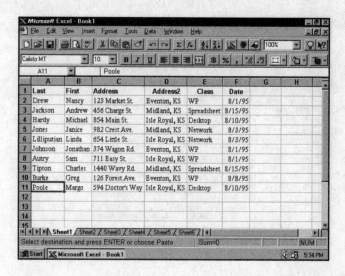

7 Repeat Steps 5 and 6 until you enter all the information you need into the data list. Then, click the **Close** button. Excel closes the data form and displays the data list you just created.

Begin Guided Tour Use a Data Form to Find and Edit Records in a Data List

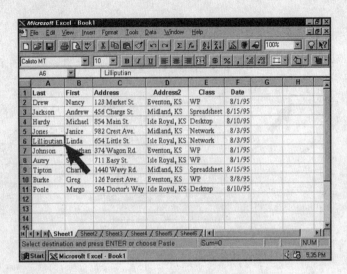

1 Place the cell pointer on any record in the data list. Open the **Data** menu and choose the **Form** command.

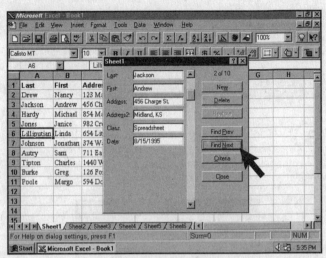

3 To cycle forward through the records one at a time, click the **Find Next** button.

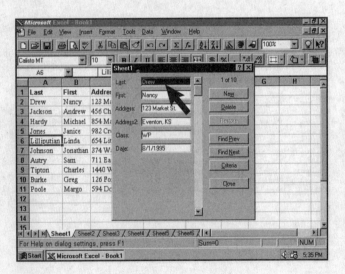

2 Excel displays a completed data form with the information from the first record in the data list.

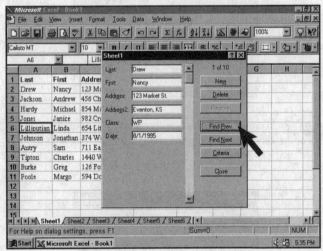

4 To cycle backward through the records one at a time, click the **Find Prev** button.

Guided Tour   Use a Data Form to Find and Edit Records in a Data List

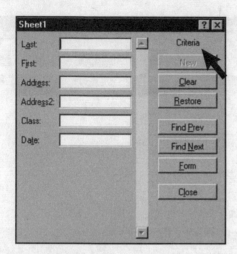

5 To find a specific record, click the **Criteria** button. Excel displays a blank criteria data form.

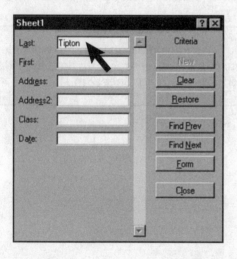

6 Fill in just enough information for Excel to find the record you want. In the example, type the last name of one student, **Tipton**.

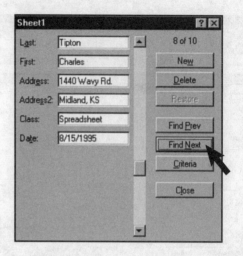

7 Click the **Find Next** button. Excel finds the record that matches your criteria.

If Excel finds more than one record that matches the criteria you specify, click **Find Next** and Excel shows you each record that matches your criteria. When Excel finishes the search, your computer beeps.

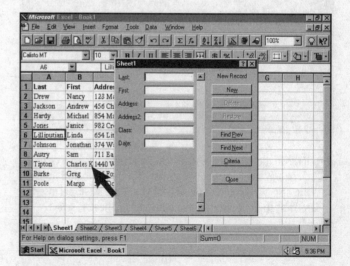

8 Type the changes you want to make and click the **New** button. Excel modifies the record and displays a blank new data entry form.

Begin Guided Tour   Create a Criteria Range

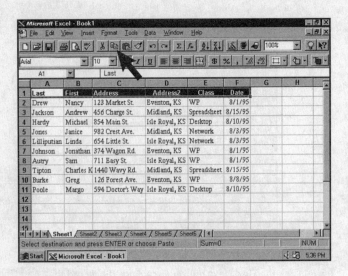

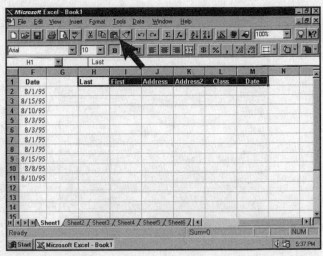

(1) Select the column headings of your data list and click the **Copy** tool on the Standard toolbar.

(3) Click the **Paste** tool on the Standard tool bar. Excel pastes a copy of your column headings into the worksheet.

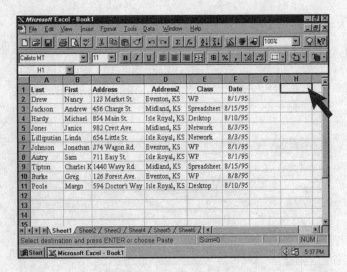

(2) Move the cell pointer to a location at least one row or one column away from your data list. If you plan to add to the data list, select a column to the side of your data list (Excel inserts new records to the bottom of the data list). In Sheet 1, select cell H1.

If you're following along with the examples, create criteria ranges for both data lists. Place the criteria range for Sheet2 in J1:Q1.

Use Database Functions to Analyze a Data List

Excel contains 12 database functions you can use to analyze a data list; here you explore the four most popular functions: DCOUNT, DMAX, DMIN, and DSUM. You may find it easier to work with these functions if you let the Function Wizard help you set up your query.

While working with the Function Wizard, you can click in the worksheet to supply your answers. You may find that the Function Wizard dialog box appears to be covering a cell you want to click. Move the Function Wizard dialog box by dragging its title bar.

Each of the database functions requires four pieces of information, and the syntax for a database function is:

Dfunction(database,field,criteria), where:

- **Dfunction** is the database function and represents the kind of information you're trying to get. The database function always appears first and outside the parentheses. The other three pieces of information appear inside parentheses, separated by a comma. The Function Wizard enables you to set up the query correctly.

- **Database** is a reference to the cells that comprise the data list, including the column headings. You find it easier to name the range containing the data list so that you can refer to it quickly.

- **Field** is a reference to the column heading you want Excel to use when performing the analysis. You can specify the field by name or by number. If you use a name, enclose the name in quotes; if you use a number, do *not* enclose it in quotes and assume the first column of data in the list is column 1, the second column is column 2, and so on. You may find it easier to simply click on

the cell that contains the column heading you want to use.

- **Criteria** is a reference to the range of cells that contain the conditions you want Excel to meet while performing the analysis. The criteria is always a range of at least two cells—the top cell contains a column heading, and the cell below contains the conditions.

When you want to count the number of records that meet a certain criteria in your data list, you use either the DCOUNT function or the DCOUNTA function. The DCOUNT function counts the cells that contain numbers only, while the DCOUNTA function counts non-blank cells. Use DCOUNTA when you want to count cells that contain labels. For example, use the Function Wizard to count the number of students who attended a particular class on a particular date. Use the information stored in the first data list shown previously in the Student Roster. By using the DCOUNTA function on the first data list, you get the information you need to complete the second data list, Classes Taught, that you stored in Sheet 2.

After entering the results of the DCOUNTA function into the second data list, you can use the DMAX function to find out how many students attended the largest class and the DMIN function to find out the lowest profit gained by any one class. You can use the DAVERAGE function to get average number of students in the classes.

You can also use the DMAX function to find out the highest profit generated by any one class and the DMIN function to find out how many students attended the smallest class.

Last, you can use the DSUM function to figure out how many students attended a particular type of class. You can repeat these steps to figure out the total profit made on each type of class by changing the criteria range slightly.

Sometimes, you just need to find information in a data list. You can find a particular record using the Data Form dialog box and setting up criteria, or you can filter the list using Excel's AutoFilter feature.

For more information on filtering a list, see "Filter a List," p. 74.

Begin Guided Tour   Naming the Data List Range

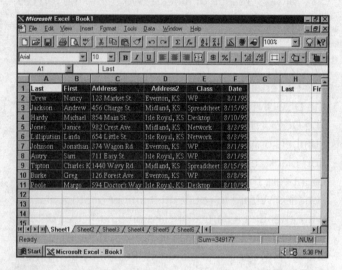

1 In Sheet 1, select all the rows and columns that you want to include in your data list. In the example, select **A1:F11**.

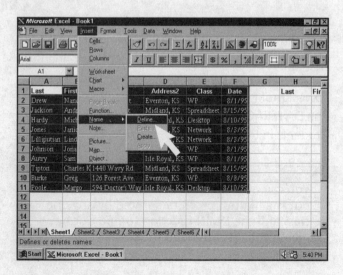

2 Open the **Insert** menu and select the **Name** command. Excel displays the Name submenu. Choose the **Define** command.

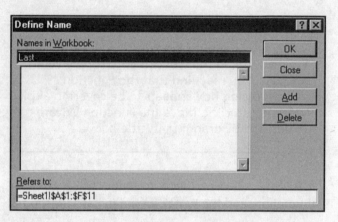

3 Excel displays the Define Name dialog box.

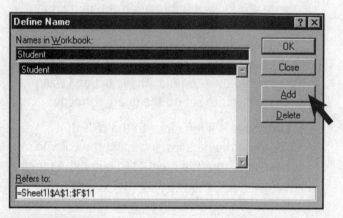

4 Type a name for the data list and click the **Add** button. Excel adds the name to the list. In the example, name the first data list Student. Click the **OK** button.

Guided Tour   Naming the Data List Range

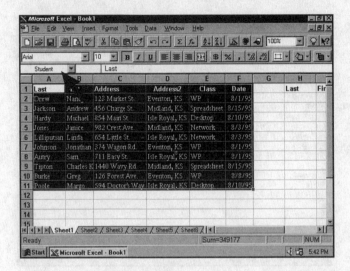

5 The name of the data list appears in the Formula bar.

> If you intend to follow along in the example, switch to Sheet2 and name the data list Class. The range for the second data list in Sheet2 includes A1:H12.

Begin Guided Tour   Count Records in the List

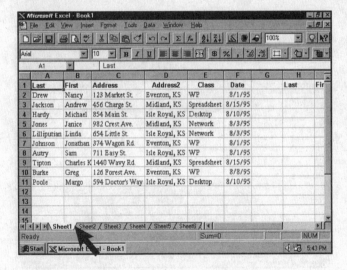

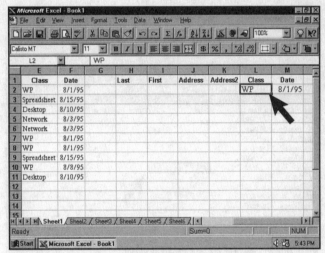

1 Display the sheet containing the data list you want to count. In the example, click **Sheet1**.

2 Set up the criteria range. In the example, you want to count the number of entries for WP on 8/1. In cell L2, type **WP**. In cell M2, type **8/1/95**.

> To make this example easier to follow, place the answer in the same sheet you are querying. Theoretically, you need to retype the answer in Sheet2 later, where you need it. You can, if you want, skip step 3 and, in step 4, select cell B2 in Sheet2 to place the result of the query directly in Sheet2. If you choose this approach, all your subsequent selections while completing the Function Wizard will be in Sheet1.

(continues)

Guided Tour Count Records in the List *(continued)*

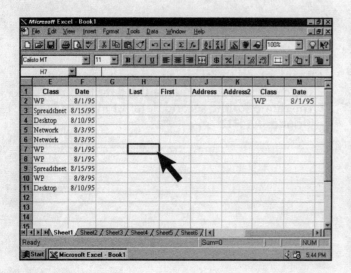

3 Select a cell where you want to place a label for the answer to your query. Select a cell several rows below the criteria range; in the example, select **H7**.

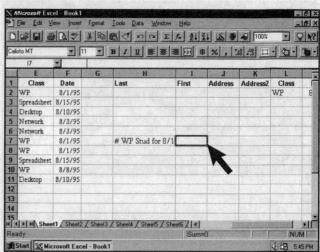

5 Select the cell immediately to the right of the label. You will place the query in this cell. In the example, select **I7**.

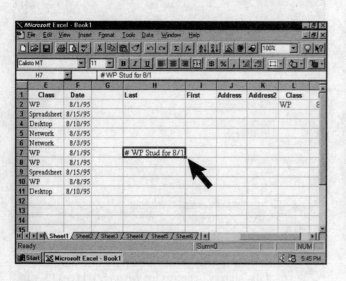

4 Type a label for what the value represents. In the example, type **# WP Stud. for 8/1**.

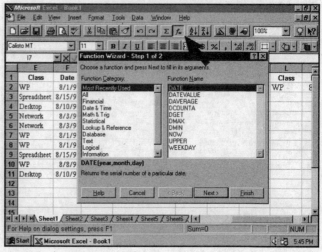

6 Click the **Function Wizard** tool on the Standard toolbar. Excel displays the Function Wizard—Step 1 of 2 dialog box.

Guided Tour   Count Records in the List

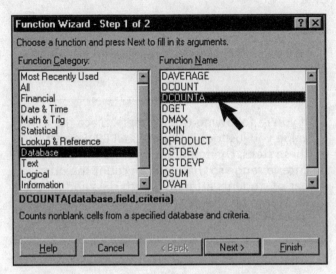

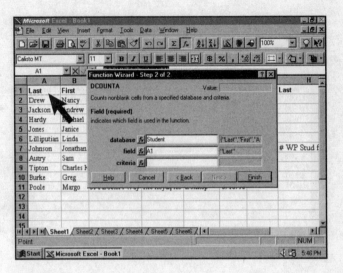

7 From the Function Category column, select **Database**. From the Function Name column, choose **DCOUNTA**. Click **Next**.

9 Press the **Tab** key to move to the field text box. Click the column heading in the worksheet that represents the Field you want to count. In this example, click **A1** to count the last names of the students who attended the class.

10 Press the **Tab** key to move to the criteria text box.

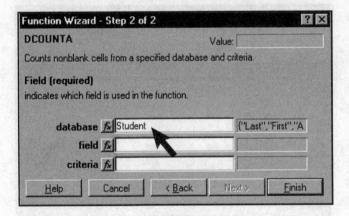

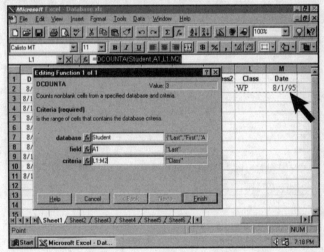

8 Excel displays the Function Wizard—Step 2 of 2 dialog box. In the database text box, type the name you defined for the data list range. In this example, type **Student**.

11 In the worksheet, select the cells that contain the criteria you want Excel to use when performing the calculation. In the example, select **L1:M2**. Click the **Finish** button.

If you need to move the dialog box out of the way, drag its title bar.

Guided Tour   Count Records in the List

(continued)

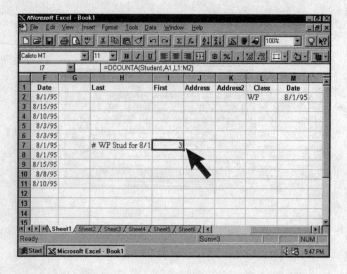

12 Excel displays the results of the function in the cell containing the pointer. In the example, the result is three. This is the number of students who attended the WP class on 8/1/95.

If you're following this example, place the value you just got in Sheet2, cell B2. Repeat these steps, changing the information in the criteria range so that you can count the number of students attending each class and fill the answer in on Sheet2 (for the sake of simplicity, you can just type the information into Sheet2).

Begin Guided Tour   Find the Record with the Largest Value

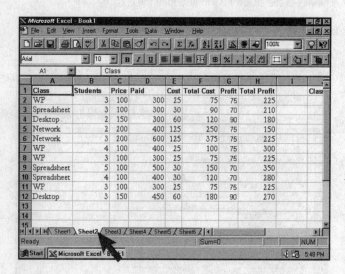

1 Display the sheet that contains the data list you want to query. In the example, click **Sheet2**.

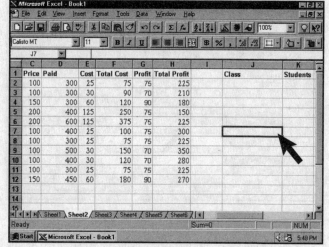

2 Select a cell where you want to place a label for the answer to your query. Select a cell several rows below the criteria range. In the example, select **J7**.

Guided Tour Find the Record with the Largest Value

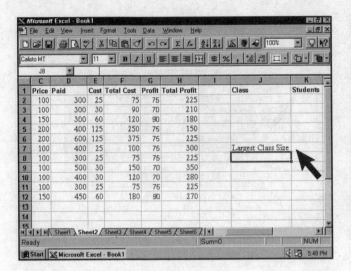

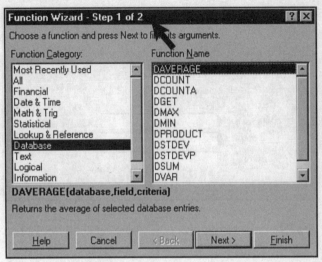

3 Type a label for what the value represents. In the example, type **Largest Class Size**.

5 Click the **Function Wizard** tool on the Standard toolbar. Excel displays the Step 1 of 2 dialog box of the Function Wizard.

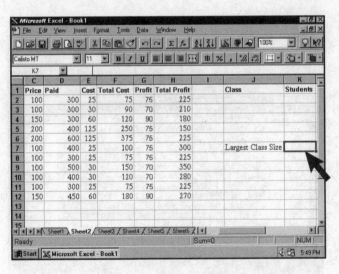

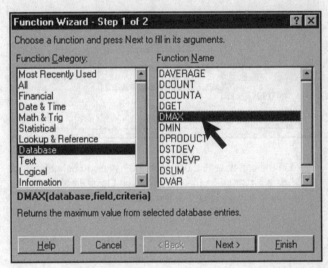

4 Select the cell immediately to the right of the label. You will place the query in this cell. In the example, select **K7**.

6 From the Function Category column, select **Database**. From the Function Name column, choose **DMAX**. Click **Next**.

(continues)

Guided Tour   Find the Record with the Largest Value

(continued)

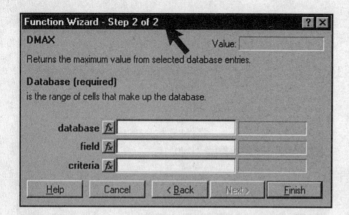

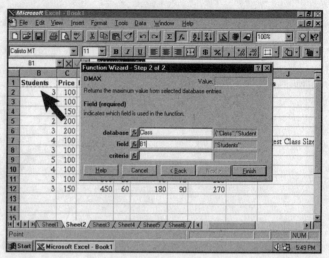

7 Excel displays the Step 2 of 2 dialog box of the Function Wizard.

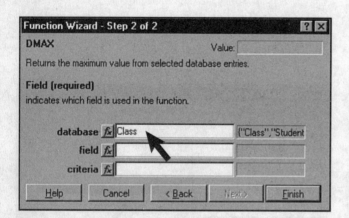

8 In the database text box, type the name you defined for the data list range. In the example, type **Class**. Press the **Tab** key to move to the field text box.

9 Click the column heading in the worksheet that represents the field for which you want to know the largest value. In the example, click **B1** to find the largest number of students who attended a class.

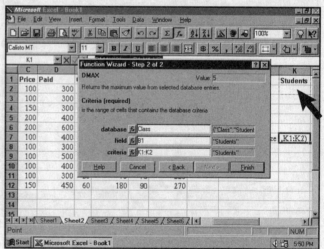

10 Press the **Tab** key to move to the criteria text box. In the worksheet, select the cells that contain the criteria you want Excel to use when performing the calculation. In the example, select **K1:K2**. Click the **Finish** button.

If you need to move the dialog box out of the way, drag its title bar.

Guided Tour   Find the Record with the Largest Value

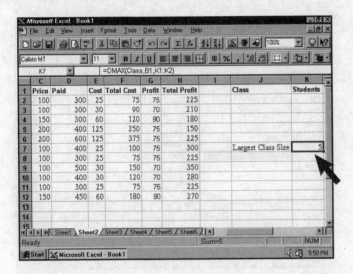

11 Excel displays the results of the function in the cell containing the pointer. In the example, the largest class contained five students.

Begin Guided Tour   Find the Record with the Smallest Value

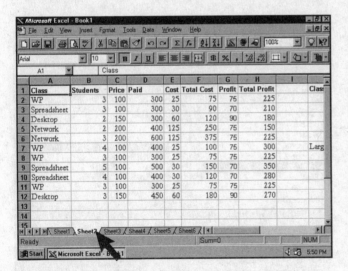

1 Display the sheet that contains the data list you want to query. In the example, click **Sheet2**.

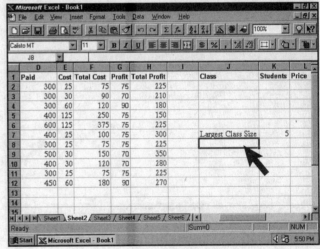

2 Select a cell where you want to place a label for the answer to your query. Select a cell several rows below the criteria range. In the example, select **J8**.

(continues)

Guided Tour   Find the Record with the Smallest Value   *(continued)*

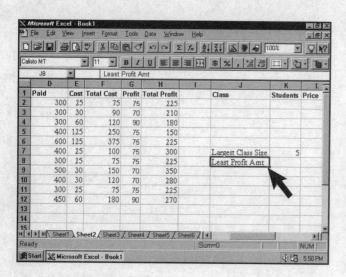

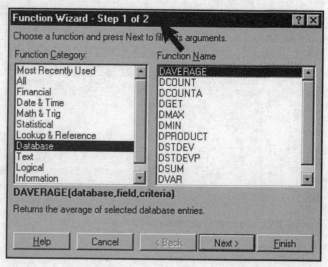

3 Type a label for what the value represents. In the example, type **Least Profit Amt**.

5 Click the **Function Wizard** tool on the Standard toolbar. Excel displays the Step 1 of 2 dialog box of the Function Wizard.

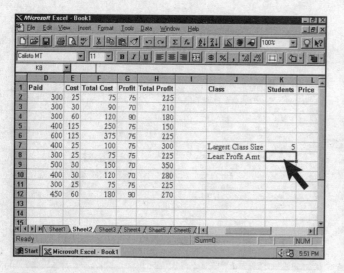

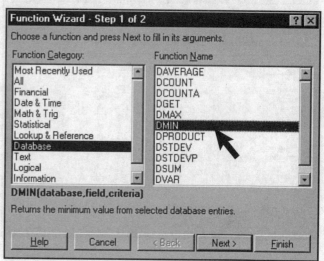

4 Select the cell immediately to the right of the label. You'll place the query in this cell. In the example, select **K8**.

6 From the Function Category column, select **Database**. From the Function Name column, choose **DMIN**. Click **Next**.

Guided Tour   Find the Record with the Smallest Value

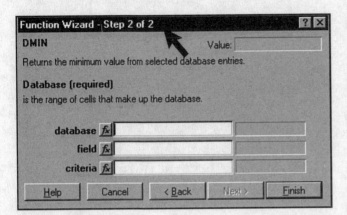

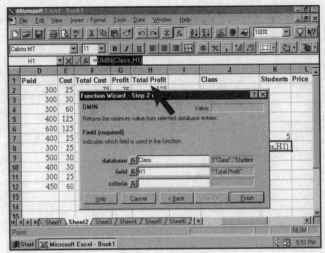

7 Excel displays the Step 2 of 2 dialog box of the Function Wizard.

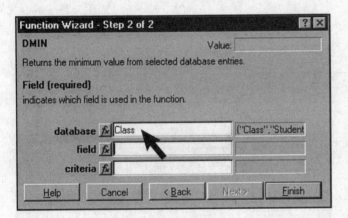

8 In the database text box, type the name you defined for the data list range. In this example, type **Class**. Press the **Tab** key to move to the field text box.

9 Click the column heading in the worksheet that represents the field for which you want to know the largest value. In the example, click **H1** to find the smallest amount of profit for a class. Press the **Tab** key to move to the criteria text box.

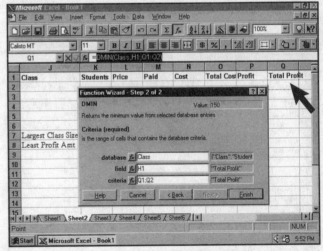

10 In the worksheet, select the cells that contain the criteria you want Excel to use when performing the calculation. In the example, select **Q1:Q2**. Click the **Finish** button.

> If you need to move the dialog box out of the way, drag its title bar.

(continues)

Guided Tour   Find the Record with the Smallest Value

(continued)

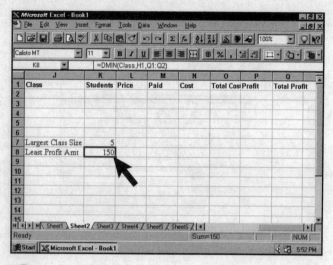

11 Excel displays the results of the function in the cell containing the pointer. In the example, the smallest amount of profit on any class was $150.00.

Begin Guided Tour   Find the Average for a Field in a Data List

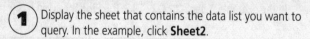

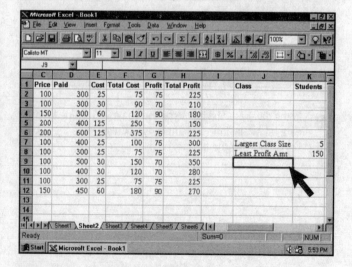

1 Display the sheet that contains the data list you want to query. In the example, click **Sheet2**.

2 Select a cell where you want to place a label for the answer to your query. Select a cell several rows below the criteria range. In the example, select **J9**.

Guided Tour   Find the Average for a Field in a Data List

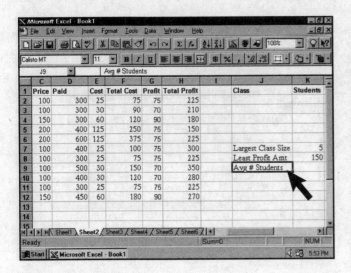

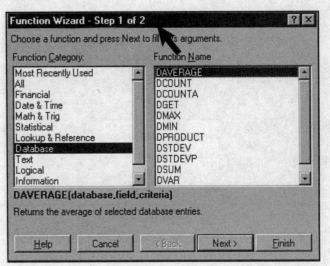

3 Type a label for what the value represents. In the example, type **Avg # Students**.

5 Click the **Function Wizard** tool on the Standard toolbar. Excel displays the Step 1 of 2 dialog box of the Function Wizard.

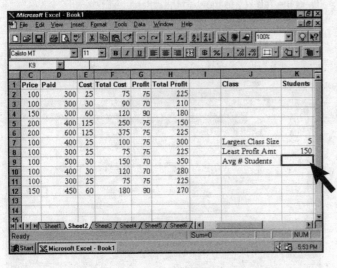

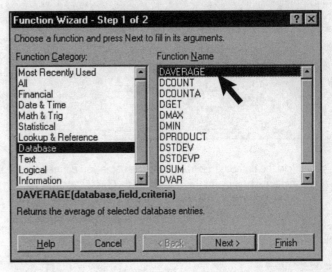

4 Select the cell immediately to the right of the label. You will place the query in this cell. In the example, select **K9**.

6 From the Function Category column, select **Database**. From the Function Name column, choose **DAVERAGE**. Click **Next**.

(continues)

Guided Tour Find the Average for a Field in a Data List *(continued)*

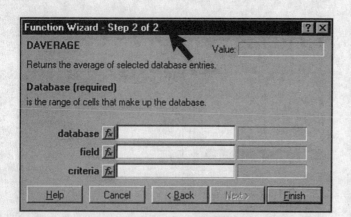

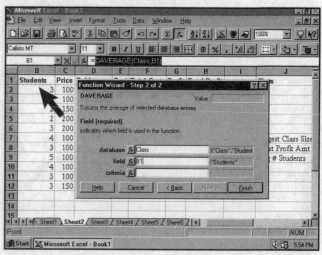

7 Excel displays the Step 2 of 2 dialog box of the Function Wizard.

9 Click the column heading in the worksheet that represents the field for which you want to know the average. In the example, click **B1** to find the average number of students in class. Press the **Tab** key to move to the criteria text box.

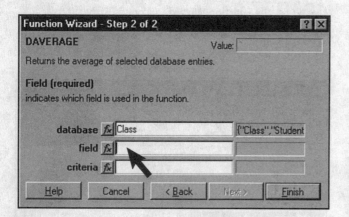

8 In the database text box, type the name you defined for the data list range. In the example, type **Class**. Press the **Tab** key to move to the field text box.

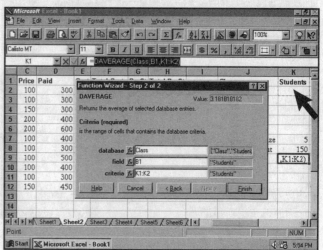

10 In the worksheet, highlight the cells that contain the criteria you want Excel to use when performing the calculation. In the example, select **K1:K2** to indicate to Excel that it needs to include all students in the calculation of the average number per class. Click the **Finish** button.

Guided Tour Find the Average for a Field in a Data List

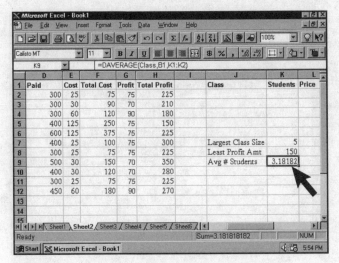

If you need to move the dialog box out of the way, drag its title bar.

11 Excel displays the results of the function in the cell containing the pointer. In the example, on the average, classes contained 3.18182 students.

Begin Guided Tour Subtotal Records in the Data List

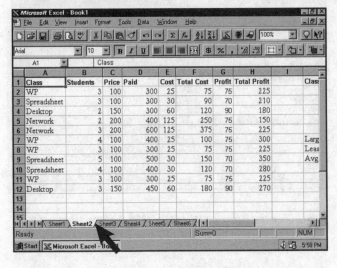

1 Display the sheet that contains the data list you want to query. In the example, click **Sheet2**.

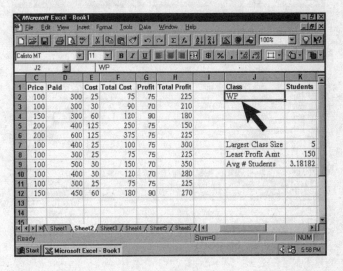

2 Set up the criteria range to identify what you want to total. In the example, type **WP** in cell J2 to indicate you want totals related to the WP class.

(continues)

Guided Tour Subtotal Records in the Data List   *(continued)*

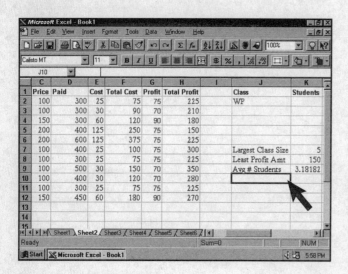

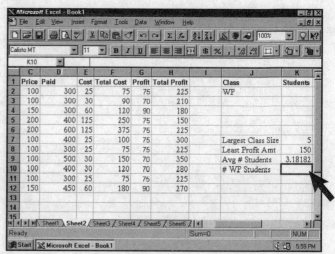

(3) Select a cell where you want to place a label for the answer to your query. Select a cell several rows below the criteria range. In the example, select **J10**.

(5) Select the cell immediately to the right of the label. You'll place the query in this cell. In the example, select **K10**.

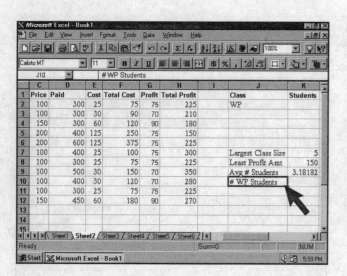

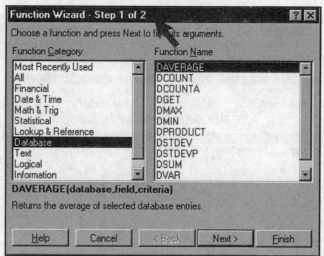

(4) Type a label for what the value represents. In the example, type **# WP Students**.

(6) Click the **Function Wizard** tool on the Standard toolbar. Excel displays the Step 1 of 2 dialog box of the Function Wizard.

Guided Tour   Subtotal Records in the Data List

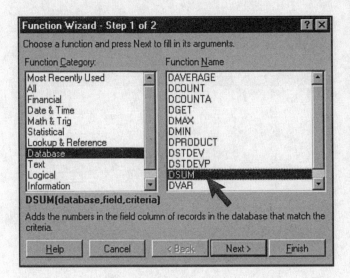

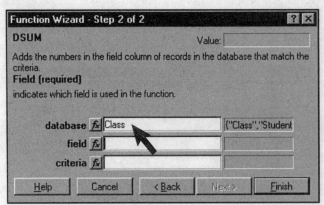

7 From the Function Category column, select **Database**. From the Function Name column, choose **DSUM**.

9 In the database text box, type the name you defined for the data list range. In the example, type **Class**. Press the **Tab** key to move to the field text box.

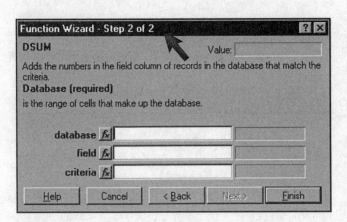

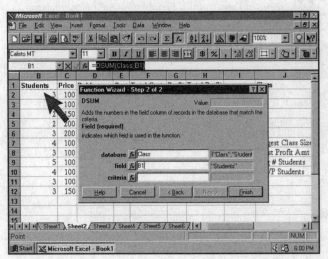

8 Click **Next**. Excel displays the Step 2 of 2 dialog box of the Function Wizard.

10 Click the column heading in the worksheet that represents the field for which you want to know the total. In the example, click **B1** to find the total number of students in a class. Press the **Tab** key to move to the criteria text box.

If you need to move the dialog box out of the way, drag its title bar.

(continues)

Guided Tour Subtotal Records in the Data List *(continued)*

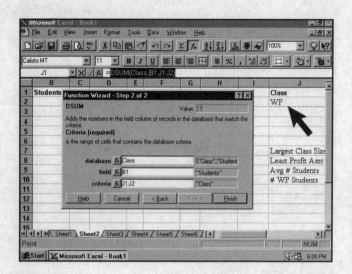

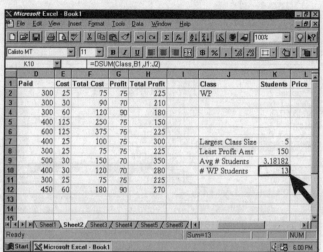

11 In the worksheet, select the cells that contain the criteria you want Excel to use when performing the calculation. In the example, select **J1:J2** to indicate that you want Excel to include entries that contain WP in the total. Click the **Finish** button.

12 Excel displays the results of the function in the cell containing the pointer. In the example, 13 students attended WP classes.

You can calculate the total profit for WP by clicking cell H1 in step 10. To find the total number of students for Spreadsheet, change J2 to Spreadsheet in step 2.

HOW TO...

Work with Charts

Worksheet information can be both useful and impressive in presentations. If you only need numerical detail, you can print just the worksheet, but remember the old adage: a picture is worth a thousand words. Consider creating a chart from the data in the worksheet. Charts are great for increasing the understanding of relationships between numerical values; at the same time, charts greatly enhance a presentation.

To create a chart quickly and easily, use the ChartWizard, which guides you step-by-step through an otherwise complex procedure. While using the ChartWizard, you preview the sample chart before you finish creating the chart, and you can make changes. Once you create a chart, use Excel's Chart AutoFormat feature to apply one of several predefined formats to your chart, making formatting faster and easier because you don't need to apply formatting to each individual chart element. Or, if you prefer, modify any individual chart feature.

What You Will Find in This Section

Create a Chart

When you create a chart in Excel, the ChartWizard walks you through the process. You select the information you want to chart from a worksheet. When you select the information, be sure to include both row and column headings as part of your selection (Excel uses this information to identify the data on your chart).

As you create the chart, you select a chart type and some formats for the chart. The type of chart you select needs to reflect the kind of information you're trying to emphasize. For example, a column chart tends to emphasize variations over time while a bar chart tends to emphasize information at a specific point in time. The formats you find available for the chart depend on the chart type you select. In any case, formats are variations of the chart type.

Understand the Parts of a Chart

Before you create a chart, you should familiarize yourself with the elements of a chart. With the exception of pie charts, all charts contain at least two axes—one vertical axis and one horizontal axis (pie charts contain no axes, and some charts contain more than one vertical or horizontal axis). The *Y axis* is the vertical axis; Excel refers to this axis as the *value axis*. This axis displays the values of the information you plot. The *X axis* is the horizontal axis; Excel refers to this axis as the *category axis,* because it contains divisions or classifications of information (categories) about your data. You'll learn more about categories in a moment.

A chart enables you to plot values from worksheet cells. Each cell represents a data point on the chart.

Charts group data points into bars, pie slices, lines, or other elements; these grouped data points are known as a *data series*. A column chart contains bars that depict a series of values for the same item, such as monthly sales figures or monthly staffing levels; each bar is a data series. You see labels describing each data series in the legend of the chart.

> You must have data in a worksheet before you can create a chart.

Categories show the number of elements in a data series. You may use two data series to compare the sales of two different offices, and four categories to compare these sales over four quarters. On a chart like this one, you see the following:

- Sales dollars appear on the value axis (the vertical or Y axis).

- Each office name appears in the legend of the chart.

- Quarter 1, Quarter 2, Quarter 3, and Quarter 4 appear as categories on the category axis (the horizontal or X axis).

Categories usually correspond to the number of columns that you select in your worksheet. *Category labels* describe the categories along the horizontal axis. These labels come from the column headings of the data you include when you select information you want to appear in the chart. By default, Excel labels the category axis and the value axis using at least one row and one column in the range you select. As you create the chart, Excel gives you the opportunity to specify additional rows and columns in the range that you want to appear as labels.

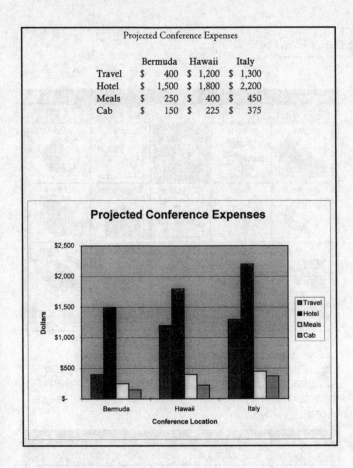

The *chart text* includes all the labels on the chart. You need to add most text to the basic chart. You can also format labels by changing the fonts, font sizes, font styles, and colors. Text is useful for explaining various elements on the chart.

Excel automatically assigns values to the value axis when you create a chart, but you can override the default settings and set the minimum and maximum values. You can also add a text label to the value axis to describe what the values represent.

The *plot area* consists of the actual bars, lines, or other elements that represent the data series. Everything outside the plot area helps explain what is inside the plot area. You can format the plot area by changing the patterns and colors of the data series.

A *legend* contains the labels for the data series in the chart and serves as a key to the chart. To create the legend, Excel uses labels in the first column of the chart range. The legend appears at the right of the chart data. However, you can move the legend anywhere you want on the chart.

Gridlines are dotted lines you can add to a chart so that you can read the plotted data more easily. You can create three types of gridlines: horizontal, vertical, and a combination of both. After you add the gridlines, you can change the colors and patterns of the gridlines.

Begin Guided Tour   Use the ChartWizard to Create a Chart

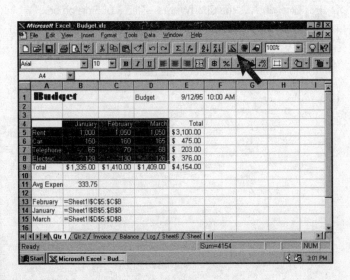

1 Select the range you want to chart. Be sure to include row and column headings in the selection. Click the **ChartWizard** button on the Standard toolbar.

Guided Tour Use the ChartWizard to Create a Chart *(continued)*

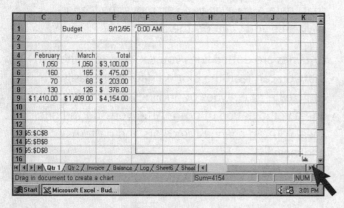

2 A marquee surrounds the selected data. The mouse pointer changes to a crosshair pointer with a tiny column chart attached.

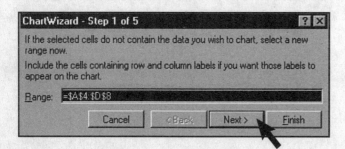

3 Starting in the cell where you want the upper left corner of the chart to appear, click and drag to the cell where you want the lower right corner of the chart to appear. While you drag, Excel displays a solid line rectangle to specify the size and shape of the chart on the worksheet. Release the mouse button.

4 The ChartWizard—Step 1 of 5 dialog box appears. In this dialog box, Excel specifies the range across which you just dragged as an absolute address in the Range text box. Click the **Next** button to confirm this selection.

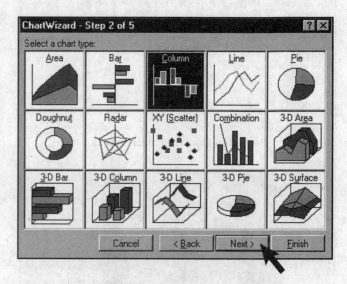

5 Excel displays the ChartWizard—Step 2 of 5 dialog box, from which you choose a chart type. The column chart is the default chart type. Click the **Next** button to confirm the type of chart.

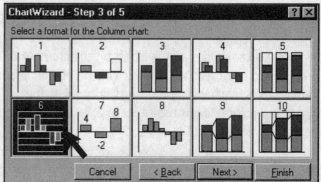

6 Excel displays the ChartWizard—Step 3 of 5 dialog box, from which you specify the format you want for your chart. Column chart 6 is the default format for the column chart type (this is a column chart with horizontal gridlines). Click the **Next** button to confirm the format for the chart type.

Guided Tour Use the ChartWizard to Create a Chart

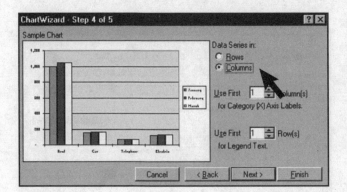

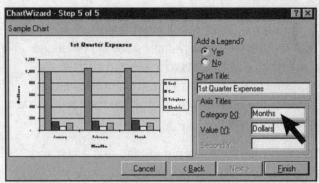

7 Excel displays the ChartWizard—Step 4 of 5 dialog box, which contains a sample chart. Initially, Excel charts the data series in columns. In the example, each bar represents a month, and you see three bars for each expense in the budget.

8 Click the **Rows** option button to view the data series in rows. Excel redisplays the chart. In the example, each bar now represents an expense in the budget, and you see four bars for each month in the chart. Click the **Next** button to confirm the options for the data series, first column, and first row.

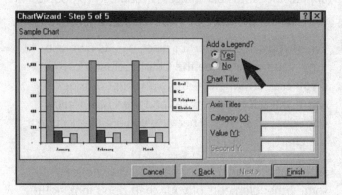

9 Excel displays the final dialog box, ChartWizard—Step 5 of 5. By default, Excel adds a legend to your chart. You can remove it by choosing the **No** option button, but since legends clarify your chart for the reader, consider displaying the legend.

10 To add titles to the chart, click in the **Chart Title** text box, or press the **Tab** key. Type the title you want on the chart. In the example, type **1st Quarter Expenses**. Excel redisplays the chart in the sample box with the title at the top. You can also add titles for each axis; type **Months** for the category (X) axis and **Dollars** for the value (Y) axis. Click the **Finish** button.

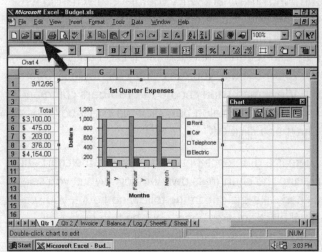

11 Excel adds the new chart to the worksheet at the specified location. You may also see the Chart toolbar on-screen. Click the **Save** button on the Standard toolbar to save the workbook.

Format a Chart

Using the Chart AutoFormat feature, you can simultaneously apply a set of predefined chart types and formats to a selected chart in the worksheet. In fact, the Chart AutoFormat feature provides the only way to change the format of a chart after you create it.

You find that the AutoFormat feature is a fast and easy way to make a chart look good. Now, you don't need to take the time to apply formatting to each individual chart element.

To change a chart in any way, including applying formatting to a chart, you work with the chart in its own window. To place a chart in its own window, double-click anywhere inside the black line that surrounds the chart. Once you place the chart in its own window, Excel replaces the thin black line that surrounds the chart with a diagonal hatched line. You may also see the Chart toolbar. If Excel doesn't display the Chart toolbar, you can display the toolbar. Open the **View** menu and choose the **Toolbars** command; in the resulting dialog box, click the check box next to **Chart** and click **OK**.

There is a difference between selecting the chart and placing the chart in its own window. When you select a chart, like the one in the following figure, you see small black squares appear on the thin black line surrounding the chart. The small black squares are *selection handles*, and the thin black line is the chart frame. Typically, Excel displays the Chart toolbar when you select a chart.

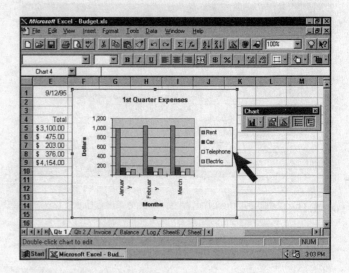

If you don't see selection handles surrounding the chart, click once anywhere inside the black line surrounding the chart, and the black selection handles appear. Notice that once selection handles appear the status bar indicates you need to double-click to edit the chart.

When you select a chart or place it in its own window, you may also see the Chart toolbar. However, if you click anywhere in the worksheet outside the chart, the selection handles and the Chart toolbar both disappear. This is because you are deselecting the chart.

After applying an autoformat, you may notice that some other elements of your chart don't look right. Other tasks in this section show you how you can fix those elements manually.

And, if you decide you don't like the formatting you applied, remove the formatting by clicking the **Undo** button on the Standard toolbar. Then, try these steps again.

Begin Guided Tour   Automatically Format the Chart

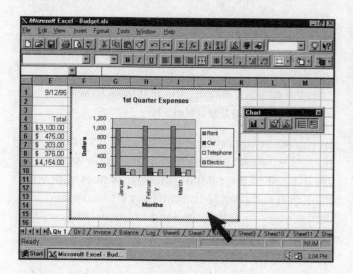

1 Make sure the chart is in its own window. If it isn't, double-click anywhere inside the chart frame. In the chart area, click the right mouse button.

2 Excel displays a shortcut menu of commands you can use to modify the appearance of the chart. Choose the **AutoFormat** command.

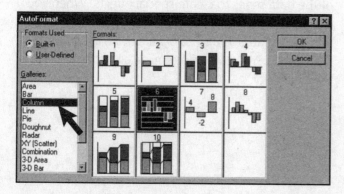

3 Excel displays the AutoFormat dialog box. A list of chart types and a palette of corresponding chart formats appear in the dialog box. The column chart 6 format is selected.

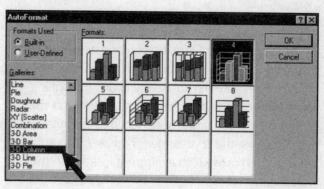

4 From the Galleries list box, choose the chart type you want to apply. In this example, choose **3-D Column**.

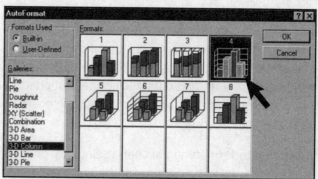

5 When you select a chart type from the Galleries list box, Excel displays a palette of formats available for that chart type. In the example, select the default format for a 3-D column chart, which is format 4. Click **OK** to confirm your choice.

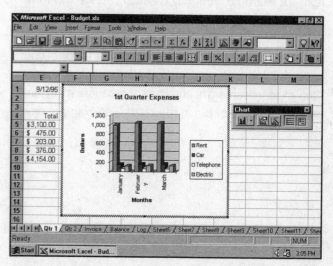

6 Excel changes the chart to the new format.

Modify a Chart

After initially creating a chart, and even after using the AutoFormat command, you may find you need to change portions of the chart. For example, when you first create the chart, the outline you drag for the chart determines the size and shape of the chart in the worksheet. You may find that you want to make the chart larger or smaller. No problem. You can even move it to a different location in the worksheet.

You find that certain chart types are best for certain situations. You may think it is more dramatic, appropriate, or meaningful to display data in a different type of chart than the one you first selected. For example, you can usually spot trends more easily with a line chart, but a pie chart is best for showing parts of a whole. A line chart, on the other hand, shows trends over time. To find out which is the best chart type for displaying your data, take an existing chart and change its chart type.

In addition to formatting the chart itself, Excel gives you several formatting options for the text that appears in a chart. For example, you can make the text print vertically, horizontally, or stacked, and you can move text anywhere you want on the chart. You can change the font, font size, style, and color of any text; for example, you may want to change the font for the title to a larger font and apply boldface to draw attention to the title. The font sizes available vary, depending on the type of printer and fonts you have. Adding text labels to a chart makes the chart's data more meaningful and may accentuate a certain bar, line, or slice of pie in the chart. For example, you

may want to add a text label to point out the highest, or lowest, value in the chart. If you change your mind and decide you don't need a text label, remove it from the chart by clicking the text label to select it, and then pressing the **Delete** key.

Excel places category labels next to the horizontal axis along the bottom of the chart. If you don't want to use the text of the category labels that goes with your chart, you can change the category labels. For instance, you can abbreviate long category labels that run into each other. That way, all the labels fit properly on the category (X) axis.

Usually, the vertical axis (the value (Y) axis) in an Excel chart represents values. Excel automatically scales the value axis for your charts to best fit the minimum and maximum values in the worksheet. Sometimes, however, you may need to customize the values along the vertical or horizontal axis. Perhaps you want to display fewer numbers in larger increments on the value axis. You also can change the look of the scale indicators on the axes. For example, you can change the style, color, and weight of the axis line. You can change the format of the numbers that appear on an axis scale by adding dollar signs, decimal points, commas, and percent signs.

You also may want to change the colors and patterns of the data series to create special effects. When you explore changing the patterns of data series, you may find some patterns and colors are more attractive than others. You can even remove all patterns and use only color.

Begin Guided Tour   Change the Chart's Size and Shape

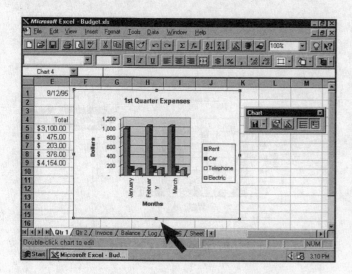

1 Select the chart, but make sure it doesn't appear in its own window by clicking anywhere outside the chart and then, if necessary, clicking once inside the chart frame. You see selection handles on the chart frame.

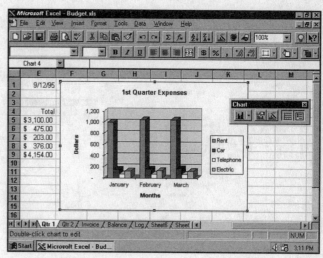

3 Drag the selection handle out from the center of the chart to make the chart larger or in toward the center to make the chart smaller.

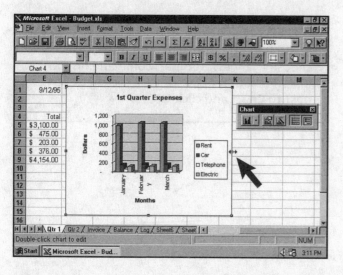

2 Position the mouse pointer over any selection handle in the thin black line that surrounds the chart. The mouse pointer changes shape and becomes a double-headed arrow.

Begin Guided Tour Change the Chart Type

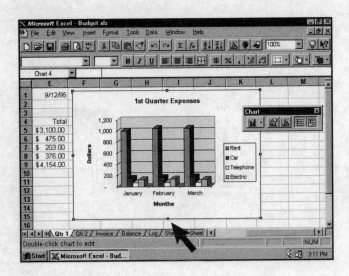

1 Select the chart. It can appear in its own window, but it doesn't have to appear in the window. You see the Chart toolbar and selection handles on the chart frame.

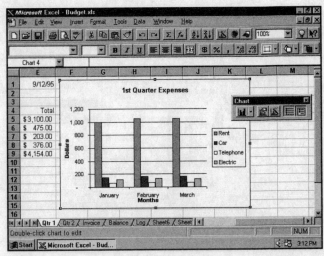

3 As soon as you make a selection, Excel changes the chart to the format you chose. In the example, choose the vertical column format (the third chart type from the top of the first column in the Chart type drop-down list).

If Excel doesn't display the Chart toolbar, choose the View, Toolbars command. In the dialog box that appears, click the check box next to Chart and click OK.

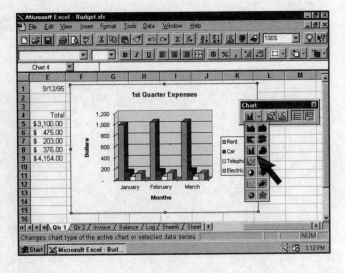

2 Click the down arrow next to the Chart Type button on the Chart toolbar. Excel displays a palette of predesigned charts. Choose the chart type you want to use.

Begin Guided Tour   Change the Size of the Chart Title

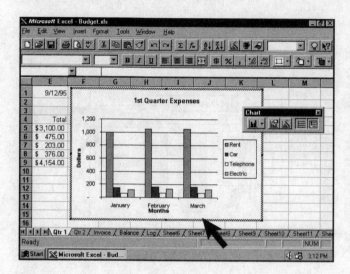

1 Make sure the chart appears in its own window. If you see the chart frame only, double-click the chart to display it in its own window.

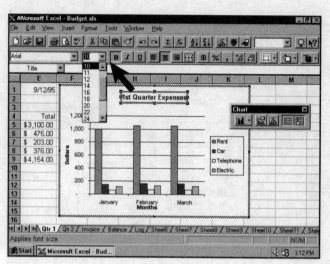

3 Click the down arrow next to the Font Size text box on the Formatting toolbar. Excel displays a list of font sizes.

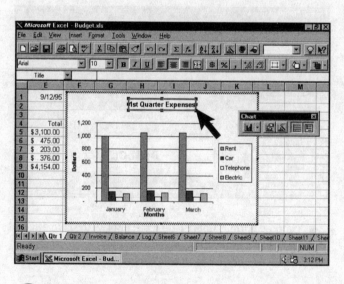

2 Click the title at the top of the chart. A border with selection handles surrounds the title.

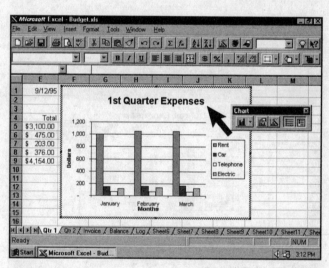

4 Click a larger number than the current size. Then press **Esc** to deselect the title. In the example, the new font size is 14.

Begin Guided Tour   Change the Font of the Chart Title

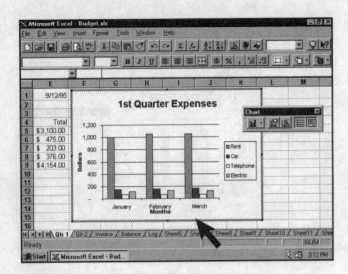

1 Make sure the chart appears in its own window. If you see the chart frame only, double-click the chart to display it in its own window.

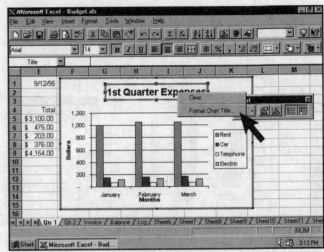

3 Point the mouse pointer at the selected title and click the right mouse button. A shortcut menu appears.

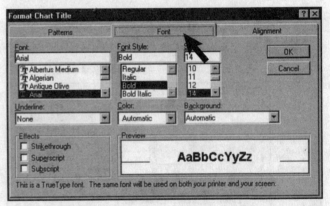

4 Choose **Format Chart Title**. Excel displays the Format Chart Title dialog box. Click the **Font** tab.

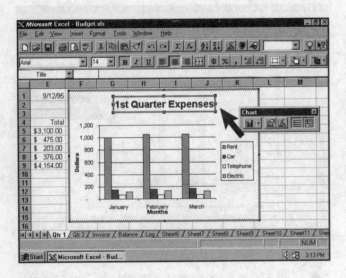

2 Click the title at the top of the chart. A border with selection handles surrounds the title.

Guided Tour Change the Font of the Chart Title

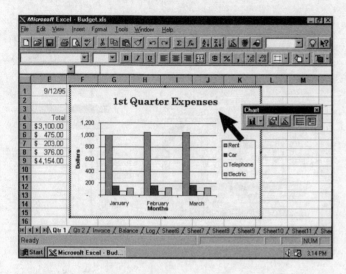

5 Make your changes and click **OK**. Press **Esc** to deselect the title. In the example, change the font for the chart title to bold, 14-point Century Schoolbook.

Begin Guided Tour Add Text Labels

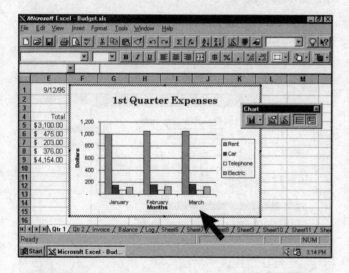

1 Make sure the chart appears in its own window. If you see the chart frame only, double-click the chart to display it in its own window.

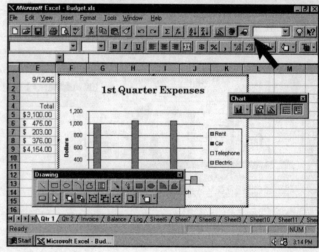

2 Click the **Drawing** tool on the Standard toolbar to display the Drawing toolbar.

(continues)

Guided Tour Add Text Labels *(continued)*

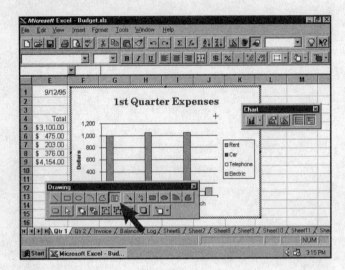

3 Click the **Text Box** button on the Drawing toolbar. This displays a crosshair pointer.

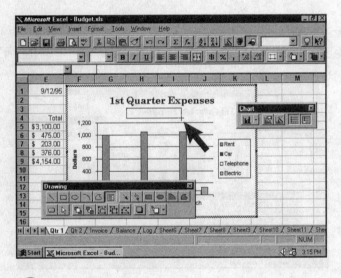

4 On the chart, drag the crosshair pointer to draw a rectangular box. In the example, the rectangular box appears just below the chart title.

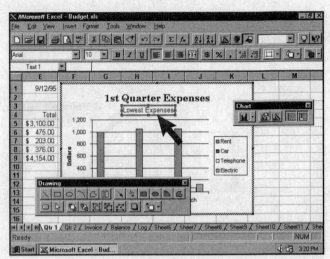

5 Release the mouse button. Excel adds the text box to the chart. Type the text you want to appear in the label and press **Esc** to indicate that you are finished typing. In the example, type **Lowest Expenses**.

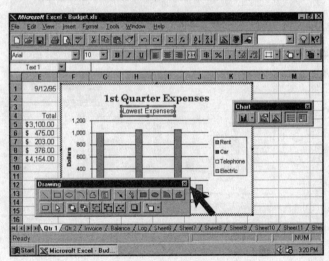

6 Close the Drawing toolbar by clicking the **Close** button (the X) in the upper right corner of the toolbar.

Guided Tour Add Text Labels

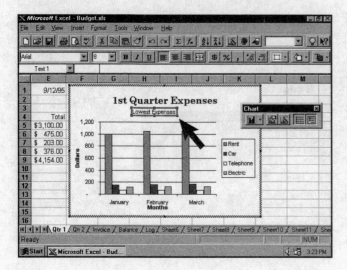 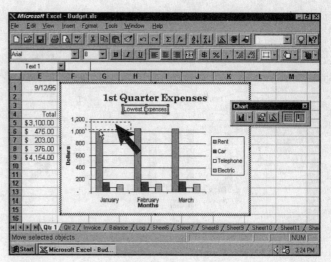

7 If a border with selection handles does not surround the text, click the text label. Then, if necessary, use the selection handles to shrink the box so that it is the same size as the text. If you want, change the font size.

8 Move the mouse pointer to the border of the box and drag the text label to its proper place on the chart. In the example, place the text label above the first set of bars—the data series for January. To remove the selection handles from the text box, press **Esc**.

To make the label easier to see, you can make the text in the label boldface. Just click the label to select it and click the Bold button on the Formatting toolbar.

Begin Guided Tour Modify the Category Labels

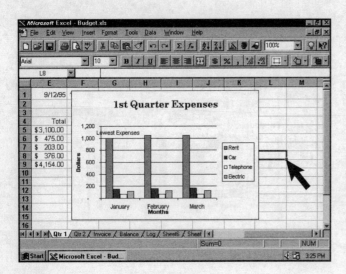

1 Click any cell in the worksheet twice to deselect the chart.

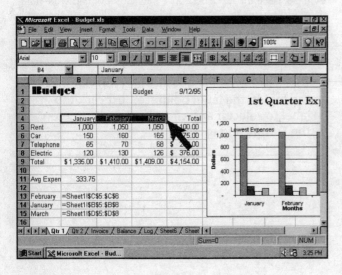

2 Select the cells that contain the category labels. In the example, select cells **B4:D4**.

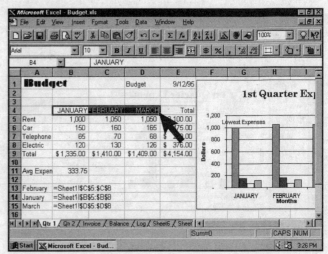

3 Make the changes you want, pressing **Enter** after you type each cell entry. In the example, retype the category labels in uppercase letters.

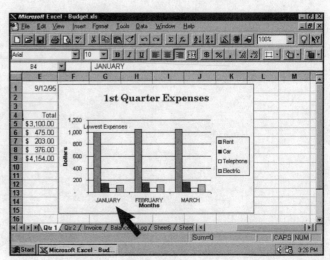

4 Scroll so that you can see the chart. As you type, Excel instantly updates the chart to reflect the changes in the worksheet. The new category labels appear at the bottom of the chart.

Begin Guided Tour   Change the Axis Scale

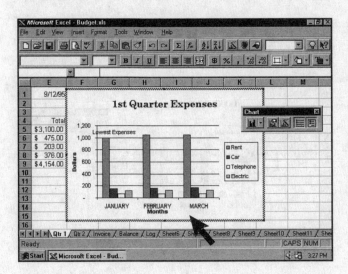

1 Make sure the chart appears in its own window. If you see the chart frame only, double-click the chart to display it in its own window.

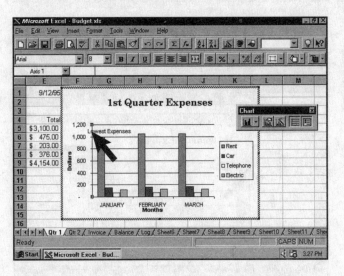

2 Click the vertical line to select the value axis. Selection handles boxes appear at each end of the value axis.

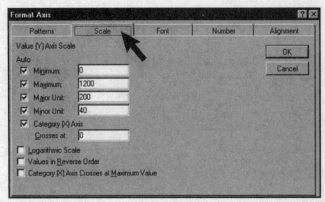

3 Double-click the value axis. Excel displays the Format Axis dialog box. Click the **Scale** tab to display the scale options.

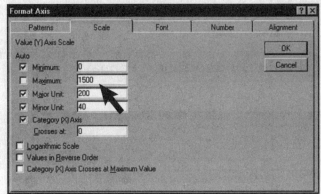

4 To change the largest value on the axis, double-click in the **Maximum** text box and type the value you want to use. In the example, type **1500**. Notice that Excel automatically clears the Auto check box when you change any of the preset values.

(continues)

Guided Tour Change the Axis Scale

(continued)

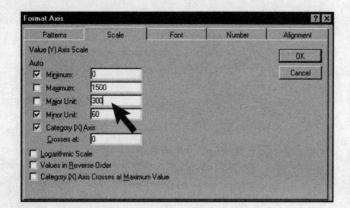

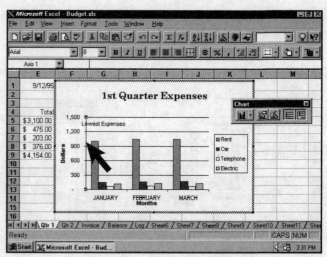

5 To change the interval between the values on the value axis, double-click in the **Major Unit** text box and type the interval you want to use. In the example, type **300**. Again, Excel clears the Auto check box. Click **OK** to accept the changes.

6 The chart reflects your changes on the vertical axis.

Begin Guided Tour Format an Axis

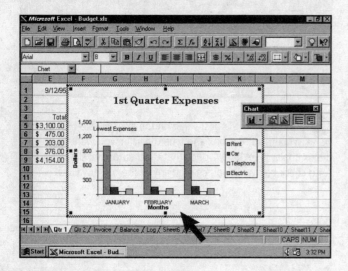

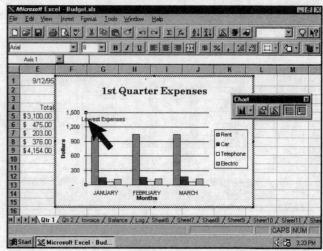

1 Make sure the chart appears in its own window. If you see the chart frame only, double-click the chart to display it in its own window.

2 If necessary, click the vertical line to select the value axis. Selection handles appear at each end of the value axis.

Guided Tour Format an Axis

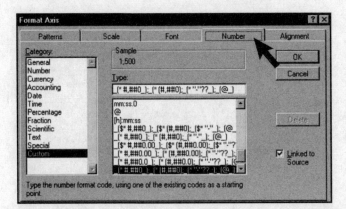

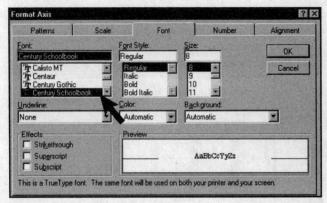

3 Double-click the value axis. Excel displays the Format Axis dialog box. Click the appropriate tab to format the axis. In the example, choose the **Number** tab to display the number options.

5 To change the font on the value axis, choose the **Font** tab. Click a font in the list. In the example, the new font is Century Schoolbook. Click **OK** to confirm your choices.

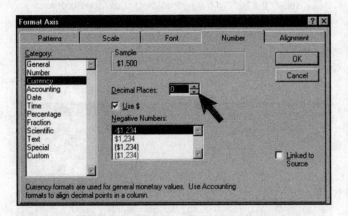

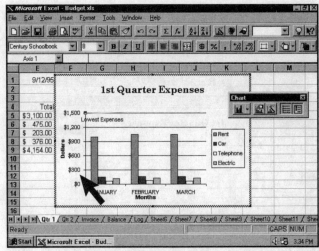

4 To display the numbers on the vertical axis as currency, choose **Currency** from the Category list. Click the **Use $** check box to use dollar sign symbols. The sample $1,500.00 appears at the top of the dialog box. Last, use the Decimal Places spinner box to change the decimal places to 0.

6 Excel updates the chart to reflect them.

Although these steps show you how to format the value (Y) axis, you can also use them to format the category (X) axis. Simply select it instead of the value axis in step 2.

Begin Guided Tour   Change the Patterns for a Data Series

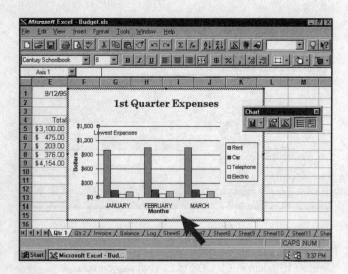

1 Select the chart, making sure it appears in its own window.

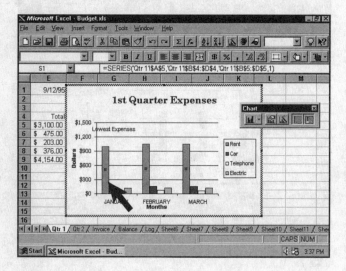

2 Click the first data series to select all the bars that represent that data series. In the example, click the bar that represents the rent for January. Selection handles appear in each of the bars.

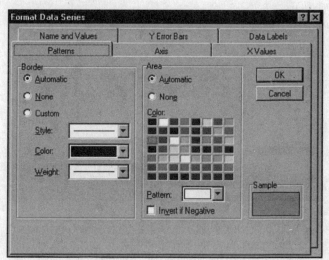

3 Double-click any selected bar. Excel displays the Patterns tab in the Format Data Series dialog box. The Border options on this tab affect the perimeter of the selected element, including the style, color, and weight of the border line. The Area options control the inside of the element, such as its pattern and color.

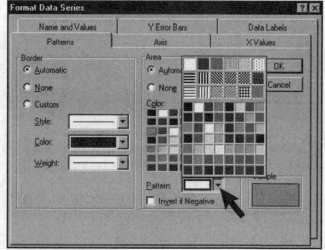

4 To change the pattern that fills the selected bar, click the down arrow next to the Pattern text box in the Area options. Excel displays a palette of patterns and colors.

Guided Tour Change the Patterns for a Data Series

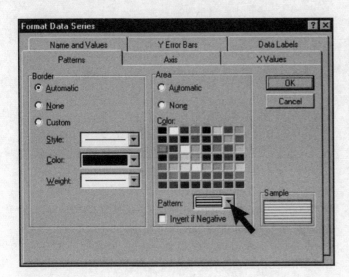

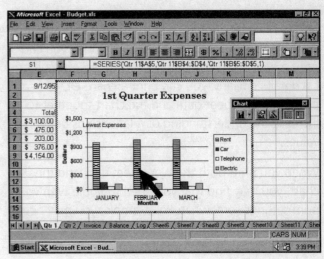

5 Select the pattern you want to use. In the example, select the horizontal striped pattern (the second pattern from the top in the first column of the palette). The sample appears in the lower right corner of the dialog box.

7 Excel applies your selections to the chart. Notice, in the figure, that the legend contains a new pattern for Rent.

If you want to change just the color in the elements that represent the data series, skip steps 4 and 5.

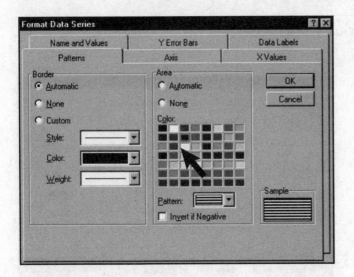

6 To change the color of this pattern, select a color from the color palette. Again, the sample box in the lower right corner changes to reflect your selection. Click **OK**.

Put Your Chart on Paper

Chart information is both useful and impressive in presentations. As you already know, you can print a worksheet if you only need to present numerical detail. Similarly, you can print a chart. Or, you can print the worksheet data and the chart together to increase the understanding of relationships between values.

When you print both the worksheet data and the chart, you may find that you need to fiddle with your print settings somewhat. For example, you may need to change the orientation of the printout from the default orientation of Portrait to Landscape. To fit everything on one page, you may need to reduce column widths, move the chart so that it appears below or to one side of the data, or even change the margins for your paper.

If a portion of the page is cut off, you may have shortened the margins too much. Laser printers require at least .5 inches around all edges of the page. Open the File menu and choose Page Setup. Then, click the Margins tab. Make sure each margin is at least .5 inches.

If you are printing a chart on a printer that doesn't print color, for example, a non-color dot matrix printer, you must change the print chart options to print in black and white. Otherwise, you do not get the printout results you want. Open the **File** menu and choose the **Page Setup** command. Then, click on the **Sheet** tab, and, in the Print text box, select the **Black and White** option. Now you can print the chart.

Begin Guided Tour   Print a Chart Without Worksheet Data

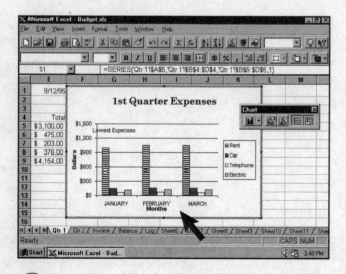

1 Select the chart, making sure it appears in its own window.

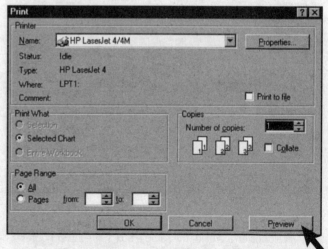

2 Open the **File** menu and choose the **Print** command. Excel displays the Print dialog box. To preview your chart before printing, choose the **Preview** command button.

Guided Tour   Print a Chart Without Worksheet Data

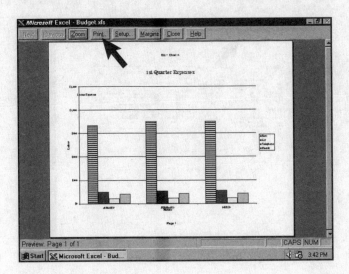

3 Choose the **Print** button from the Preview window to print your chart on paper.

Begin Guided Tour   Print a Chart and the Worksheet

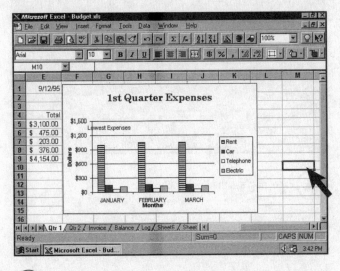

1 Click any cell in the worksheet twice to deselect the chart.

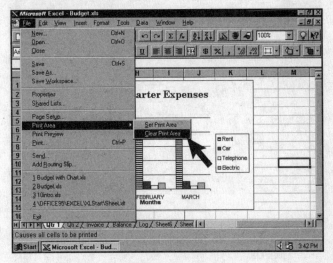

2 Choose **File**, **Print Area**, **Clear Print Area** to remove automatic page breaks.

(continues)

Guided Tour   Print a Chart and the Worksheet

(continued)

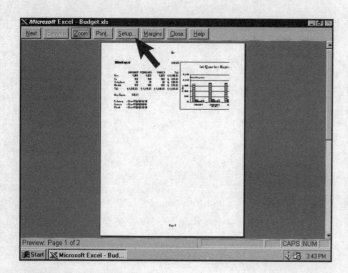

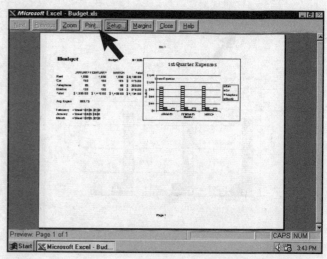

3 Click the **Print Preview** button on the Standard toolbar to display the worksheet on-screen (the fifth button from the left). This is how the worksheet will look when you print it. To change the print orientation to landscape, click the **Setup** button to display the Page Setup dialog box.

5 Excel redisplays the worksheet in landscape orientation. Now you can see the worksheet data and the chart. Click the **Print** button.

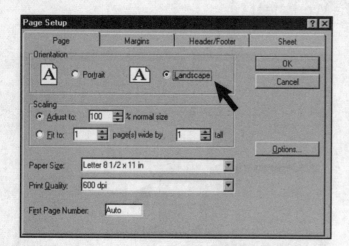

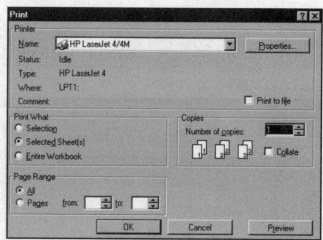

4 In the Page Setup dialog box, click the **Page** tab. Then, click the **Landscape** button in the Orientation options. Click **OK**.

6 Excel displays the Print dialog box.

Guided Tour   Print a Chart and the Worksheet

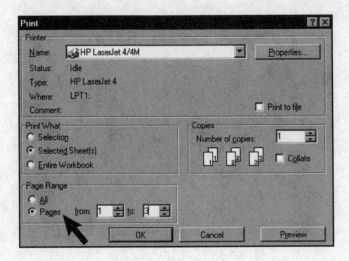

7 In the Page Range options, click the **Pages** option button, and, in the from box, type the number of the first page you want to print. Press the **Tab** key to move to the to box and type the number of the last page you want to print. Click **OK** to confirm your choices. Excel prints the worksheet and the chart.

HOW TO...

Work with Maps

Mapping is a new feature in Excel 7. Just as charts help you visualize and analyze data, you can use maps to visualize and analyze the geographic impact of your data. With this new feature, you can easily show information like sales data for a particular region. To set up mapping in Excel, one column of your data needs to contain some kind of geographic information, such as state names or countries; other columns need to contain numbers Excel can use on your map.

To use Excel's mapping feature, you must install it. If you don't see the Map tool on the Standard toolbar, you need to run the Setup program again and make sure you install the mapping feature. You need your original Excel disks or CD. You can start the Setup program by opening the Windows 95 **Start** menu and selecting **Settings**. From the Settings menu, click **Control Panel**. In the Control Panel window, double-click **Add/Remove Programs**. On the Install/Uninstall tab, click **Excel** and click the **Add/Remove** button.

Excel also comes with demographic data such as population trends that you can add to your map to help show trends or market potential. This type of information can help you plan sales and marketing efforts. And, in addition to the data supplied with Excel, you can purchase additional mapping information from MapInfo Corporation, One Global View, Troy, NY 12180-8399, 1-800-488-3552 (U.S. only) or 518.285.7110 (International).

What You Will Find in This Section

Create a Map

Whenever you work with data that is geographic in nature, displaying the data on a map is a most effective tool. Using Excel's new mapping feature, you can enter data into a worksheet and instruct Excel to draw a map that includes your data.

To create a map, you need to select a range of cells that includes one column of geographic data. Geographic data can be country names, state names, or postal codes. As you create the column that contains the geographic data, you can use standard abbreviations for state names, such as FL for Florida. If you are unsure about the spelling or abbreviation for a geographic name, you can find the information you need in a worksheet Microsoft provides. The worksheet, MAPSTATS.XLS, is in the \Program Files\Microsoft Shared\Datamap\Data folder.

If you decide to use U.S. postal codes (zip codes), be sure you format the codes as text, not numbers. This prevents Excel from removing leading zeros.

You can also select data values you want Excel to include on the map. Suppose you want to map sales for several states, and your data contains one column of geographic data (state names or abbreviations), and one column of sales values (one for each state). To create the map, you select the two columns and any column titles you included in the data.

> You can create a map without selecting any data in the worksheet, but in the long run, you find that creating a map is easier if you select geographic data.

To work with the map, it must appear in its own window. The map is in its own window if you see the Mapping toolbar and short diagonal lines and handles surrounding the map. If you aren't sure the map is in its own window, click once anywhere in the worksheet, and a thin black line, or frame, surrounds the map. You also see the Standard and Formatting toolbars. Then, double-click inside the frame.

Begin Guided Tour   Draw a Map

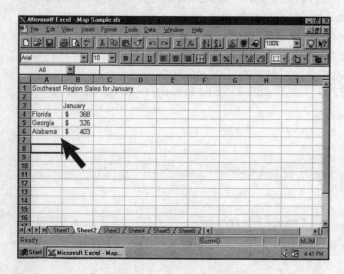

1 Set up a worksheet that contains at least one column of geographic data.

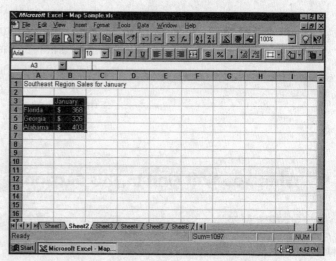

2 Select the geographic data and any other data you want Excel to map. Include row and column titles, if they appear in your data.

Guided Tour   Draw a Map

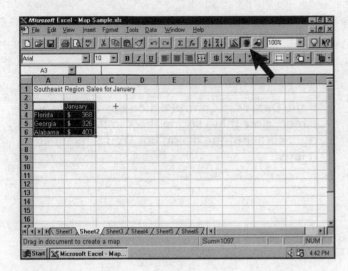

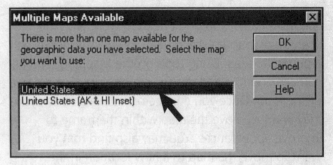

5 Release the mouse button. Excel creates a window for the map and, depending on the geographic data in your selection, displays either the Multiple Maps Available dialog box or the Unable to Create Map dialog box. Both are similar and give you the opportunity to specify the map you want Excel to use. Select a map for Excel and click **OK**.

3 Click the **Map** tool on the Standard toolbar and position the mouse pointer over the worksheet area. The mouse pointer shape changes to a plus sign.

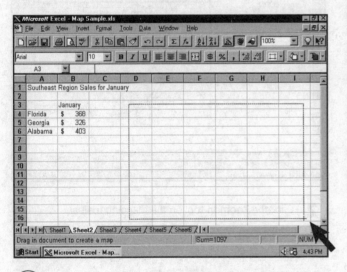

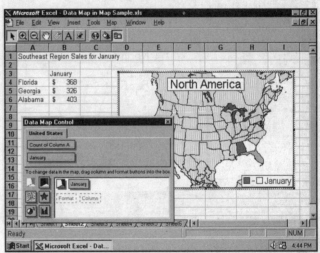

6 Excel displays the map and, if you selected data, the Data Map Control dialog box. If the Data Map Control dialog box appears on-screen, close it by clicking the X in the upper right corner of the dialog box.

4 Position the mouse pointer so that it appears over the cell where you want the upper left corner of the map to appear. Click and drag the mouse pointer to the cell where you want the lower left corner of the map to appear.

Zoom In and Out

In most cases, you don't need to work with the entire map that Excel draws. You want to focus on a particular area. Using tools on the Mapping toolbar, you can zoom in and out to enlarge or reduce an area of the map. Once you enlarge or reduce an area, you may want to move the map within the frame to improve appearances. You may also find that you want to move the map to a new location in the worksheet—for example, near data that is associated

with the map so that you can print both the map and the data on the same page.

> If the Data Map Control dialog box appears on-screen, close it by clicking the X in the upper right corner of the dialog box. You can reopen it later.

Begin Guided Tour Enlarge an Area of a Map

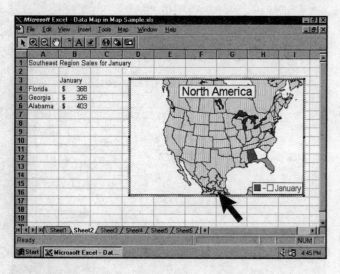

1 Make sure the map appears in its own window. If it isn't, double-click anywhere inside the map's frame.

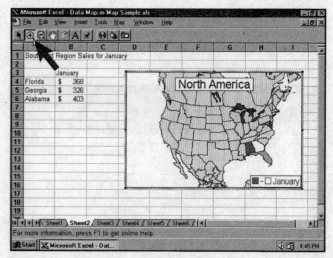

2 Click the **Zoom In** tool on the Mapping toolbar.

Guided Tour Enlarge an Area of a Map

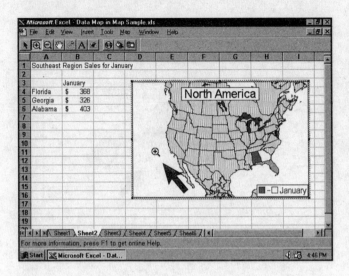

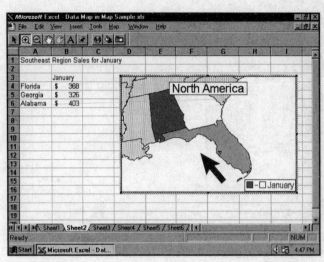

3 Position the mouse pointer over the map. The mouse pointer shape changes to a magnifying glass containing a plus sign. It looks just like the Zoom In tool.

5 Release the mouse button. Excel redraws the map, focusing on the area you selected.

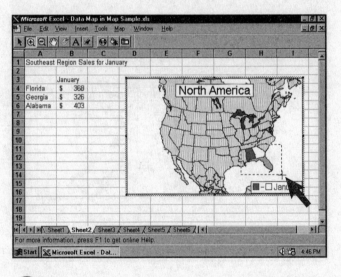

4 Drag to draw a rectangle around the area you want to enlarge.

Begin Guided Tour   Reduce a Map

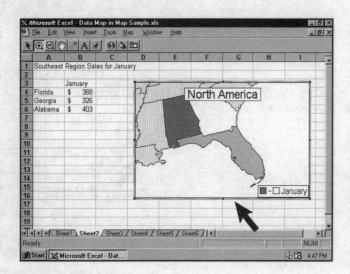

1 Make sure the map appears in its own window. If it isn't, double-click anywhere inside the map's frame.

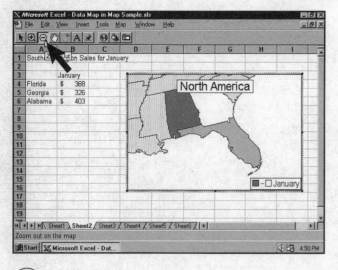

2 Click the **Zoom Out** tool on the Mapping toolbar.

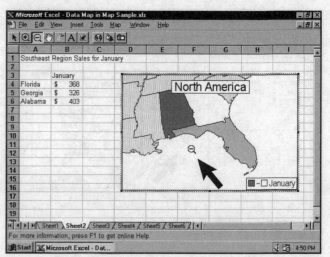

3 Position the mouse pointer over the map. The mouse pointer shape changes to a magnifying glass containing a minus sign; it looks just like the Zoom Out tool.

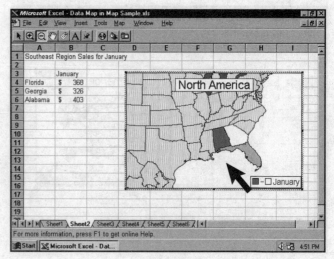

4 Click on the map to reduce the view.

Begin Guided Tour   Move the Map within the Frame

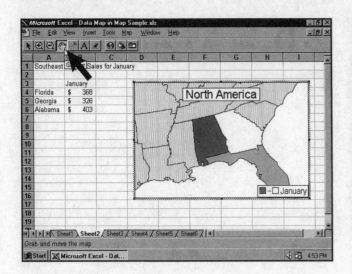

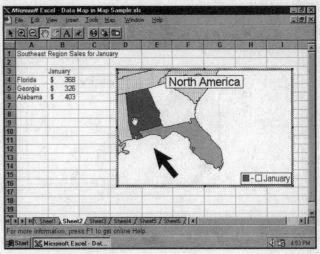

1 With the map in its own window, click the **Grabber** tool on the Mapping toolbar.

2 Drag the map inside the map frame until it's in the position you want. Release the left mouse button.

Begin Guided Tour   Move the Map to a New Location in the Worksheet

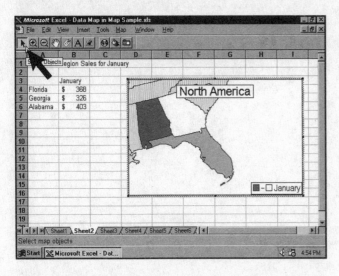

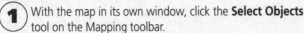

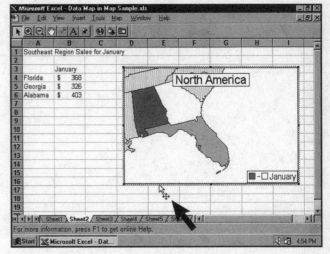

1 With the map in its own window, click the **Select Objects** tool on the Mapping toolbar.

2 Position the mouse pointer over the short diagonal lines that border the map window. The mouse pointer changes to a four-headed arrow.

(continues)

Guided Tour   Move the Map to a New Location in the Worksheet

(continued)

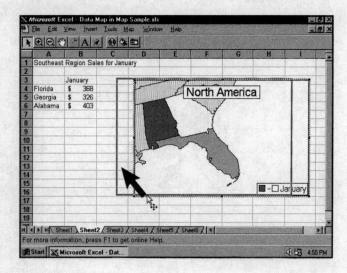

3 Drag the map window border until it is located where you want it. Don't drag a handle on the map window border—this resizes the map instead of moving it. Release the left mouse button.

Add Features to a Map

Once you create a map, you may want to add features to it. Excel ships with several features you can add, such as highways and major cities. Or, you may want to add other features, such as remarks or geographic labels, to clarify information for the reader.

Be careful about adding too many additional features to your map. Too many features can clutter the map. A cluttered map is very difficult to read and may distract the reader from the actual information you are trying to show and the point you're trying to make.

Begin Guided Tour Add Highways to a Map

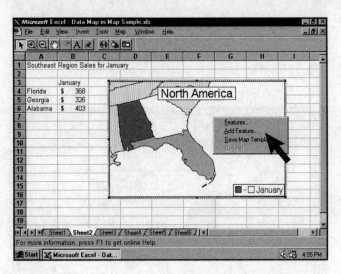

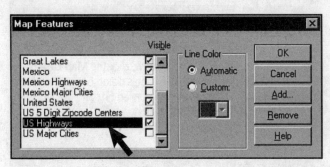

3 Scroll down the list box in this dialog box until you see the feature you want to display on the map. Place a check mark in the check box next to that feature. In the example, select **U.S. Highways**. Click **OK**.

1 With the map in its own window, move the mouse pointer anywhere inside the map window and press the right mouse button. A shortcut menu appears.

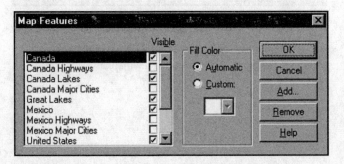

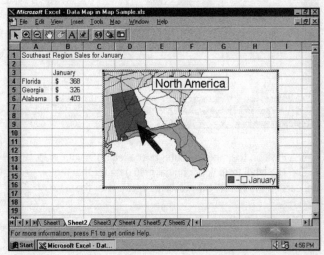

2 Choose the **Features** command. Excel displays the Map Features dialog box.

4 Excel adds the feature to your map.

5 To hide a feature, remove the check mark from the check box in the Map Features dialog box.

Begin Guided Tour   Add Map Labels

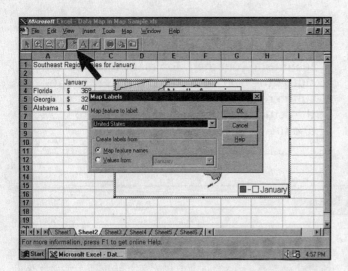

1 With the map in its own window, click the **Map Labels** tool. Excel displays the Map Labels dialog box. Click **OK** to accept the default information in the dialog box and use labels based on the map you originally created.

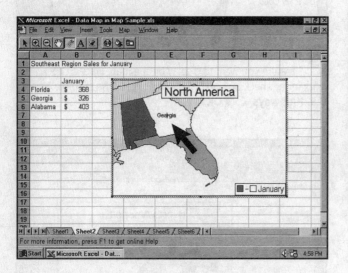

2 Position the mouse pointer over a region in your map. The label from your original map data for that region appears. In the figure, the mouse pointer is over the state of Georgia.

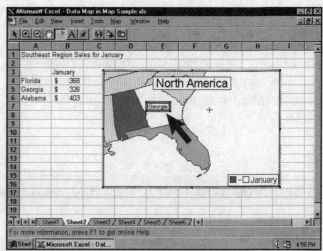

3 Click in the region to place the label on the region.

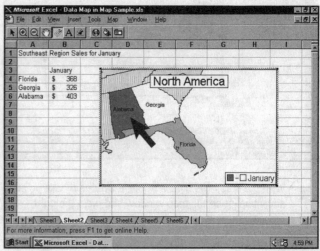

4 Repeat steps 2 and 3 until you label all the regions on your map that you want. Excel continues to display labels as you move the mouse pointer around the map until you choose another tool from the Mapping toolbar.

Begin Guided Tour   Add Remarks to the Map

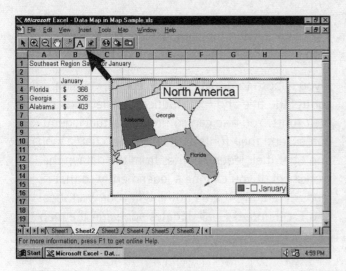

1 With the map in its own window, click the **Add Text** tool on the Mapping toolbar.

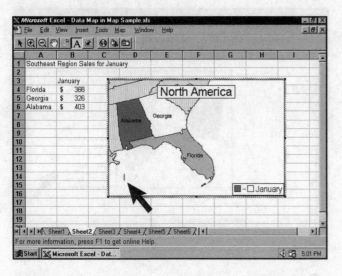

2 Inside the map window, click at the location where you want the left edge of the remark to appear. Excel displays a flashing insertion point.

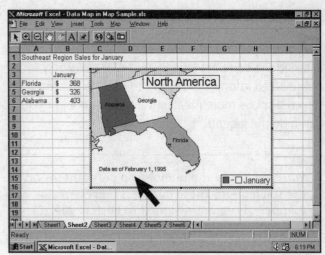

3 Type the remark you want to appear on the map. Excel continues to display the flashing insertion point as you move the mouse pointer around the map until you choose another tool from the Mapping toolbar.

Change the Legend

By default, Excel displays a legend on the map when you create it. The legend you see initially is called the *compact legend*, and it displays only abbreviated information. You can use the full legend, which displays more meaningful information, or you can hide the legend.

> You may notice the numbers in parentheses on the full legend. These numbers represent the number of regions assigned to each range.

If you are viewing the compact legend, you can modify the title of the legend and its font.

If you choose to display the full legend, you can control the title and the subtitle of the legend and their fonts. You also can control the actual legend entries (and their fonts as well). Unlike charts, maps don't get their legend entries from the data in the worksheet. If you change a legend entry so that it reads differently, there's nothing in your worksheet that Excel updates—all updates appear in the map legend only.

Begin Guided Tour   Display the Full Legend

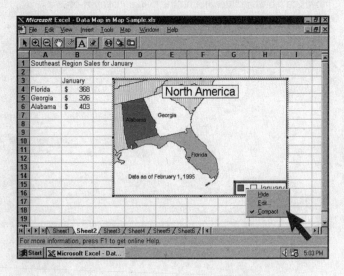

1 With the map in its own window, position the mouse pointer over the legend and press the right mouse button. Excel displays a shortcut menu. Choose the **Compact** command to display the full legend.

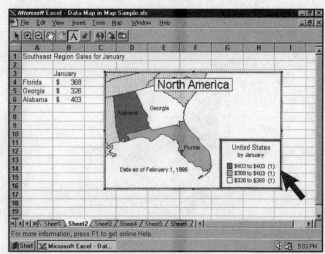

2 Excel displays the full legend.

Begin Guided Tour   Hide (and Redisplay) the Map Legend

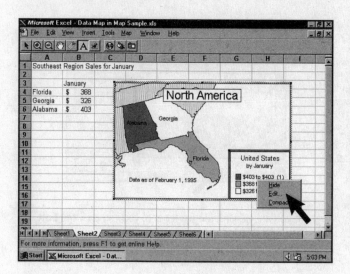

1 With the map in its own window, position the mouse pointer over the legend and press the right mouse button. Excel displays a shortcut menu. Choose the **Hide** command.

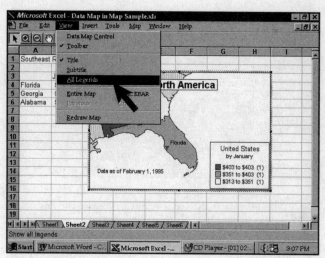

3 To redisplay the legend, open the **View** menu and choose the **All Legends** command. Excel redisplays the legend.

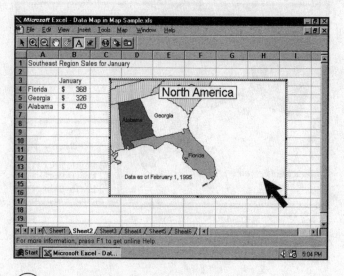

2 The legend disappears from the map.

Begin Guided Tour   Modify the Map Legend

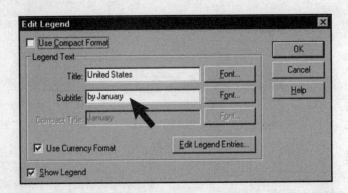

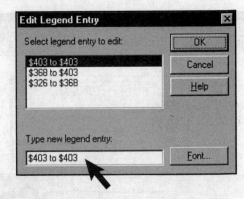

1 With the map in its own window and the legend on-screen, double-click the legend. Excel displays the Edit Legend dialog box. The legend you are viewing determines what you can modify.

2 If you are viewing the full legend, you can click the **Edit Legend Entries** button to change the entries that actually appear in the legend box or their fonts.

Begin Guided Tour   Move or Resize the Legend

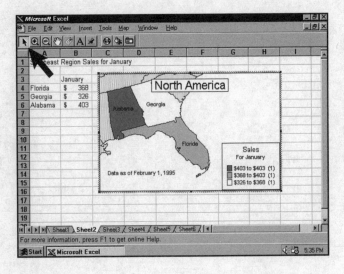

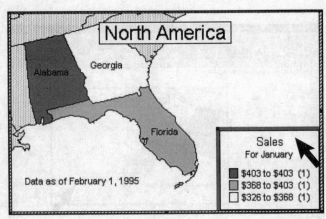

2 Click the legend to select it.

1 With the map in its own window, click the **Select Objects** tool on the Mapping toolbar.

Guided Tour   Move or Resize the Legend

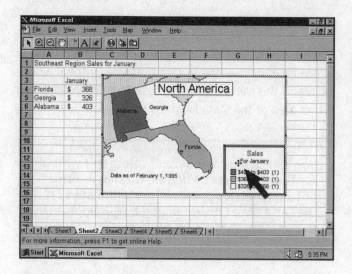

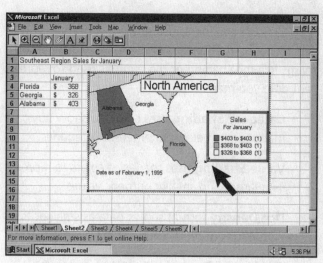

3 To move the legend, position the mouse pointer over the center of the legend. The mouse pointer turns into a four-headed arrow.

5 To resize the legend, position the mouse pointer over a handle of the legend. The pointer turns into a double-headed arrow.

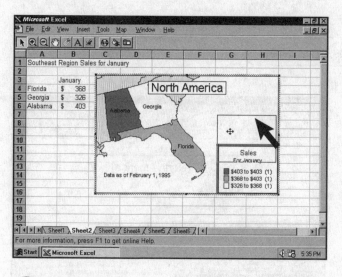

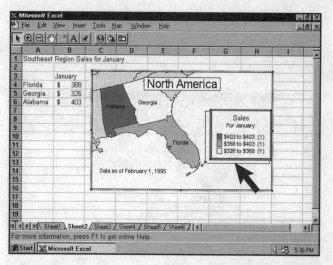

4 Drag the legend to a new location and release the mouse button.

6 Drag a corner of the legend in toward the center to make the legend smaller or out from the center to make the legend larger. Excel automatically resizes text within the legend.

Modify the Map

If you don't like the appearance of your map, you can change the formats of the map, which control things like the shading or the symbols used to represent data you map:

Category Shading uses colors to show how map regions belong to different categories.

Value Shading uses shades of colors to represent larger and smaller numeric values.

Dot Density format shows data as small dots, with each dot representing some quantity.

Graduated Symbol format shows data as various-sized symbols, with larger symbols representing larger quantities.

You can switch between these various formats using the Data Map Control dialog box. The format buttons available appear at the bottom left side of the dialog box, and the format button in use appears in the white area of the Data Map Control dialog box.

You can change the default colors and symbols for these formats by double-clicking a format button when it appears in the white area of the Data Map Control dialog box. It appears in the white area if you apply it.

You also can modify text (such as the map title) that appears on the map, and, if the data you mapped changes, you can update the map to reflect the changes.

Begin Guided Tour   Change the Formats on a Map

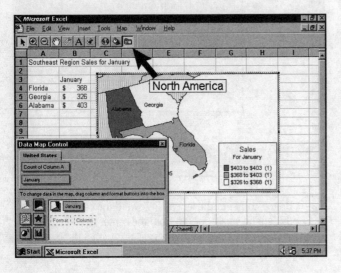
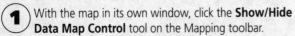

1 With the map in its own window, click the **Show/Hide Data Map Control** tool on the Mapping toolbar.

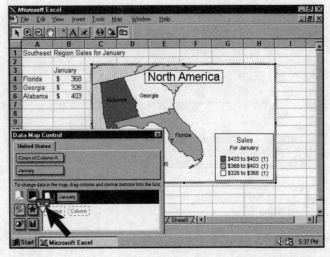

2 In the Data Map Control dialog box, drag a format button from the bottom left side of the dialog box onto the format button in the white area of the dialog box.

Guided Tour   Change the Formats on a Map

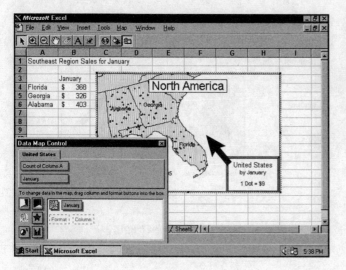

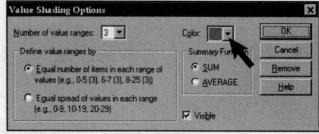

4 To change the default colors or symbols after you apply a format, double-click the format button in the white box and make changes in the resulting dialog box.

3 When you release the mouse button, Excel updates your map.

Begin Guided Tour   Modify the Map Title

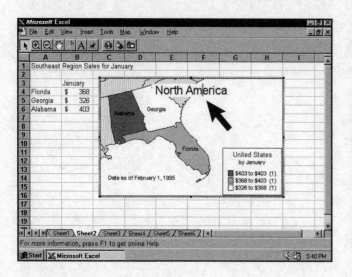

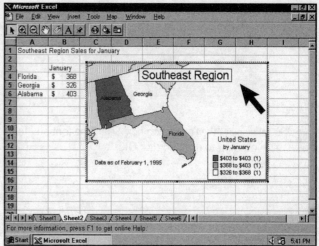

1 With the map in its own window, double-click the map title. An insertion point appears.

2 Type your changes, using the Backspace and Delete keys to remove unwanted characters. Press **Enter** when you finish.

(continues)

Guided Tour Modify the Map Title *(continued)*

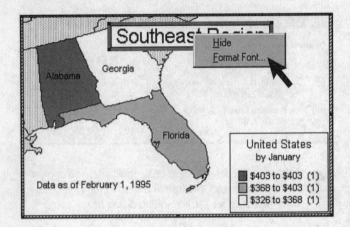

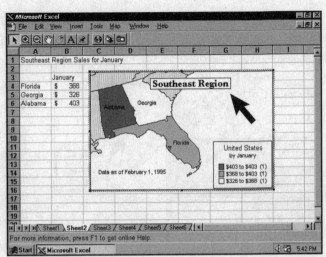

3 To change the font or font size of the title, point at the title and press the right mouse button. Excel displays a shortcut menu. Choose **Format Font**.

5 Excel makes your changes.

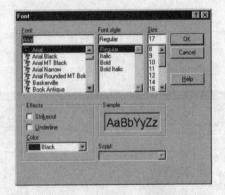

4 Excel displays the Font dialog box. Select the font and font size you want to use, and click **OK**.

Begin Guided Tour   Change the Data that Appears on the Map

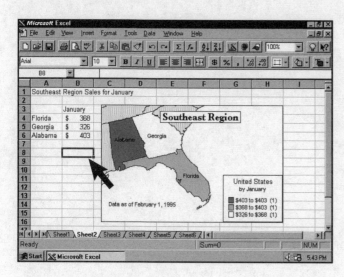

1 Click in the worksheet. Excel stops displaying the map in its own window.

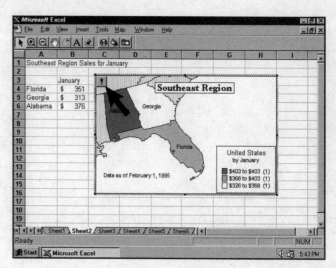

3 Double-click inside the map frame to place the map in its own window. Then click the **Map Refresh** button in the upper left corner of the map.

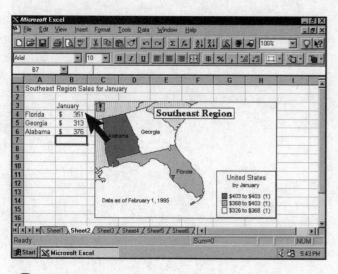

2 In the worksheet, update the map data as necessary.

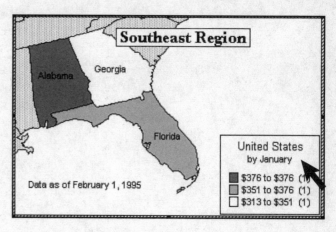

4 Excel updates the map to reflect the changes you made in the worksheet.

Excel Housekeeping

While "housekeeping" is still a dirty word for most of us, it's also a necessary evil. From time to time, you need to do some cleaning and arrange things just the way you like them. This applies whether you're talking about your living space or your Excel workspace. With a bit of practice, you'll find Excel housekeeping more pleasant than picking up those dirty tube socks that you threw in the corner a month ago.

This section introduces you to the options you have for controlling numerous features in Excel—from how Excel looks on-screen to making custom lists for speedy data entry. To set most of these options, you work with the many tabs in the Options dialog box. This section offers the following Guided Tours explaining how you can manage your Excel housekeeping with minimal muss and fuss:

What You Will Find in This Section

Show and Hide Parts of a Window

Sections 1 and 2 introduced you to the various and sundry parts of the Excel workspace. Because Excel is so sophisticated now, it offers not only a myriad of commands but also more view features and options than you may want to use. If one look at your Excel screen makes your head spin, you can change it to keep your work in focus.

This Guided Tour explains how to control the elements of the Excel screen. First, you'll learn how to choose whether to view the Formula bar or status bar on-screen. Choosing not to display these features leaves more room on-screen for your work in Excel.

Next, you'll learn how to choose which of Excel's eight toolbars appear on-screen at any time. You can choose to display only the toolbar you need for the task at hand, hiding other toolbars to leave a greater work area on-screen. For example, you can display the drawing toolbar and the map toolbar and hide other toolbars while you're working on a map you want to include in a worksheet. You also have some control over the size and appearance of the toolbar buttons.

> You can move any Excel toolbar to the bottom of the Excel window or to a floating palette simply by dragging it to the location you want. Point to a space on the toolbar, press and hold the left mouse button, and drag.

Excel gives you the option of using the Full Screen view. When you specify this view as explained later, Excel hides non-essential screen features such as the Excel title bar and the Windows 95 taskbar, leaving only the menu bar and workbook window, including its tabs and scroll bars, to fill the screen.

The Guided Tour moves on to show you how you can change the zoom for your workbook. When you change the *zoom* for a worksheet, you change its magnification on-screen. For example, you can view a workbook at 200% its actual size to make it easier to view cell contents, or you can view a workbook at 25% to take a look at the overall worksheet layout. Excel not only enables you to select preset zoom percentages but also enables you to specify the custom percentage of your choice. Or, you can select a cell or range of cells and zoom to magnify those cells using the Fit Selection check box in the Zoom dialog box. The selected cells fill the entire screen.

Use the View Tab in the Options Dialog Box to Change What Appears

Finally, the Guided Tour explains how to use the View tab in the Options dialog box (you can display this dialog box by opening the **Tools** menu, choosing **Options**, and clicking **View**) to determine whether specific features appear on-screen. To choose whether an item appears on-screen, you click to place a check mark in the check box beside the option. The first area within this tab, the Show area, offers the following four options:

- **Formula Bar**   Determines whether the Formula bar for data entry appears on-screen.
- **Status Bar**   Enables you to specify whether Excel should show the status bar with information below the open workbook(s).
- **Note Indicator**   When this option is enabled, Excel displays a red note indicator in the upper-right corner of any cell where you've inserted a note.

- **Info Window** Opens the Info window in addition to the workbook window. The Info window displays statistical information about the on-screen cell (such as any formula it contains, the contents of any notes it contains, and so on).

The next area of the View tab, Objects, controls whether Excel displays objects you've placed on a worksheet, such as drawings, charts, or graphics. Choose one of the following three options in this area by clicking it:

- **Show All** Displays all objects as you place them on the worksheet.

- **Show Placeholders** Shows a gray placeholder box rather than the object contents. Select this choice to help Excel appear to run and scroll a bit more quickly, as some objects may require quite a bit of working memory (RAM) to display on-screen.

- **Hide All** Removes objects from display without deleting them from the worksheet. This choice takes the least amount of memory, therefore enabling the screen display and scrolling to be more responsive.

The final area of the Options dialog box View tab is called Window Options. In this area, click to place a check beside any screen element you want to appear automatically; remove the check beside any element that you don't want to view. Excel offers the following Window Options:

- **Automatic Page Breaks** Controls whether Excel displays page breaks it automatically inserts in a worksheet as you fill more cells than the current page can hold.

- **Formulas** Choosing this option means Excel displays the formula you entered into cells rather than the calculated results that normally appear.

- **Gridlines** Enables you to choose whether or not to display gridlines between cells, but does not affect whether gridlines print. Turning this option off provides a clean, attractive on-screen appearance for your worksheets. If you leave the Gridlines check box selected, you can use the Color drop-down list just below it to choose the color you want for the gridlines.

- **Row & Column Headers** Remove the check mark beside this option if you want to hide the row numbers and column letters appearing along the top of and down the left side of the workbook window.

- **Outline Symbols** When you check this option, Excel displays symbols for any outline you create in a worksheet.

- **Zero Values** If you have a worksheet that contains numerous formulas and you only want to show formula results that are not equal to 0 (zero), remove the check beside this option.

- **Horizontal Scroll Bar** To ensure that Excel displays the horizontal scroll bar along the bottom of the workbook windows, check this option.

- **Vertical Scroll Bar** To ensure that Excel displays the vertical scroll bar along the right side of the workbook window, check this option.

- **Sheet Tabs** To see the worksheet tabs at the bottom of the workbook window, check this option.

Begin Guided Tour   Hide the Formula Bar and Status Bar

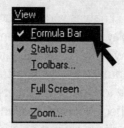

1 To hide the Formula bar from view, open the **View** menu and click **Formula Bar**. The menu closes, and Excel removes the Formula bar from the screen.

3 To redisplay either the Formula bar or status bar, open the **View** menu. Click the command corresponding with the bar to redisplay. Doing so places a check mark beside that command on the menu and redisplays the selected bar.

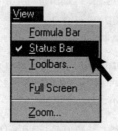

2 To hide the Excel status bar, open the **View** menu and click **Status Bar**. The menu closes, and Excel removes the status bar from the screen.

Begin Guided Tour   View and Hide Toolbars

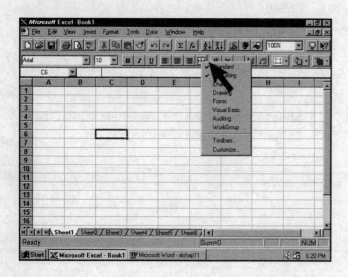

1 Right-click on any toolbar to display the toolbar shortcut menu. A check mark appears to the left of each toolbar that presently appears on-screen. (If no toolbars appear, use the steps under "Work with Toolbar Display," p. 257 to display one.)

Guided Tour   View and Hide Toolbars

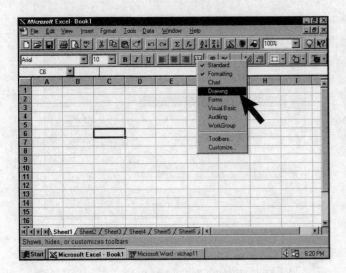

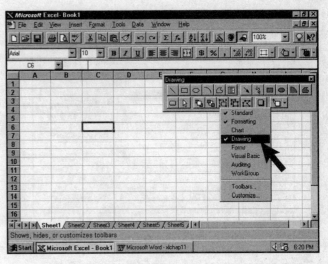

2 To display a toolbar that doesn't currently appear on-screen, click its name in the shortcut menu.

3 The toolbar appears. To hide a toolbar, display the toolbar shortcut menu and click the toolbar name (notice the toolbar name has a check mark beside it before you click it).

Begin Guided Tour   Work with Toolbar Display

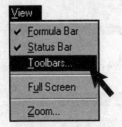

1 Open the **View** menu and click **Toolbars**. Or, display the toolbar shortcut menu and click **Toolbars**. The Toolbars dialog box appears.

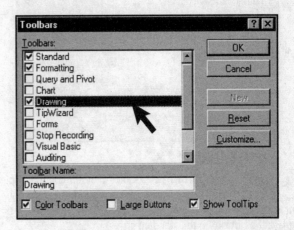

2 To choose to display a toolbar that doesn't have a check beside its name, click its name in the Toolbars list. To hide a toolbar (one that has a check beside its name), click its name in the Toolbars list (this removes the check mark beside it).

(continues)

Guided Tour Work with Toolbar Display *(continued)*

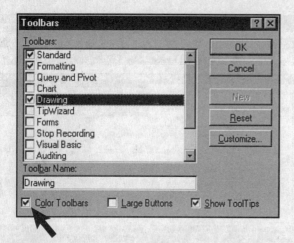

3 If you want to change whether or not the toolbar icons appear in color or in shades of gray, click the **Color Toolbars** check box. A check in the box means colors appear; removing the check removes the colors.

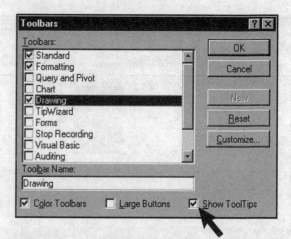

5 The **Show ToolTips** option controls whether yellow ToolTips identifying the purpose of the tool (similar to on-screen sticky notes) appear when you point to a toolbar button. Make sure the check mark appears in the box if you want to see ToolTips. Click to clear this check box if you don't need those tips.

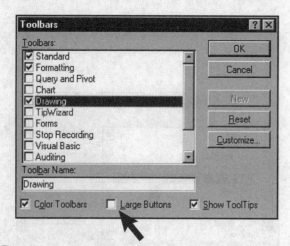

4 Use the **Large Buttons** check box to determine the display size of the buttons on the toolbars. Clicking to check this option displays the buttons in the large size; removing the check displays the buttons in the standard size.

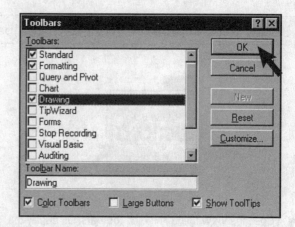

6 Click **OK** to close the Toolbars dialog box.

Begin Guided Tour   Choose Full-Screen View

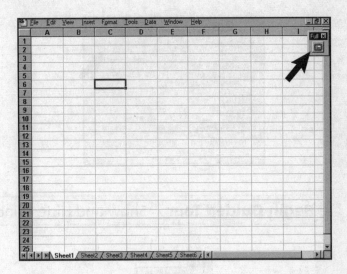

1 Open the **View** menu and click **Full Screen**. Excel removes all elements from the screen except the workbook window and the menu bar. It adds the Full toolbar in a floating window on-screen.

2 To return to the regular view for your workbook, click the **Full Screen** button on the Full toolbar. Or, open the **View** menu and click **Full Screen**.

Begin Guided Tour   Zoom In and Out

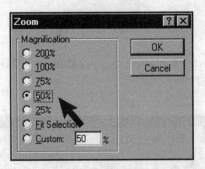

1 Open the **View** menu and choose **Zoom**. The Zoom dialog box appears.

2 Click the zoom percentage you wish to use. If you want to zoom in on a cell or range you selected before displaying the dialog box, click **Fit Selection**. Or, click **Custom** and enter a custom zoom percentage in the text box beside it.

(continues)

Guided Tour   Zoom In and Out   *(continued)*

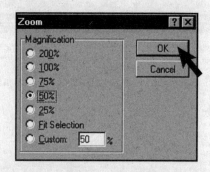

3 Click **OK** to close the Zoom dialog box.

Begin Guided Tour   Show and Hide Window Parts Using the View Options

1 Open the **Tools** menu and click **Options**. The Options dialog box appears.

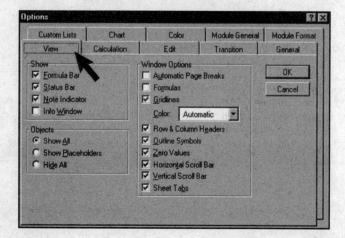

2 **(Optional)** Click the **View** tab, if it isn't in front.

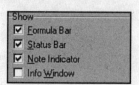

3 If needed, click to select or deselect the check boxes you want in the Show area of the dialog box.

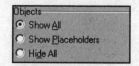

4 If you wish, click to choose one of the option buttons in the Objects area of the dialog box.

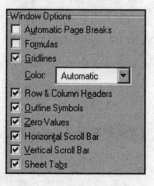

5 Select and deselect check boxes as needed in the Window Options area of the dialog box.

6 Click **OK** to close the Options dialog box. Excel changes on-screen to reflect the elements you've selected to display or hide.

Control When and How Excel Calculates

When you used your faithful old hand calculator, you usually had to press the = key to finish every equation. Otherwise, the calculator wouldn't perform the required calculation for the last number you entered. In a similar way, when you press the Enter key or click the entry check mark on the Formula bar, Excel completes the formula you're entering into a cell and displays the formula's results in that cell—assuming, of course, that you've entered all the values the formula needs to calculate.

Otherwise, Excel automatically calculates the formula's results as soon as you enter the data needed for the calculation. At any time, if you change the entry for a cell that a formula in another cell uses, Excel recalculates the formula results immediately. (For more details about making cell entries, see "Enter Information," p. 40.)

Most Excel users welcome this particular feature. It's satisfying to see the results for a calculation right after you complete the formula or enter the data. Normally this automatic calculation doesn't slow Excel down in any way. However, in some situations, you may experience a noticeable delay each time Excel recalculates formulas. You may experience such delays if:

- Your computer has eight megabytes of RAM or less.

- You're using a workbook that's very complex in nature, with hundreds of calculations or calculations that are long and complicated.

- Your workbook has numerous charts, based on worksheet data, that redraw on screen each time you change the data. (See "Create a Chart," p. 208, to learn about Excel's tools for charting your data.)

- Data on the current worksheet is linked to another worksheet or workbook, and you therefore want to control when calculation occurs.

- You're using Excel's Goal Seek feature to find the best answer to a particular problem that requires Excel to perform dozens of calculations.

In any of these cases, Excel's default automatic recalculation can cause you to have to wait while Excel updates formula results, charts, and the like on-screen. If you have 100 cell entries to change, you have to wait after making each change. You have better things to do!

> Excel's Goal Seek feature helps you look for a specific solution to a formula. When you use goal-seeking, you adjust the value of one cell to derive the value of another cell. Goal Seek is an advanced feature beyond the scope of this book.

Use the Calculation Tab in the Options Dialog Box

The Calculation tab in the Options dialog box in Excel enables you to prevent Excel from calculating automatically. You also can choose how Excel handles particular situations when it does recalculate.

The Calculation area of the Calculation tab enables you to specify whether or not calculation occurs automatically. Select the **Automatic** choice to return to automatic calculation, if you've been using another option. If you select the **Automatic Except Tables** option button, Excel automatically recalculates all workbook formulas except for Excel data tables. Click the **Manual** option to prevent Excel from calculating except when you tell it to calculate (more on this later in the task). When you select the **Manual** option, Excel enables the **Recalculate before Save** check box beneath it. Leave this box checked so that Excel recalculates the workbook anytime you save in addition to other manual recalculations you specify.

The next area of the Calculation tab enables you to control how many times Excel tries a calculation when performing a Goal Seek and when searching to resolve a *circular reference* (a formula that refers to part of itself, such as if you enter =sum(A1:A15) into cell A1). Select the **Iteration** check box to override Excel's defaults for these operations. Then, change the entry in the **Maximum Iterations** text box to set the total number of times Excel can try a given calculation. Alter the **Maximum Change** text box entry, if needed, to control the size of each iteration—that is, the maximum increment Excel can adjust a changing value by to try to resolve the calculation.

The Workbook Options area of the Calculation tab provides control over some miscellaneous calculation features, which are in effect whenever you click to place a check mark in the check box beside the feature:

- **Update Remote References** Excel always updates formulas that use information from other applications, such as when a formula includes a reference to a table of numbers in a Word document. If you want Excel to recalculate without affecting the Word document, deselect this option.

- **Precision as Displayed** At recalculation, truncates cell contents and formula results to

the number of decimal places called for by the present cell formatting.

- **1904 Date System** Use this option to have Excel calculate dates based on a 1/2/1904 starting date rather than the 1/1/1900 date that's typically used. Excel for the Mac uses the 1904 Date System. You need to select this option only if you are working with a workbook that is using the 1904 date system. If you are trading files with an Excel for the Mac user who has version 2.0 or later, both Excel for the Mac and Excel for Windows recognize the differences in the date systems and compensate accordingly by converting the dates in the worksheet to the appropriate default date system.

- **Save External Link Values** Causes Excel to save existing data from another document (worksheet or other application data) linked to the current workbook before recalculation.

Finally, two command buttons appear near the center of the Calculation tab. Click the **Calc Now** (F9) button to recalculate the current workbook at any time; as the button's name indicates, pressing the F9 key enables you to recalculate without opening the Options dialog box. Click the **Calc Sheet** button to recalculate the formulas on the current worksheet only.

Now that you understand all the calculation options available in Excel, take the Guided Tour for a look at how to find and choose them.

Begin Guided Tour Set Calculation Options

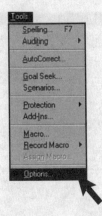

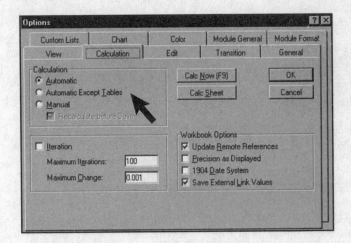

1 Open the **Tools** menu and choose **Options**. Excel's Options
dialog box appears.

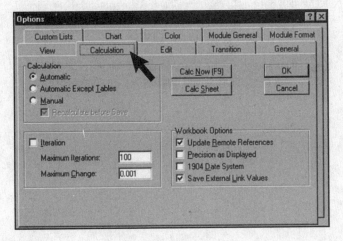

3 In the Calculation area of the dialog box, choose **Automatic**, **Automatic Except Tables**, or **Manual**. If you
choose **Manual**, use the **Recalculate before Save** check box
below it to specify whether you want Excel to recalculate formulas
before you save your workbook.

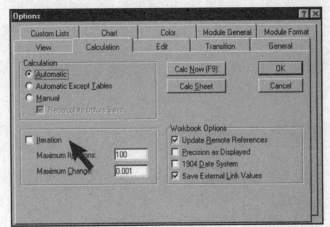

2 Click the **Calculation** tab to display its options.

4 To increase or reduce the amount of time Excel attempts to
solve a Goal Seek or circular reference, click to check the
Iteration check box. Then change the **Maximum Iterations** and
Maximum Change settings as needed.

(continues)

Guided Tour   Set Calculation Options

(continued)

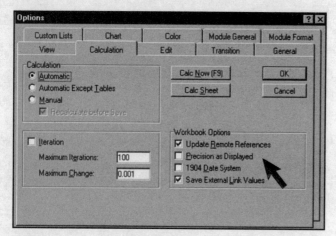

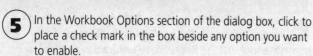

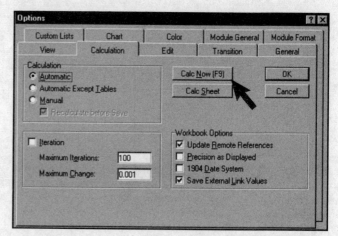

5 In the Workbook Options section of the dialog box, click to place a check mark in the box beside any option you want to enable.

6 To recalculate the entire workbook, click the **Calc Now** (F9) button. To calculate only the current worksheet, click the **Calc Sheet** button. In either case, Excel closes the Options dialog box and recalculates as specified.

7 If you didn't choose to recalculate in step 6, click **OK** to close the Options dialog box so the Calculation options you specified take effect.

Change Excel's Editing Settings

In the dawn of the spreadsheet era, users survived with little more than their wits and the primitive tools granted them by the software deities. With only their arrow keys to guide them, they traversed the barren cells and persevered in entering data using the time-honored, tedious methods handed down from generation to generation.

Now, users can rough it or choose to use all the modern conveniences in Excel. These conveniences include numerous features to speed your ability to enter and edit data, as well as to control what actions and warnings Excel issues in response to your edits.

As with the features you learned about in the previous two tasks, you control Excel's editing capabilities in the Options dialog box. In this case, the Edit tab of the dialog box offers eight different options for specifying editing shortcuts, messages, and more. In a nutshell, here are those options and what each does when it's enabled (checked):

- **Edit Directly in Cell** Enables you to edit cell contents in the cell by double-clicking the cell; otherwise, you have to perform the editing in the Formula bar.

- **Allow Cell Drag and Drop** Enables you to take advantage of drag and drop for moving and copying cell contents. When you enable this option, turn on the **Alert before Overwriting Cells** check box to ensure that Excel warns you to confirm that you want to move or copy information over existing information.

- **Move Selection after Enter** Use this option, and the accompanying **Direction** drop-down list, to control which direction the cell selector moves after you press Enter to complete a cell entry.

- **Fixed Decimal** Use this option if you want to have Excel automatically add the number of decimal places you specify in the accompanying **Places** text box. Entering a positive number of places moves the decimal point to the left, and a negative number of places moves the decimal to the right. Even if you use this option, you can enter a number with as many decimal places as you want simply by typing the decimal when you make the cell entry.

- **Cut, Copy, and Sort Objects with Cells** Includes inserted objects like charts along with the surrounding cells during operations like sorts, rather than leaving the object stationary and sorting only the surrounding cells. This feature may be useful when you sort a product database where each product (record) in the database has an object like a logo attached to it.

- **Ask to Update Automatic Links** Displays a message so you can confirm whether to update a link.

You can link information contained in two different files created in two different programs. When you make a change in the source file (the one where the information originated), you may or may not want to update the target file. This feature in Excel lets you decide how you want to handle linked data in workbooks.

- **Animate Insertion and Deletion** Shows you all the actions Excel takes when it executes an edit; only choose this option when you have memory (RAM) and time to burn.

- **Enable AutoComplete for Cell Values** Tells Excel to complete any text entry when the initial part of the entry matches a predefined AutoComplete list or Custom List in Excel.

The Guided Tour illustrates where to find the Edit options in Excel.

For more information about how the editing features covered in this task affect your real-world work in Excel, see "Enter Information," p. 40; "Fix a Mistake," p. 45; and "Move and Copy Information," p. 56.

For more information about how the editing features covered in this task affect your real-world work in Excel, see "Enter Information," p. 40; "Fix a Mistake," p. 45; and "Move and Copy Information," p. 56.

Begin Guided Tour   Change Editing Settings

1 Open the **Tools** menu and choose **Options**. Excel's Options dialog box appears.

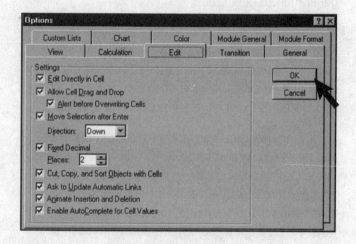

4 Click **OK** to close the Options dialog box. Your editing options take effect in Excel.

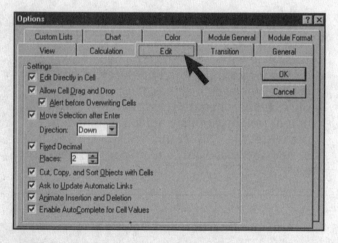

2 Click the **Edit** tab to display its options.

3 Choose the options you want. To enable an option, click in its check box so a check mark appears. To disable an option, click on the check box beside it to remove the check mark.

Set Up the General Options

You say toe-may-toe, I say toe-mah-toe. Each of us has preferences regarding seemingly small details in life. In reality, any detail that makes you more comfortable—no matter how small it is—can make you more efficient and productive in your work. Acknowledging your right to be the master of your own details, Excel enables you to adjust several miscellaneous aspects of how it works to increase your comfort level when working with Excel. For example, if you prefer that your cell entries always appear in a larger font to make them easier to read, you can change the default font size.

In the Options dialog box, the General tab offers you control over several details, most of them involving menus and files. You can change these options on the General tab:

- **Reference Style**   The choices here control how Excel names columns, rows, and cells. The **A1** choice causes Excel to use letters to label columns and numbers to label rows; cell addresses are a combination of the column letter and row number. Choosing **R1C1** means that Excel uses numbers to identify both columns and rows, so that each cell address becomes a combination of the row number and the column number.

- **Menus**   You can determine whether Excel's **File** menu includes the **Recently Used File List**. When this option is enabled, the File menu includes the names of the files that you've worked with most recently (usually two to four file names) near the bottom. To open a file, you simply click its name in the menu. Checking **Microsoft Excel 4.0 Menus** means that Excel displays the menus used in version 4.0 of Excel, which runs under Windows 3.1x. This choice can make it easier for you to become comfortable working with Excel for Windows 95.

- **Ignore Other Applications**   Check this option if you want to temporarily disable Dynamic Data

Exchange (DDE) links to documents from other applications. This ensures that you can make changes to your Excel workbook and other documents without updating the linked information, saving the time it normally takes to update links.

- **Prompt for File Properties**   When you check this option, Excel asks you to provide information (called *properties*) about a workbook file the first time you save it. For example, you can enter comments about a file, or keywords to describe a file. File properties provide more information about a file that can be useful when you're searching for the file using the Find file capabilities of the Open dialog box.

- **Reset TipWizard**   Enable this check box if you want the TipWizard to repeat tips you've previously viewed. You can control the display of the TipWizard bar using the TipWizard button on the Standard Toolbar.

- **Sheets in New Workbook**   Each time you use the **File**, **New** command or the **New** icon on the Standard toolbar, Excel opens a new, blank workbook file in its own window on-screen. By default, each new workbook has 16 worksheet pages, each identified by its own tab. To adjust the number of worksheets in a new workbook, type a new value beside this option on the General tab. You also can click the up arrow to increase the value or the down arrow to reduce the value.

> If you don't routinely use more than a few workbook pages, reduce the number of default workbook sheets. This makes your workbook files smaller, saving disk space. See "Create a New Workbook," p. 88, to learn more about creating and setting up new workbooks.

- **Standard Font/Size**   Each of these options offers a drop-down list of choices you can use to control the font and letter size Excel uses for entries you type. The font is the lettering style, and the size is measured in *points*, with each point equaling 1/72 of an inch. By default, Excel uses the Arial font in a 10-point size. If your worksheets typically involve only small values, and you want to make the worksheet easier to read, choose another font, like Times New Roman in a larger size like 12. On the other hand, if you learn through practice that most of your worksheets fit on one printed page if you use 9-point lettering, you can specify that size here.

- **Default File Location**   The *working folder* is where Excel assumes you store all your workbook files. So, when you open or save a new workbook, Excel displays this folder first in the Open or Save As dialog box. You can change the working folder by typing its full path and name into this text box. For example, if you have a folder called c:\budget and typically use Excel only to calculate budget information, enter **c:\budget** here so that Excel assumes you want to save files to that folder unless you tell it otherwise.

- **Alternate Startup File Location**   By default, any workbook files in the XLStart folder open automatically when you start Excel. If you want Excel to automatically open files from another folder, enter the full path and name for that folder here.

- **User Name**   As was mentioned earlier in this section, Excel stores file properties when you save a file. One of these properties is the name of the user who created the file. If you want to change the user name that Excel uses as a file property, type your changes in this text box.

Begin Guided Tour Set Up Options

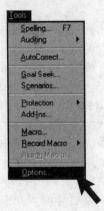

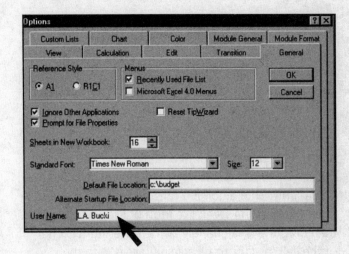

1 Open the **Tools** menu and choose **Options**. Excel's Options dialog box appears.

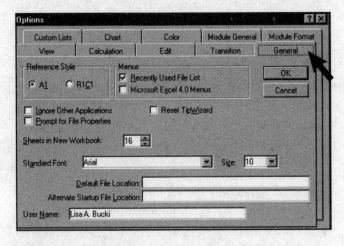

3 Choose the options you want, clicking check boxes or option buttons to enable features mentioned in the discussion. Enter your changes directly into options that offer text boxes.

4 Click **OK** to close the Options dialog box. The General options you specified take effect in Excel.

2 Click the **General** tab to display its options.

Create Custom AutoFill Lists

Data entry is a more hazardous business than you'd think. Not only does it cause your fingers to cramp up, but it also dramatically increases the likelihood of typos and the time that it takes you to finish your work and start to play.

Excel now offers the AutoFill feature, which automates data entry. "Enter Information," p. 40, introduced you to using AutoFill to enter *lists,* or series of similar entries, in adjoining cells. For example, if you enter a day of the week like Mon or Monday, you can then drag the small handle at the lower right corner of the cell selector to fill adjoining cells with the remaining days of the week (Tue or Tuesday in the second cell, Wed or Wednesday in the third cell, and so on). Selecting a range, using the **Edit Fill Series** command (for more, see "Work with Ranges," p. 50) and then choosing **AutoFill** also enables you to fill the range of cells with the subsequent days of the week.

In addition to day, date, and time AutoFill series, Excel also enables you to fill numerical series or even alphanumeric series that combine a pattern of similar entries Excel can recognize. For example, if you enter **Game 1** in a cell and use AutoFill to create entries for the next three cells, Excel enters **Game 2**, **Game 3**, and **Game 4,** respectively. AutoFill looks at the first entry and identifies the pattern you want it to follow to fill the adjoining cells.

The only lists that AutoFill can't work with are lists that are completely random and those that include entries that follow more than one pattern. In this newest version of Excel, AutoFill offers the smarts to handle these kinds of lists in another way. You can save highly specialized lists as *custom lists* that AutoFill can automatically recall.

For example, suppose you have a list you use often that's completely random, such as the social security

numbers of your family members or the names of the teams in your volleyball league. There's no way that Excel can take the name Spikers and fill the next three cells with Setters, Servers, and Diggers. Or, say you coach a little league team where the kids each pick a jersey number so you have a roster consisting of Jones 26, Smith 00, Thomas 32, and Miller 99. A million monkeys with a million typewriters would take a million years to come up with that combination, so it's no wonder Excel can't figure it out!

To enable AutoFill to deal with a unique list, you need to save that list as a custom AutoFill list. Then, when you enter a list item into a cell using AutoFill, it fills the adjoining cells with the custom list entries, in the exact order you entered them.

You create a custom list using the Custom Lists tab in the Options dialog box. You can type the list entries directly into this tab, or use entries that you've already typed into cells in a worksheet. No matter which method you use to create the list, keep these guidelines in mind:

- Excel saves only the list items you enter. For example, say you create a list that contains AA01, AB02, AC03, and AD04. If you AutoFill that list to eight adjoining cells on the worksheet, it does not extend the series and create new entries like AE05. Instead, in the fifth cell, it begins repeating the list, starting with the first item, AA01.

- The lists are not case-sensitive. For example, if you create the same custom list mentioned in the last item (AA01, AB02, AC03, and AD04), AutoFill completes the series when you enter either **aa01**, **Aa01**, or **AA01**. AutoFill simply matches the capitalization you used for your first entry.

• AutoFill works whether you enter the first custom list item or any other item in the list into a worksheet cell. Using the example list again (AA01, AB02, AC03, and AD04), you enter **AC03** into a cell. Then, if you use AutoFill to make entries in the next three cells, those entries are AD04, AA01, and AB02, in that order. Excel simply continues the list from the starting point you designate and repeats the earlier entries when needed.

The Guided Tour shows you both methods for creating a custom AutoFill list, as well as explaining how to edit a list and remove one you no longer need.

> After AutoFill enters your custom list in a worksheet, you may need to format the list cells. To learn how to change the font, alignment, number formatting and more, refer to "Format Worksheets," p. 99.

Begin Guided Tour   Create an AutoFill List

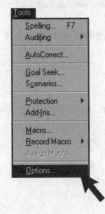

1 Open the **Tools** menu and choose **Options**. The Options dialog box appears.

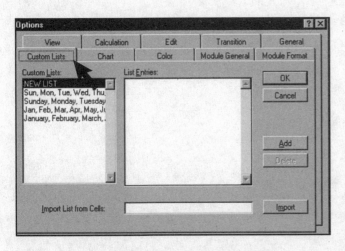

2 If needed, click the **Custom Lists** tab to display its options. Make sure **NEW LIST** is selected (highlighted) in the Custom Lists list box.

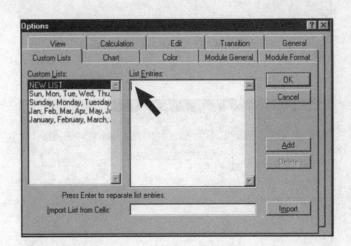

3 Click in the **List Entries** text box to position the insertion point there.

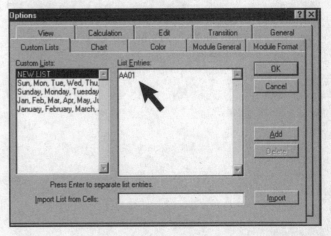

4 Type the first entry for your custom list and press **Enter**.

(continues)

Guided Tour Create an AutoFill List   *(continued)*

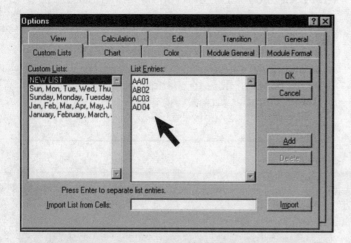

5 Type the remaining list entries, pressing **Enter** after each one.

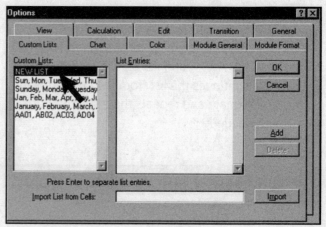

7 **(Optional)** To create additional lists, click **NEW LIST** to select it and use steps 4 through 7 for each list you want to create.

8 When you finish creating all the custom lists you want, click **OK** to close the Options dialog box.

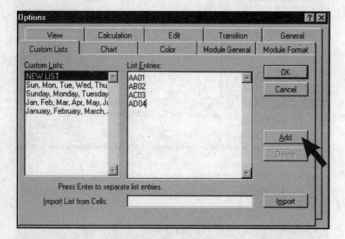

6 Click the **Add** button to add the new list to the choices in the Custom Lists list box.

Begin Guided Tour   Use Cell Entries to Make an AutoFill List

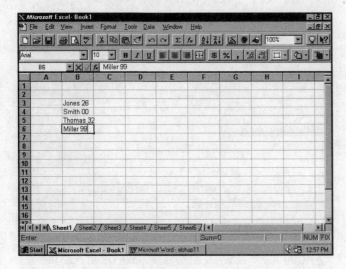

1 In the current worksheet, type the cell entries you want to save as a custom AutoFill list.

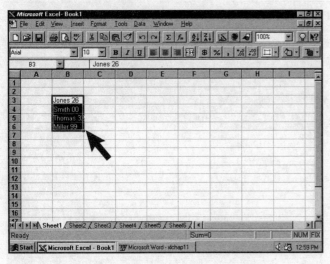

2 Select all the list entries by dragging over them.

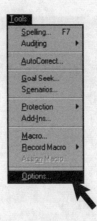

3 Open the **Tools** menu and choose **Options**. The Options dialog box appears.

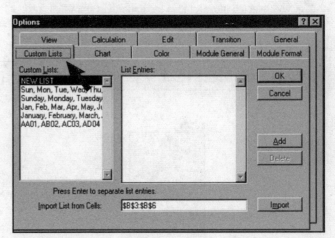

4 If needed, click the **Custom Lists** tab to display its options.

(continues)

Guided Tour Use Cell Entries to Make an AutoFill List

(continued)

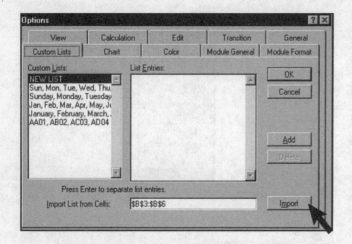

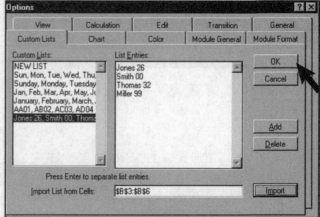

5 Click the **Import** button to place the entries from the cells you selected (now listed in the Import List from Cells text box) in both the **Custom Lists** and **List Entries** list boxes.

6 The new custom list is complete. Click **OK** to close the Options dialog box.

Begin Guided Tour Make Changes to a Custom List

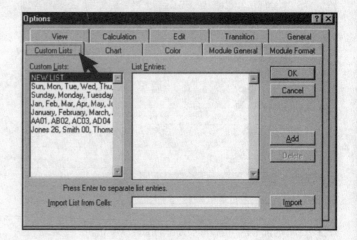

1 Open the **Tools** menu and choose **Options**. The Options dialog box appears.

2 If needed, click the **Custom Lists** tab to display its options.

Guided Tour   Make Changes to a Custom List

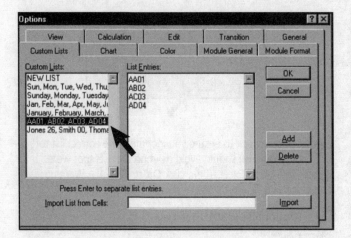

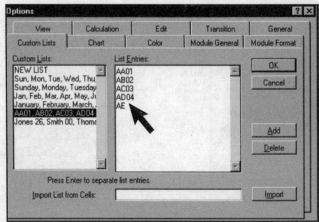

3 In the Custom Lists list box, click on the list to which you want to make changes.

4 Click in the **List Entries** text box to position the insertion point there. Make the edits you choose. For example, to add a new list entry click just to the right of the last list entry, press **Enter** and type the new entry.

5 **(Optional)** When you finish editing the list, you can click **Add** and use steps 3 and 4 to edit another list.

6 When you finish editing, click **OK** to close the Options dialog box.

Begin Guided Tour   Delete a Custom List

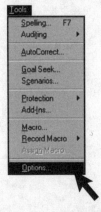

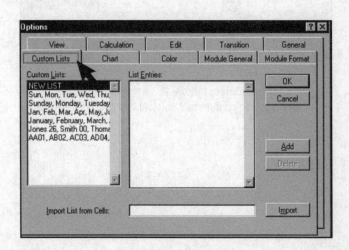

1 Open the **Tools** menu and choose **Options**. The Options dialog box appears.

2 If needed, click the **Custom Lists** tab to display its options.

(continues)

Guided Tour Delete a Custom List

(continued)

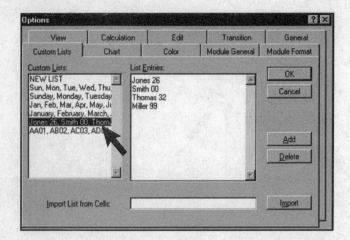

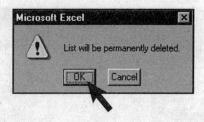

5 Double-check to ensure you identified the correct list for deletion. You should avoid deleting the lists that were already defined by Excel. Then, click **OK** to close the Warning dialog box and delete the list.

6 **(Optional)** Use steps 3 through 5 to delete other lists as you wish.

3 In the Custom Lists list box, click on the list you'd like to delete.

7 Click **OK** again to close the Options dialog box.

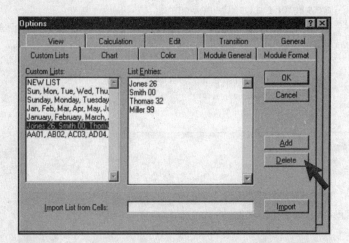

4 Click on the **Delete** button. A warning dialog box appears, asking you to confirm that you want to permanently delete the list.

Set Up the Colors in a Workbook

Kids engage in an annual back-to-school ritual of choosing just the right school supplies. Everything has to be just the right color; otherwise, doing homework just isn't possible. If you feel the same way about the colors in your workbook, then this is the task for you!

It's nice—and practical—for adults to be able to choose the colors in the workbook. As you may already have learned, Excel offers you a palette of 56 colors. You use the colors in the palette to format cell entries, cell backgrounds, elements of charts, and more. The palette also controls which colors Excel applies by default to certain elements until you format them otherwise. For example, the palette defines eight default fill colors for chart series. When you create a chart, Excel colors the first series with the first fill color, the second series with the second fill color, and so on.

Using the Color tab of the Options dialog box, you can change the palette for a workbook, adjusting the colors it offers and the brightness and tone of those colors. You can change as many of the colors on the palette as you wish. Excel automatically reformats any existing workbook elements affected by a change in a particular color. To continue with the example just discussed, if your worksheet contains a chart, and you change the first fill color or hue in the workbook color palette, Excel changes the color of the first chart series using the new palette color. After you change the palette, you should save your workbook to ensure Excel saves the palette changes.

So, why would you want to change the palette colors (other than to make your workbook more appealing on-screen)? Here are just a few examples:

- You want to change the colors you use for particular chart elements.

- A particular color is too light to be legible when it prints, so you want to eliminate it from the palette and use another one.

- You have a color printer, and you want to change the colors you typically use in a workbook.

- You've formatted entries on several workbook sheets with a particular color, and you want to change that text globally. Changing it via the palette saves you the trouble of selecting each sheet, selecting the cells containing the entries, and then changing the font color.

You use the Color tab in the Options dialog box to change the colors for a workbook. Excel even streamlines the process of creating and using color palettes. Once you create a palette for a workbook, you can automatically copy the colors from that palette to any other workbook. You can even reset palette colors simply by clicking a command button in the tab. The Guided Tour for this task walks you through the ins and outs of changing and copying workbook color palettes.

The formatting toolbar's Color and Font palettes immediately display your changes to the workbook palette so you can put the new colors to work. For more on these toolbar buttons, see "Change and Enhance Fonts," p. 109, and "Shade Cells," p. 115.

Begin Guided Tour   Change a Workbook's Colors

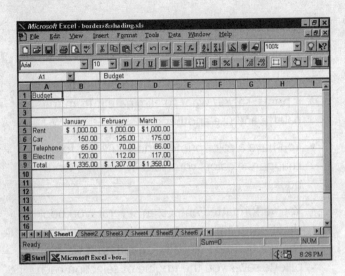

1 Open or select the workbook that contains the color palette you want to change. Or, create a new workbook, enter the data for it, and save it. (See "Manage Workbooks and Worksheets," p. 81.) If you want to see the effects of changing the color palette as you follow these steps, apply a color to some cells in your worksheet. The sample figure shows cells colored in the yellow you find in the top row of the palette.

2 Open the **Tools** menu and click **Options**. The Options dialog box appears.

3 Click the **Color** tab to select it. The tab offers four separate groups of colors. The first three include colors that you may automatically assign to workbook elements. The last, Other Colors, offers colors available for manual color formatting.

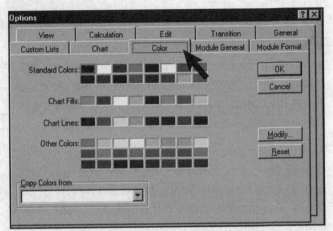

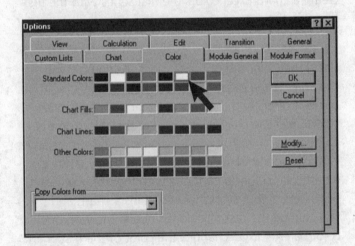

4 To change a color, double-click on it, or click it and then click the **Modify** button. If you applied color in step 1, make sure you choose that color to change. The Color Picker dialog box appears.

Guided Tour   Change a Workbook's Colors

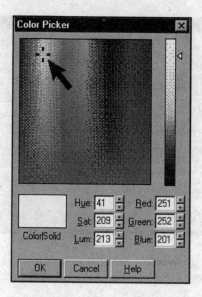

5 Click in the picker area to choose a new color.

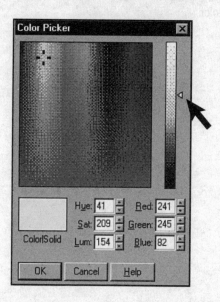

6 To adjust the brightness of the color you've chosen, drag the arrowhead along the intensity bar at the right side of the Color Picker dialog box. Dragging up makes the color lighter; dragging down darkens it.

7 Click **OK** to close the Color Picker dialog box and make the color change take effect.

8 Repeat steps 4 through 7 to change other colors in the palette.

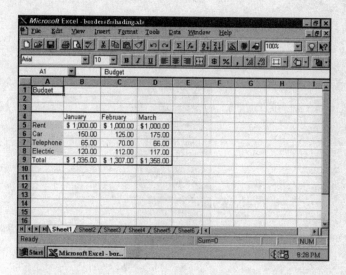

9 Click **OK** to close the Options dialog box after you change all the palette colors you wish. If you had applied the color you changed to elements in the worksheet, you see the effects of the color change, which may not be apparent in the black and white figure.

10 Click the **Save** button on the Standard toolbar to save your workbook and its palette changes. You can now use any of the new colors you specified in the palette to format elements in the workbook.

Begin Guided Tour   Choose the Default Color Palette

1 Open or select the workbook that contains the color palette you want to change back to the default colors.

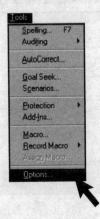

2 Open the **Tools** menu and click **Options**. The Options dialog box appears.

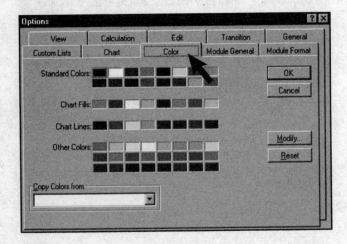

3 If needed, click the **Color** tab to select it.

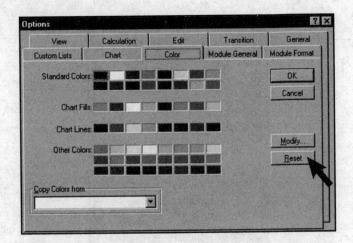

4 Click the **Reset** button. Excel reverts any colors you changed to their original shade, brightness, and so on.

5 Click **OK** to close the Options dialog box. Excel resets the color palette. Excel returns any worksheet items that you formatted with a custom color to the corresponding default color.

Begin Guided Tour Copy the Colors from One Workbook to Another

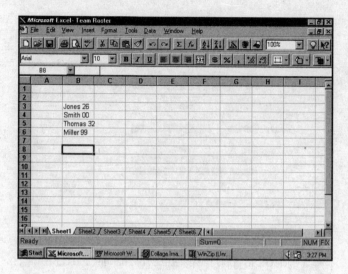

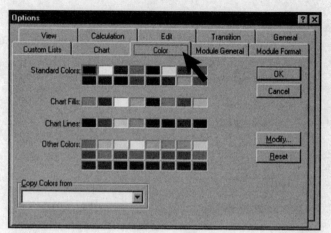

④ Click the **Color** tab to select it.

1 Open the workbook that contains the color palette you want to copy.

2 Open or select the workbook to which you want to copy the color palette.

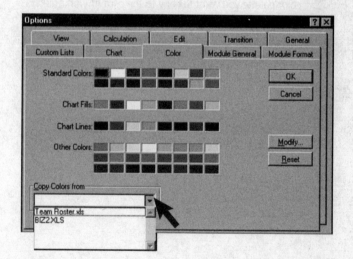

5 Click the down arrow on the **Copy Colors from** drop-down list to display its list. The list shows open workbooks (other than the one to which you're copying the palette). You can copy the color palette from any of the workbooks that appear in the list.

3 Open the **Tools** menu and click **Options**. The Options dialog box appears.

(continues)

Copy the Colors from One Workbook to Another *(continued)*

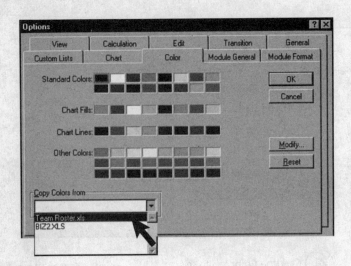

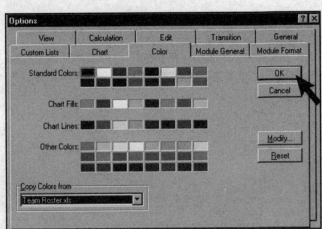

6 In the Copy Colors from list, click the workbook with the color palette you want to copy to the current workbook. The list closes, and the workbook you clicked appears in the Copy Colors from text box.

7 Click **OK** to apply the palette color changes and close the Options dialog box.

PART 2

Do It Yourself

"If you want something done right, you have to do it yourself." How many times have you muttered those words when something's gone wrong? The reality is that you very often need to "do it yourself" to accomplish a task. This part of *The Big Basics Book of Excel for Windows 95* shows you how to put the techniques you learned in Part 1 to work.

This part teaches you how to create more than 40 projects in Excel. These projects are geared not only to reinforce Excel skills that will help you work more efficiently, but also to enable you to build a portfolio of useful workbooks that you can use and modify over and over. Some of the tasks you'll learn here are more technical and practical, such as learning how to create an Excel macro or build a workbook to track an investment. Other projects will spur your creativity, introducing you to new ways to use Excel, such as for tracking your family schedule or creating math flash cards.

What You Will Find in This Part

DO IT YOURSELF

Improve Your Working Environment

Excel's awesome flexibility has helped it rise to the top of the spreadsheet program heap. In fact, the program offers more features than most users ever bother to try or learn. This section calls some of these features to your attention.

We've selected some Excel features you can use to streamline your work in Excel. You'll learn how to automate printing features using reports, supplement the Excel Help system with your own notes, and more. If you have spare time to experiment, and you prefer to work smarter, not harder, check out these Do It Yourself projects:

What You Will Find in This Section

Make Your Own Notes in Help

Computer monitors are great holders for sticky notes. That plastic edging around the monitor fills up faster with reminders of which function key is the shortcut for what; the exact menu and command you choose to do X, Y, or Z; and the secret ingredient for your Texas chili. (Well, maybe not that last one.) But what's a poor user to do when a reminder is too long to fit on a sticky note?

Excel offers its online Help system, but you can't add your own notes to it—or can you? Of course you can! It's simply a little-known fact. Adding your own personal comments to most Help topics is almost as easy as jotting down a sticky note and slapping it on your monitor.

Annotations provide you the opportunity to customize and expand the amount of online Help available in Excel. Even better, you can copy information from Excel or from another application and paste it in as an annotation. The annotations you create are limited only by your imagination and can help reduce your sticky note budget. The only Help topics you can't annotate are those that offer interactive illustrations rather than text, or those that are handled by the Answer Wizard. Although you'll probably find many situations where Help annotations are useful, here are a few ideas to get you started:

- You finally figure out how to use a particular function in a formula (and actually get that formula to work!). You can copy the function from the workbook and paste it into Help as an annotation. Then, when you need to use that function again, your example is there along with the Help Excel provides.

- You contact technical support or get help from a pal because you're having trouble working with a particular feature. Rather than writing the solution down on paper and risking misplacing

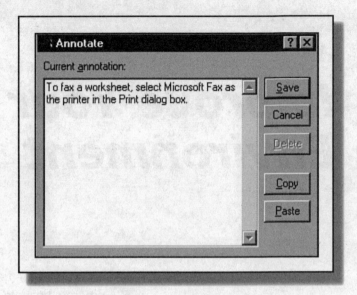

it, you can create an annotation to ensure it's available when you need it.

- You've found a document on the Internet, CompuServe, or another online service that gives you some great ideas and examples for using a feature. You can copy that information from the document file and paste it into Excel as a Help annotation.

Annotated Help topics contain a small green paper clip icon, usually located beside the Help topic title, to indicate there's a note "clipped" to the topic. You select the paper clip icon to read the annotation. The Do It Yourself steps explain how to add and work with annotations in Excel.

Even though you may be quite comfortable with using Help in Windows programs, if you need a refresher see "Get Help Performing a Task," p. 26, and "Get Help on Menu Commands and Dialog Box Choices," p. 27.

Begin Do It Yourself   Annotate a Help Topic

1 If you want to copy information from Excel or another application document, select the information and copy it to the Clipboard by choosing **Edit**, **Copy** or clicking the **Copy** button on the toolbar.

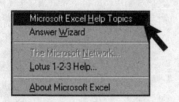

2 Open the **Help** menu and click **Microsoft Excel Help Topics**. The Help Topics: Microsoft Excel window appears on-screen.

3 Navigate through the Help System to find the topic you want. Double-clicking closed book icons displays additional book icons or lists of Help topics indicated by question mark document icons.

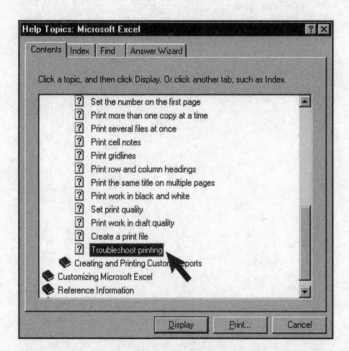

4 When you see the topic you want to annotate, double-click it. The window for the Help topic appears on-screen.

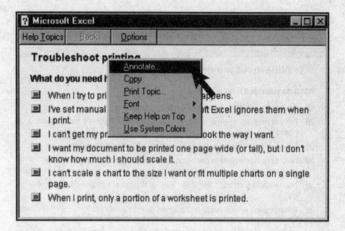

5 Right-click on the topic to display its shortcut menu, or click the **Options** button near the top of the Help topic window. Click **Annotate** in either menu. The Annotate dialog box appears.

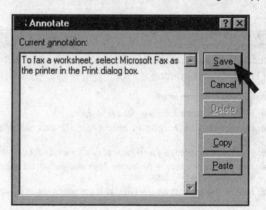

6 Type your notes in the **Current annotation** text box. If you copied information in step 1, click in the text box and then click **Paste**. Click **Save**. The Annotate window closes, and the paper clip icon appears in the topic.

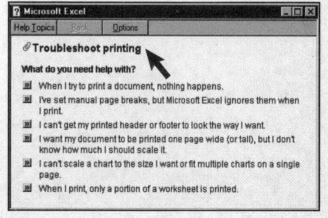

7 Click the **Close** button for the Help topic window to close the Help topic you've annotated.

Begin Do It Yourself Read a Help Annotation

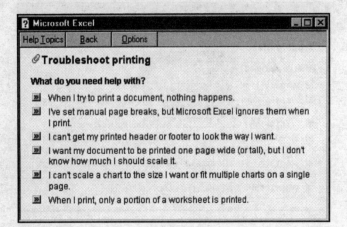

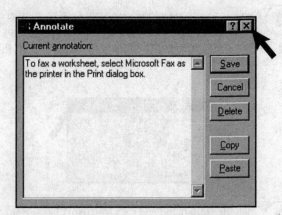

(1) Navigate through the Help system to display the Help topic with the annotation (it's the one with the paper clip icon).

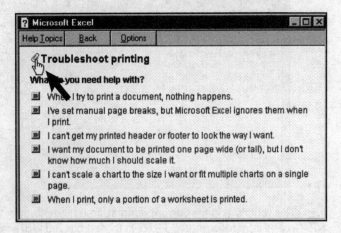

(2) Move the mouse pointer over the paper clip icon for the annotation until the pointer turns to a hand.

(3) Click the paper clip icon. The Annotate dialog box opens so you can view the annotation.

(4) After you finish reading the annotation, click the **Cancel** button or the Annotate dialog box's **Close** button.

(5) Click the **Close** button for the Help topic window.

Begin Do It Yourself Edit or Copy an Annotation

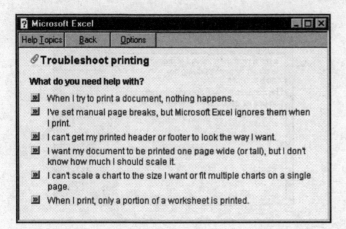

1 Navigate through the Help system to display the Help topic with the annotation.

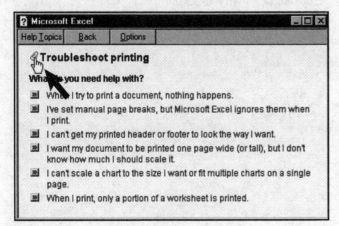

2 Move the mouse pointer over the paper clip icon for the annotation until the pointer turns to a hand.

3 Click the paper clip icon. The Annotate window opens so you can view the annotation.

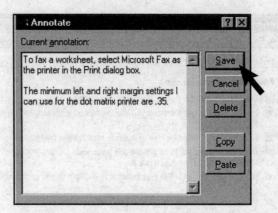

4 Click in the **Current annotation** text box, type your changes, and click **Save**. Or, to copy information from the annotation to paste into a document, select the annotation information and click **Copy**. Close the Annotate dialog box.

5 Click the **Close** button for the Help topic window to close the Help topic you've annotated.

6 If you copied information from the annotation, click to select the location where you want to paste the information and then choose **Edit**, **Paste** or click the **Paste** button on the toolbar.

You can paste this information into any application because it's plain text.

Begin Do It Yourself Delete an Annotation

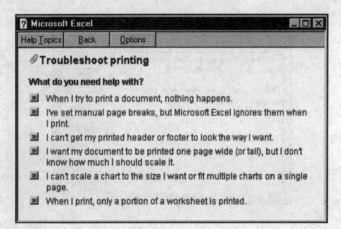

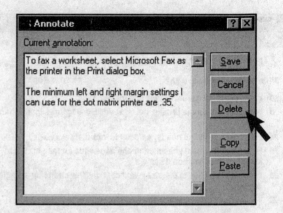

1 Navigate through the Help system to display the Help topic with the annotation.

4 Click **Delete**. Excel removes the annotation and the paper clip icon, and closes the Annotate dialog box.

5 Click the **Close** button for the Help topic window to remove it from your screen.

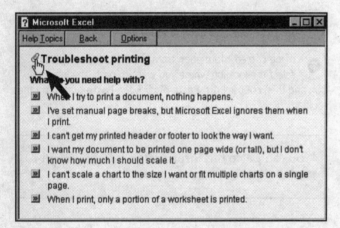

2 Move the mouse pointer over the paper clip icon for the annotation until the pointer turns to a hand.

3 Click the paper clip icon. The Annotate dialog box opens so you can view the annotation.

Create and Use File Properties

If you have a drawer full of socks and each pair is a different color, it's relatively easy to find the pair you want. But pulling the right pair out of a drawer full of black and navy dress socks provides a larger challenge because it's harder to grab the right pair with only a quick glance.

Similarly, searching for a workbook file among a folder full of files with nothing but the names to guide you can take some time. Even though Windows 95 enables you to use long file names of up to 85 characters, file names alone may not give you the information you need to find a file when you need it.

In Excel, you create *file properties* to store more descriptive information about the workbook file. Properties can help individual users find files; the Open dialog box enables you to search for a file based on a property and the information you've entered for that property. Properties also can be important if you're sharing your files with other users. For example, if you open a workbook file and have a question about it, but you can't remember who you got it from, you can check the properties to find out who the file's author is.

Excel automatically stores some of the properties for the file, including the file's creation date, its last opened and modified dates, and its author. You can create the rest of the properties, adding such items as a title, subject, keywords, and comments. This version even enables you to create custom file properties. For example, if you're working with a workbook related to a certain project, you can create a custom date property to record the completion date for the project.

You create the properties using the workbook's Properties dialog box. This dialog box offers five different tabs:

- **General**   Offers options stored by Excel, such as the file's long name and DOS file name, the

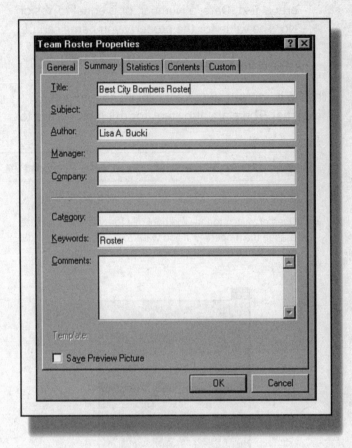

type and size of the file, creation and modification dates, and the attributes assigned to the file. File attributes include Read Only (so no one can edit the file), Archive, Hidden, and System.

- **Summary**   Offers numerous text boxes into which you enter information. For example, you can enter a workbook title and subject, manager and company names, comments, keywords, and a category for the workbook.

- **Statistics**   On this tab, Excel tells you when the file was last created, accessed, modified, or printed. It records who last saved a file, a file revision number (if any), and the total time spent editing the file.

- **Contents**   Lists the name of each worksheet, from the worksheet tab, in the workbook.

• **Custom** Enables you to create a property using several suggested property names or the name you specify. You can specify whether the property is Text, Date, a Number, or is equal to Yes or No. The value for the property you name can be text you typed or the contents of a cell you've copied from the workbook.

The Do It Yourself steps here explain how to enter properties. There are also steps for using properties to

find a particular workbook file when you want to open it.

This task assumes that you're comfortable with the basic techniques for opening files. If you need a refresher, see "Open an Existing Workbook," p. 89.

Begin Do It Yourself Edit File Properties

1 Open or switch to the workbook file for which you want to change the properties. If you want to create a property that relates to the contents of a cell, copy those contents.

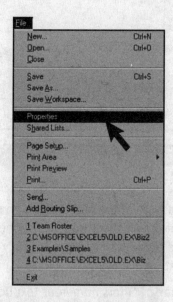

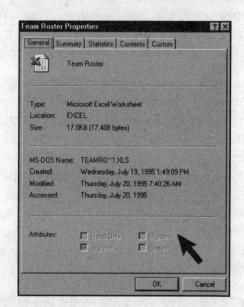

3 While this tab doesn't enable you to create any properties, it does provide useful properties you can view and use when trying to find the file.

2 Open the **File** menu and click **Properties**. The Properties dialog box appears. Click on the General tab to bring it to the front, if necessary.

Do It Yourself Edit File Properties

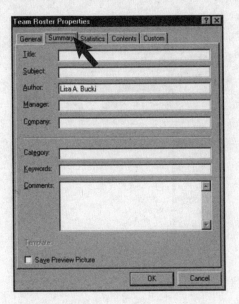

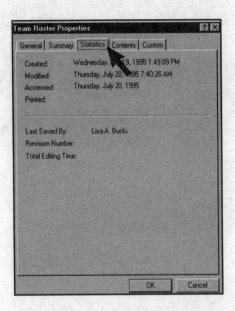

4 Click the **Summary** tab to display its options.

7 Click the **Statistics** tab to view the information it offers. This tab is similar to the General tab—it doesn't enable you to create any properties, but it does provide useful properties you can view and use when trying to find the file.

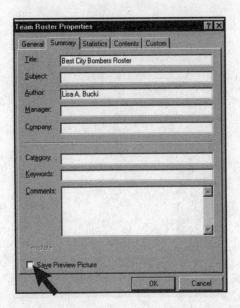

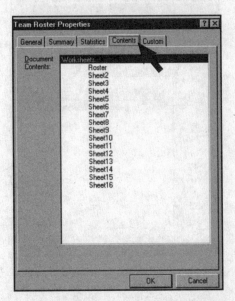

5 To create or edit a property, click in the text box for the property and type or edit the text (the *value* for the property). Repeat this process for as many properties as you wish to change on the tab.

6 If you want to be able to quickly preview the worksheet in dialog boxes that offer preview pictures, click to check the **Save Preview Picture** check box.

8 Click the **Contents** tab to display a list of the worksheets in the current workbook. This list enables you to get an overall view of the overall positioning of information in the workbook.

(continues)

294 DO IT YOURSELF ...Improve Your Working Environment

Do It Yourself Edit File Properties *(continued)*

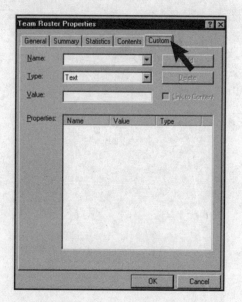

9 Click the **Custom** tab. This tab enables you to create as many custom properties as you wish, as described in the next few steps.

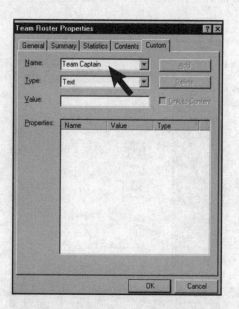

10 Specify a **Name** for the property. You can type a name in the text box. Or click the down arrow beside the box to display a list of suggested properties and click a property name.

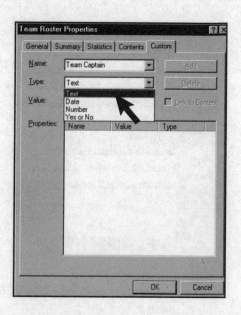

11 Specify the **Type** of property, if needed, by clicking the drop-down list arrow and clicking the type you want.

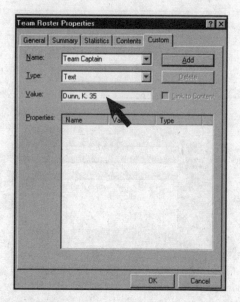

12 Type the contents in the **Value** text box. If you copied a cell in step 1, right-click the text box and choose **Paste**; clicking **Link to Contents** tells Excel to update the property when the cell changes.

13 Click the **Add** button to add the new property to the Properties list.

Do It Yourself   Edit File Properties

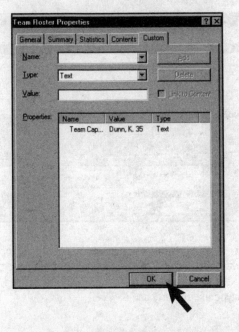

14 Repeat steps 10 through 13 to create other properties. Or, to edit existing custom properties, click the property in the Properties list and use steps 10 through 13, changing rather than creating the entries.

15 Click **OK** to finish creating properties and close the worksheet Properties dialog box.

Begin Do It Yourself   Find a File Using Properties

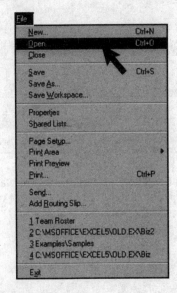

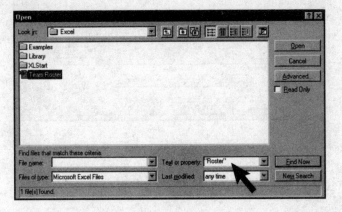

1 Open the **File** menu and choose **Open**. The Open dialog box appears on-screen. Or, click the **Open** button on the Standard toolbar.

2 If you are searching for a file based on one property, type the property's contents, in quotation marks, in the Text or property text box. Then go to step 12 to finish.

3 To search for a file with property contents matching two or more properties, click the **Advanced** button. The Advanced Find dialog box appears.

(continues)

Do It Yourself   Find a File Using Properties *(continued)*

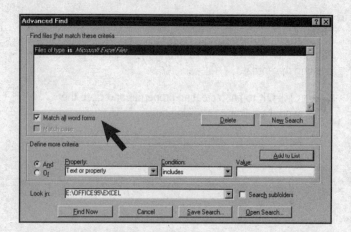

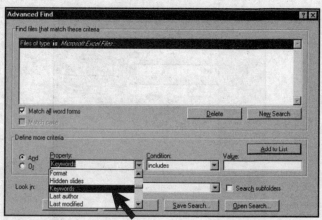

4 **(Optional)** Click to choose **Match all word forms** (returns *working*, *works*, etc. when you enter *work*) or **Match case**.

6 In the Property text box, type the name of the property you want to search for or select a property from the drop-down list. If you're searching for a custom property you created, you have to type the property name.

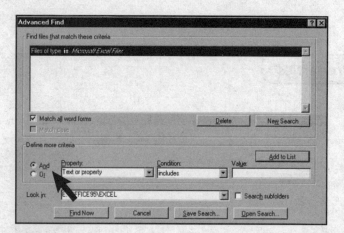

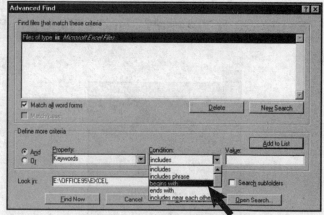

5 In the Define more criteria area, choose **And** if you want the search to return files that must match the property you're adding or **Or** to return files that match the property you're specifying or any other properties you've specified.

7 Specify a **Condition**, such as whether you want Excel to return only entries that begin with the exact value you specify in the next step.

> **Do It Yourself** Find a File Using Properties

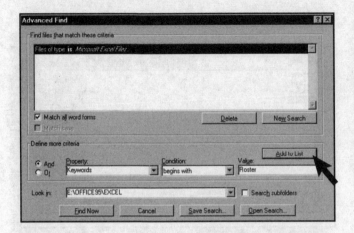

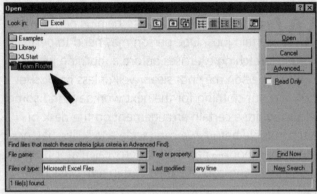

8 Type the **Value** (contents) of the property for which you want Excel to search. You do not need to enclose the value in quotation marks in this instance.

9 Click the **Add to List** button to add the criteria you just created to the Find files that match these criteria list box.

10 Repeat steps 5 through 9 if needed to specify additional criteria (specific matching properties) for Excel to find.

11 Specify any other options for the search, such as whether you want Excel to look in a particular folder for the workbook file.

13 If Excel finds more than one file that matches your properties, click on the name of the file you want in the files list.

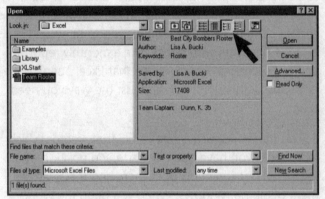

14 Click the **Properties** button in the open dialog box to view a list of the properties for the file to review them, if needed. Then click **Open** to open the workbook file and close the dialog box.

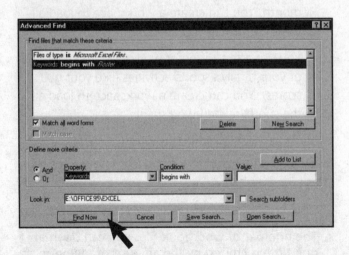

12 Click the **Find Now** button. Excel searches for the workbook file(s) using the properties you specified. When it finds matching files, it highlights them and displays them in the Open dialog box.

Create a Custom Workspace

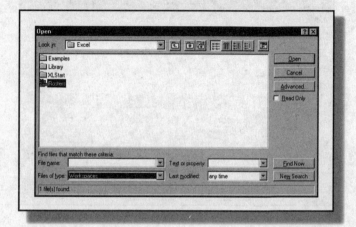

We all rely on little rituals to help us perform certain jobs. One person may need to perform certain stretching exercises before a morning job. Another person may not sleep well unless he or she first lays out clothing for the next workday. And some of us require a certain arrangement on the desk or kitchen table before we can tackle a task like balancing a checkbook—paperwork here, calculator there, and a steaming cup of coffee within arm's reach.

You may find you have a ritual when you work with Excel; for example, you open certain workbook files in a certain order and arrange them in a certain way. ("Manage Workbooks and Worksheets," p. 81, sheds some light on opening, closing, and arranging workbooks.) If you do have an Excel ritual, or if you have a certain periodic task that requires you to open and arrange the same workbooks (like a monthly report), you can save your *workspace* so that Excel opens and positions all the workbook files just the way you need them.

Saving the workspace creates a file that records which workbooks you have open, the size and position of each workbook window on-screen, and the arrangement of all the windows. When you open the workspace file, Excel opens each of the workbooks it keeps track of and positions them perfectly so you can move on to your work. The obvious advantage here is that you can open a single workspace file rather than having to go through all the steps of opening and positioning several workbooks on-screen.

Even better, if you save the workspace file to Excel's startup folder, which is called XLSTART and is located in the main Excel folder, Excel automatically opens that workspace when it starts. The only file that has to be in the XLSTART folder is the workspace file, not the workbook files it tracks.

Here are just a few examples where workbooks come in handy:

- You're responsible for updating two daily sales

reports and e-mailing them to others by 10 a.m. You can set up a workspace that loads these workbooks when you start Excel, so you'll be reminded each morning of this priority task.

- You create the "Budget without Pain" (p. 419), "Discover Your Net Worth" (p. 374), and "Check Your Checking" (p. 384) projects later in this section, and generally use them all when you're paying your bills a couple of times a month. You can create a workspace to load all these files when you need them.

- You use a few different workbooks to keep track of your family's sports activities (like your golf scores). You can create a workspace to load all the sports-related worksheets.

Forge ahead to the Do It Yourself steps when you're ready to create a workspace and learn how to open it later.

The number of workbook files you can open at one time is limited by the amount of memory on your computer. If you have 12M of memory or less, Excel may limit you to only a few workbooks in a workspace.

Begin Do It Yourself   Save a Workspace

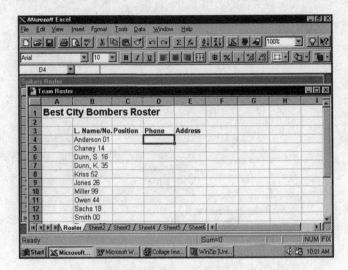

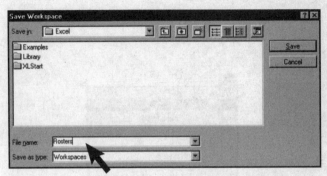

④ Type a name for the workspace file in the File name text box.

⑤ Click the **Save** button to save the workspace.

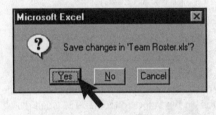

⑥ If the workspace contains any files with changes you haven't saved, Excel displays a dialog box asking whether you want to save those changes to the individual workbook file (not to the workspace file). Click **Yes**. Excel finishes saving the workspace.

⑦ When you're finished working with the workbooks, you must close each workbook window individually by using the **File**, **Close** command or by clicking the **Close** button on the workbook window.

① Open and arrange any workbooks you want to save as a workspace. For example, you can open two or more worksheets and cascade them on-screen.

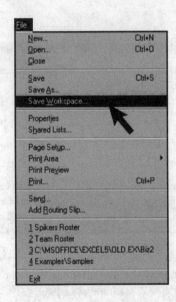

② Open the **File** menu and choose **Save Workspace**. The Save Workspace dialog box appears.

③ Navigate to the folder where you want to save the workspace file. If you want the workspace to load automatically each time you start Excel, choose the **XLSTART** folder within the Excel folder.

Begin Do It Yourself Open a Workspace

1 Start Excel.

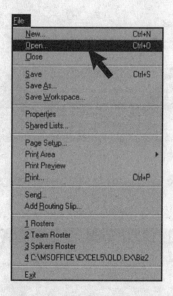

2 Open the **File** menu and click **Open**. Or, click the **Open** button on the Standard toolbar. The Open dialog box appears.

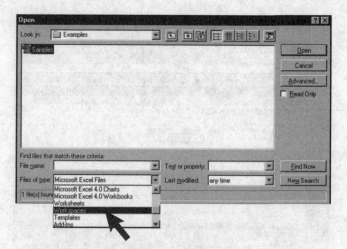

3 **(Optional)** To show only workspace files in the file list, open the **Files of type** drop-down list and click **Workspaces**.

4 Navigate to the folder that holds the roster file you want to open.

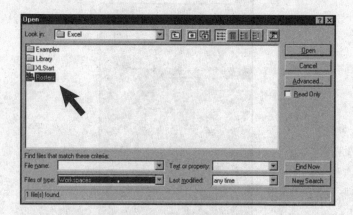

5 The file list shows the roster files. Notice the workspace icon that appears to the left of the file. Double-click on the workspace file name to open the workspace, or click the file name and click **Open**.

Customize the Excel Toolbars

No matter how high the quality of a tool, it isn't worth a darn unless it's the right tool for the job. If you've ever tried to use a metric socket wrench to free up a standard-sized nut or have tried to slice an apple with a butter knife, you're familiar with this problem.

Although Excel offers eight toolbars, there's no guarantee that any of them offer the right tools for every job. True, you can display all the toolbars at once to have the tools you need at your disposal, but then you're left with only a few square inches of space to display the current worksheet. Anticipating that you'd be less than pleased with such an arrangement, the makers of Excel built in the capability for you to customize toolbars and even create new ones.

On any toolbar, you can change the order in which buttons appear. You can also add and delete buttons on any toolbar. Let's say you don't use the Map tool on the Standard toolbar. Get rid of it and use that space for another tool you do use frequently. Further, you can create and name unique toolbars for highly specialized operations. If you use Excel to create database lists, you could create your own data management toolbar.

Excel offers several categories of buttons you can add to any toolbar. These categories offer all the tools from the existing Excel toolbars plus other tools that you may want to explore using:

- **File** Buttons for working with files, including operations such as automatically mailing a workbook, changing a workbook between read-only and write-enabled, and finding a workbook file.

- **Edit** Includes the common editing tools (Cut, Copy, and so on) along with tools for clearing selection contents only, inserting and deleting selected rows and columns, and more.

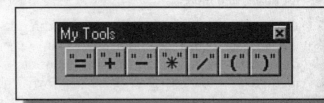

- **Formula** Offers formula tools like the Sum tool and others for inserting math operators in the formula bar as you build a formula.

- **Formatting** Buttons for adding borders, shading, styles, and more to cells.

- **Text Formatting** Tools for formatting cell contents, such as text font, style, color, and alignment.

- **Drawing** Provides all the tools you need to create drawings in Excel.

- **Macro** Not only provides tools for recording and editing macros, but also offers customization tools that insert Visual Basic modules, enable you to edit the workbook menus, and more.

- **Charting** The tools from the Chart toolbar for creating and working with charts.

- **Utility** Your grab bag of tools, including ones for switching quickly to other applications, working with scenarios, sorting, calculating, and so on.

- **Data** Tools for working with pivot tables, filtering, and more.

- **TipWizard** For adding the TipWizard button or display box.

- **Auditing** Buttons for managing workbook auditing functions such as tracer arrows, as well as tools for adding cell notes and showing the info window.

- **Forms** Offers the tools from the Forms toolbar, which enables you to create interactive workbooks with command buttons, option buttons, list boxes, and more.

- **Custom** Offers button graphics that you can use to create toolbar tools from macros you create. You'll learn how to create these kinds of macro tools in the task called "Build Your Own Macro Button," p. 332.

To get a handle on changing the buttons on a toolbar and creating and deleting your own toolbars, tackle

the Do It Yourself steps. Note that Excel does not enable you to delete any of its built-in toolbars. However, you can reset a built-in toolbar you've changed by displaying the Toolbars dialog box, selecting the toolbar, and clicking **Reset**.

"Show and Hide Parts of a Window," p. 254, provides information on moving, hiding, and displaying different toolbars.

Begin Do It Yourself   Move, Delete, and Add Toolbar Buttons

1 Display the toolbar that you want to change. For example, you can display the Workgroup toolbar.

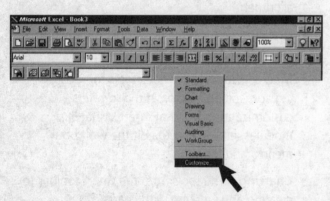

2 Right-click the toolbar and click **Customize**. The Customize dialog box appears.

3 (Optional) If the Customize dialog box covers up any part of the toolbar you want to modify, point to the dialog box's title bar and drag it out of the way.

4 To move a button on a toolbar, drag it to a new location on the current toolbar or another toolbar. Excel moves the button to the location specified; a gray outline of the button appears while you drag.

5 (Optional) To leave a gray space between buttons, ensure there's space between toolbar buttons before you release the left mouse button.

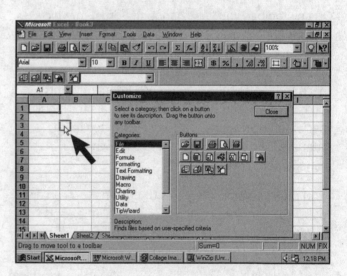

6 To delete a button from a toolbar, drag it off the toolbar onto the worksheet and release the mouse button. Excel removes the button from the toolbar.

Do It Yourself Move, Delete, and Add Toolbar Buttons

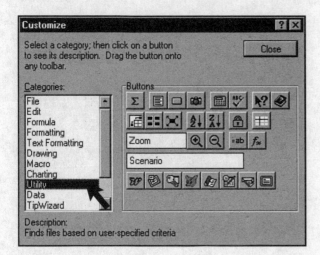

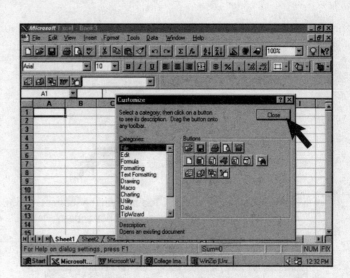

7 To add a button to a toolbar, start by scrolling through the **Categories** list and clicking a button category. For example, you can click on the Utility category. The buttons available in that category appear.

10 Click the **Close** button to close the Customize dialog box and put into effect the toolbar changes you've made.

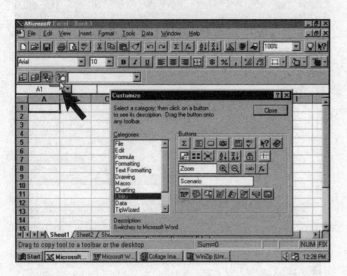

8 Drag a button from the Customize dialog box to a toolbar. A plus sign appears with the mouse pointer. Releasing the mouse button places the button in the location specified by the gray outline that appeared while you were dragging.

9 Repeat steps 4 through 8 to make other toolbar changes.

Begin Do It Yourself Make a New Toolbar

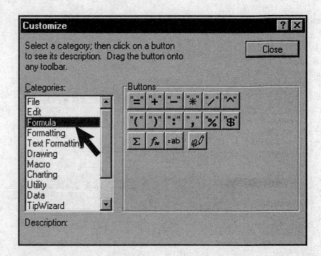

1 Right-click a toolbar and click **Toolbars** on the shortcut menu that appears. The Toolbars dialog box appears.

4 Scroll through the **Categories** list and click a button category.

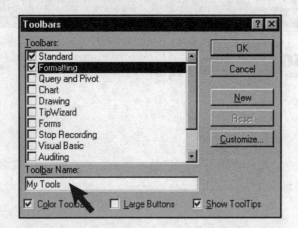

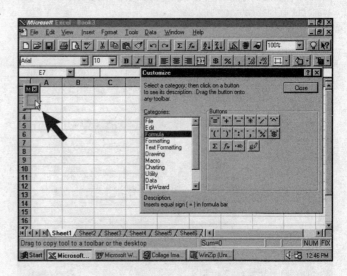

2 Double-click in the **Toolbar Name** text box and type a name for the new toolbar.

3 Click the **New** button. Excel closes the Toolbars dialog box, displays a new toolbar on-screen, and displays the Customize dialog box.

5 Drag a button from the Customize dialog box to the new toolbar.

Do It Yourself   Make a New Toolbar

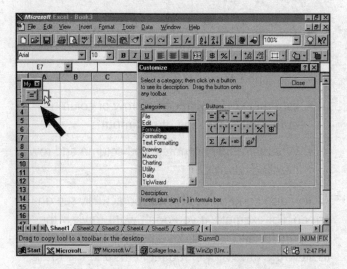

6 Continue selecting categories and dragging buttons as needed. The toolbar automatically increases in size to accommodate each button you add.

7 Click **Close** to close the Customize dialog box and finish creating the toolbar.

Begin Do It Yourself   Delete a Custom Toolbar

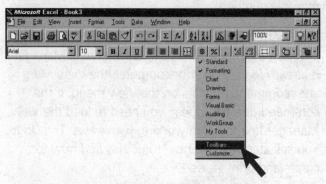

1 Right-click a toolbar and click **Toolbars** from the shortcut menu that appears. The Toolbars dialog box appears.

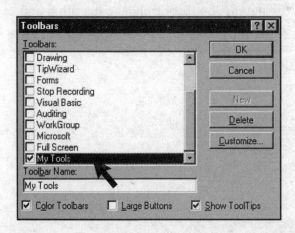

2 Scroll through the **Toolbars** list and click on the name of the custom toolbar you want to delete.

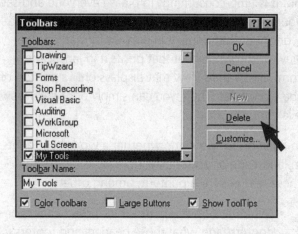

3 Click the **Delete** button. Excel asks if you really want to remove the toolbar. If you choose Yes, Excel removes the toolbar from the list.

4 Click **OK** to close the Toolbars dialog box.

Create a View You Can Use

View is probably a slightly misleading name for the feature described in this project. Excel views have as much to do with what you get on paper as with what you see on-screen. When you create an Excel view, you tell Excel to display or print all or a specified part of a workbook using specific formatting features you specify.

For example, suppose you create a worksheet that you plan to update monthly and provide to various people. Some of the recipients prefer a copy printed in the regular portrait (tall rather than wide) format. Others want to receive the printout in a landscape (wide rather than tall) format. Still others don't want the entire worksheet. Changing the page setup every month to accommodate your recipients isn't difficult, but it is time-consuming. To please everyone and save yourself some time, you can create one view of the worksheet that prints it in portrait format, another view of the worksheet that prints it in landscape form, and a third view that displays only a portion of the worksheet. Then, you can simply print each view every month.

In addition to specifying whether a worksheet prints in landscape or portrait layout, a view can specify these features for a printout, among others:

- Whether or not a printout includes headers or footers, and what those headers and footers contain. That is, you can create two views that use headers, but the header for each view can be different.

- The size of margins and the percentage at which the document prints.

- The range of cells that print.

- Whether you repeat certain row or column entries on each page of a printout.

- Whether gridlines, notes, and column and row headings print.

A view also controls what data you actually see on-screen. For example, if you don't want to view the numbers for each month of a budget, but you want to view the titles of the budget items and the totals, you can hide the monthly columns and then save the totals only view. That way, whenever you want to see only totals, you display the view that hides the monthly numbers.

You control views with the View Manager, an Add-In program that comes with Excel. If the View Manager is already loaded on your computer, the View Manager command appears on the View menu. If the command doesn't appear, you need to load the View Manager first to begin working with views. The Do It Yourself steps explain how to do this and how to create and print views.

"Print Worksheets," p. 125, provides many of the details about controlling page setup and printing a workbook.

Begin Do It Yourself Load the View Manager

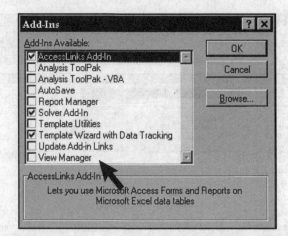

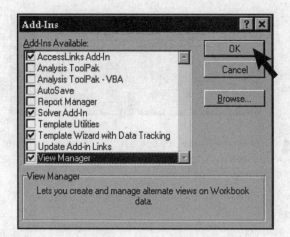

1 Open the **Tools** menu and click **Add-Ins**. The Add-Ins dialog box appears.

2 In the Add-Ins Available list, click **View Manager**.

3 Click **OK** to finish loading the View Manager.

Begin Do It Yourself Save a View

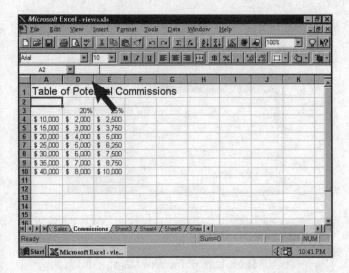

1 Display the information on-screen that you want to include in the view. If you want to include print settings with your view, select the worksheet area to print. If you do not specify a print area, Excel includes the selected sheet as the print area of the view.

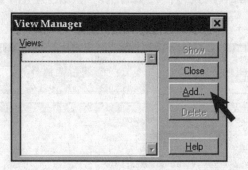

2 Open the **View** menu and click View Manager. The View Manager dialog box opens.

3 Click the **Add** button. The Add View dialog box appears.

(continues)

Do It Yourself Save a View

(continued)

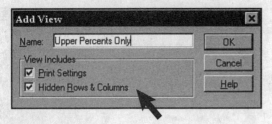

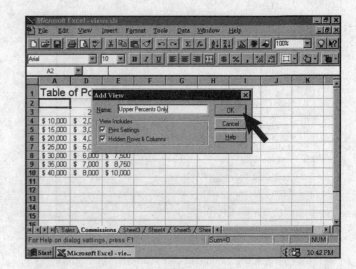

4 Type, in the **Name** text box, a name for the view. Giving names that correspond with the purpose of the view is one naming method to use.

5 Under View Includes, select the options you want to include in the view.

6 Click **OK** to finish creating the view.

Begin Do It Yourself Load and Print a View

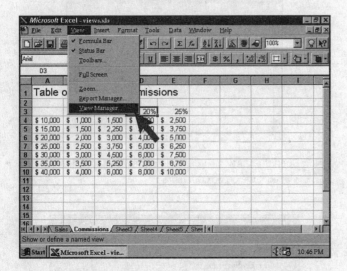

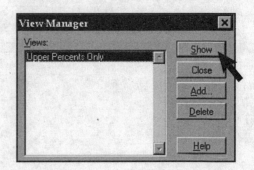

2 Click the name of the view you want to load in the Views list.

3 Click the **Show** button. The View Manager dialog box closes, and Excel displays the selected view.

1 Open the **View** menu and click **View Manager**. The View Manager dialog box appears.

Do It Yourself Load and Print a View

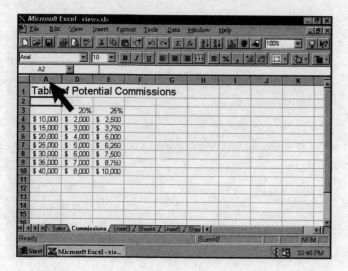

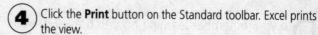
4 Click the **Print** button on the Standard toolbar. Excel prints the view.

Create Your Own Formatting Styles

Do you remember learning how to draw with crayons when you were a kid? You probably started out scribbling in a couple of different crayon colors. Then you graduated to drawing shapes like circles and blobs, claiming charmingly that you were drawing Mommy. At some point, you achieved the ability to combine shapes and colors that actually resembled Mommy.

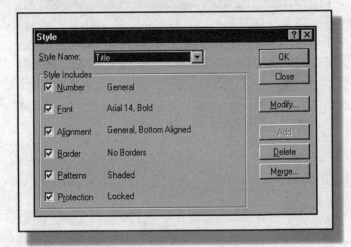

A similar process evolves as you learn to use a computer program like Excel. You start out using just the features you need to accomplish a particular task. One or two features may even do it. As you gain experience, you try other crayons—er, features—to make your workbooks more sophisticated and attractive. In particular, many users tend to allocate more effort toward formatting worksheet cells once they master the nuts and bolts aspects of entering data. Formatting not only makes a worksheet more attractive but also enables you to visually group data or call attention to important data. For example, you may want to shade the background of a cell that displays the result of an important calculation.

"Format Worksheets," p. 99, explains how to apply individual formatting characteristics to selected cells. However, selecting cells and applying your favorite formatting over and over is time-consuming, especially if you're applying numerous formatting characteristics. As usual, Microsoft is thinking ahead, so it provides *styles* in Excel.

A style is a saved collection of formatting characteristics. To format a cell with all the style's characteristics, you simply select the cell and choose the style. Voilà! Attractively formatted text. You can create styles for

workbook headings, subheadings, calculation results, and more. If you want to change the formatting characteristics of a style later, you can. Doing so automatically reformats all cells using that style.

By default, Excel saves the styles you create only in the workbook you're working in when you create them. To use those styles in another workbook, you have to copy the style to that workbook. If you want to make particular styles automatically available to all workbooks, you have to save those styles in an autotemplate that automatically loads the styles when you start Excel. The following Do It Yourself explains exactly how to create, apply, and copy styles.

You can add a drop-down list of available styles to any toolbar. It's in the Formatting category of buttons available for addition to toolbars. See "Customize the Excel Toolbars," p. 301, to learn to modify toolbars.

Begin Do It Yourself   Create a Style

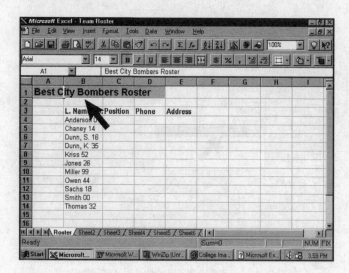

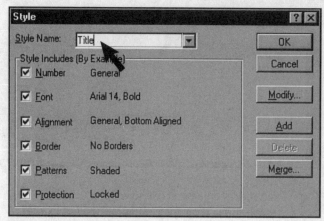

1 Select a worksheet cell with an entry in it and format that cell with all the characteristics (font, size, fill, and so on) that you want.

2 Open the **Format** menu and click **Style**. The Style dialog box appears on-screen. Excel automatically highlights the contents of the Style Name box.

3 Type a new name for the style, such as **Title**.

4 Click **Add** to add the style to the workbook.

5 Click **OK** to close the Style dialog box.

Begin Do It Yourself   Apply a Style

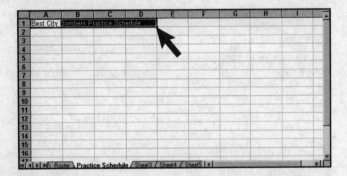

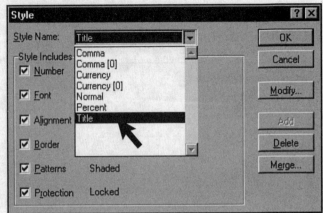

1 Select the cell or range of cells to which you want to apply the style. (If you're applying a style with shading to a cell entry that spills over into adjoining cells, select all the cells to shade behind the full entry.)

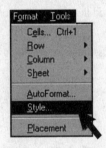

2 Open the **Format** menu and click **Style**. The Style dialog box appears on-screen.

3 Click the down arrow on the **Style Name** list to display its drop-down list and click the style you want to apply.

4 **(Optional)** If you don't want to apply all the style's characteristics to the selected cells, click to remove the check box beside the formatting you don't want to apply.

5 Click **OK** to close the Style dialog box and apply the style of your choice.

Begin Do It Yourself Edit a Style

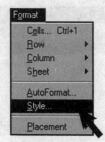

1 Open the **Format** menu and click **Style**. The Style dialog box appears on-screen.

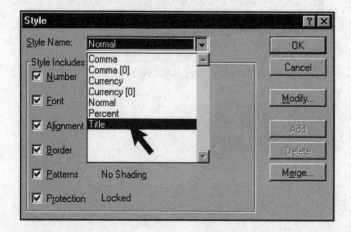

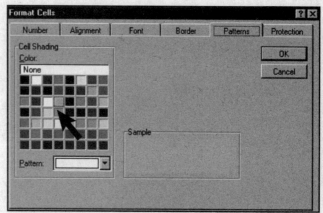

4 Click a tab to display its options and change the option you wish. Repeat this to change options on as many of the tabs as you want.

5 When you finish specifying the formatting options, click the **OK** button to close the Format Cells dialog box. The lists of formatting characteristics in the Style dialog box may reflect some of your changes.

6 Click **OK** to close the Style dialog box and save and apply your style changes.

2 Click the down arrow on the **Style Name** list to display its drop-down list and click the style you want to edit.

3 Click the **Modify** button. Excel displays the Format Cells dialog box, which offers six different tabs full of formatting options.

Begin Do It Yourself Copy a Style to a Workbook

1 Open the workbook that contains the style(s) you want to copy. Open the workbook to which you want to copy the styles, making sure it's the current workbook.

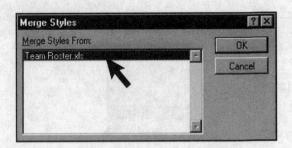

4 Click the name of the workbook to merge styles from in the Merge Styles From list.

5 Click **OK** again to close the Merge Styles dialog box and return to the Style dialog box. The styles you merged now appear on the Style Name list.

2 Open the **Format** menu and click **Style**. The Style dialog box appears on-screen.

6 Click **OK** to close the Style dialog box. You can now apply the merged style in the current workbook.

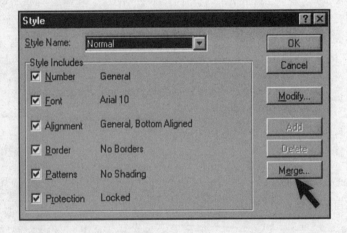

3 Click the **Merge** button. The Merge Styles dialog box appears. It lists the names of open workbooks from which you can copy styles.

Begin Do It Yourself Make Styles Available in All Workbooks

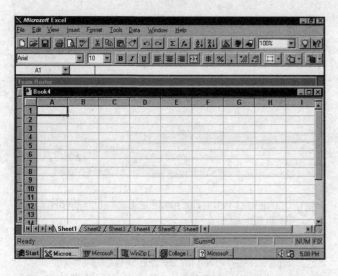

1 Open the workbook that contains the style(s) you want to copy. Open a new workbook to save as the autotemplate that will make styles available to all workbooks, making sure it's the current workbook.

2 Open the **Format** menu and click **Style**. The Style dialog box appears on-screen.

3 Click the **Merge** button. The Merge Styles dialog box appears. It lists the names of open workbooks from which you can copy styles.

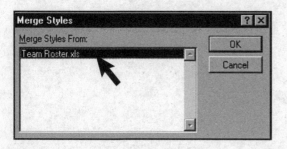

4 Click the name of the workbook to merge styles from in the Merge Styles From list.

5 Click **OK** again to close the Merge Styles dialog box and return to the Style dialog box. The styles you merged now appear on the Style Name list.

6 Click **OK** to close the Style dialog box. You can now save the new workbook as the autotemplate.

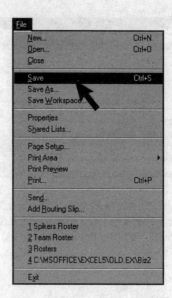

7 Open the **File** menu and choose **Save**, or click the **Save** button on the Standard toolbar. The Save As dialog box appears.

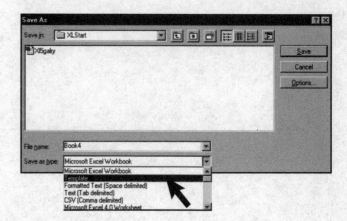

8 Open the **Save as type** list and click **Template**.

(continues)

Do It Yourself   Make Styles Available in All Workbooks *(continued)*

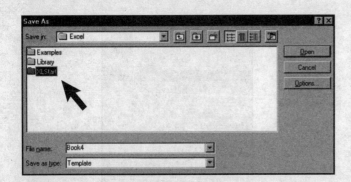

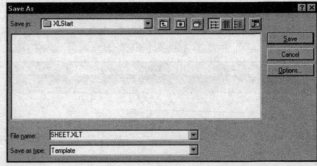

9 Navigate to the **XLSTART** folder. When that folder appears in the file list, double-click it to make it the current folder where you'll save the autotemplate.

10 Double-click in the **File name** text box and type **SHEET.XLT** (in all capitals).

11 Click **Save** to finish creating the autotemplate. The next time you start Excel, the styles in SHEET.XLT are available to all worksheets. In the future, you can update the styles in SHEET.XLT or merge other styles to it.

Create Custom Number Formats

In a task earlier in this book called "Format Numbers," p. 104, Excel provides numerous number formats you can use to apply decimals, dollar signs, colors, and more to numbers and dates you enter in Excel. As you may have seen on the Number tab of the Format Cells dialog box, Excel uses a *number format code* to define each format. You can create custom number format codes, if needed, to apply to entries in your workbooks.

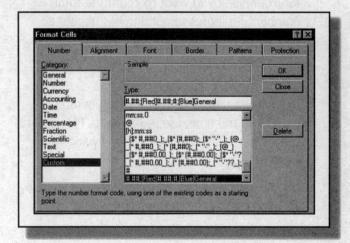

You divide each number format code into up to four sections (for positive numbers, negative numbers, zeros, and text), separating each section with a semicolon. Here's an example of a four-section number code: 0.00;[RED]0.00;#;[RED]@. That code formats positive numbers with two decimal places, negative numbers in red with two decimal places, zeros do not appear, and text appears in red. (More on the coding in a moment.)

You can include only the first section to apply the format to all numbers. When you include two sections, the first defines the format for positive numbers and zeros and the second section defines negative numbers.

When you construct your number format code, you use certain characters to represent the numbers and punctuation to use for the format. Here are the characters that you'll use most:

- Insert a decimal point (.) to set the number of decimal places appearing in the format.

- Insert a pound sign (#) to represent digits. Using a pound character to the right of the decimal point means Excel does not display a zero to the right of the last decimal character if the cell entry contains fewer decimal places than the format.

- Use a zero (0) to the right of the decimal to ensure that Excel does display a zero to the right

of the last decimal character if the cell entry contains fewer decimal places than the format.

- Use a question mark (?) to display extra zeros and add spacing for zeros to the left and right of the decimal point. Question marks combined with the division symbol display a fraction.

- Insert a comma (,) in the format to create a thousands separator.

- You have to use an expression in a section of the number format code if you want that section to appear in a certain color (such as setting the second section to display negative values in red). Simply type the color name in square brackets in the section: [BLACK], [BLUE], [CYAN], [GREEN], [MAGENTA], [RED], [WHITE], or [YELLOW]. To use one of the 56 colors from the current workbook palette, type **[COLOR n]**; n is a number between 0 and 56 corresponding to that color's position in the color palette (use **Tools**, **Options**, **Colors** to view the palette).

- Use m, d, and y to display characters in the month, day, and year respectively.

- Use h (hour), m (minute), and s (second) to create number codes (yes, when the m follows an h code, it can represent the minutes). You have to separate the parts of the time with a colon. Square brackets around a number code enable it to exceed the limitation for one unit; for example, if you want to count the total number of minutes something has happened, you use [mm] to let the display show a value like 75 minutes. A period in a time lets you show a fraction of a second.

- To display a time only as a morning (a.m.) or evening (p.m.) time, use a, AM, A, p, PM, or P to specify the capitalization and abbreviation you want to use.

- Use the percent sign (%) to multiply the value by 100 and display the percent sign with it.

- Add an asterisk (*) to repeat the character to the right of it to fill the cell to full column width.

- E-, E+, e-, e+—followed by 0 or # codes for the number of digits you want— displays the number in scientific notation.

- Use double quotations around or a backslash before any character you want to include (such as a "K" to represent thousands). You don't need to use quotes for these characters: $ - + / ( ) : space. Excel enters the backslash for you before these characters: ! ^ & ` ' ~ { } = < >.

- When some numbers contain parentheses and others don't, they may not line up in the worksheet. To correct for this with parentheses or other characters, type an underscore and then the character (like the parenthesis) that may or may not appear in the number format code.

- If you plan to apply a number format to cells holding text or numbers and you want the code formatting (like a color you've specified) to apply to the text entries, type the at symbol (@) in the section of the number format code that holds the formatting to apply.

- You can apply a section format based on the value entered into a cell by setting up a condition. Start the format code section with square brackets enclosing and expression with <, >, =, >=, <=, or <> plus a number. To display numbers greater than 5,000 with an exclamation point, the code section could read: [<5000]\!. Remember, Excel adds the backslash character for you.

The table that follows shows several example number format codes. The Do It Yourself steps clarify how to put one together on your own.

Example Number Format Codes

Format Code	Cell Entry	Displays as
#,###.##	7295.777	7,295.78
#.0	7	7.0
???/???	.50	1/2
00#.##	1.5	001.5
mmmm d, yyyy	8/7/95	August 07, 1995
hh:mm	2:53	02:53

Begin Do It Yourself   Create Custom Number Formats

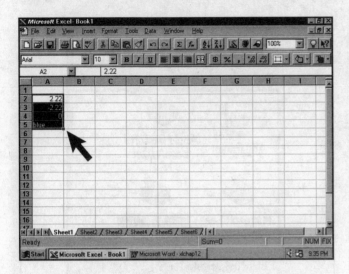

1 **(Optional)** Enter a value like the one you want to format and select the cell containing it.

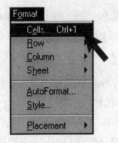

2 Open the **Format** menu and click **Cells**. The Format Cells dialog box appears.

3 Click the **Number** tab to display its options, if needed.

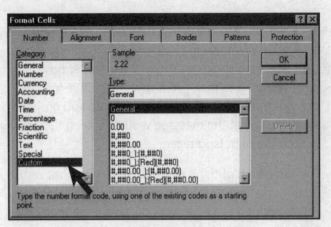

4 In the Category list, click on **Custom**.

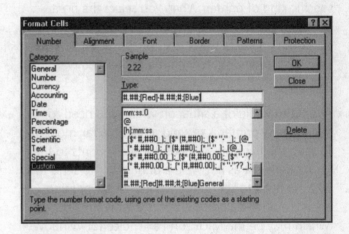

5 Double-click in the **Type** box and enter your formatting code.

6 Click **OK** to close the Format Cells dialog box and save the new format code.

Choose Another Printer

Have you ever answered the phone and found yourself speaking to a person from the Ukraine or Beijing who spoke no English? No matter how basic you tried to make your sentences, little information got through, and after you hung up you probably wondered what the message would've been had you spoken the right language.

The same kind of thing occurs if you try to print an Excel worksheet to the wrong printer, such as when you are printing to a network or have more than one printer connected to your computer. That's because Windows needs a very specific piece of software called a *printer driver* to communicate with each specific kind of printer. When you select the right printer in Excel's Print dialog box, Windows automatically finds and uses the correct printer driver so that Excel can communicate with the printer you want to use.

A great example of a situation where you need to select a new printer is to send a fax via a fax modem. To send the fax, your computer actually prints to the fax modem just as if it were a printer. So, to send the fax, you need to set up the worksheet for printing, open the print dialog box, select the fax print driver (which may be the Microsoft Fax choice for Windows 95), and print. After you specify the phone number to dial, Windows sends your worksheet as a fax. After Windows finishes sending the fax, you can use the Print dialog box to specify your usual printer.

To be able to select a printer to use with Excel, that printer (actually, its driver) needs to be installed to

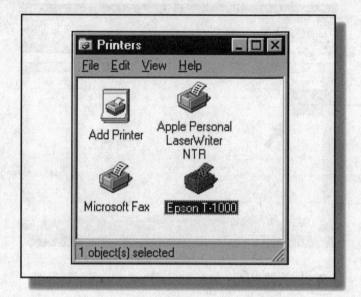

work with Windows 95. To help you survive this foray into the technical jungle, Windows provides the Add Printer Wizard to walk you through the process.

Move on now to the Do It Yourself to learn how to choose a new printer while printing or add another printer to use with Windows 95. For more on the basics of printing, see "Print Worksheets," p. 125.

You can set up various properties for your printer, such as the size of the paper you're using, but that subject is beyond the scope of this book. See the Windows 95 online Help to learn more.

Begin Do It Yourself   Select Another Printer and Print

1 Select the worksheet you want to print.

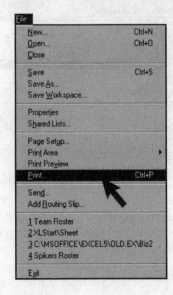

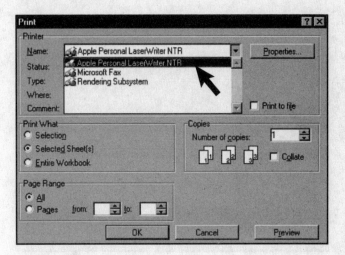

3 In the Printer area of the dialog box, click the drop-down list arrow to display the printers in the **Name** list and click the printer you want to use.

4 Specify any other printing options you want to choose and click **OK** to close the Print dialog box and send the worksheet to the selected printer.

2 Open the **File** menu and choose **Print**. The Print dialog box appears.

Begin Do It Yourself   Set Up Another Printer to Work with Windows

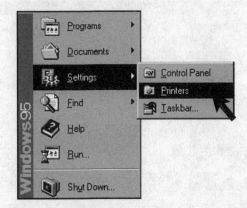

1 Click the **Start** button on the taskbar. Point to **Settings** and click **Printers**. The Printers window appears on-screen.

2 Double-click the **Add Printer** icon. The first dialog box for the Add Printer Wizard appears.

(continues)

Do It Yourself Set Up Another Printer to Work with Windows *(continued)*

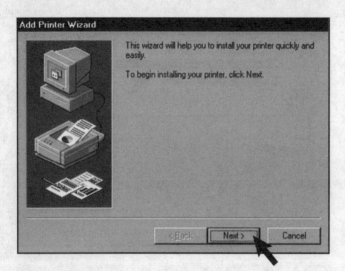

3 Click the **Next>** button to continue adding a printer.

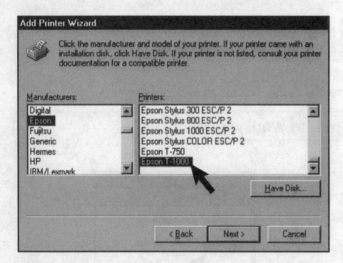

4 Scroll through the **Manufacturers** list and click the name of the maker of your printer. In the **Printers** list, click your printer model. Then, click the **Next>** button.

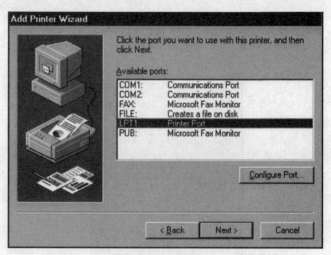

5 In the **Available ports** list, if needed, click the port to which the printer is connected. Often, you don't need to change this setting.

6 Click **Next>**.

7 **(Optional)** Type a descriptive name for the printer in the **Printer name** text box. If you want the printer to be the default printer for your system, click **Yes**.

8 Click **Next>**.

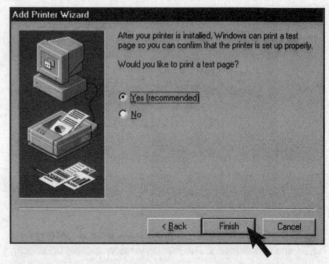

9 To confirm that you want to print a test page, simply click **Finish**.

Do It Yourself Set Up Another Printer to Work with Windows

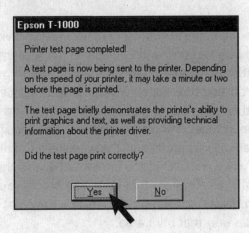

Epson T-1000

Printer test page completed!

A test page is now being sent to the printer. Depending
on the speed of your printer, it may take a minute or two
before the page is printed.

The test page briefly demonstrates the printer's ability to
print graphics and text, as well as providing technical
information about the printer driver.

Did the test page print correctly?

Yes   No

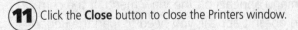

10 In the box that appears, click **Yes** to confirm the test page
printed out well. Windows 95 automatically adds an icon
for the printer to the Printers dialog box. You can select the new
printer in Excel's Print dialog box.

11 Click the **Close** button to close the Printers window.

Set Up a Report

Reports can be torture, no matter whether they're for school, the boss, or a client. It's bad enough that you have to pull together and summarize reams of data. To add insult to injury, you usually have to format it in a very specific way. Ugh! I'm sure you have better ways to spend your time than wrangling with Excel.

In the project called "Create a View You Can Use," p. 306, you saw how to save a particular on-screen representation of your data, including print area and print settings in a *view* that you can use on-screen and print. In Excel, a *report* is similar but more sophisticated than a view. Whereas a view helps you display the data in a single worksheet in a particular way, a report helps you print multiple sheets, views, and even scenarios where Excel automatically inputs various sets of data to enable you to compare the results. Not only do reports enable you to create multiple pages, but they also (depending on the views the report prints out) enable you to use the same worksheet to print different representations of your data on numerous pages using different page setup options, such as different headers or footers.

To use the Report Manager, you tell Excel to divide the report into sections, and Excel prints the sections in the order that you list them in the Add Report or Edit Report dialog box. For each section, you can specify a worksheet, view, or scenario to print. When a report section includes a single worksheet with a specified print area, Excel prints only the worksheet's print area. So, if you want to limit the printout of a worksheet to a specific area, specify that print area *before* you add the worksheet to a report. Or create a view that includes only that print area.

Reports are controlled by the Report Manager, an Add-In program that comes with Excel. When the Report Manager is loaded, the Report Manager command appears on the View menu. If the command doesn't appear, you need to load the Report Manager first to begin working with Reports. This Do It Yourself explains how to do it and how to create and print views.

"Print Worksheets," p. 125, provides many of the details about controlling page setup and printing a workbook.

Begin Do It Yourself   Load the Report Manager

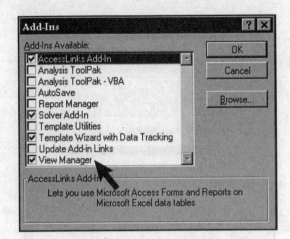

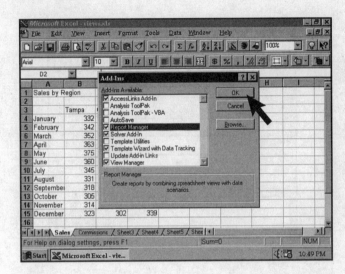

1 Open the **Tools** menu and click **Add-Ins**. The Add-Ins dialog box appears.

2 In the Add-Ins Available list, click **Report Manager**.

3 Click **OK** to finish loading the Report Manager.

Begin Do It Yourself   Create a Report

1 Create the worksheets, views, and scenarios you want to save in the report.

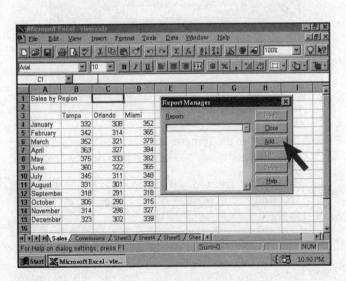

2 Open the **View** menu and click **Report Manager**. The Report Manager window appears.

3 Click **Add**. The Add Report dialog box appears.

(continues)

Do It Yourself   Create a Report

(continued)

4 In the Report Name text box, type a name for the report.

5 From the Sheet list box, click the name of the sheet you want to print as the first section of the report.

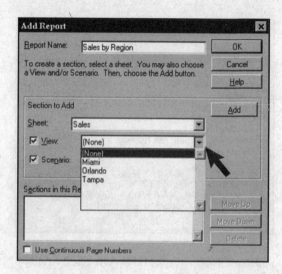

6 Click to open the **View** check box and click the name of the view (if any) to include in the first report section.

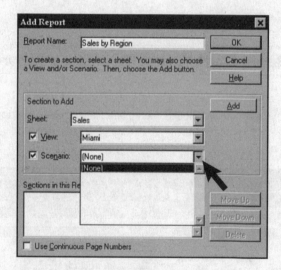

7 Click to open the **Scenario** check box and click the name of the scenario (if any) to include in the first report section.

8 When you've specified all the components for the section, click **Add**. Report Manager adds the name of that section to the Sections In This Report list.

Do It Yourself   Create a Report

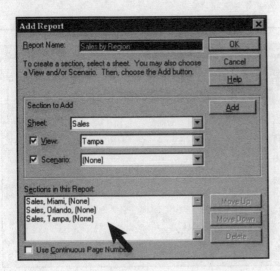

9 Repeat steps 4 through 8 until you've created all of the sections you want in the report.

10 Click **OK** to indicate you've finished creating the report and redisplay the Report Manager window with your report defined and appearing in the list.

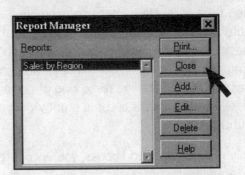

11 To add other reports, repeat these steps. Click **Close** to close the Report Manager window.

Begin Do It Yourself   Print a Report

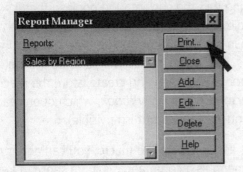

1 Open the **View** menu and click **Report Manager**. The Report Manager window appears.

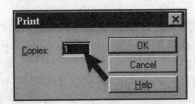

2 In the Reports list box, click the name of the report to print.

3 Click the **Print** button. The Print dialog box appears, enabling you to choose the number of copies to print.

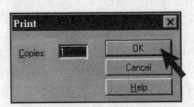

4 In the **Copies** text box, type the number of copies you want the Report Manager to print and choose **OK**. The Report Manager sends your report to the printer and its window closes.

Record and Run an Easy Macro

Most people don't mind doing something repetitive when the task is associated with a hobby. Pounding tons of nails and spending hours sanding feels productive when you're creating a beautiful piece of carpentry. Making small, even stitches doesn't wrack your patience when you're creating an heirloom quilt. On the other hand, when you're working or handling some kind of personal business, repetitive tasks become grunt work you can do without.

When you work with workbooks, you encounter some repetitive tasks or tasks that you'd simply prefer not to think about again. So what's you're strategy for avoiding some of your Excel grunt work when you want to? Macros!

Macros are like mini-programs that store a series of steps you take in Excel. Suppose you're doing something that takes ten steps. If you save those steps in a macro, you can accomplish the macro with just a step or two that's required to run the macro. To create basic macros in Excel, you can simply record the steps to save as a macro. The Do It Yourself steps that follow explain how to record a basic macro.

As you spend more time working in Excel, you'll learn which tasks you'd like to automate. For example, you may want to create a macro to handle operations like these:

- You've created a formatting style and saved it in the autotemplate so it's available to all workbooks (see "Create Your Own Formatting Styles," p. 310). Now you want a shortcut for applying the style.

- You need to frequently print a particular range in a workbook. You can create a macro to select and print that range.

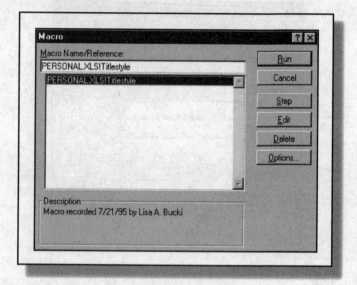

- You frequently use a complex formula, and you want a shortcut for entering it.

When you record a macro, Excel gives you the option of saving it in the current workbook so that it's available in that workbook only. You can store the macro in a new workbook that Excel automatically creates. But, if you want a macro to be available to all workbooks you open and create, store the macro in the *Personal Macro Workbook*, which opens each time you start Excel (but isn't visible).

Finally, as you create the macro, you can add it to the Tools menu as a command, assign a shortcut key combination that you can press to run the macro, or both. The Do It Yourself steps review all of these options.

You can create a button on a worksheet or on a toolbar to run a macro. The next task, "Build Your Own Macro Button," p. 332, explains how to do so.

Begin Do It Yourself   Record a Macro

1 If you want to record a macro that's available to a particular workbook only, open that workbook and make it the current workbook.

2 **(Optional)** Review the steps you plan to record so you can perform them smoothly while creating the macro.

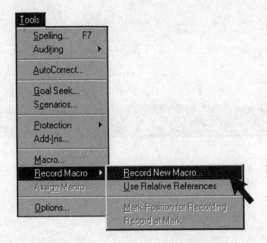

3 Open the **Tools** menu, point to **Record Macro**, and click **Record New Macro**.

4 In the Record New Macro dialog box, change the entries in the **Macro Name** text box and **Description** text box, if you wish.

5 Click the **Options** button. The Record New Macro dialog box expands to provide you with choices for specifying how to run the macro and where to store the macro.

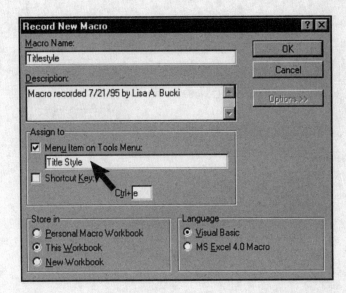

6 If you want to add a command to the Tools menu that runs the macro, click to select the **Menu Item on Tools Menu** check box and click in the text box below to type a name for the command.

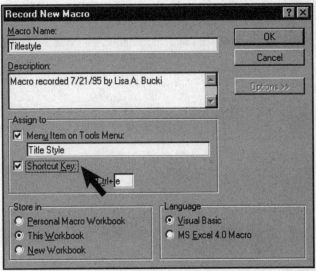

7 **(Optional)** Select the **Shortcut Key** check box. To change the default choice for the second shortcut combination character, change the **Ctrl+** text box entry. The shortcut is **Ctrl+***character*. Pressing **Shift** and entering the second character makes the shortcut **Ctrl+Shift+***character*.

(continues)

Do It Yourself   Record a Macro

(continued)

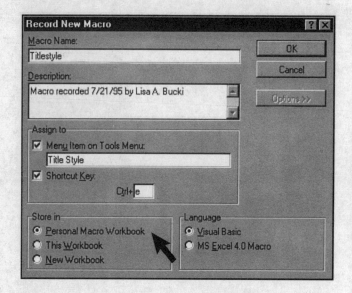

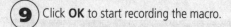

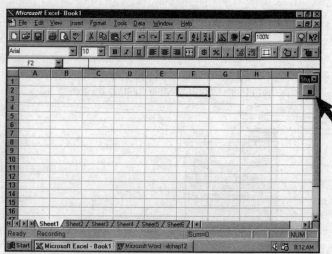

8 To specify where Excel saves the macro you're creating, click a choice in the Store in area. Personal Macro Workbook, the choice shown here, loads the macro automatically and makes it available to all workbooks.

9 Click **OK** to start recording the macro.

10 Perform the steps you want to store in the macro.

11 When you finish the steps you want to record, click the **Stop** button on the Macro toolbar that appears.

Begin Do It Yourself   Run a Macro

1 Prepare to run the macro. For example, if the macro formats text, select some text.

2 Press the shortcut key combination you assigned for the macro, or

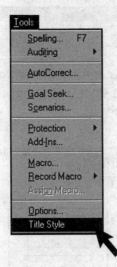

open the **Tools** menu and click the name of the command you created for the macro, or

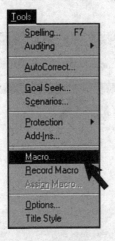

open the **Tools** menu and choose **Macro**.

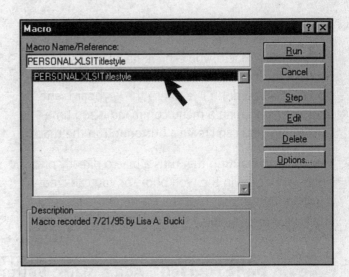

3 In the Macro dialog box, click on the name of the macro to run in the Macro Name/Reference list and click **Run**. Excel runs the macro.

Build Your Own Macro Button

As you learned in the last project, when you create a macro, you can create a keyboard shortcut for it or add a command to a macro for it. However, if you don't like to use the keyboard, and think even choosing a menu command is too time-consuming, you can create a button to run the macro.

You can add a button that runs a macro directly on a single worksheet in the workbook, or you can create a toolbar button that runs the macro and adds it to any toolbar—including a custom toolbar you create

yourself (see "Customize the Excel Toolbars," p. 301). The Do It Yourself steps, next, prepare you to become a macro button genius.

Begin Do It Yourself   Add a Macro Button to the Worksheet

1 Record and save the macro you want for the workbook you want to run it in. Make sure the workbook you want to run it in is the current workbook.

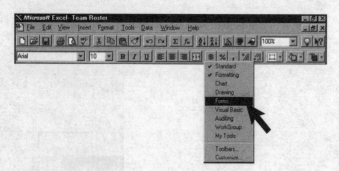

2 Right-click a toolbar and click **Forms**. The Forms toolbar appears on-screen.

3 Click the **Create Button** button on the Forms toolbar. The mouse pointer turns to a crosshair.

4 Drag on the worksheet to draw the button in the size you want. The Assign Macro dialog box appears automatically.

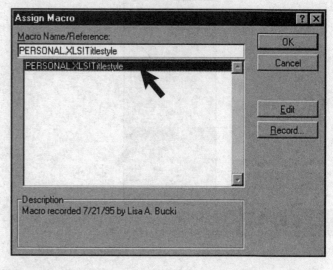

5 In the Macro Name/Reference list, click on the name of the macro you want to assign to the button. Then click **OK**.

Do It Yourself   Add a Macro Button to the Worksheet

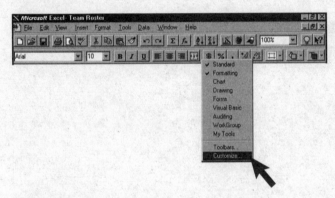

Title Style

6 Drag over the descriptive text on the button and type a new name for the button.

7 Click outside the button to finish it. You can then use the button to apply the macro on the worksheet that holds the button.

Begin Do It Yourself   Add a Macro Button to a Toolbar

1 Record and save the macro you want for the workbook you want to run it in. Make sure the workbook you want to run it in is the current workbook.

2 Display the toolbar to which you want to add the macro button.

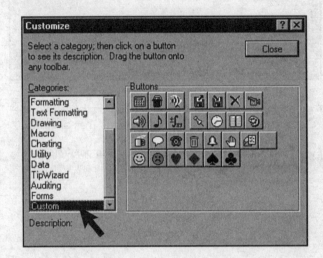

3 Right-click the toolbar and click **Customize**. The Customize dialog box appears on-screen.

4 In the Customize dialog box, scroll down through the **Categories list** and click **Custom**.

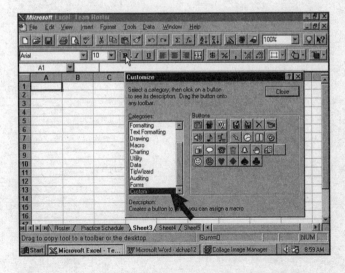

5 Drag the button of your choice onto the toolbar you want to add it to. The Assign Macro dialog box appears automatically.

(continues)

Do It Yourself Add a Macro Button to a Toolbar

(continued)

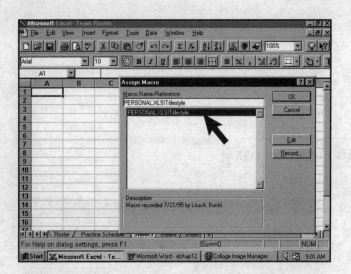

5 In the Macro Name/Reference list, click on the name of the macro you want to assign to the button. Then click **OK**.

6 Click **Close** to close the Customize dialog box. You can then use the button to apply the macro in any workbook where that macro is available.

DO IT YOURSELF

Track Personal Information in Excel

Even if you have a deep aversion to making lists to track your time and possessions, sometimes you have a compelling reason to gather information. Still, the thought of sitting down and writing out reams of information by hand is often enough to make you postpone the inevitable…one more time.

This section offers projects that show you ways to use Excel's features to take some of the pain out of making and managing lists. "Build a Database," p. 181, covers many of the basic database techniques you'll use in many of the projects you find here. Although you can use database programs like Access to perform some of the operations described in the projects, you may find Excel more convenient if you know how to work with Excel and don't want to learn a new program. The following Do It Yourself projects show you how to manage all the data that clutters up your life.

What You Will Find in This Section

Keep Your Address Book

Many people have address books that are loose-leaf affairs, with little pieces of paper slipped in here or there between the alphabetical tab dividers. This system works—sort of. If you use a handwritten address book, you can usually find an address when you need it. But there are several drawbacks to Ye Olde Address Book:

- If you want to make changes to an address, you have to erase it or cross it out and rewrite it.

- You can run out of space for names beginning with a particular letter.

- If the book or some pages in the book become worn, you have to replace the book or pages and rewrite all the names and addresses.

- You have to be able to read your own handwriting—and be sure that other family members can, as well.

- You don't have any way to sort the names if you need to.

If you use Excel's data management features to create an electronic address book, you can overcome all of these shortcomings. The electronic address book expands as much as you need it to, and you can sort, update, and print entries anytime you want. Even better, you can add special information that you can later use to sort the addresses or select certain addresses later.

The Do It Yourself steps here explain how to build an address book database in Excel. You'll learn to alphabetize your addresses, as well as how to find, add,

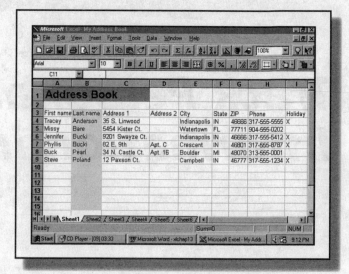

and update addresses. As an example, the address book offers a Holiday field. In this field, you type an X for any person to whom you'd like to send a holiday card. Then, when the time comes, you can print a list that only includes those holiday card recipients. You can use this technique and add fields that enable you to create and print lists for specific purposes. For example, you can include birthday and anniversary fields and compile a list each month of people to whom you want to send cards for those occasions.

If you're using Word for Windows 95, you can merge the information from your Excel address book in a Word mail merge. Word's online Help can walk you through that process.

Begin Do It Yourself Build Your Address Book Form

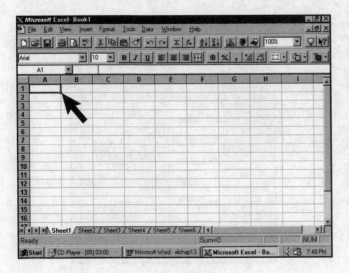

1 If needed, click the **New Workbook** button on the Standard toolbar to start a new, blank workbook.

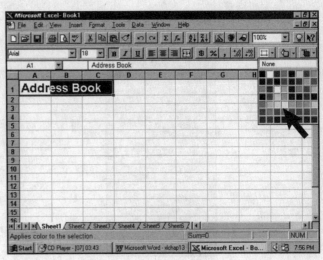

3 Select cells **A1:C1** and use the **Color** button on the Formatting toolbar to apply a background color to the cells.

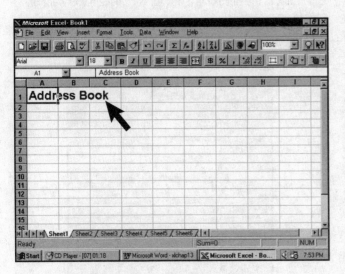

2 In cell A1, enter **Address Book**. Then, with cell A1 selected, use the Formatting toolbar to change the font size to 18 and apply boldface to the cell.

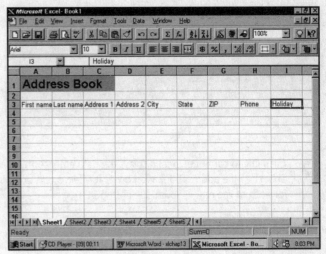

4 Make these entries in row 3: A3, **First name**; B3, **Last name**; C3, **Address 1**; D3, **Address 2**; E3, **City**; F3, **State**; G3, **ZIP**; H3, **Phone**; and I3, **Holiday**.

5 Click the **Save** button on the Standard toolbar to save and name the workbook. In the Save As dialog box, specify the folder to save in and type a file name like **My Address Book**. Click **Save** to close the dialog box.

(continues)

Do It Yourself Build Your Address Book Form

(continued)

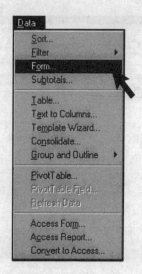

6 Select a cell anywhere in the range A3:I3. Then, open the **Data** menu and choose **Form**. Excel displays a message asking whether it should assume the top row of the current selection is the header row.

8 Enter the first address and press the **Tab** key when you complete the entry. Repeat this process for each entry. Enter an **X** in the Holiday text box for each person you want on your Holiday card list.

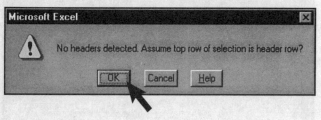

7 Click **OK** to continue. Excel displays the data entry form for Sheet1 of the address book workbook. It offers a text box for each of the entries you made in step 4.

9 Click **New** to finish adding the address, or record, and clear the text boxes. Excel adds the address to the address book list automatically.

10 Repeat steps 8 and 9 to add as many other addresses as you wish.

Do It Yourself   Build Your Address Book Form

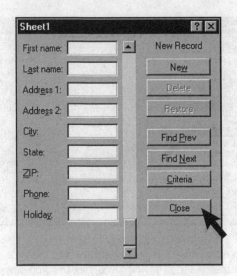

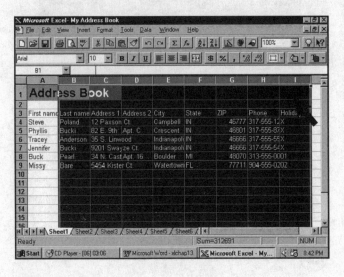

11 When you finish adding addresses, click **Close**.

12 Click the **Save** button on the Standard toolbar to save the records you added to your address book.

13 Add a few finishing touches to make your address book easier to use. First, select columns **B** through **I** by dragging over the column heading (column letters).

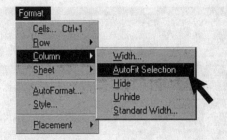

14 Click to open the **Format** menu, point to **Column**, and click **AutoFit Selection**. Excel automatically adjusts all the selected columns so the entries are fully visible.

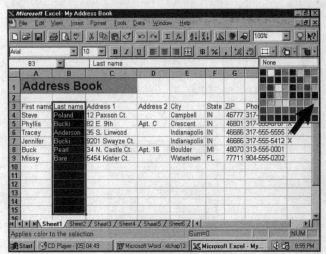

15 Select column **B** from cell B3 through the end of your list (or further) and use the **Color** button on the Formatting toolbar to apply a light shading to the Last name column. This makes it easier for you to find last names when you view or print the list.

16 Click the **Save** button on the Standard toolbar to save changes.

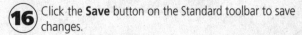

Begin Do It Yourself Alphabetize Your Address Book

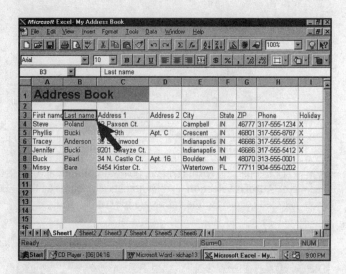

1 Click to select cell **B3**. Selecting this cell tells Excel which field you want to sort by. In this case, you select Last name, because most address books are alphabetized by last name.

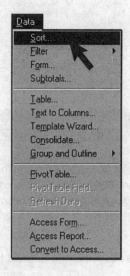

2 Open the **Data** menu and click **Sort**. The Sort dialog box appears. The Last name field and Ascending sort order are selected for you as the first sort to perform.

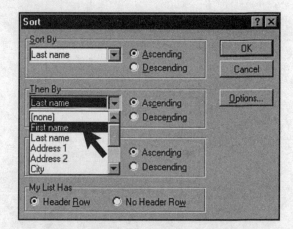

3 To ensure that addresses for people with the same Last name are sorted by First name, click the drop-down list arrow for the first Then By list and click **First name**.

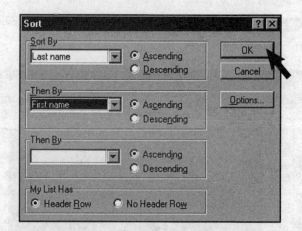

4 Without changing any other options, click **OK**. Excel sorts all the addresses in the address book, first by Last name and then by First name.

5 Save and print your sorted address book.

Begin Do It Yourself   Add an Address

1 Click a cell anywhere in the address book list.

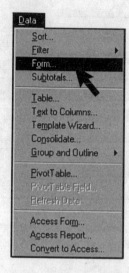

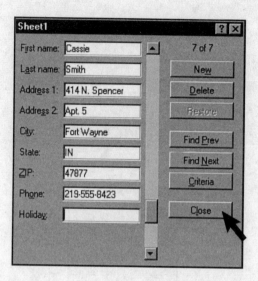

6 Click **Close** when you finish adding the last new address.

2 Open the **Data** menu and click **Form**. The data entry form for the worksheet appears, with the entries for the first address.

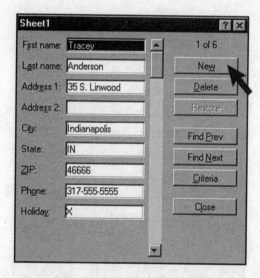

3 Click **New**. Excel clears the form to receive the new address.

4 Enter the new address you want to store. Press the **Tab** key after you complete the entry for each text box.

5 Repeat steps 3 and 4 to add other addresses.

Begin Do It Yourself Find, Update, or Delete an Address

1 Click a cell anywhere in the address book list.

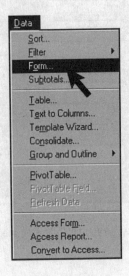

2 Open the **Data** menu and click **Form**. The data entry form for the worksheet appears, with the entries for the first address.

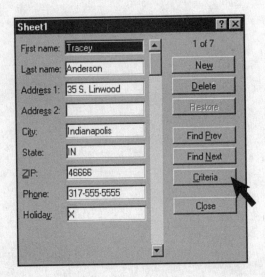

3 Click **Criteria**. Excel displays the Criteria form for the worksheet. Here, you type the entry you want Excel to search for, such as the address with the last name **Pearl**.

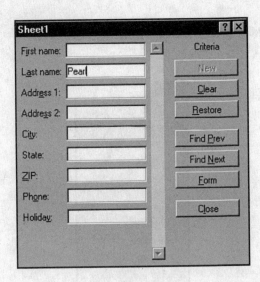

4 Enter the field information for the entry to search for. For example, you can enter **Pearl** in the Last name text box to find the address for Pearl.

5 **(Optional)** Make entries in other text boxes to make the search more specific. For example, if you know you have addresses for more than one person with the last name you're searching for, enter a first name, too.

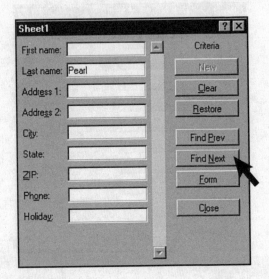

6 Click **Find Next**. Excel displays the matching address in the data entry form.

Do It Yourself Find, Update, or Delete an Address

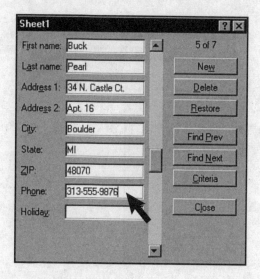

7 Either type changes to an entry for the address, or click the **Delete** button to remove the address from the address list.

8 Click **Close** when you finish making changes to the address book.

Begin Do It Yourself Print Your Holiday Card List

1 Click a cell anywhere in the address book list.

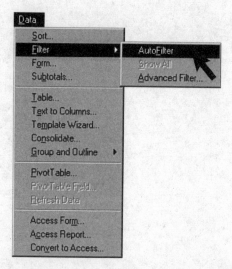

2 Open the **Data** menu, point to **Filter**, and click **AutoFilter**. AutoFilter drop-down list arrows appear beside the name for each field in the header row (row 3) at the top of the address book.

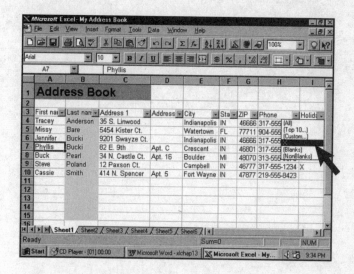

3 Click the **AutoFilter** drop-down arrow for the Holiday field on cell I3 and click **X** or **NonBlanks**. Excel displays only the addresses you marked with X in the Holiday field. These are your holiday card recipients.

(continues)

Do It Yourself Print Your Holiday Card List *(continued)*

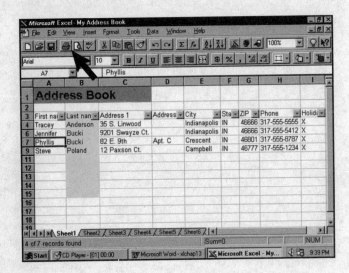
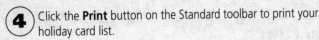
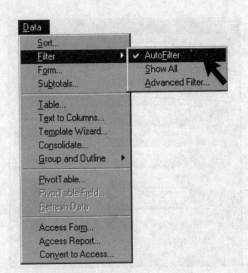

4 Click the **Print** button on the Standard toolbar to print your holiday card list.

5 To return to the normal address book display of all the records, open the **Data** menu, point to **Filter**, and click **AutoFilter**. The AutoFilter drop-down arrows disappear, and you can see all the addresses.

Track Your Household Stuff

It's inevitable as the passage of time. We all tend to accumulate more and more "stuff" as we go along in life. Now, it's generally not productive to spend your time oohing and ahhing over how great your possessions are. On the other hand, keeping some records about your possessions can be useful if you ever need to use your homeowner's or renter's insurance.

Tracking your possessions for insurance reasons serves two purposes. First, it enables you to have a realistic idea of what your possessions are worth to determine how much insurance you need and whether it's in your best interest to consider adding riders to your insurance policy to cover special items like jewelry. Second, you can use the list to track the present value of those possessions, so if you do experience a robbery, fire, or other loss, you can provide documentation to your insurance company to ensure you are paid in full for your stuff.

Here are a few guidelines for creating and using a list to track your possessions:

- Have special items like jewelry or antiques appraised to determine the present value. For other possessions, keep an eye on advertisements for similar items to determine a fair replacement cost.

- Take a photograph of each item you add to the list.

- Print a copy of the list and place it, along with the photographs you took and the written

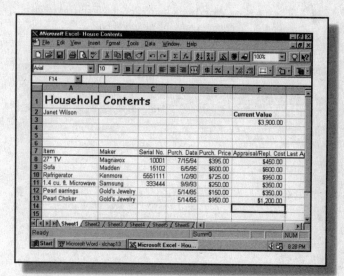

appraisals for items, in your safe deposit box at your bank. This ensures that your records won't be destroyed in a fire, tornado, or other disaster.

- You should have items that require appraisal reappraised at least every five years to ensure you have an accurate assessment of the item's value, which may fluctuate over time.

So, without further ado, use the Do It Yourself steps to learn how to create and update your Excel list for tracking your household possessions.

If working with Excel database features still leaves you scratching your head, check out "Build a Database," p. 181 for a refresher.

Begin Do It Yourself Create Your List of Possessions

1 Click the **New Workbook** button on the Standard toolbar, if needed, to create a new, blank workbook.

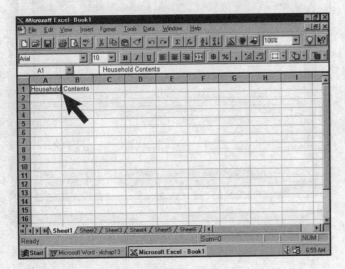

2 Enter **Household Contents** in cell A1 and click the green entry check mark on the Formula bar to finish the entry.

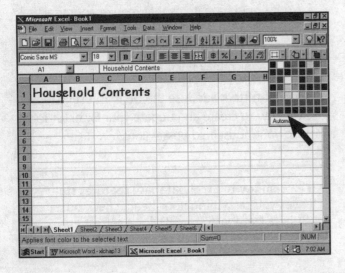

3 With cell A1 still selected, you can change its formatting, apply a color to it, or apply a fill color for the cells behind it, if you wish.

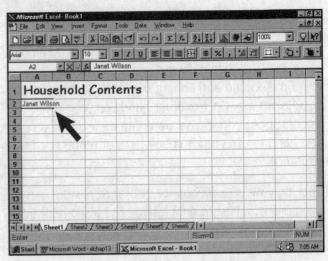

4 Enter your name (and your spouse's name, if needed) in cell A2.

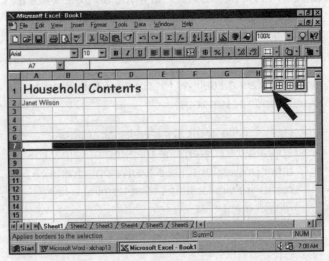

5 **(Optional)** Select row 7 by clicking on its row number header. Use the **Borders** button on the Formatting toolbar to apply a border along the bottom (and top, if desired) of the row.

Do It Yourself Create Your List of Possessions

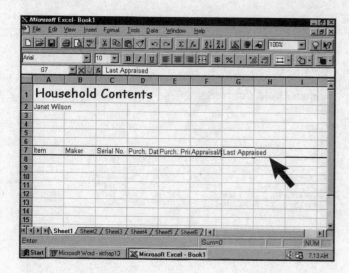

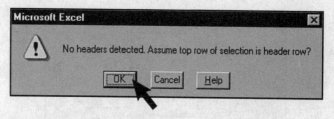

6 Make these entries in row 7: A7, **Item**; B7, **Maker**; C7, **Serial No.**; D7, **Purch. Date**; E7, **Purch. Price**; F7, **Appraisal/Replace. Cost**; and G7, **Last Appraised**. Don't worry about the fact that some cell entries may overlap.

9 Click **OK** to continue. Excel displays the data entry form for Sheet1 of the House Contents workbook. It offers a text box for each of the entries you made in step 6.

7 Click the **Save** button on the Standard toolbar to save and name the workbook. In the Save As dialog box, specify the folder to save in and type a file name like **House Contents**. Click **Save** to close the dialog box.

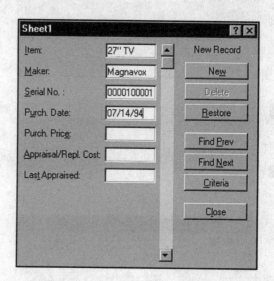

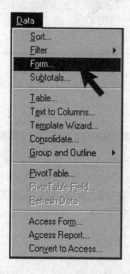

8 Select any cell in the range A7:G7. Then, open the **Data** menu and choose **Form**. Excel displays a message asking whether it should assume the top row of the current selection is the header row.

10 Enter the information about the first item, pressing the **Tab** key after you complete each text box entry. Make sure you enter dates in a format like mm/dd/yy or mm-dd-yy. Also add a dollar sign and two places for dollar values so Excel formats them automatically.

(continues)

Do It Yourself Create Your List of Possessions *(continued)*

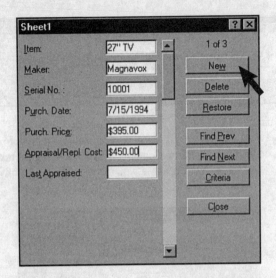

11 Click **New** to finish adding the item, or record, and clear the text boxes. Excel adds the item to the House Contents list automatically.

12 Repeat steps 10 and 11 to add as many other items as you wish.

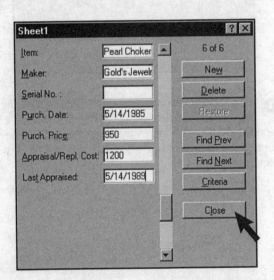

13 When you finish adding items, click **Close**.

14 Click the **Save** button on the Standard toolbar to save the records you've added to your House Contents list.

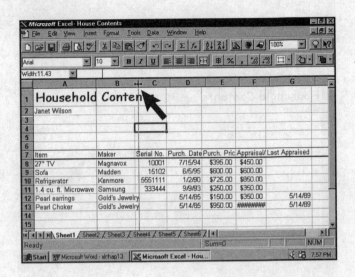

15 Notice that you can't read all the entries for some columns. To fix the width of any column, drag the right boundary of its column header letter to a new location. Or, double-click the right column boundary in the column head.

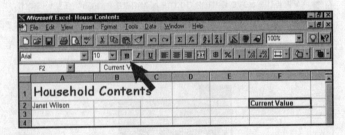

16 Enter **Current Value** in cell F2 and format it in bold.

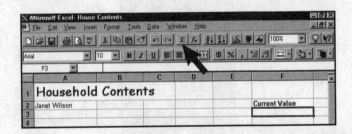

17 To find the minimum amount of insurance you need to have, click cell **F3** and then click the **AutoSum** button on the Standard toolbar. Excel starts the SUM function for you.

Do It Yourself Create Your List of Possessions

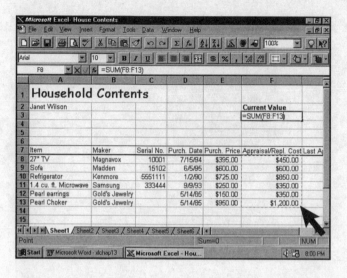

18 Drag to select the column below the Appraisal/Repl. Cost heading. After you select the range, press **Enter** to finish the formula. Note that if you add more items to the list, you need to update this formula to ensure it includes all the items.

19 Click the **Save** button on the Standard toolbar to save the records you've added to your House Contents list.

Begin Do It Yourself Find Out When to Reappraise Things

1 Click a cell anywhere in the House Contents list.

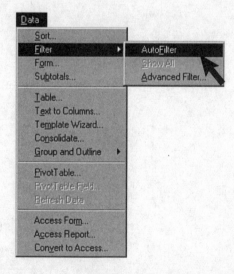

2 Open the **Data** menu, point to **Filter,** and click **AutoFilter.** AutoFilter drop-down list arrows appear beside the name for each field in the header row (row 7) at the top of the House Contents list.

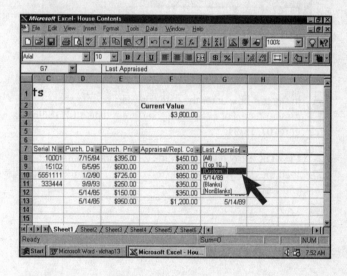

3 Scroll over so the Last Appraised column comes into view. Click the **AutoFilter** drop-down arrow for the Last Appraised field on cell G7 and click **Custom**. The Custom AutoFilter dialog box appears.

(continues)

Do It Yourself Find Out When to Reappraise Things (continued)

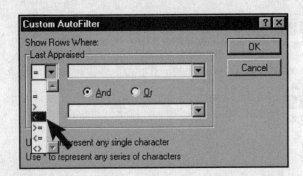

4 Click the drop-down list arrow beside the = sign to display a list of math operators. Click <, the less than choice.

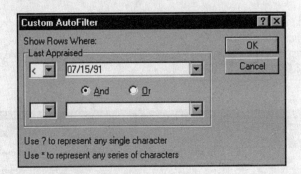

5 In the text box, enter the date five years prior to the present date. For example, if the current date is 07/15/96, enter **07/15/91**.

6 Click **OK**. Excel displays records with appraisal dates older than the date you specified. You can then print the list, if you wish.

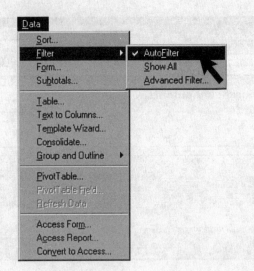

7 To return to the normal House Contents display of all the records, open the **Data** menu, point to **Filter**, and click **AutoFilter**. The AutoFilter drop-down arrows disappear, so you can see all the items.

Begin Do It Yourself   Update an Item in the List

1 Click a cell anywhere in the House Contents list.

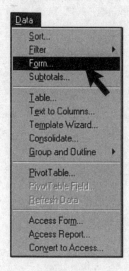

2 Open the **Data** menu and click **Form**. The data entry form for the worksheet appears, with the entries for the first item.

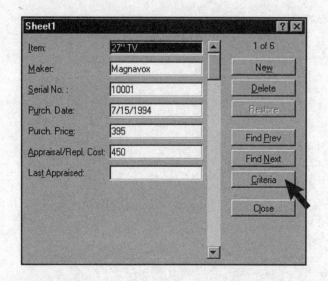

3 Click **Criteria**. Excel displays the Criteria form for the worksheet. Here, you type the entry you want Excel to search for, such as the refrigerator.

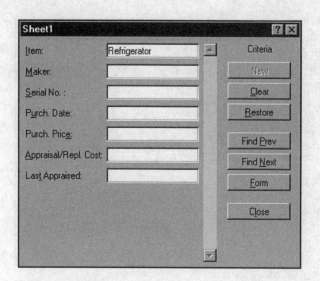

4 Enter the field information for the entry to search for. For example, you can enter **Refrigerator** in the Item text box to find its record.

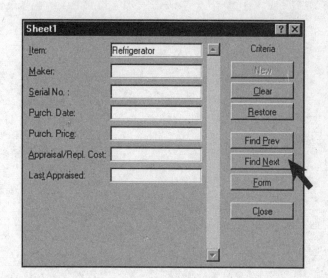

5 Click **Find Next**. Excel displays the matching item in the data entry form.

(continues)

Do It Yourself Update an Item in the List *(continued)*

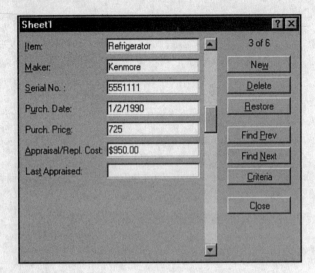

6 Type changes to an entry for the item.

7 Click **Close** when you finish making changes to the household contents.

Keep Your Family Planner

The average family now has more going on than some multimillion dollar corporations. Family schedules brim over with dance lessons, sports, music lessons, pizza parties, and more—not to mention that parents have to fit a work schedule around providing limo service for the young 'uns. Let's face it: nothing is more troubling to parents than the thought of unintentionally leaving a child stranded without a ride.

To avoid oversights like this and to impose some control over your family's chaotic commitments, you can use Excel to create a weekly master schedule of family activities. Post a copy on the fridge and print additional copies for each family member.

If you make a habit of putting together the schedule once a week, it can help in these ways:

- You can identify schedule conflicts ahead of time, so you'll have plenty of time to change plans or make other accommodations.

- You can decide in advance which parent will be driving which child where and when.

- You can use the schedule to assign chores for the week, thereby cutting down on family spats.

- You give yourself a tool for reminding yourself of special events when the kids need to take extra money or other items to school or to another activity.

- The kids can take more responsibility in family planning. They can check the schedule *before*

asking to go to a pajama party on the same night that there's a scouting camp out.

The Do It Yourself steps explain how to set up a weekly schedule worksheet and save it as a template. Then, you can use the template weekly to create a new schedule.

This project provides an example of setting up a template so you can use a worksheet and its formats over and over. For more about creating and using templates, see the section "Use Templates," page 165.

Begin Do It Yourself   Create the Calendar Template

1 Click the **New Workbook** button on the Standard toolbar, if needed, to create a new, blank workbook.

2 Enter **Weekly Schedule** in cell A1.

3 Click cell **A2** and click the **Function Wizard** button on the Standard toolbar.

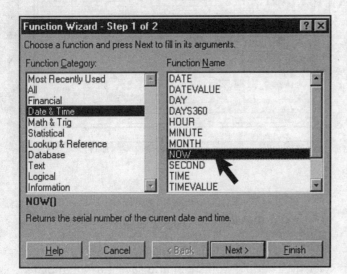

4 In the Function Category list, click **Date & Time**. In the Function Name list, click **NOW**. Click **Finish** to enter the function, which automatically updates to display the current date when you open the workbook.

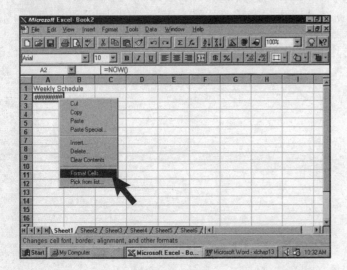

5 With cell A2 still selected, right-click the cell to display its shortcut menu and click **Format Cells**. The Format Cells dialog box appears, with the Number tab selected.

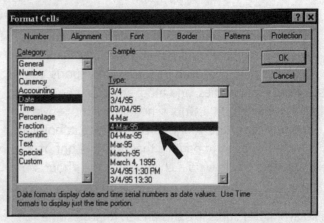

6 In the Type list, click a shorter format, such as **4-Mar-95**. Click **OK** to finish changing the format for the date.

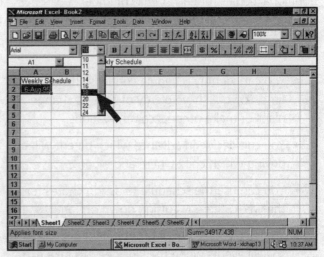

7 Select cells **A1:A2** and change the formatting using the Formatting toolbar, if you wish. If you need to adjust the column width, do so by dragging the right border of the column A heading.

Do It Yourself Create the Calendar Template

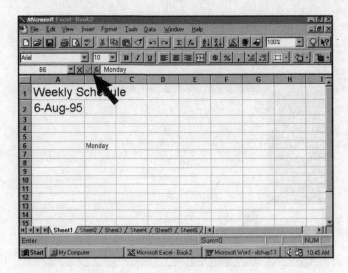

8 Select cell **B6** and enter **Monday**. Click the green entry check box to finish the cell entry and leave the cell selected.

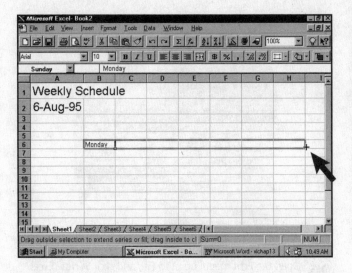

9 Point to the square fill handle at the lower-right corner of the cell selector so the mouse pointer turns into a small cross and then drag to select the cells through cell H6. When you release the mouse button, Excel fills the cells with the days of the week.

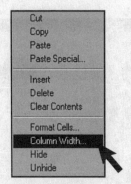

10 Select columns **B** through **H** by dragging over the column headers. Right-click on the selected columns to display a shortcut menu and click **Column Width**.

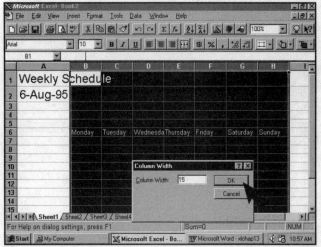

11 In the Column Width text box of the Column Width dialog box, enter **15** and then click **OK**.

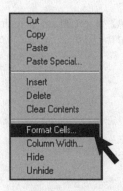

12 Right-click the selection again to display the shortcut menu and then click **Format Cells**. The Format Cells dialog box appears.

(continues)

Do It Yourself Create the Calendar Template *(continued)*

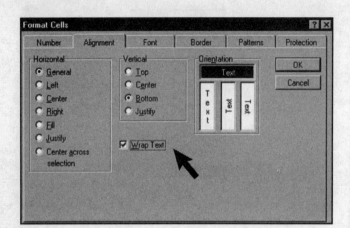

13 Click the **Alignment** tab to display its options. Click to select the **Wrap Text** check box. Click **OK**. This causes Excel to automatically wrap long cell entries to the next line and adjust the row height.

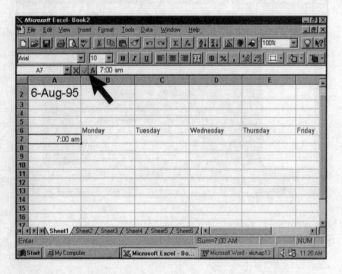

14 Click in cell **A7**, type **7:00 am**, and click the green entry check box on the Formula bar to complete the cell entry.

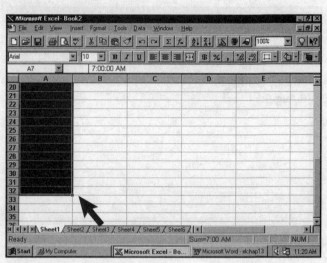

15 Select the cell range **A7:A32**.

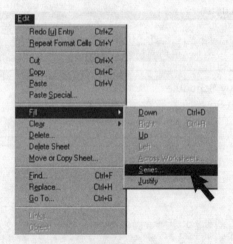

16 Open the **Edit** menu, point to **Fill**, and click **Series**. Excel displays the Series dialog box.

17 Enter **.02083333** in the Step Value text box and click **OK**. (This value is the equivalent of 1/48 for 1/2-hour in a day.) Excel fills in half-hour increments through 7:30 PM.

⬭ **Do It Yourself** Create the Calendar Template

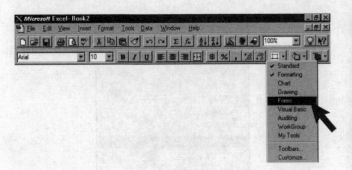

18 Right-click a toolbar and click **Forms** to display the Forms toolbar.

19 Enter **Take Out Trash** in cell D2 and press **Enter**.

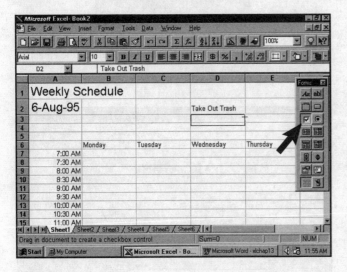

20 Click the **Check Box** button on the Forms toolbar and then drag within cell D3 to place a check box there.

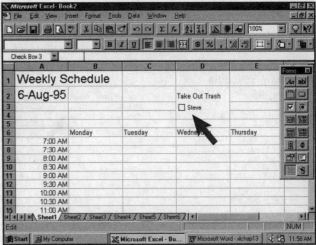

21 Drag to highlight the words **Check Box 1** and replace those words by typing the name of one household member who is responsible for taking out the trash. Click outside the cell to finish the check box.

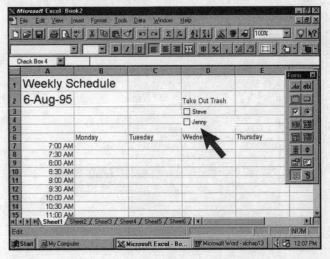

22 Repeat steps 20 and 21 to add one or more additional check boxes for the Take Out Trash chore.

(continues)

Do It Yourself Create the Calendar Template *(continued)*

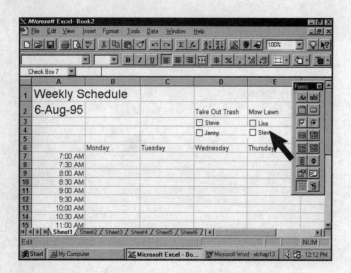

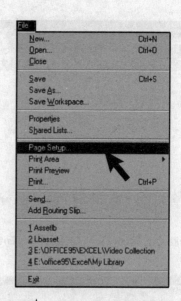

23 If you want to add additional chores, add a chore name in a cell in row 2 and follow steps 20 and 21 to add the check boxes for each person who will be performing the chore.

24 **(Optional)** Close the Forms toolbar by clicking its **Close** button, or by right-clicking it and then clicking **Forms**.

26 Open the **File** menu and choose **Page Setup**. The Page Setup dialog box appears.

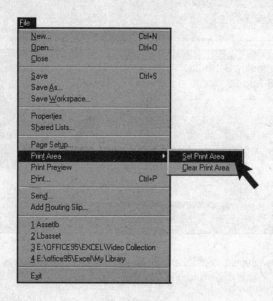

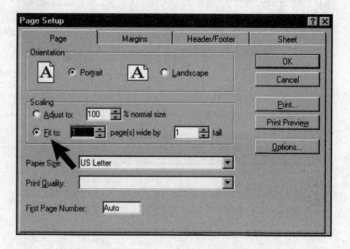

25 Select the cell range **A1:H32**. Open the **File** menu, point to **Print Area**, and click **Set Print Area**.

27 On the Page tab, click to select the **Fit to** option button and leave the other settings at 1 page wide by 1 page tall.

Do It Yourself Create the Calendar Template

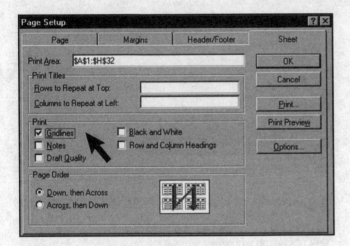

28 Click the **Sheet** tab to display its options and click to check the **Gridlines** check box. Click **OK**.

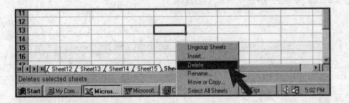

29 Delete all the worksheets but Sheet1 by clicking the **Sheet2** tab, scrolling to the last tab, and pressing **Shift** and clicking it. Then, click the right mouse button and choose **Delete**.

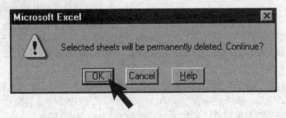

30 Excel displays a message telling you that it will delete all the worksheets. Click **OK** to continue.

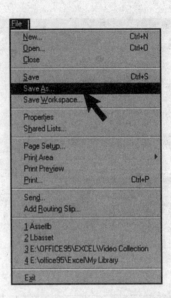

31 To save the schedule as a worksheet template, open the **File** menu and click **Save As**. Excel displays the Save As dialog box.

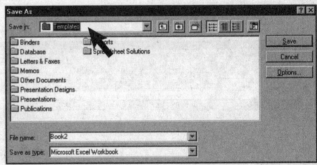

32 Navigate to select the **Templates** folder within the MSOffice folder as the folder in which to save the schedule.

(continues)

Do It Yourself   Create the Calendar Template

(continued)

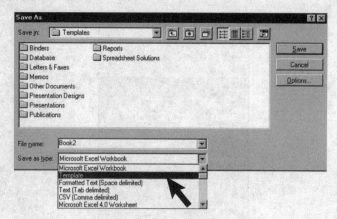

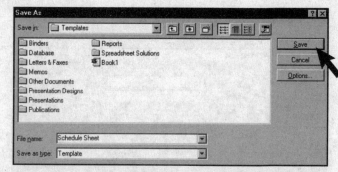

33 Open the **Save as type** drop-down list and click **Template**.

34 Type a file name, such as **Schedule Sheet** and click **Save** to finish saving the worksheet template.

35 Close the worksheet template.

Begin Do It Yourself   Create and Print a New Weekly Calendar

1 Click the **New Workbook** button on the Standard toolbar, if needed, to create a new, blank workbook.

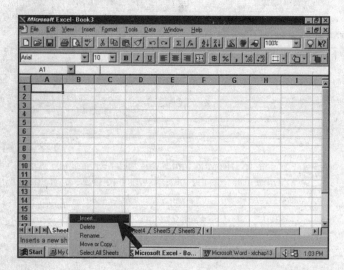

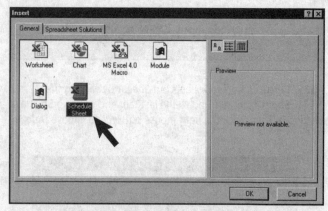

3 Click the **Schedule Sheet** icon (or the icon for the name you gave your schedule sheet template) and click **OK**. Excel inserts a copy of the schedule sheet on a new worksheet in your workbook.

2 Right-click on the **Sheet1** tab and click **Insert**. The Insert dialog box appears.

Do It Yourself   Create and Print a New Weekly Calendar

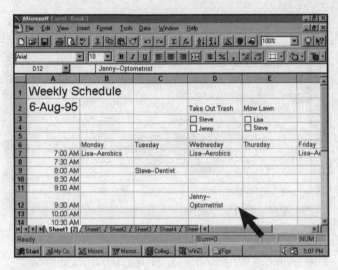

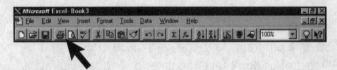

7 Click the **Print** button on the Standard toolbar to print the schedule. Repeat to print additional copies of the schedule for other family members.

4 Enter your family's appointments for the week.

5 Click the check box beside the name of each person who you want to assign to a particular chore for the week.

6 **(Optional)** Save the new schedule workbook.

Whip Yourself into Shape

Most of us know that many diet and exercise programs fail. One key reason may be that most of us don't take the time to set goals or track progress. That's why schools use report cards and companies use performance reviews. To feel a sense of accomplishment or to get a sense of the progress you still need to make, it helps to see on paper precisely where you stand.

Using Excel, you can create a worksheet to track your weekly workouts. If you set up the worksheet as a template, as explained in the Do It Yourself steps, you can insert a new worksheet template to set up your workouts and track your performance. You can chart your progress in a particular area, such as weight or speed.

The Do It Yourself steps show how to create a Weekly Trainer workout template for a runner. The worksheet tracks such things as miles run, time per mile, total miles per week, and average weight. You can just as easily create templates for other kinds of workouts, such as:

- Weight training   Track the number of sets, reps, and weight you perform for each particular exercise each workout.

- Bodybuilding   Track your weight workouts, plus add tracking for your body fat percentage, or measurements such as the size of your biceps.

- Biking   Track your mileage and average speed.

- Walking   Focus in on distance and time per mile, so you can gauge how you're improving your fitness level.

- Stair-climbing   Track your time and intensity level when you use the mean machine.

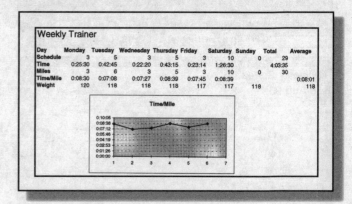

The example Weekly Trainer developed through the Do It Yourself steps includes a chart for tracking the daily time per mile. You can use the Weekly Trainer template to add multiple Weekly Trainer worksheets into a single workbook. Then, you can chart data from several weeks, such as total mileage, on a separate chart (in its own worksheet). The Do It Yourself steps provide an example of pulling a chart like this together, as well.

One last note about the Weekly Trainer: Excel is very finicky when it comes to working with times. Pay careful attention to the instructions on formatting cells for times and entering times in the Do It Yourself steps.

For more details about working with different number formats, see "Format Numbers," p. 104. To get started with charting, see "Work with Charts," p. 207.

Begin Do It Yourself   Create Your Weekly Trainer Template

1 Click the **New Workbook** button on the Standard toolbar, if needed, to create a new, blank workbook.

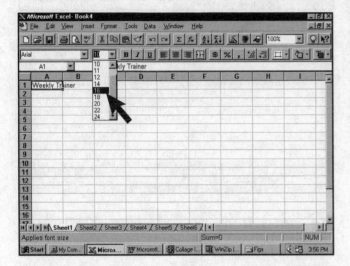

2 Enter **Weekly Trainer** in cell A1 and format that cell the way you want.

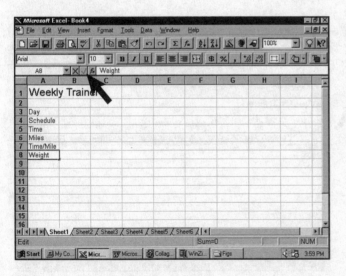

3 Click in cell A3 and make these entries in column A: A3, **Day**; A4, **Schedule**; A5, **Time**; A6, **Miles**; A7, **Time/Mile**; and A8, **Weight**.

4 Select cells **A3:A8** and click the **Bold** button on the Formatting toolbar to format those cells as bold.

5 Enter **Monday** in cell B3.

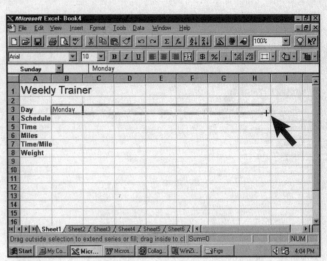

6 With cell B3 still selected, point to the fill handle on the lower right corner of the cell selector and drag the fill handle to select cells **B3:H3**. Release the mouse button. Excel fills the cells with the days of the week.

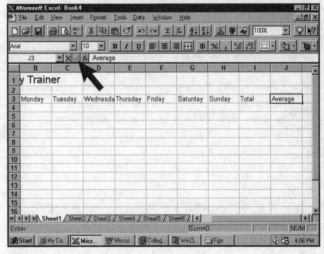

7 Enter **Total** in cell I3 and **Average** in cell J3.

8 (Optional) Format cells **B3:J3** with bold. Adjust any column widths by dragging the appropriate column border beside its column header.

(continues)

Do It Yourself   Create Your Weekly Trainer Template *(continued)*

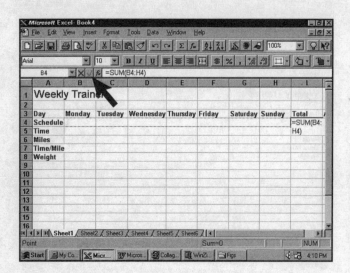

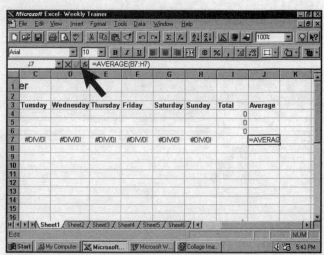

9 Select cell **I4**, click the **AutoSum** button on the Standard toolbar, drag to select cells **B4:H4**, and click the green entry check mark on the Formula bar to finish the formula.

11 Select cell **J7**. Enter the formula **=average(b7:h7)** and click the green check mark in the Formula bar. When you finish entering the formula, you see the #DIV/0 error. Don't worry about it for now.

12 Copy the formula from J7 to J8 by selecting cell **J7** and dragging its fill handle.

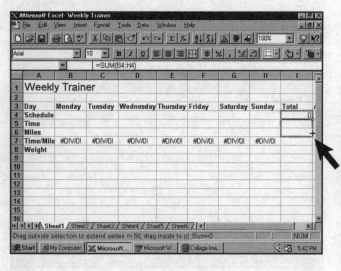

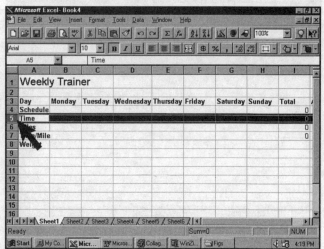

10 With cell I4 still selected, drag the fill handle to copy its formula to cells **I5:I6**.

13 Click the row header for row 5 to select the whole row.

Do It Yourself Create Your Weekly Trainer Template

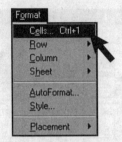

14 Open the **Format** menu and choose **Cells**. The Format Cells dialog box appears. Click on the **Number** tab if necessary.

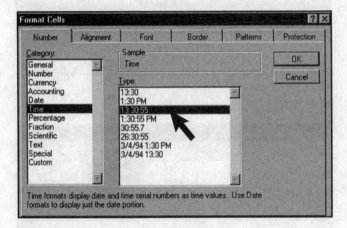

15 In the Category list, click **Time**. In the Type list, click **13:30:55**. Click **OK**.

16 Click the row header for row 7 to select that row. Repeat steps 14 and 15 to format the cells for this row.

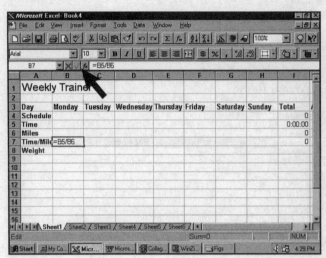

17 Select cell **B7** and enter the formula **=B5/B6**.

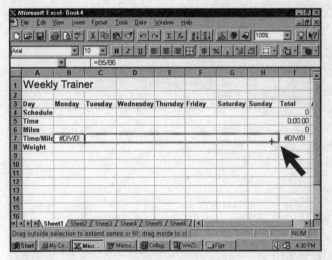

18 Copy the formula from cell B7 to cells C7:H7. Don't worry about the #DIV/0 error.

(continues)

Do It Yourself   Create Your Weekly Trainer Template   *(continued)*

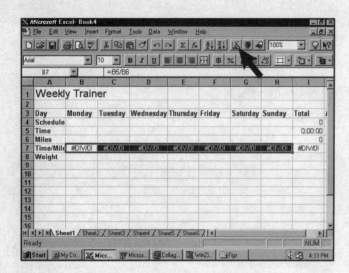

19 Select cells **B7:H7** and click the **ChartWizard** button on the Standard toolbar. This is the first step for creating a chart illustrating your Time/Mile for each workout. You choose other cells to chart other data.

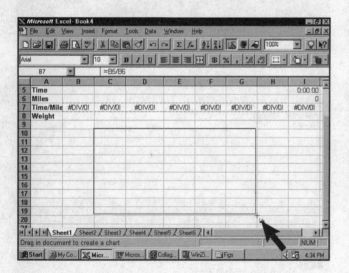

20 Drag to define a chart area on the worksheet. The first ChartWizard dialog box appears. Simply click **Next>** to continue, as you've already selected the range to chart.

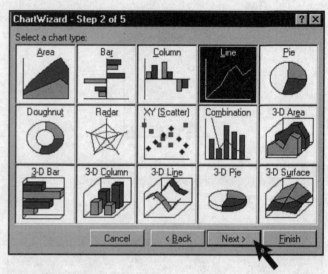

21 In the dialog box for step 2, click the line chart thumbnail sketch and click **Next>**.

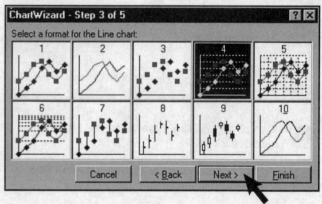

22 Simply click **Next>** again in the dialog box for step 3.

Do It Yourself   Create Your Weekly Trainer Template

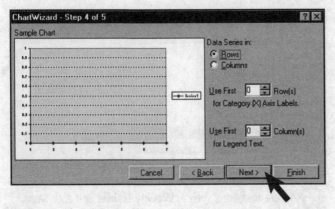

 Simply click **Next>** again at the dialog box for step 4.

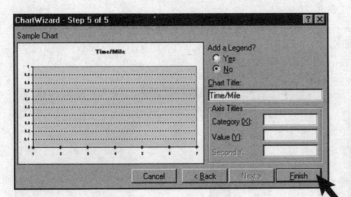

 In the final ChartWizard dialog box, click **No** under Add a Legend?. Enter **Time/Mile** in the Chart Title text box and click **Finish**. Excel sets up the chart. The chart automatically adjusts to reflect data you enter.

25 Delete all the worksheets but Sheet1 by clicking the Sheet2 tab, scrolling to the last tab, and pressing **Shift** and clicking it. Then, click the right mouse button and choose **Delete**.

26 Excel displays a message telling you it will delete all the worksheets. Click **OK** to continue.

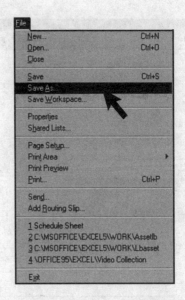

27 To save the training sheet as a worksheet template, open the **File** menu and click **Save As**. Excel displays the Save As dialog box.

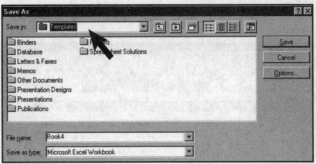

28 Navigate to select the **Templates** folder within the MSOffice folder as the folder in which to save the training sheet.

(continues)

Do It Yourself   Create Your Weekly Trainer Template   *(continued)*

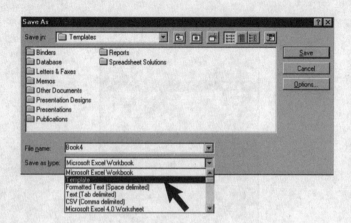

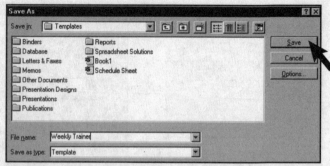

29 Open the **Save as type** drop-down list and click **Template**.

30 Type a file name, such as **Weekly Trainer** and click **Save** to finish saving the worksheet template.

31 Close the worksheet template.

Begin Do It Yourself   Set Up a New Week

1 Click the **New Workbook** button on the Standard toolbar, if needed, to create a new, blank workbook.

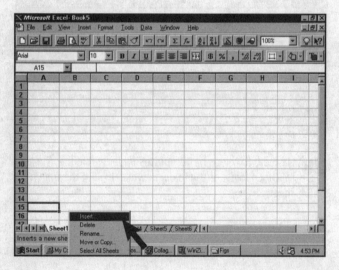

2 Right-click on the **Sheet1** tab and click **Insert**. The Insert dialog box appears.

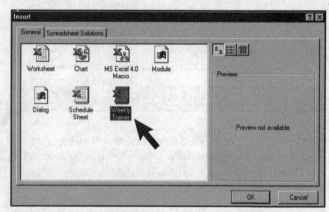

3 Click the **Weekly Trainer** icon (or the icon for the name you gave your training sheet template) and click **OK**. Excel inserts a copy of the Weekly Trainer on a new worksheet in your workbook.

Do It Yourself   Set Up a New Week

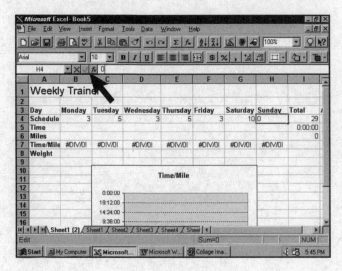

4 Enter your scheduled mileage for the week in cells B4:H4.

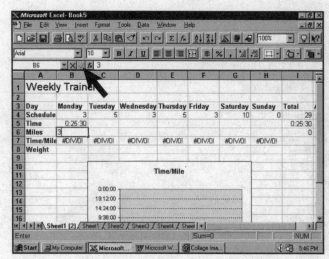

6 Enter the total miles run in row 6. When you finish entering the value, Excel automatically calculates the Time/Mile value and updates your chart.

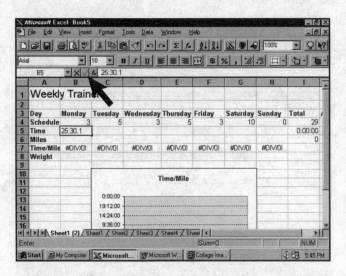

5 For each workout day, enter the total running time in row 5. You need to enter all times in the mm:ss.0 format for Excel to interpret it correctly. Do not enter hours; convert them to minutes (enter 1:06:30.0 as 66:30.0).

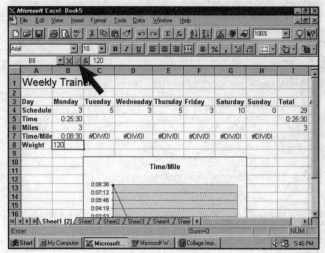

7 Enter your weight in row 8 for the workout day.

8 Save the workbook and close it until your next workout update.

(continues)

Do It Yourself Set Up a New Week

(continued)

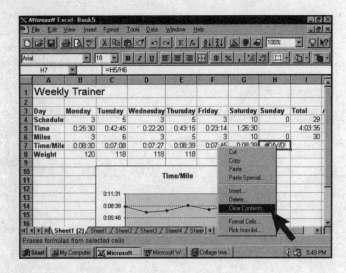

9 Open and fill in the appropriate cells for each daily workout. For days when you don't run, select the **Time/Mile** cell in row 7, right-click, and choose **Clear Contents**. This removes the #DIV/0 error without disturbing any formatting.

10 Save and print your Weekly Trainer as needed.

Begin Do It Yourself Chart Multiple Weeks of Data

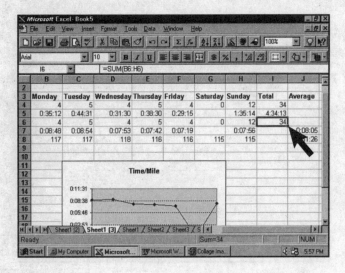

1 Insert Weekly Trainer additional worksheets for more weeks in your workbook and enter the data.

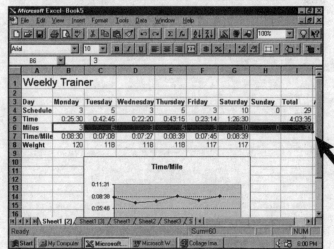

2 Select the data you want to chart on the first Weekly Trainer worksheet, such as the mileage run in B6:I6.

Do It Yourself   Chart Multiple Weeks of Data

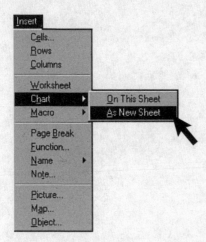

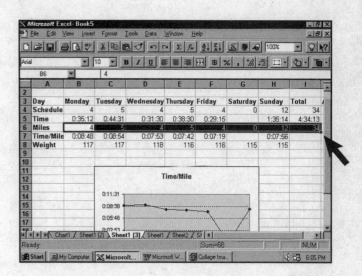

3 Open the **Insert** menu, point to **Chart**, and click **As New Sheet**.

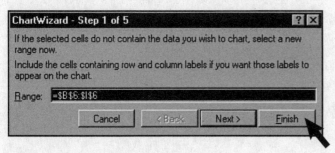

4 The first ChartWizard dialog box appears. You can go through all the ChartWizard steps, or simply click **Finish** to insert the chart using the default chart type.

5 Click the tab for the worksheet that has additional mileage you want to chart. Select cells **B6:I6** and click the **Copy** button on the Standard toolbar.

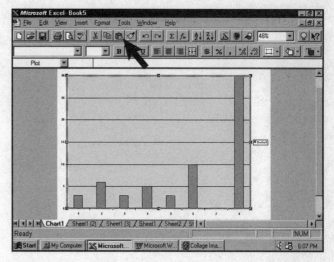

6 Click the tab for the chart worksheet and click to select the chart plot area. Click the **Paste** button on the Standard toolbar. Excel pastes in the miles for the next week into the chart.

7 Repeat steps 4 through 6 to chart cells B6:I6 from other Weekly Trainer worksheets you've inserted in the current workbook.

8 Save your workbook.

DO IT YOURSELF

Manage Your Money

Excel provides so much calculating power that it can be intimidating—so many functions, so little time. But you shouldn't hesitate to put Excel to work tracking your dollars and cents. By creating some relatively straight-forward worksheets, you can get a clearer picture of where you stand financially and make better financial decisions.

This section shows you how to create different worksheets for counting your pennies. So, throw away your abacus or whatever other method you've been using to track your finances and build some worksheets instead.

What You Will Find in This Section

Discover Your Net Worth

During the course of your life, you may set numerous financial goals. Some may be small in scale, like striving to pay off a particular credit card by a particular date. Others may require years of effort. You may want to save to pay cash for a car. You may want to pay your mortgage off five years early. Or, you may want to increase your net worth to a certain amount by a certain date.

Great, you say. But what's *net worth,* and why do I care about it? Simply stated, your net worth reflects the total value of your investments and assets, minus your total debts. This calculation gives you a realistic picture of what you *really* own. For example, your neighbor may have more stuff than you do (a great car, a boat, jet skis, and more), but if that neighbor has borrowed large sums of money for all these

Assets as of Lisa A. Bucki			8/20/95 19:08
Asset Name	**Account No.**	**Balance**	
Savings Account	555-55-31	$	12,015.62
Checking Account	555-55-30	$	3,314.12
Certificate of Deposit	x1278	$	1,514.00
IRA	52-52-0004	$	6,712.32
Stock Account			
Mutual Fund Account			
U.S. Savings Bonds		$	500.00
Home Value		$	99,500.00
Other			
Total Assets		**$**	**123,556.06**
Liability Name	**Account No.**	**Balance**	
Mortgage	222-2243-222	$	71,552.00
Car Loan	154-451	$	9,949.00
VISA			
MasterCard	5555-2222-0001-001	$	125.00
Discover	8383-3333-4141	$	500.00
Other			
Total Liabilities		**$**	**82,126.00**
Net Worth		**$**	**41,430.06**

Cell Entries for Your Net Worth Worksheet

Cell	Entry	Cell	Entry
A1	Assets as of	A14	Total Assets
C1	=NOW()	C14	=SUM(C5:C13)
A2	Your name	A16	Liability Name
A4	Asset Name	B16	Account No.
B4	Account No.	C16	Balance
C4	Balance	A17	Mortgage
A5	Savings Account	A18	Car Loan
A6	Checking Account	A19	VISA
A7	Certificate of Deposit	A20	MasterCard
A8	IRA	A21	Discover
A9	Stock Account	A22	Other
A10	Mutual Fund Account	A23	Total Liabilities
A11	U.S. Savings Bonds	C23	=SUM(C17:C22)
A12	Home Value	A25	Net Worth
A13	Other	C25	=C14–C23

purchases, your net worth may be larger if you have substantially less debt.

It's important to keep your eye on your net worth, especially if you're planning to borrow money in the future for a new home or to start a business. When you borrow money, your bank takes a look at your net worth to see how much debt you have and how responsible you are in managing your money. If your net worth is a negative number, which can occur if you have few assets but accumulate a lot of credit card debt, you may have trouble getting additional credit unless your income greatly exceeds your monthly debts.

If you have additional assets and liabilities to include, insert rows for them in the appropriate section of the net worth worksheet. See "Insert and Delete Rows and Columns," p. 64 for a reminder of how to insert rows.

Begin Do It Yourself   Create and Use the Net Worth Worksheet

1 Save the workbook and name it Net Worth after you complete all the cell entries in the table.

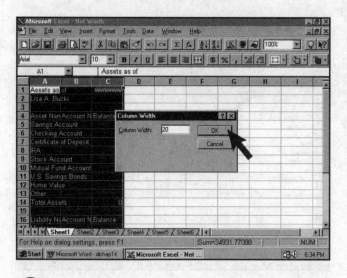

2 Select columns **A** through **C** by holding down the **Shift** key and clicking each column letter. Right-click the selection and click **Column Width**. Enter **20** in the Column Width text box and click **OK**.

3 Select column **A**. Press and hold the **Ctrl** key while you use the mouse to select cells **B4:C4**, **B14:C14**, **B16:C16**, **B23:C23**, and **B25:C25**. Click the **Bold** button on the Formatting toolbar.

(continues)

Do It Yourself   Create and Use the Net Worth Worksheet   *(continued)*

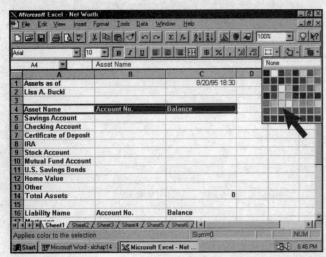

4. Apply any additional formatting you wish (such as a border, shading, or font color) to the following ranges: **A4:C4**, **A14:C14**, **A16:C16**, **A23:C23**, and **A25:C25**.

6. Complete the Assets portion of the worksheet by filling in the account number and latest balance (from your monthly statement) for each asset. Use the most recent appraisal for the Home Value balance.

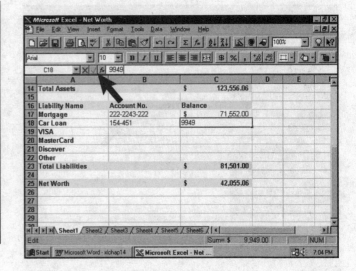

5. Use the **Currency Style** button on the Formatting toolbar to format cell ranges **C5:C14** and **C17:C23** and cell **C25**.

7. Complete the Liabilities section by entering the account number and balance due (from your monthly statement) for each. If you need to amortize your mortgage to check the balance, see "Make Smart Decisions with the Loan Manager," p. 399.

Do It Yourself   Create and Use the Net Worth Worksheet

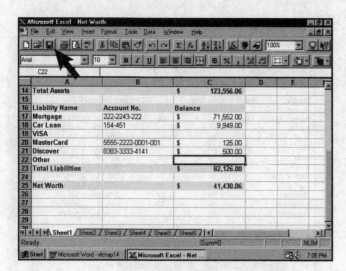

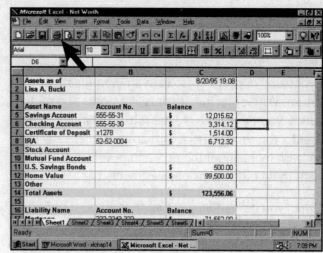

8 Excel automatically calculates your net worth. Click the **Save** button on the Standard toolbar to save your entries.

10 Click the **Print** button on the Standard toolbar to print the Net Worth worksheet.

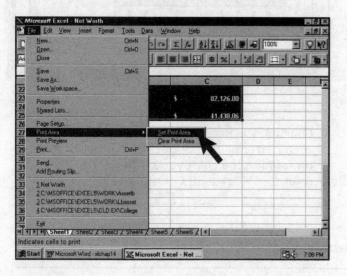

9 Select the cells with the net worth entries and calculations (this includes A1:C25, unless you've added rows to the worksheet). Open the **File** menu, point to **Print Area**, and click **Set Print Area**.

Track Investment Values

Your basic savings account or certificate of deposit is a fine, safe place to park your investment dollars. However, safety has a price—namely, you bypass the opportunity to earn an even greater return. With other investments like stocks and mutual funds, you can earn a greater return on your investment. (You should check with an investment advisor to learn more about the risks and rewards associated with these other kinds of investments.)

When you have money in a savings account or buy a CD, the bank tells you exactly what interest rate it will pay you. With investments like stocks and mutual funds, it's up to you to figure out how quickly your investment is growing and to determine when to sell a particular investment or buy more.

This Do It Yourself shows you how to track the value of an investment, including the year-to-date increase or decrease (as a percentage) in the value of the investment. Armed with this information, you can make intelligent investment decisions.

Start by creating a new, blank workbook and making the cell entries listed in the table. Then use the Do It Yourself steps to finish the Investment Value worksheet and track one or more investments.

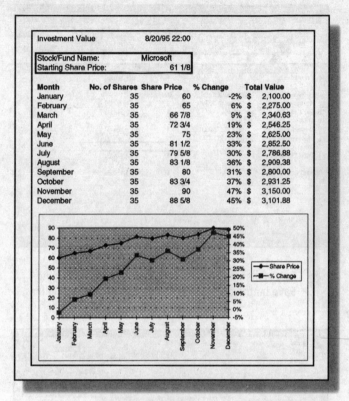

Charting the investment's progress provides an even better picture of how it's doing. For more on refining the chart you create in this task, refer to, "Work with Charts," p. 207.

Cell Entries for Your Investment Value Worksheet

Cell	Entry
A1	Investment Value
C1	=NOW()
A3	Stock/Fund Name:
A4	Starting Share Price:
A6	Month
B6	No. of Shares
C6	Share Price

Cell	Entry
D6	% Change
E6	Total Value
A7	January
D7	=IF(C7<$C$4,–(1–(C7/$C$4)), ((C7/$C$4)–1))
E7	=B7*C7

Begin Do It Yourself   Finish the Investment Worksheet

1 After you complete the cell entries, save the workbook and name it Investment Value.

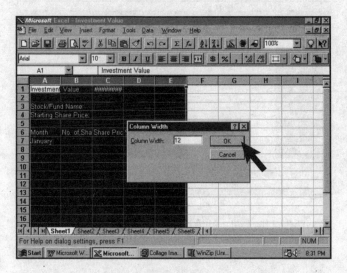

2 Select columns **A** through **E**. Right-click the selection and click **Column Width**. Enter **12** in the Column Width text box and click **OK**.

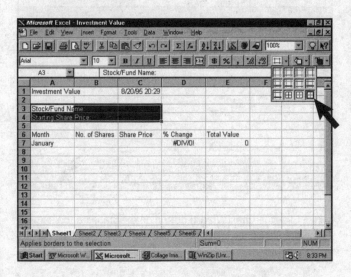

3 Select cells **A3:C4** and use the **Borders** button on the Formatting toolbar to add a border around the range.

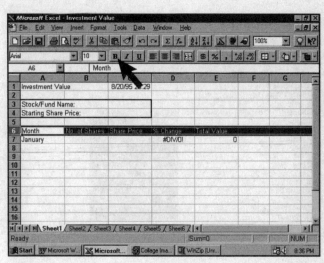

4 Select row **6** and click the **Bold** button on the Formatting toolbar.

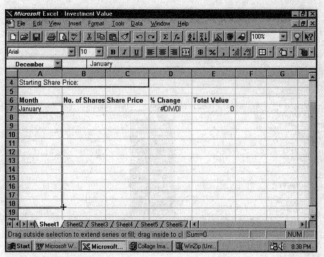

5 Select cell **A7**. Drag the fill handle down to fill the range **A7:A18**.

(continues)

Do It Yourself Finish the Investment Worksheet *(continued)*

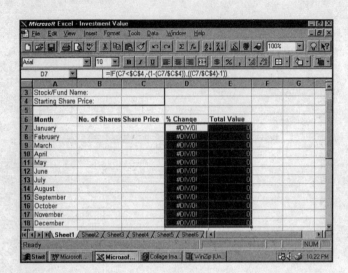

6 Select cells **D7:E7**. Drag the fill handle down to fill the range **D7:E18**.

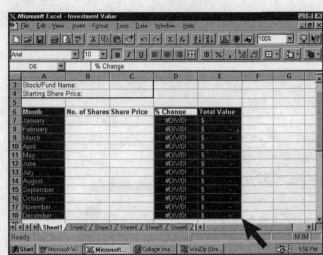

8 Select the range **A6:A18**. Press and hold the **Ctrl** key while you drag to select the range **C6:D18**.

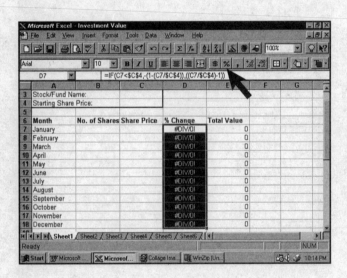

7 Select cells **D7:D18**. Click the **Percent Style** button on the Formatting toolbar. You can also format cells **E7:E18** with the **Currency Style** button.

9 Click the **ChartWizard** button on the Standard toolbar and drag to define a chart area below the cell entries you've created.

Do It Yourself Finish the Investment Worksheet

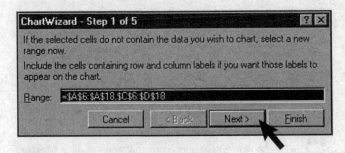

10 The ChartWizard—Step 1 of 5 dialog box appears. Click **Next>**.

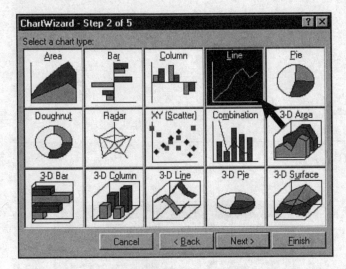

11 In the ChartWizard—Step 2 of 5 dialog box, click the **Line** option and then click **Next>**.

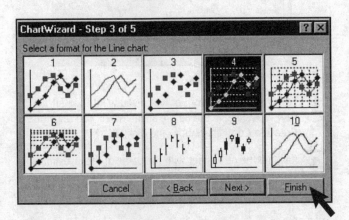

12 In the ChartWizard—Step 3 of 5 dialog box, simply click **Finish**.

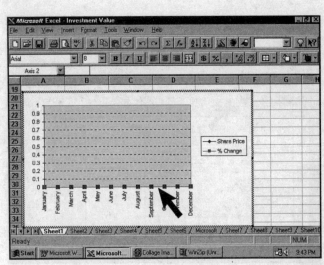

13 Double-click the chart and then click on the line for the **% Change** series so that selection handles appear for each data point.

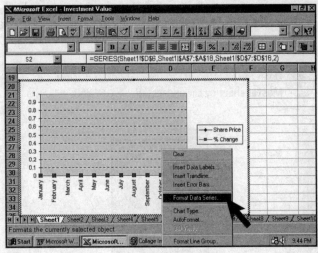

14 Right-click the axis to display a shortcut menu. Click **Format Data Series**.

(continues)

Do It Yourself Finish the Investment Worksheet *(continued)*

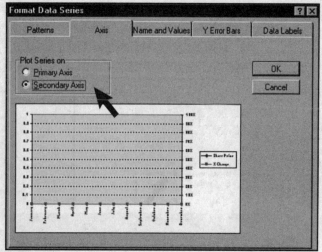

16 Double-click the tab for the Investment Value worksheet. In the Rename Sheet dialog box that appears, type **Master** and click **OK**.

17 Save the workbook.

15 In the Format Data Series dialog box, click the **Axis** tab and click to select the **Secondary Axis** option button. Click **OK**.

Begin Do It Yourself Track an Investment

1 Open the Investment Value workbook and select the **Master** sheet by clicking its tab.

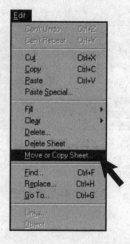

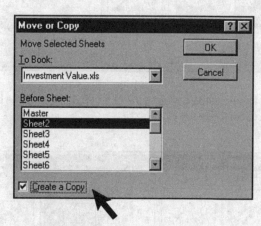

2 Open the **Edit** menu and click **Move or Copy Sheet**. The Move or Copy dialog box appears.

3 Select the sheet in front of which you want to insert the new worksheet in the Before Sheet list, click to select the **Create a Copy** check box, and click **OK**.

4 Rename the new sheet with the name of the investment you're tracking, such as the name of the stock or mutual fund.

Do It Yourself Track an Investment

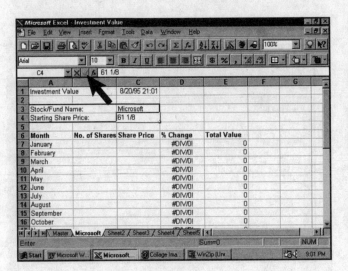

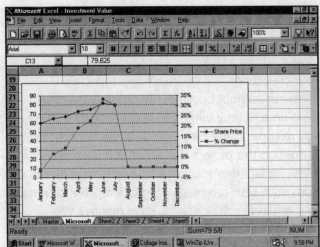

5 Enter the name of the investment and the closing price from the end of the prior year in cells C3 and C4, respectively. You can enter the value in fractions. Excel displays the fraction but calculates using the equivalent decimal value.

6 Save the workbook.

8 Scroll down to view the chart. It displays the change in Share Price, measured against the axis on the left, and the % Change, measured against the axis on the right. The axes adjust to fit the range of the values you enter.

9 Save the workbook and print the worksheet for each investment when you need to.

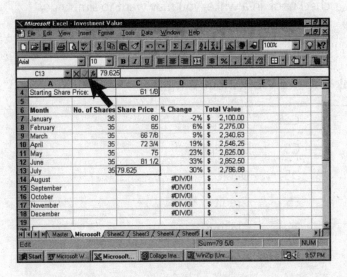

7 Each month, open the workbook, select the worksheet for the investment by clicking its tab, and enter the **No. of Shares** and **Share Price** values for the month.

Check Your Checking

Do you consider balancing your checkbook right up there with going to the dentist on your list of "Ways I'd Least Like to Spend My Time"? Balancing your checkbook is a necessary evil, especially if your checking account becomes mysteriously overdrawn from time to time when you don't anticipate it. Hey, if you're comfortable being off by a few hundred dollars or so, skip this project altogether. But for most of us, knowing whether you're "a little light" this month or flush with cash can make a big difference with regard to spending decisions (read: Have money? Will spend!)

Because balancing your checkbook involves relatively simple math, you can create an Excel worksheet to do the dirty deed. Then, if you save that worksheet as a template, you can use it each month to compare the *debits* (cash withdrawals, or checks written) and *credits* (deposits) to and from your checking account.

The Do It Yourself steps explain how to set up the Checkbook Balance worksheet. After you set up the worksheet and save it as a template, you should use it

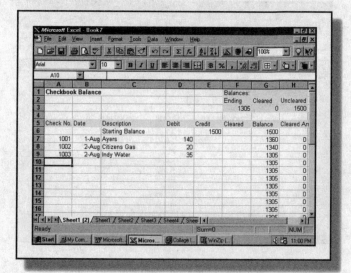

monthly. The first month, use your checkbook balance from the last time you balanced your checkbook as the starting balance. (If you haven't balanced your checkbook in a while, you may want to simply go with the bank's balance, as that's the one that counts).

Cell Entries for Your Checkbook Balance Worksheet Template

Cell	Entry	Cell	Entry
A1	Checkbook Balance	C5	Description
F1	Balances:	D5	Debit
F2	Ending	E5	Credit
G2	Cleared	F5	Cleared
H2	Uncleared	G5	Balance
H3	=E6+G3	H5	Cleared Amt.
F3	=G36	G6	=E6
G3	=SUM(H6:H36)	G7	=G6–D7+E7
A5	Check No.	H7	=IF(F7="X",–D7+E7,)
B5	Date		

After the first month, you'll need to set up a new worksheet for each month, using the ending balance from the prior month (not the cleared balance) as the starting balance. To clear transactions from a prior month, go back to the worksheet for that month.

To start the worksheet template, open a new, blank workbook and delete all the sheets except the sheet on which you'll create the template. (Click the first sheet to delete, press **Shift**, click the last sheet to delete, right-click, and choose **Delete**.) Then, enter the values and formulas detailed in the following table.

The task called "Work with Your Own Templates," p. 175, provides more information about saving a particular worksheet as a template.

One point to clarify: the Ending Balance in Cells F2 and F3 represents your checkbook's ending balance at the time you are balancing your statement. The Uncleared Balance in Cells H2 and H3 represents the ending balance on your bank statement after you have cleared the items shown on the bank statement.

Begin Do It Yourself Create the Checkbook Balance Template

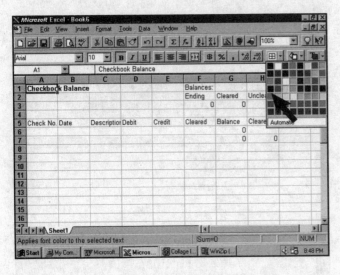

① Apply the formatting you want to cell **A1**, changing the size and color of the text using the Formatting toolbar.

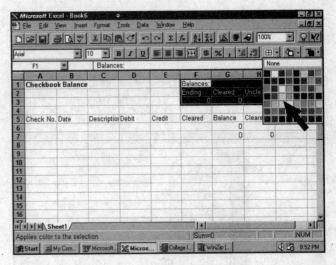

② Select cells **F1:H3**. Either apply a background fill or border around those cells using the Formatting toolbar. If you opt for a fill color, select a light color to avoid printing problems.

(continues)

Do It Yourself   Create the Checkbook Balance Template   *(continued)*

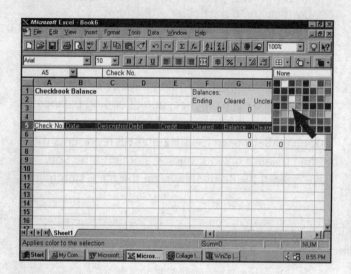

3 Click the row header for row 5 and apply a background fill using the **Color** button on the Formatting toolbar.

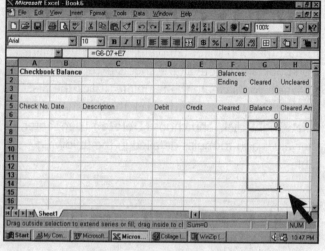

6 Click cell **G7**. Drag the fill handle down to copy its formula to cells **G8:G36**.

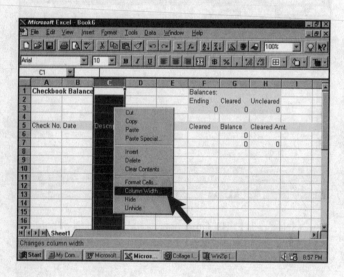

4 Click the column head for column C to select the column, right-click to display the shortcut menu, and click **Column Width**.

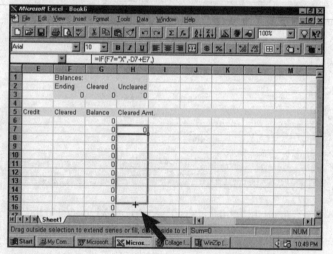

7 Click cell **H7**. Drag the fill handle down to copy its formula to cells **H8:H36**.

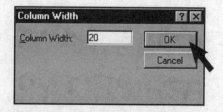

5 In the Column Width text box of the Column Width dialog box, type **20**. Click **OK**.

Do It Yourself   Create the Checkbook Balance Template

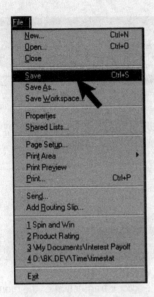

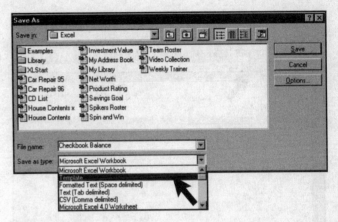

10 Open the **Save as type** drop-down list and click **Template**.

11 Click the **Save** button to save the worksheet as a template.

12 Close the template.

8 Open the **File** menu and choose **Save**, or click the **Save** button on the Standard toolbar. The Save As dialog box appears.

9 Enter a name like **Checkbook Balance** in the File name text box.

Begin Do It Yourself   Use the Checkbook Balance Template Each Month

1 Click the **New Workbook** button on the Standard toolbar, if needed, to create a new, blank workbook.

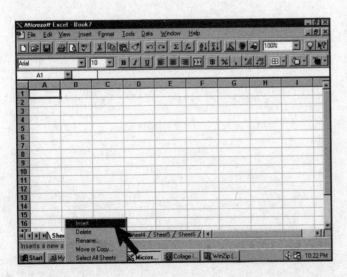

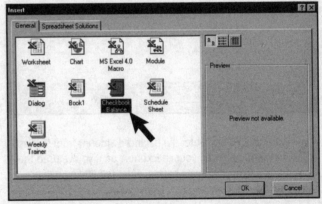

3 Click the **Checkbook Balance** icon (or the icon for the name you gave your schedule sheet template) and click **OK**. Excel inserts a copy of the Checkbook Balance template on a new worksheet in your workbook.

(continues)

2 Right-click on the **Sheet1** tab and click **Insert** from the shortcut menu that appears. The Insert dialog box appears.

Do It Yourself   Use the Checkbook Balance Template Each Month

(continued)

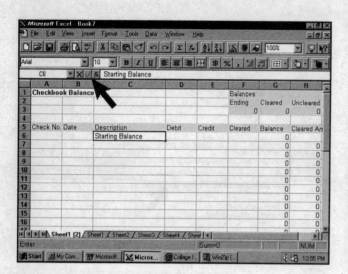

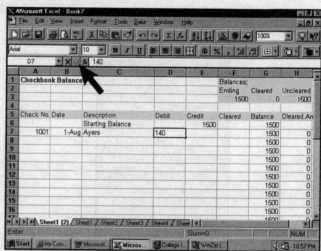

4 Click cell **C6** and enter **Starting Balance**. You enter the starting balance for the month in this row.

6 For each checkbook transaction of the month, enter the check number, date, and description in the appropriate columns. For ATM withdrawals, cash withdrawals, or checks written, enter the amount in the Debit column.

7 For deposits into the checking account, enter the date, description, and credit amount. After debits and credits, the balance value changes.

8 After you have made all the entries you need to make, save and close the workbook.

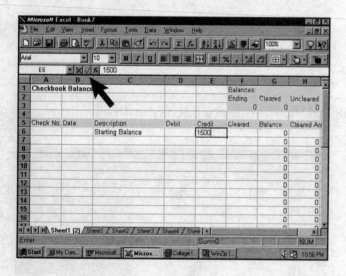

5 Click cell **E6** and enter the balanced amount from the last time you balanced your checkbook; or, if you've used the Checkbook Balance template before, enter the ending balance from the prior month.

Begin Do It Yourself   Balance the Checkbook Balance Sheet

1 Open the checkbook workbook for the month.

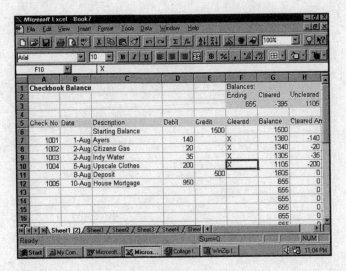

2 Comparing your entries in the current worksheet to your monthly checking account statement, enter an "X" in the cleared column for each entry that appears on the checking account statement.

3 The Uncleared balance amount in cell H3 should match the ending balance on your checking account statement. If not, check to make sure you've cleared other transactions. Otherwise, check for errors from other months.

Use Excel's Pre-Built Templates

I f you worked with the last few sections of this book, you've learned to put together worksheets to handle a variety of tasks. If you paid attention (and we know you did), you learned a little bit about entering text and values, creating formulas, and working with some of Excel's other features like charting and working with maps.

If you survived those sections, then this one should be a no-brainer. This section of *The Big Basics Book of Excel for Windows 95* walks you through the process of using Excel's built-in *templates*, which contain all the formulas and formatting for fairly complex calculations. All you have to do is fill in some data that's specific to the operation you're performing, save, and print.

Three templates install automatically when you perform a typical installation of Excel or Microsoft Office. You can add the others using the Add/Remove Programs feature in the Windows 95 Control Panel or the Microsoft Office shortcut bar. Here's the rundown of the available templates covered in this section; the first three are those that install automatically.

What You Will Find in This Section

Bill a Customer with the Invoice

Technically speaking, all you need to create a legally enforceable invoice is a pen and a piece of paper. However, if you want your business image to convey more sophistication than a fifth-grade homework assignment, Excel comes to the rescue for you.

One of the templates that installs automatically with Excel is an invoice. Not only will Excel's Invoice template lend professional polish (which should make it easier for your customers to figure out how much they owe you so they can pay you more quickly), but also it tracks the contents of each invoice you create in the Template Wizard database workbook. Excel saves this database, called invdb.xls, in the Library folder within the Excel folder. This database enables you to capture data about products and services you sell to customers and keep a record of all the invoices you send. The Invoice template displays its own toolbar when you open it; it also has buttons and cell notes (point to a red cell note indicator to see one) that enable you to work more easily with the template.

> You can open the invdb.xls file just as you would open any other workbook file. See "Open an Existing Workbook," p. 89.

You should start by customizing the Invoice template with your changes and saving it under a new name. You can:

- Add your company name and logo to the invoice.

- Change the font for the company address.

- Specify which credit cards you accept for customer purchases.

- Adjust the sales tax figures you use to calculate the invoice total.

- Automatically add shipping charges.

After you save and rename the customized Invoice template, you can use it to create individual invoices and add data to the invdb.xls database, a file you can open and work with like any other list in Excel.

The Do It Yourself steps explain how to customize and use Excel's Invoice template.

> See "Build a Database," p. 181, for several tasks that provide information about working with database lists in Excel.

Begin Do It Yourself   Open and Customize the Invoice Template

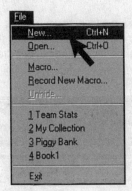

1 Open the **File** menu and click **New**. The New dialog box appears.

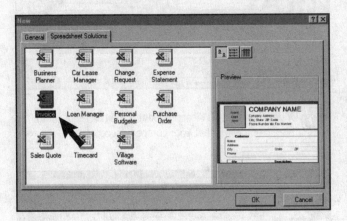

2 Click the **Spreadsheet Solutions** tab and then click the **Invoice** icon. The Preview area displays the template.

3 Click **OK** to open the template.

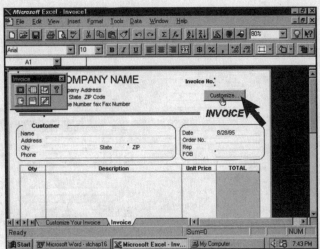

4 Click the **Customize** button on the template. The contents of the Customize Your Invoice tab appear.

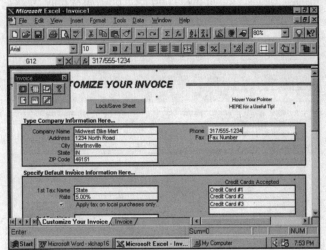

5 In the Type Company Information Here… section, enter the information for your company so your company's name and contact information appears on the invoice. You can leave cells blank if you wish.

(continues)

Do It Yourself Open and Customize the Invoice Template *(continued)*

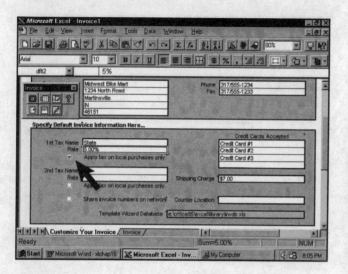

6 Scroll down to the Specify Default Invoice Information Here... section. The 1st Tax Name entry enables you to specify taxes for customers in your state. Change the rate if needed. Deselect the **Apply tax on local purchases only** check box to apply the 1st tax to all invoices.

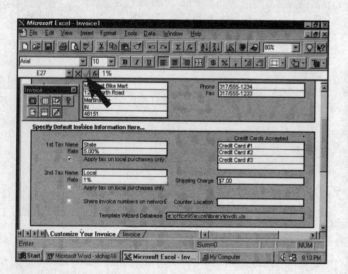

7 The 2nd Tax Name entry enables you to specify local (city) taxes. Enter the name and rate. Click to check the **Apply tax on local purchases only** check box to apply the 2nd tax only to customers from your company's area.

8 Check the **Share invoice numbers on network** check box if more than one user on a network will use the template and you want the template to automatically number the invoices.

9 If you're working on a network, use the Counter Location cell to specify the path for the folder that will hold the file that counts the invoices. (Excel automatically creates the counter file.)

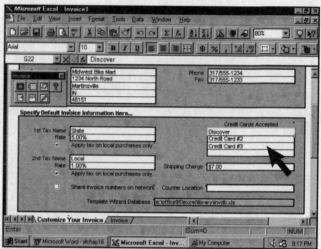

10 Under Credit Cards Accepted, enter the names of up to three credit cards that your company accepts.

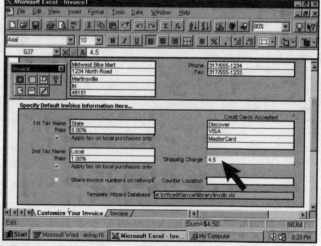

11 Change the default shipping charge, if needed.

Do It Yourself Open and Customize the Invoice Template

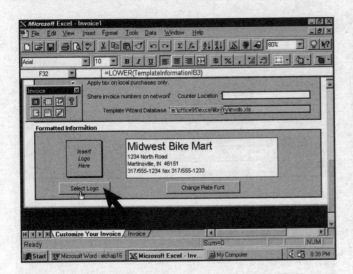

12 Scroll down to the Formatted Information section. Click the **Select Logo** button if you want to add your logo image to your invoices. The Picture dialog box appears.

14 Click the **Change Plate Font** button to change the font for your company's name and address on the invoice. The Format Cells dialog box appears.

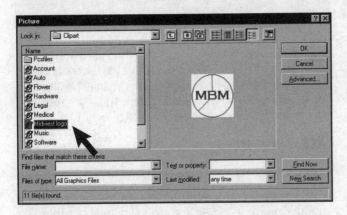

13 Navigate to the directory that holds the picture file for your logo. Click the file in the Name list and click **OK** to insert it.

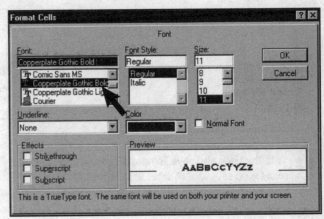

15 Select the new font from the Font drop-down list. If you want, change the size of the font using the Size list box. Then, click **OK**. Excel applies the new font.

(continues)

Do It Yourself Open and Customize the Invoice Template *(continued)*

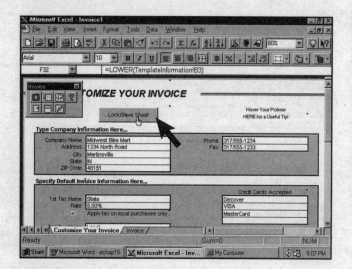

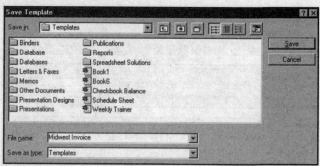

18 The Save Template dialog box appears. In the File name text box, type a name for your custom Invoice template, if needed, and click **Save**.

16 Scroll back up to the top of the sheet. Click the **Lock/Save Sheet** button. Excel displays the Lock/Save Sheet dialog box.

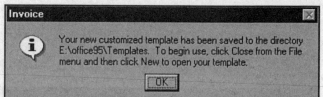

19 An Invoice message box appears, telling you that Excel saved your invoice template and that you can use it. The location you see in the figure is for Excel as a part of MSOffice. The location for the template will be different on your screen if you are working with a stand-alone version of Excel. Click **OK**.

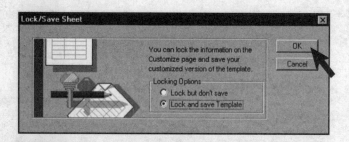

20 Close the template.

17 With the **Lock and save Template** option button selected, click **OK** to save your changes to the template.

The folder you specify as the counter location must be on a server in a universally accessible place.

Begin Do It Yourself   Create an Invoice

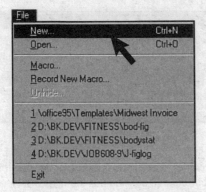

1 Open the **File** menu and click **New**. The New dialog box appears.

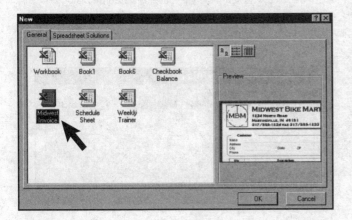

2 Click the icon for the custom Invoice template and click **OK**.

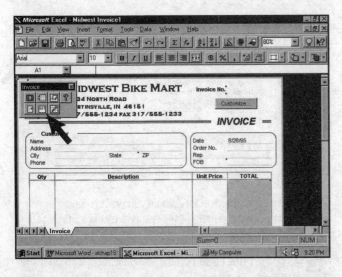

3 To number the invoice, click the **Assign a Number** button on the Invoice toolbar.

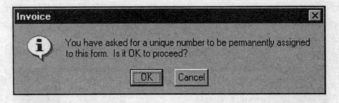

4 In the message box that asks if it's OK to permanently assign a number to the form, click **OK**.

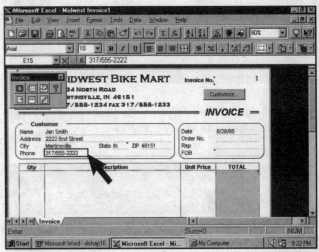

5 Enter information about the customer in the Customer area.

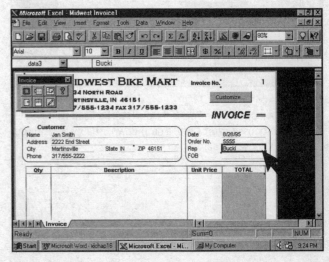

6 Enter the information about the order number, freight, and so on.

(continues)

Do It Yourself Create an Invoice *(continued)*

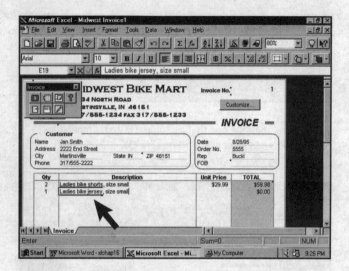

7 Enter the items that are part of the order with the pricing information. Enter one item per row.

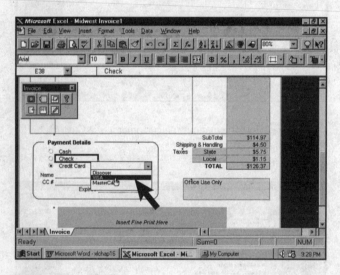

8 Scroll down to the Payment Details section and fill it in. If you choose **Credit Card**, a drop-down list appears and you can choose the card type.

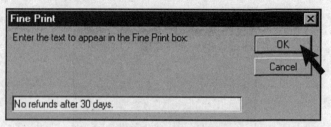

9 Make Insert Fine Print Here and Insert Farewell Statement Here entries, if needed. For example, click the **Insert Fine Print Here** button; in the dialog box that appears, type the text you want and click **OK**.

10 Click the **Save** tool on the Standard toolbar to save the invoice. The Template File–Save to Database dialog box appears so you can specify whether to save the invoice data to the invoice tracking database.

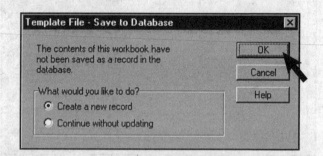

11 Leave the **Create a new record** option selected and click **OK**. The Save As dialog box appears.

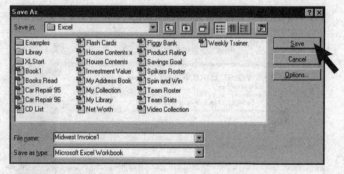

12 Navigate to the directory where you want to save the invoice. Type a name in the File name text box, if needed, and click **Save**.

13 Click the **Print** button on the Standard toolbar to print the invoice.

Make Smart Decisions with the Loan Manager

A couple of years ago, interest rates hit the lowest levels in years. Thousands of people flocked to mortgage companies to refinance high interest rate loans for loans with lower interest rates. Refinancing resulted in a windfall for homeowners, each of whom has been saving hundreds of dollars a year in interest per mortgage since.

The burst of refinancing activity has caused mortgage companies to do more to compete for your business. Not only have lenders offered a greater variety of options in loan choices (5/25, 7/23, 1-year ARM, 3-year ARM, and so on), but they've also developed very attractive home equity loan programs.

Unless you've got a calculator for a brain, it's unlikely that you'll be able to compare the payments based on the principal you borrow and the interest rate you pay. In fact, it's better to have a good idea of what these figures will be before you meet with a lender.

If you really want to impress your loan officer, you can use the Loan Manager template to take a look at payment amounts at varying principal and interest rates. The Loan Manager template installs automatically when you perform the typical Excel install. The Loan Manager template offers several sophisticated features:

- You can create a custom version of the template that contains your family name and other basic information.

- After you make a few basic entries on the Loan Data sheet, the template quickly calculates the total payment, including interest and principal amounts.

- Using the Loan Amortization Table sheet, you can enter the amount of any additional principal payments you make using the **Refinance/Prepay** button. The template automatically

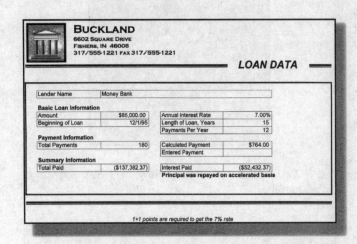

calculates the actual loan balance, taking into account your extra payments.

- If you have an adjustable rate mortgage, use the **Refinance/Prepay** button to specify rate changes (which in essence refinance the loan). The template calculates the new payments for you.

- The Summary Graph sheet depicts the total of the interest and principal you've paid to the lender up to the present date.

You can use the Loan Manager template to evaluate car and mortgage loan choices, or to get an up-to-date snapshot of how much you owe on your current loan. The Do It Yourself steps explain how to customize and use this template.

Because the cost to refinance a loan can be high, use the Loan Manager template to look at how much you would save by prepaying principal and compare the savings with the savings from refinancing.

Begin Do It Yourself   Open the Template and Customize It

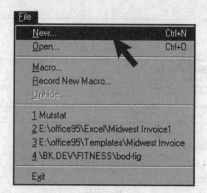

1 Open the **File** menu and click **New**. The New dialog box appears.

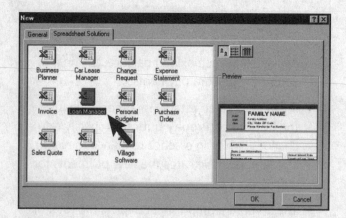

2 Click the **Spreadsheet Solutions** tab and then click the **Loan Manager** icon. The Preview area displays the template.

3 Click **OK** to open the template. The Loan Manager template opens with the Loan Data sheet selected.

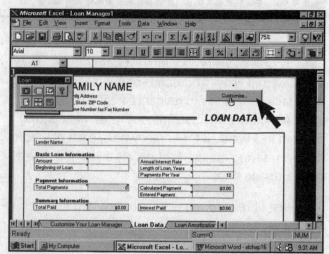

4 Click the **Customize** button on the template. The contents of the Customize Your Loan Manager tab appear.

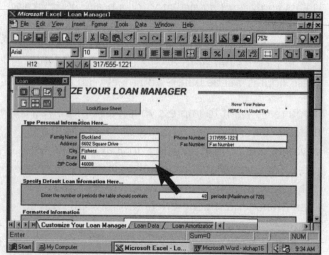

5 In the Type Personal Information Here... section, enter your name, address, and other data so your contact information appears on the Loan Data sheet. You can leave cells blank if you wish.

Do It Yourself Open the Template and Customize It

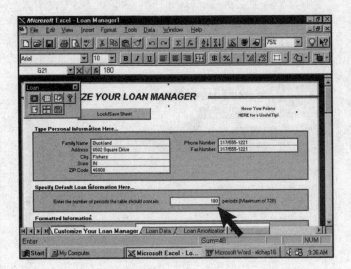

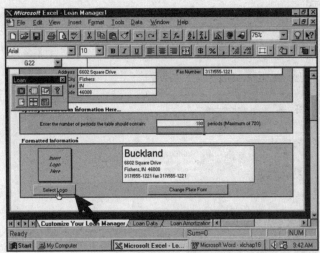

6 In the Specify Default Loan Information Here... section, enter the number of months in the life of the loan. For example, enter **60** for a five-year loan, **180** for a 15-year loan, or **360** for a 30-year loan. (This sets the maximum number of lines on the Loan Amortization Table sheet.)

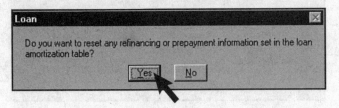

7 When you finish entering the number of payments, Excel displays a message box asking whether you want to update any refinancing or prepayment information in the Loan Amortization Table sheet. Click **Yes** to do so.

8 Scroll down to the Formatted Information section. Click the **Select Logo** button if you want to add a logo image to your Loan Manager template. The Picture dialog box appears.

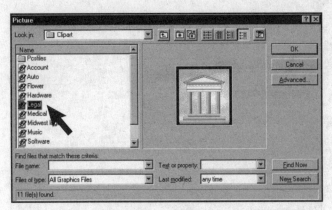

9 Navigate to the directory that holds the picture file you want to insert. Click the file in the Name list and then click **OK** to insert it.

(continues)

Do It Yourself Open the Template and Customize It *(continued)*

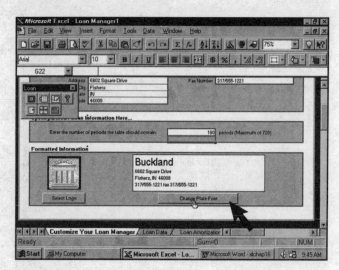

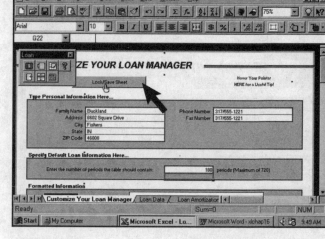

10 Click the **Change Plate Font** button to change the font for your name on the Loan Manager worksheets. The Format Cells dialog box appears.

12 Scroll back up to the top of the sheet. Click the **Lock/Save Sheet** button. Excel displays the Lock/Save Sheet dialog box.

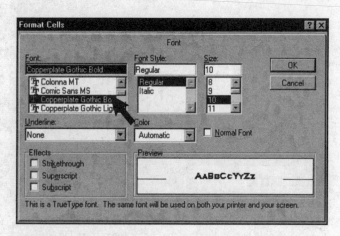

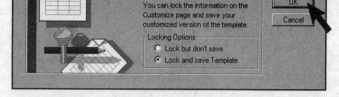

13 With the **Lock and save Template** option button selected, click **OK** to save your changes to the template.

11 Select the new font from the Font drop-down list and click **OK**. Excel applies the new font.

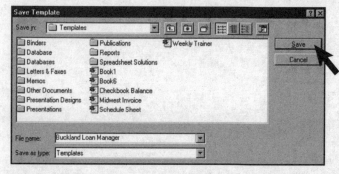

14 The Save Template dialog box appears. In the File name text box, type a name for your custom Loan Mananger template, if needed, and click **Save**.

Do It Yourself   Open the Template and Customize It

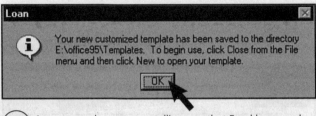

15 An message box appears telling you that Excel has saved the template and that you can use it. Click **OK**.

16 Close the template.

Begin Do It Yourself   Enter and View Loan and Payment Information

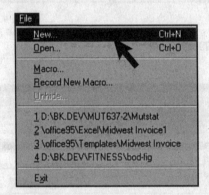

1 Open the **File** menu and click **New**. The New dialog box appears.

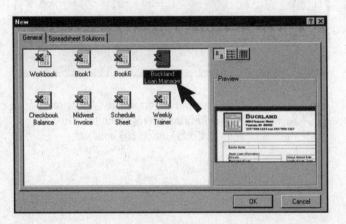

2 Click the icon for the custom Loan Manager template and then click **OK**. A new, blank workbook based on the template appears.

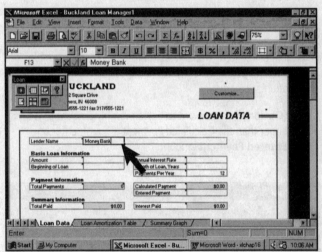

3 Enter the name of the lender.

(continues)

Do It Yourself Enter and View Loan and Payment Information

(continued)

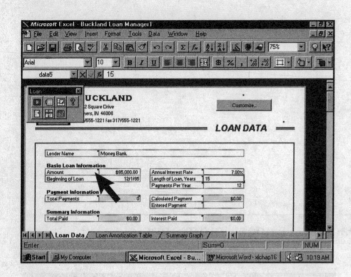

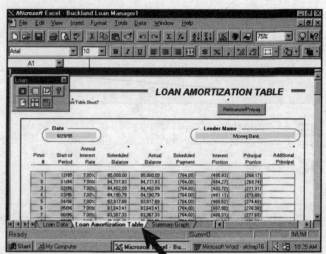

4 In the Basic Loan Information area, enter the amount you're borrowing, the date (mm/dd/yy) you plan for the beginning of the loan, the annual interest rate (7, for example), and the length of the loan in years. Excel calculates the loan information.

7 To view the payment breakdown, click the **Loan Amortization Table** tab.

5 (Optional) If you want to pay a monthly amount that's larger than the Calculated Payment amount, enter an **Entered Payment** amount.

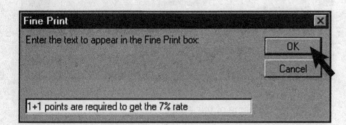

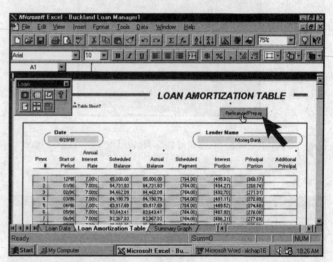

6 To insert fine print details about the loan, click the **Insert Fine Print Here** button, type the text to insert, and click **OK**. Use this box to place information on the Loan Data sheet that doesn't fit into any of the other categories on the sheet, but is important to the terms of the loan.

8 To refinance the loan or make an additional principal payment, click the **Refinance/Prepay** button. The Change the Loan During its Course dialog box appears.

> **Do It Yourself**   Enter and View Loan and Payment Information

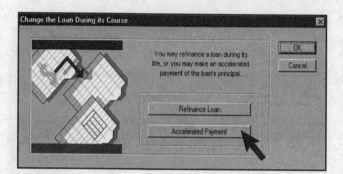

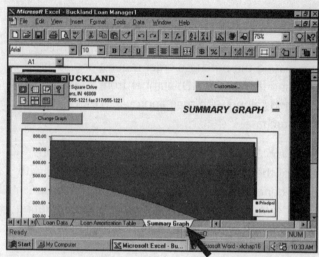

9 Click either **Refinance Loan** or **Accelerated Payment**. The options in the dialog box change.

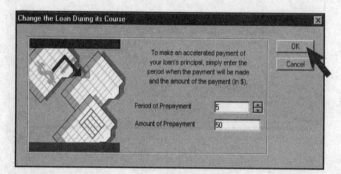

10 Specify the payment period for refinancing or repayment. Also specify the new interest rate or the amount of extra principal you're paying. Click **OK**. If you're making a prepayment, Excel recalculates the Actual Balance column.

11 To view a chart of how the interest compares to the principal in your loan payments over the life of the loan, click the **Summary Graph** tab.

12 Click the **Save** tool on the Standard toolbar to save the Loan Manager workbook. The Save As dialog box appears.

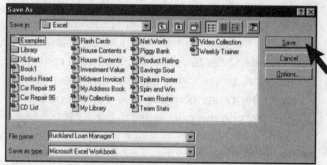

13 Navigate to the directory where you want to save the Loan Manager workbook. Type a name in the File name text box, if needed, and click **Save**.

Buy It with a Purchase Order

Purchase orders proliferate as a painful form of paperwork, both from the standpoint of filling in or creating the purchase order request and in terms of securing the correct P.O. number from your company's P.O. gods along with their approval to proceed with the purchase.

Excel for Windows 95 comes to the rescue again! One of the templates that installs automatically with Excel generates purchase orders. Excel's Purchase Order template automates the process of generating the purchase order paper work. It also checks your math, because it automatically calculates appropriate totals based on the number of units, unit cost, tax, shipping, and other information you enter.

The Purchase Order template tracks the contents of each purchase order you generate in the Template Wizard database workbook for the template. Excel saves this database, called podb.xls, in the Library folder within the Excel folder. The template also enables you to assign a permanent purchase order number to the purchase order. If your company uses the Purchase Order template database via a central-ized network server folder, then multiple users can automatically create purchase orders and generate P.O. numbers. In this case, you can use a centralized numbering file to assign a unique P.O. number to each order—eliminating the need for a warm body to control and dole out P.O. numbers.

You should start by customizing the Purchase Order template and saving it under a new name with your changes. You can:

- Add your company's name and logo to the purchase order.

- Change the font for the company's name and address.

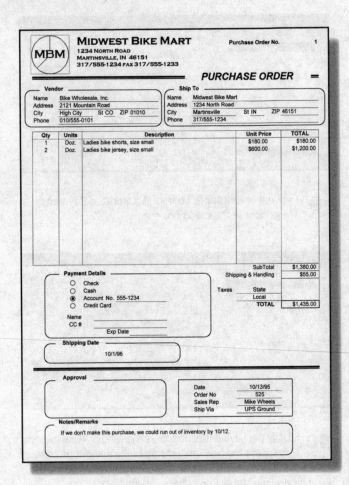

- Specify which credit cards your company may use to pay for the purchase.

- Adjust the sales tax figures your company uses to calculate the purchase total.

- Specify whether to use a central P.O. numbering file on a network.

- Specify whether the shipping address is the same as the company address.

After you save and rename the customized Purchase Order template, you can use it to create individual purchase orders and add data to the podb.xls data-base, a file you can open and work with like any other list in Excel.

The Do It Yourself steps explain how to customize Excel's Purchase Order template and use it to provide purchase orders to the vendors with whom you do business.

If you have any questions about a particular cell entry and a red dot appears adjacent to or above the cell, point to the dot to see a cell tip with information about how to make the entry.

Begin Do It Yourself   Open and Customize the Purchase Order Template

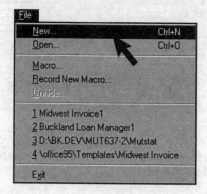

1 Open the **File** menu and click **New**. The New dialog box appears.

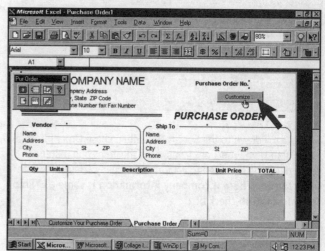

4 Click the **Customize** button on the template. The contents of the Customize Your Purchase Order tab appear.

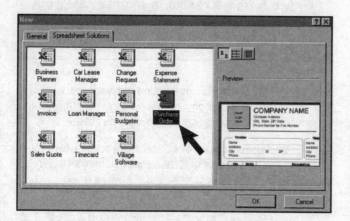

2 Click the **Spreadsheet Solutions** tab and then click the **Purchase Order** icon. The Preview area displays the template.

3 Click **OK** to open the template.

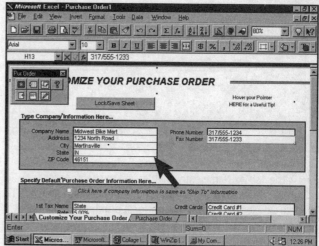

5 In the Type Company Information Here… section, enter the information for your company so your company's name and contact information appears on the purchase order. You can leave cells blank if you wish.

(continues)

Do It Yourself Open and Customize the Purchase Order Template *(continued)*

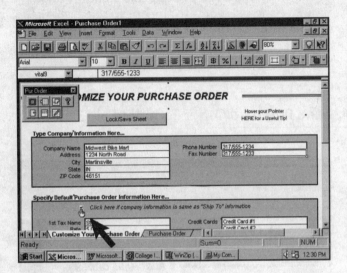

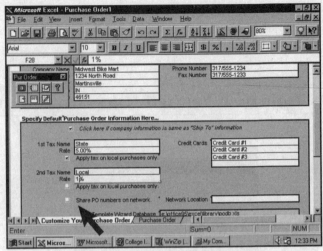

6 Scroll down to the Specify Default Purchase Order Information Here... section. If you want the items and materials you order to be delivered to your main company address, click to select the **Click here if company information is same as "Ship To" information** check box.

8 The 2nd Tax Name entry enables you to specify local (city) taxes. Enter the name and rate. Click to check the **Apply tax on local purchases only** check box to apply the 2nd tax only to purchases from companies in your company's area.

If you don't have a local tax and you consistently buy from a vendor in another state, you can use the 2nd tax name to store the other state's tax rate.

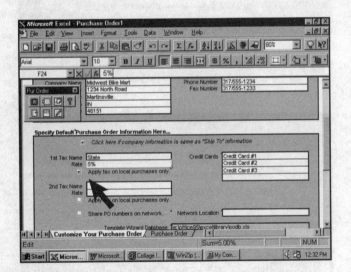

9 Check the **Share PO numbers on network** check box if more than one user on a network will use the template and you want to automatically number the purchases.

10 In the Network Location cell, specify the folder where you want to hold the file that counts the P.O. numbers. (Excel automatically creates the file.)

The folder you specify as the network location must be on a server in a universally accessible place.

7 The 1st Tax Name entry enables you to specify taxes for purchases from companies in your state. Change the rate if needed. Deselect the **Apply tax on local purchases only** check box to apply the 1st tax to all invoices.

Do It Yourself Open and Customize the Purchase Order Template

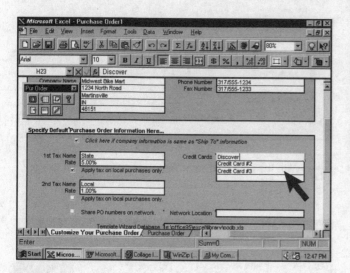

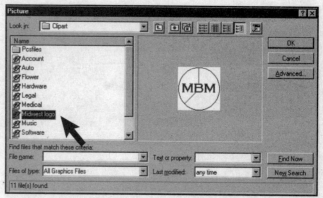

13 Navigate to the directory that holds the picture file for your logo. Click the file in the Name list and click **OK** to insert it.

11 Under Credit Cards Accepted, enter the names of up to three credit cards that people in your company may use to pay for purchases.

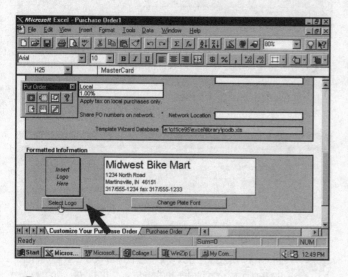

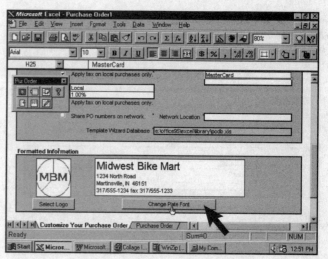

14 Click the **Change Plate Font** button to change the font for your company's name and address on the purchase order. The Format Cells dialog box appears.

(continues)

12 Scroll down to the Formatted Information section. Click the **Select Logo** button if you want to add your logo image to your invoices. The Picture dialog box appears.

Do It Yourself Open and Customize the Purchase Order Template (continued)

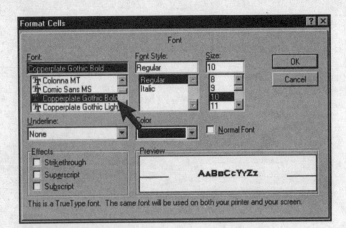

15 Select the new font from the Font drop-down list and click **OK**. Excel applies the new font.

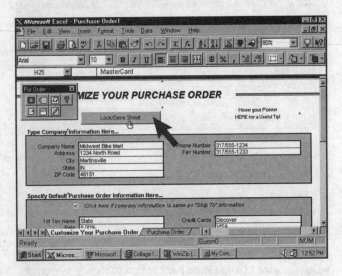

16 Scroll back up to the top of the sheet. Click the **Lock/Save Sheet** button. Excel displays the Lock/Save Sheet dialog box.

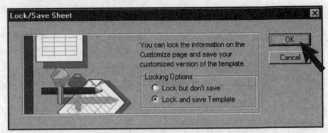

17 With the **Lock and save Template** option button selected, click **OK** to save your changes to the template.

18 The Save Template dialog box appears. In the File name text box, type a name for your custom Purchase Order template if needed, and click **Save**.

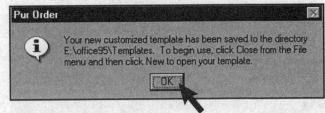

19 A Pur Order message box appears telling you that Excel has saved the Purchase Order template and that you can use it. If you are working with the stand-alone version of Excel, the path name you see will be different from the one in the figure. Click **OK**.

20 Close the template.

Begin Do It Yourself Create a Purchase Order and Update the Database

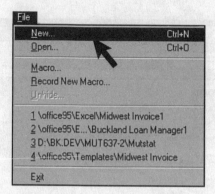

1 Open the **File** menu and click **New**. The New dialog box appears.

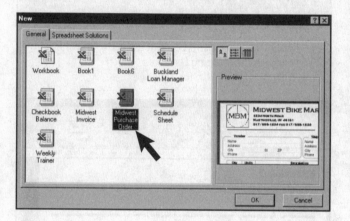

2 Click the icon for the custom Purchase Order template and click **OK**.

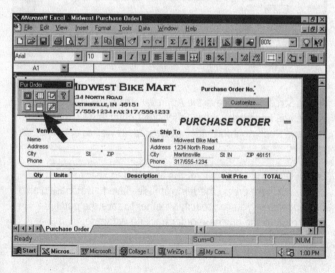

3 To number the purchase order, click the **Assign a Number** button on the Pur Order toolbar.

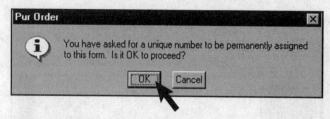

4 In the message box that asks if it's OK to permanently assign a number to the form, click **OK**.

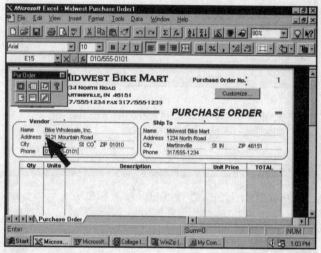

5 Enter information about the vendor from whom you're purchasing goods or services in the Vendor area. If you need to change the Ship To information, do this now as well.

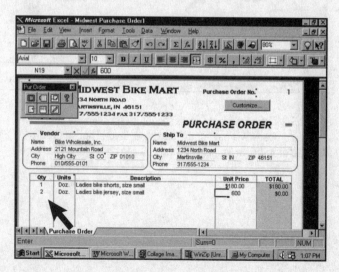

6 Enter the information about the items you're purchasing. Note that the Units column refers to the minimum unit size—gross, dozen, and so on. The Unit size should correspond to the Unit Price you enter.

(continues)

Do It Yourself   Create a Purchase Order and Update the Database   *(continued)*

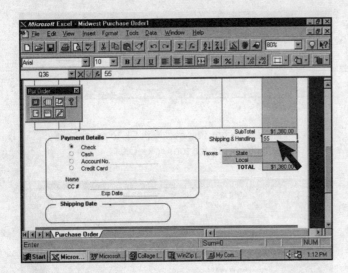

7 Scroll down the worksheet and enter shipping and handling charges that apply, if any.

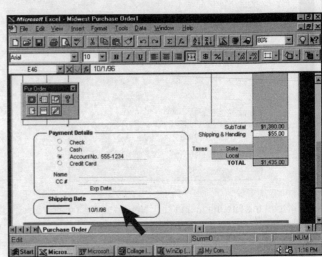

9 Specify the latest date you want the items to ship from the vendor in the Shipping Date area.

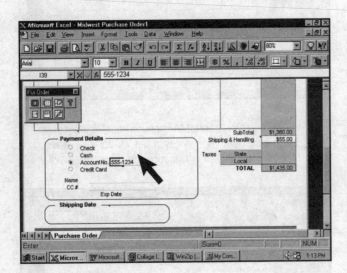

8 Fill in the Payment Details section to specify how your company will pay for the purchase. If you choose **Credit Card**, a drop-down list appears and you can choose the card type.

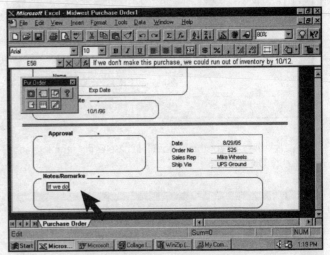

10 Scroll down. Leave the Approval area blank for sign-offs and approval stamps. Enter order number, sale representative, and shipping information, if needed, as well as any notes or remarks.

11 Click the **Save** tool on the Standard toolbar to save the purchase order. The Template File–Save to Database dialog box appears so you can specify whether to save the purchase order data to the purchase order tracking database.

Do It Yourself   Create a Purchase Order and Update the Database

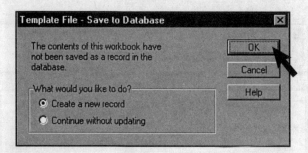

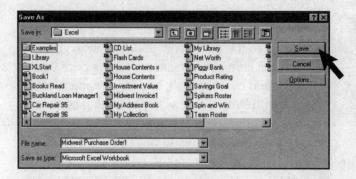

12 Leave the **Create a new record** option selected and click **OK**. The Save As dialog box appears.

13 Navigate to the directory where you want to save the purchase order. Type a name in the File name text box, if needed, and click **Save**.

14 Click the **Print** button on the Standard toolbar to print the purchase order.

Compare Car Leases

In the olden days when you wanted to buy a car, you'd go to the dealer with your money in your pocket, do a little horse tradin' to get the price you wanted, hand over the cash, and drive home in your new model T. With the newfangled leasing options that dealers offer today, it practically takes an MBA in Finance to decide whether to buy or lease a car. If you do lease, it takes some work to arrive at a leasing program that suits your needs and price range.

Thanks to Excel, there's now no need to enroll for that advanced degree just to lease a car! The Car Lease Manager template can demystify the whole process. You simply enter the facts and figures, such as the cost of the car and the monthly payment. By changing some of the values, you see what you need to do to get more favorable closed-end lease terms. Excel also offers four different options you can play with to pinpoint a particular item you may want to negotiate for, such as a lower interest rate.

This template works much as the other three described earlier in this section do. You open the template, customize it with your name and address, and save it as a custom template. Then you open the template you saved and enter the information you want to evaluate. You need to enter the terms offered by the Lessor (the car dealer) in the INITIAL OFFER column. The table below describes the entries you need to make (because they're less than self-explanatory in some cases).

Follow the Do It Yourself steps now for an overview of how to use the Loan Manager template.

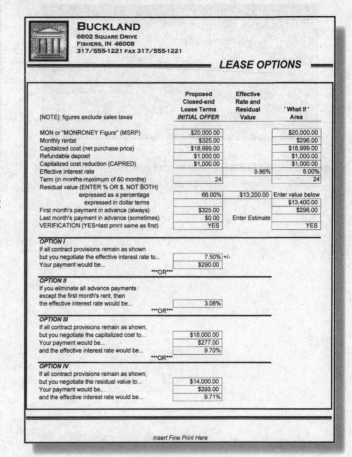

To install this template, open the **Control Panel**. Double-click **Add/Remove Programs**. On the Install/Uninstall tab, click **Microsoft Office** in the list of installed software. Insert the Office disk or CD in your drive and click **Add/Remove**. Follow the prompts on screen to add more Excel templates.

Entries for the Proposed Closed-End Lease Terms INITIAL OFFER

In This Cell...	Enter This...
MON or "MONRONEY Figure" (MSRP)	The car's sticker price
Monthly rental	The monthly payment
Capitalized cost (net purchase price)	The cash price for the car (if you negotiated and paid for it now)
Refundable deposit	A deposit against damage you may do to the car
Capitalized cost reduction (CAPRED)	Your down payment
Term (in months-maximum of 60 months)	The number of months for the lease contract
Residual value (ENTER % OR $, NOT BOTH)	The value the car will have at the end of the lease, expressed either in a dollar amount or as a percentage of the sticker price (enter either the dollar value or the percentage)
First month's payment in advance (always)	The amount you'll pay for the first month
Last month's payment in advance (sometimes)	Any advance payment you pay for the last month; enter 0 if you don't have to pay this payment in advance

Begin Do It Yourself   Evaluate a Car Loan

1 Open the **File** menu and click **New**. The New dialog box appears.

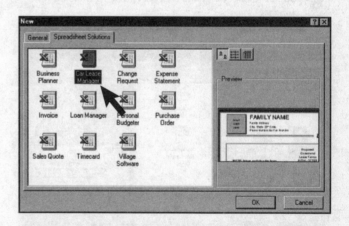

2 Click the **Spreadsheet Solutions** tab and click the **Car Lease Manager** icon. The Preview area displays the template.

3 Click **OK** to open the template.

(continues)

Do It Yourself   Evaluate a Car Loan   (continued)

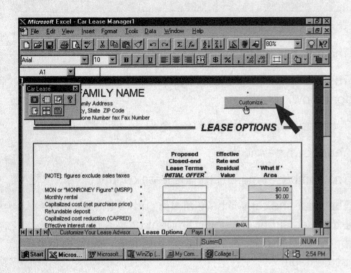

4 Click the **Customize** button on the template. The contents of the Customize Your Lease Advisor tab appear. As described in "Make Smart Decisions with the Loan Manager," p. 399, enter your address and a picture to customize the template.

5 Use the **Lock/Save Sheet** button to save and name the template as described in "Make Smart Decisions with the Loan Manager," p. 399. Close the customized template.

6 Open the **File** menu and click **New**. The New dialog box appears.

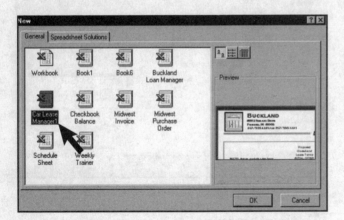

7 In the General tab, click the icon for the custom Car Lease Manager template and click **OK** to open a new, blank workbook based on the template.

8 Enter the information for the lease offer as described in Closed-End Lease Terms table. Note: Do not enter anything in any of the shaded cells in the template.

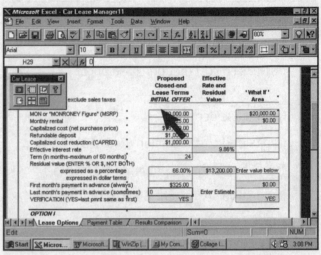

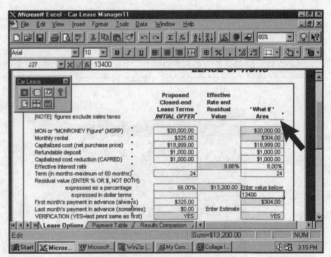

9 If you want to experiment with changes to the terms, such as entering a lower interest rate and higher residual value, make entries in the cells in the 'What If' Area column.

Do It Yourself   Evaluate a Car Loan

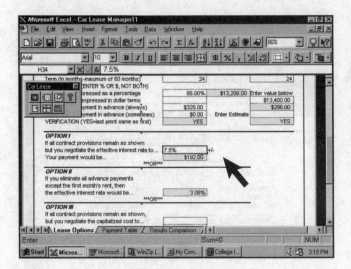

10 To begin examining options, scroll down to the OPTION I area. To see the impact of a different interest rate on the monthly payment, enter the interest rate in the specified cell.

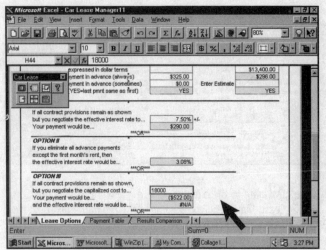

12 In the Option III area, you can look at what your monthly payment and the interest rate will be if you negotiate for a smaller capitalized cost (the price you would pay if you paid cash for the car).

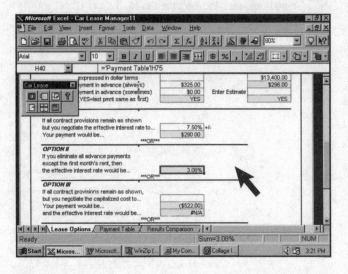

11 Scroll down to the OPTION II area. It's already calculated for you what the maximum payment will be if you eliminate advance payments other than the first month's lease payment.

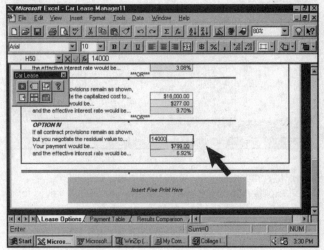

13 Scroll down to the Option IV area. Enter a different (presumably higher) residual value to see how negotiating that issue affects the payment and interest rate.

14 **(Optional)** Enter fine print if you want to by clicking the **Insert Fine Print Here** button, typing the text, and clicking **OK**.

15 Click the **Save** tool on the Standard toolbar to save the Car Lease Manager. The Save As dialog box appears.

(continues)

Do It Yourself   Evaluate a Car Loan   *(continued)*

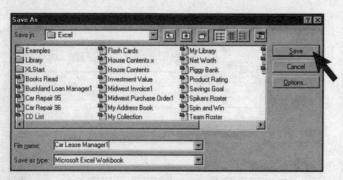

16 Navigate to the directory where you want to save the Car Lease Manager. Type a name in the File name text box, if needed, and click **Save**.

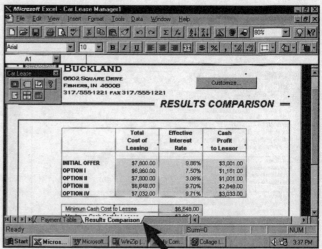

18 To compare the total results for the four options you've examined, click the **Results Comparison** tab.

19 To print any information from the Car Lease Manager workbook, click to select the tab for the worksheet you want to print and then click the **Print** button on the Standard toolbar.

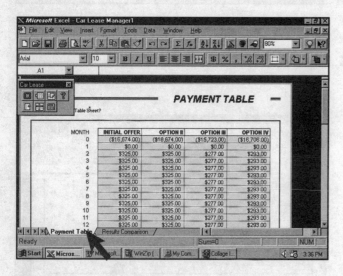

17 To compare the payments for the four options you've explored (including the capitalized and residual values for the car), click the **Payment Table** tab to view it.

Budget without Pain

We've all been there. It's a week before you'll get the next paycheck. You've got $5 in your pocket, no gas in the car, and a stack of bills that even Donald Trump would have trouble handling. You've got to get your money under control!

You may have tried to create and stick with a budget in the past. You may even have tried to use a previous version of Excel to cook up a worksheet to help whip your finances into shape. That worksheet may have been too simplistic and a bit too boring to use. So, you stopped using it.

Excel's Personal Budgeter template gives you the perfect setup to count your chickens and feather your nest. The template offers multiple worksheets to track and evaluate different aspects of your income, expenses, and budget:

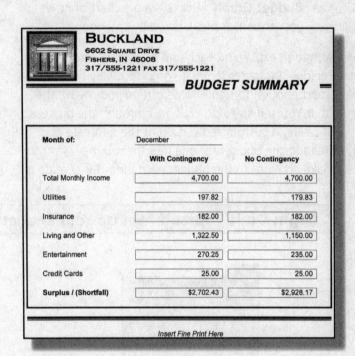

- **Income Data**   Enter monthly income and tax information for you and your spouse.

- **Utilities Data**   Enables you to find averages for common utility payments for the budget by entering the utility bills from the past six months. This sheet also enables you to enter a contingency percentage to provide extra money in case expenses in this area run over for the month.

- **Insurance Data**   Enables you to enter information about each of the insurance policies you own, including the approximate amount you must pay for each policy each month. Keep in mind that if you don't pay monthly for a policy (such as if you pay your car insurance each six months), you need to accumulate the budgeted amount in the bank until the next installment is due. This sheet also enables you to enter a contingency percentage to provide extra money in case expenses in this area run over for the month.

- **Living Expenses Data**   Here, enter rent or mortgage, car payments, expenses for commuting and groceries, and miscellaneous expenses such as having the kid next door mow the lawn. This sheet also enables you to enter a contingency percentage to provide extra money in case expenses in this area run over for the month.

- **Entertainment Data**   Track the money you spend dining out, going to movies, and more. You can enter a contingency percentage here, as well.

- **Credit Cards Data**   Enter credit card balance and payment information, as well as a contingency percentage.

- **Budget Summary**   Displays the summary of all the income and expenses you've entered and lets you know whether there's a surplus (extra cash!) or shortfall (you're in the hole—bummer!). This sheet also compares the actual budgeted amount to the totals including the contingency amounts (which are a percentage of the actual budget amounts you've entered).

- **Budget Graph**   Displays a pie chart of how your expenses break down by category.

Although explaining each and every entry in the Personal Budgeter template is unnecessary (you're smart enough to figure these out on your own), the Do It Yourself steps do walk you through the process of saving a customized version of the template and creating the budget for one month. You may want to make changes to the budget each month (or create a

new workbook based on the customized template) to review how your expenses change from month to month.

To install this template, open the **Control Panel**. Double-click **Add/Remove Programs**. On the Install/Uninstall tab, click **Microsoft Office** in the list of installed software. Insert the Office disk or CD in your drive and click **Add/ Remove**. Follow the prompts on screen to add more Excel templates.

Begin Do It Yourself   Set Up Your Budget

1 Open the **File** menu and click **New**. The New dialog box appears.

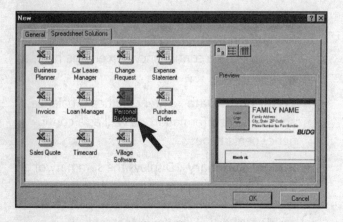

2 Click the **Spreadsheet Solutions** tab and then click the **Personal Budgeter** icon. The Preview area displays the template.

3 Click **OK** to open the template.

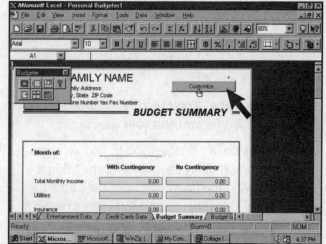

4 Click the **Customize** button on the template. The contents of the Customize Your Budget Advisor tab appear. As described in "Make Smart Decisions with the Loan Manager," p. 399, enter your address and a picture to customize the template.

5 Enter your first name and your spouse's first name. Use the **Lock/Save Sheet** button to save and name the template as described in "Make Smart Decisions with the Loan Manager," p. 399. Close the customized template.

6 Open the **File** menu and click **New**. The New dialog box appears.

Do It Yourself   Set Up Your Budget

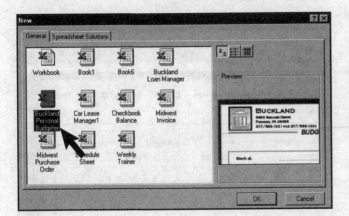

7 In the General tab, click the icon for the custom Personal Budgeter template and then click **OK** to open a new, blank workbook based on the template.

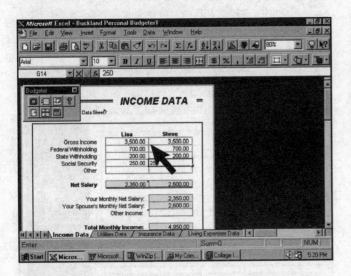

8 Scroll to display the very first workbook tab, Income Data, and click the tab. Enter the income and tax data for you and your spouse. Don't forget to enter other income, such as gifts or interest income.

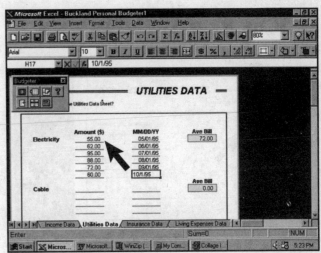

9 Click the next tab, **Utilities Data**, and enter the information you need to calculate average utility bills.

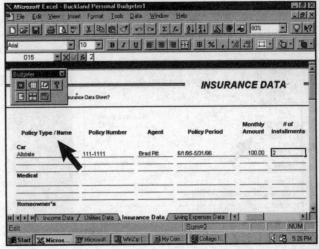

10 Click the **Insurance Data** tab and enter information about all your insurance policies.

(continues)

Do It Yourself   Set Up Your Budget   *(continued)*

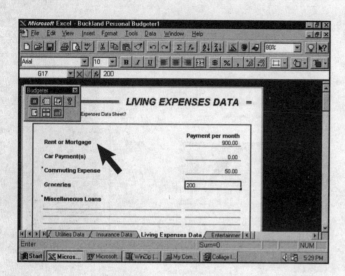

11 Select the **Living Expenses Data** tab and enter your "cost of living" expenses.

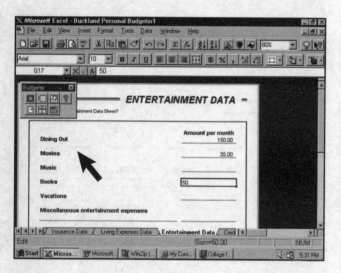

12 Click the **Entertainment Data** tab and enter the various entertainment expenses you anticipate.

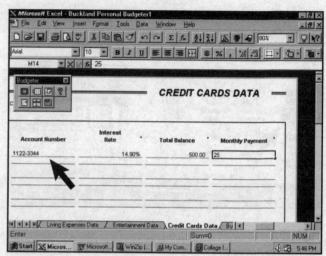

13 Click the **Credit Cards Data** tab and enter the information about the credit cards you owe on, including the interest rate and minimum payment for each.

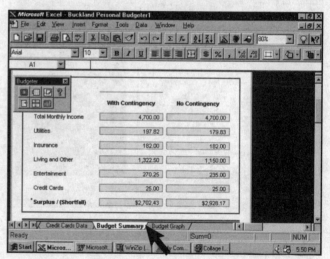

14 Click the **Budget Summary** tab to see how your income and expenses stack up. Scroll down to see if you have a shortfall or surplus.

Do It Yourself   Set Up Your Budget

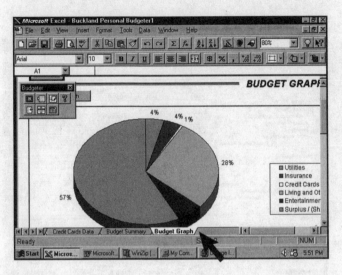

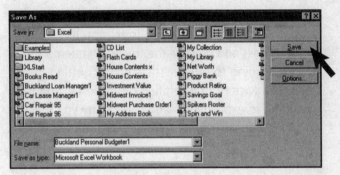

15 Click the **Budget Graph** tab to view a pie chart of your expenses.

16 Click the **Save** tool on the Standard toolbar to save the Personal Budgeter workbook. The Save As dialog box appears.

17 Navigate to the directory where you want to save the Personal Budgeter workbook. Type a name in the File name text box, if needed, and click **Save**.

18 To print any information from the Personal Budgeter workbook, click to select the tab for the worksheet you want to print and click the **Print** button on the Standard toolbar.

Mind Your Business

Let's get an admission out of the way right off the bat. This book is not going to tell you how to run your business and prepare the financial statements for it. It's not going to serve in the stead of getting good financial advice from a certified professional, and it's not going to explain each and every entry you make into the Business Planner template you can install to use with Excel.

True, the Business Planner template provides many of the worksheets you need to capture and calculate data to indicate the performance and financial health of your business. The Do It Yourself steps here will help you get started using this template. But, if you have questions about a specific entry or calculation, get advice from a financial professional.

The Business Planner template offers several different worksheets for you to use to enter information and calculate data automatically:

- **Data Sheet** On this worksheet, you enter certain fundamental information about the number of days it takes for certain operations events, expense percentages for certain categories, and more.

- **Data Chart** This worksheet charts the days you entered for certain operating events on the Data Sheet. Click a button to perform what-if analyses to see how changes in the number of days affect other financial information in the template.

- **Balance Sheet** Enter balance sheet information for the current period here, and the worksheet forecasts a balance sheet for the next four quarters.

- **Asset Chart** This worksheet charts how assets break out per quarter.

- **Income Statement** This worksheet calculates net income based on entries you made on previous worksheets and sales and other information you entered here.

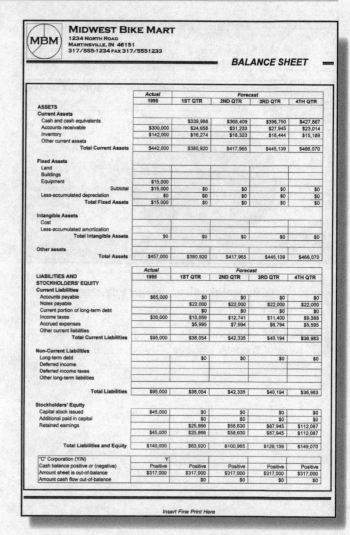

- **Income Chart** This worksheet depicts income by quarter for the company.

- **Cash Flow Sheet** This worksheet calculates quarterly and total cash flow based on previous entries.

To install this template, open the **Control Panel**. Double-click **Add/Remove Programs**. On the Install/Uninstall tab, click **Microsoft Office** in the list of installed software. Insert the Office disk or CD in your drive and click **Add/Remove**. Follow the prompts on screen to add more Excel templates.

Begin Do It Yourself   Track Business Financial Information

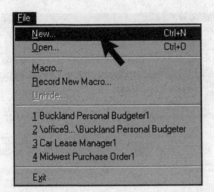

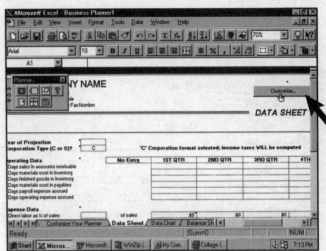

1 Open the **File** menu and click **New**. The New dialog box appears.

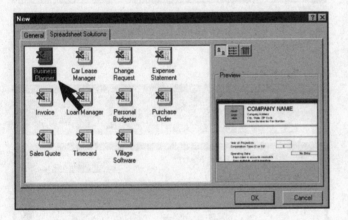

4 Click the **Customize** button on the template. The contents of the Customize Your Planner tab appear. As described in "Bill a Customer with the Invoice," p. 392, enter company information to customize the template.

5 Use the **Lock/Save Sheet** button to save and name the template as described in "Bill a Customer with the Invoice," p. 392. Close the customized template.

6 Open the **File** menu and click **New**. The New dialog box appears.

2 Click the **Spreadsheet Solutions** tab and then click the **Business Planner** icon. The Preview area displays the template.

3 Click **OK** to open the template. It appears, with the Data Sheet worksheet selected.

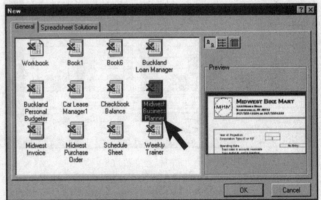

7 In the General tab, click the icon for the custom business planner template you just created and click **OK** to open a new, blank workbook based on the template.

(continues)

Do It Yourself Track Business Financial Information *(continued)*

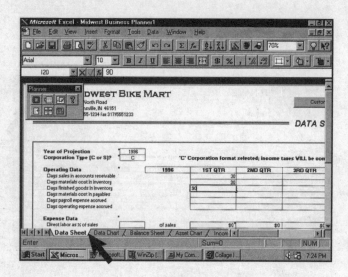

8 On the first tab, Data Sheet, enter operations and expense information for your business. Remember, the shaded cells already contain formulas to perform calculations, so don't make any entries in these cells.

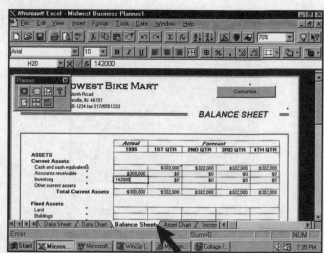

10 Click the **Balance Sheet** tab and enter actual values for the prior year.

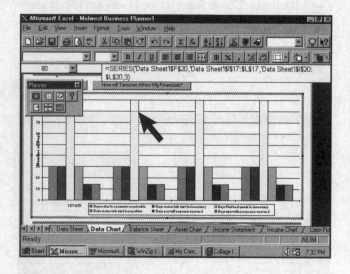

9 Click the next tab, **Data Chart**, to view a chart of the entries you made on the Data Sheet. If you click the **How will Turnover Affect My Financials?** button and then click **OK**, you can drag to change the size of the columns on the chart, and Excel adjusts the entries you made on the Data Sheet.

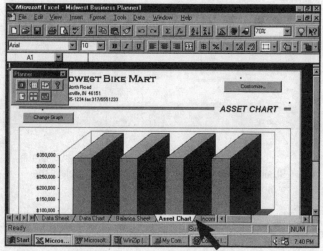

11 Click the **Asset Chart** tab if you want to view a chart of the business assets by quarter.

Do It Yourself   Track Business Financial Information

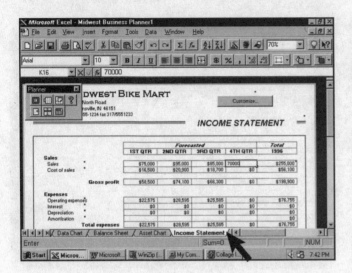

12 Select the **Income Statement** tab and enter the quarterly sales you anticipate, amortization to be expensed, dividends to be distributed, and more.

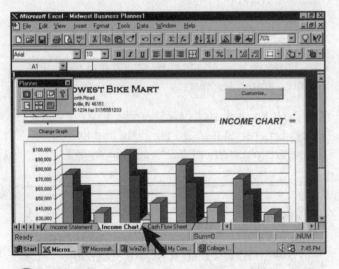

13 Click the **Income Chart** tab to view that graph if you wish.

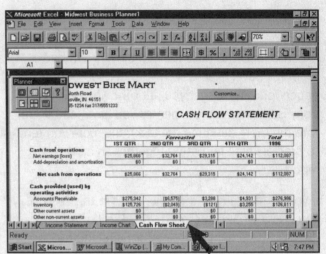

14 Click the **Cash Flow Sheet** tab to view the projected cash flow for the next year.

15 Click the **Save** tool on the Standard toolbar to save the Business Planner workbook. The Save As dialog box appears.

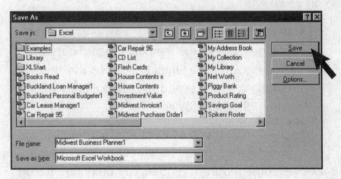

16 Navigate to the directory where you want to save the Business Planner workbook. Type a name in the File name text box, if needed, and click **Save**.

17 To print any information from the Business Planner workbook, click to select the tab for the worksheet you want to print and click the **Print** button on the Standard toolbar.

Track Work Expenses

Paperwork aversion can cost you big bucks. Many people who travel on the job have to submit an expense report to have their employers reimburse them for travel expenses. The longer you put off this paperwork, the longer you put off being paid. The irony is that the more expenses you have (and therefore the more daunting the task), the more you tend to procrastinate in putting together an expense report.

If you've read any of the other tasks in this section, you know what comes next. Yes, Excel offers an Expense Statement template for preparing expense reports. The Expense Statement template provides categories for all typical travel expenses. It calculates mileage for you and totals all your expenses automatically.

The Expense Statement template provides a few features that make it perfect to use for multiple users on a network:

- It tracks the contents of each expense report you generate in the Template Wizard database workbook for the template. Excel saves this database, called expdb.xls, in the Library folder within the Excel folder.

- The template also enables you to assign a permanent expense statement number to the expense report. A centralized numbering file on the network assigns a unique number to each expense report.

- Finally, you can enter all the employees for the company in a centralized list file in the Library folder within the Excel folder so you can choose an employee rather than typing in that information. This file is called Common.xls. Simply open this workbook, click the **Employee Info** tab,

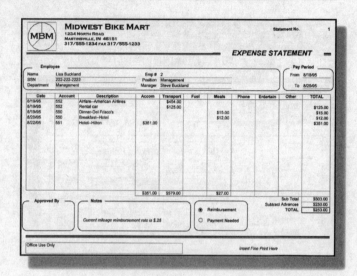

delete the sample data, enter the real information about your employees, and save and close the workbook.

You should start by customizing the Expense Statement template, adding your company name and the like. Preserve your changes by saving and renaming the customized template.

The Do It Yourself steps explain how to work with Excel's Expense Statement template and use it to request reimbursement from your employer.

To install this template, open the **Control Panel**. Double-click **Add/Remove Programs**. On the Install/Uninstall tab, click **Microsoft Office** in the list of installed software. Insert the Office disk or CD in your drive and click **Add/Remove**. Follow the prompts on screen to add more Excel templates.

Begin Do It Yourself Customize and Use the Expense Statement

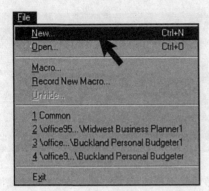

1 Open the **File** menu and click **New**. The New dialog box appears.

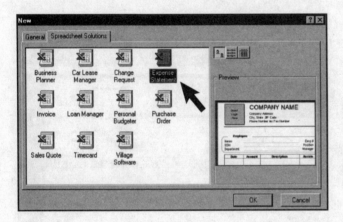

2 Click the **Spreadsheet Solutions** tab and then click the **Expense Statement** icon. The Preview area displays the template.

3 Click **OK** to open the template.

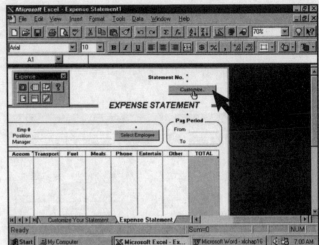

4 Click the **Customize** button on the template. The contents of the Customize Your Statement tab appear.

5 Enter your company information as described in "Bill a Customer with the Invoice," p. 392. Add a logo and choose a plate font.

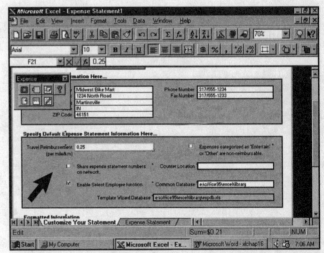

6 In the Specify Default Expense Statement Information Here… section, enter the mileage reimbursement rate.

7 Using the check boxes, choose whether or not to reimburse entertainment and other expenses, whether to use a counter file on the network (enter a folder for the file), and whether to enable you to select employees from the Common.xls list.

Do It Yourself   Customize and Use the Expense Statement *(continued)*

8 Use the **Lock/Save Sheet** button to save and name the template as described in "Bill a Customer with the Invoice," p. 392. Close the customized template.

9 Open the **File** menu and click **New**. The New dialog box appears.

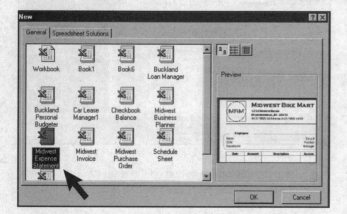

10 Click the icon for the custom Expense Statement template and click **OK**. A new, blank expense statement workbook appears.

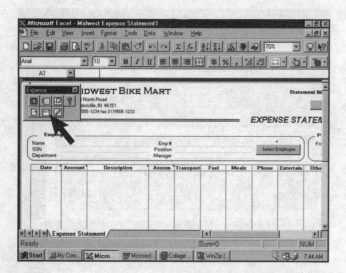

11 To number the expense statement, click the **Assign a Number** button on the Expense toolbar. In the message box that asks if it's OK to permanently assign a number to the form, click **OK**.

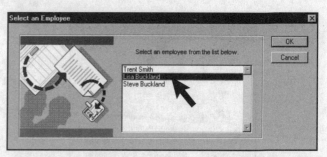

12 Enter your employee information in the Employee area. Or, if you've enabled the Select Employee feature, click the **Select Employee** button and then double-click on your name from the Select an employee from the list below list that appears.

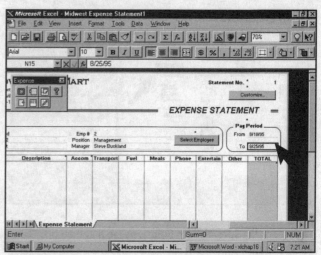

13 Scroll to the right and enter the Pay Period information.

> Specify a counter location if you intend to use this form on a network and want to allow multiple users to create expense forms.

Do It Yourself Customize and Use the Expense Statement

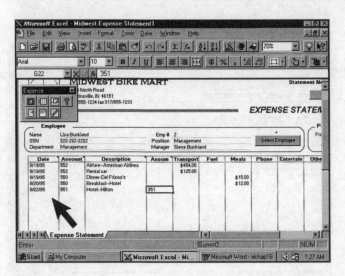

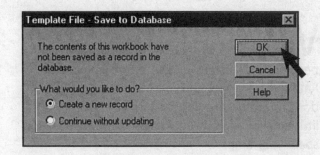

14 Enter each expense item on a separate line. Note that the Account column contains the company accounting code to which you are charging the expense.

17 Leave the **Create a new record** option selected and click **OK**. The Save As dialog box appears.

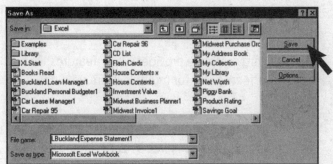

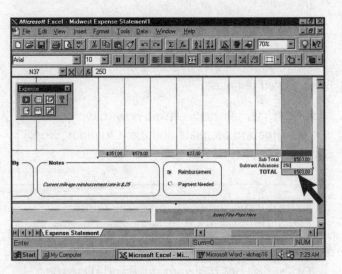

18 Navigate to the directory where you want to save the expense statement. Type a name in the File name text box, if needed, and click **Save**.

19 Click the **Print** button on the Standard toolbar to print the expense statement so you can submit it.

15 Scroll down and enter the amount for any cash advance you received, so that Excel can subtract this amount from the amount due you. Excel calculates the amount due you, or the amount you owe the company.

16 Click the **Save** tool on the Standard toolbar to save the expense statement. The Template File–Save to Database dialog box appears so you can specify whether to save the expense data to the expense tracking database.

Fill Out Your Timecard

When you work in a service business and bill by the hour, tracking your time each day becomes a distasteful and time-consuming chore. Rather than spending your time getting more work done (presumably billable work), you have to fill in little squares on a sheet of paper to justify how you spent your time.

Excel's Timecard template provides a way to automate tracking your work hours. The template enables you to track daily time spent on work related to a particular account number and calculates weekly totals plus any overtime hours.

The Timecard template provides a few features that make it perfect to use for multiple users on a network:

- It tracks the contents of each timecard you generate in the Template Wizard database workbook for the template. Excel saves this database, called timedb.xls, in the Library folder within the Excel folder.

- The template also enables you to assign a permanent timecard number to the timecard report. A centralized numbering file on the network assigns a unique number to each timecard file.

- Finally, you can enter all the employees for the company in a centralized list file in the Library folder within the Excel folder so you can choose an employee rather than typing in that information. This file is called Common.xls. Simply open this workbook, click the **Employee Info** tab, delete the sample data, enter the real information about your employees, and save and close the workbook.

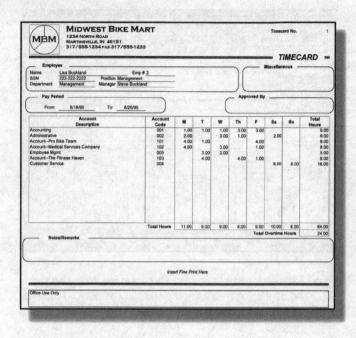

You should start by customizing the Timecard template, adding your company name and the like. Preserve your changes by saving and renaming the customized template.

The Do It Yourself steps explain how to work with Excel's Timecard template and use it to report work hours.

To install this template, open the **Control Panel**. Double-click **Add/Remove Programs**. On the Install/Uninstall tab, click **Microsoft Office** in the list of installed software. Insert the Office disk or CD in your drive and click **Add/ Remove**. Follow the prompts on screen to add more Excel templates.

Begin Do It Yourself   Customize and Use the Timecard Template

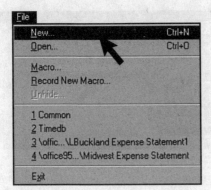

1 Open the **File** menu and click **New**. The New dialog box appears.

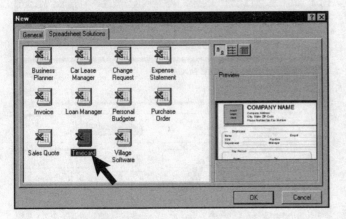

2 Click the **Spreadsheet Solutions** tab and then click the **Timecard** icon. The Preview area displays the template.

3 Click **OK** to open the template.

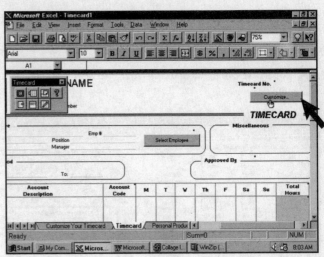

4 Click the **Customize** button on the template. The contents of the Customize Your Timecard tab appear.

5 Enter your company information as described in "Bill a Customer with the Invoice," p. 392. Add a logo and choose a plate font.

6 In the Specify Default Timecard Information Here… section, change the number of standard hours in a work week if needed.

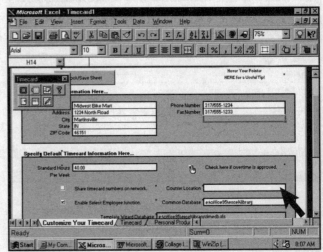

7 Using the check boxes, choose whether or not to automatically approve overtime, whether to use a counter file on the network (enter a folder for the file), and whether to enable users to select employee information from the Common.xls list.

(continues)

Do It Yourself   Customize and Use the Timecard Template   *(continued)*

8 Use the **Lock/Save Sheet** button to save and name the template as described in "Bill a Customer with the Invoice," p. 392. Close the customized template.

9 Open the **File** menu and click **New**. The New dialog box appears.

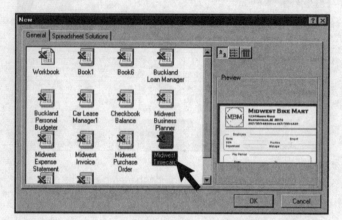

10 Click the icon for the custom Timecard template and click **OK**. A new, blank timecard workbook appears.

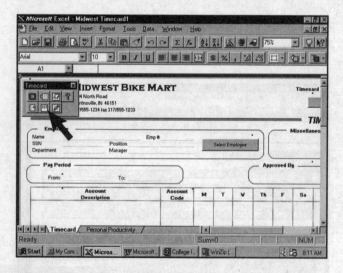

11 To number the timecard, click the **Assign a Number** button on the Timecard toolbar. In the message box that asks if it's OK to permanently assign a number to the form, click **OK**.

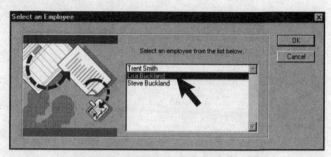

12 Enter your employee information in the Employee area. Or, if the select employee feature is enabled, click the **Select Employee** button and double-click your name in the Select an employee from the list below list that appears.

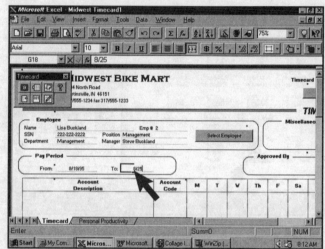

13 Enter the pay period information.

Specify a counter location if you intend to use this form on a network and want to allow multiple users to create timecards.

Do It Yourself   Customize and Use the Timecard Template

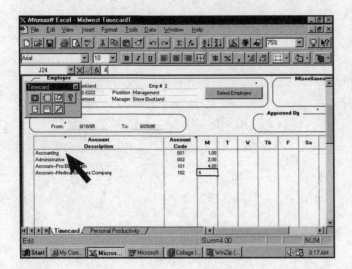

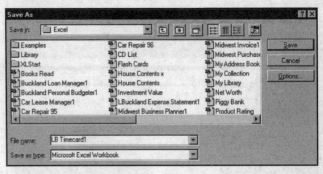

17 Navigate to the directory where you want to save the timecard. Type a name in the File name text box, if needed, and click **Save**.

14 Enter the information for each account on a separate line. Note that the categories you enter relate to job numbers +or different kinds of work rather than different clients. For the Monday column, enter the number of days you work for each account.

15 Click the **Save** tool on the Standard toolbar to save the Timecard. The Template File–Save to Database dialog box appears so you can specify whether to save the timecard data to the timecard tracking database.

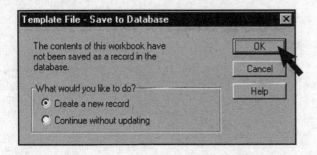

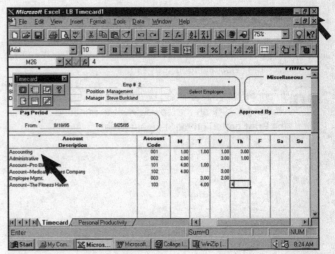

18 Each day of the week, open the current timecard workbook, add the information about your work for the day, and save the workbook.

(continues)

16 Leave the **Create a new record** option selected and click **OK**. The Save As dialog box appears.

Do It Yourself Customize and Use the Timecard Template

(continued)

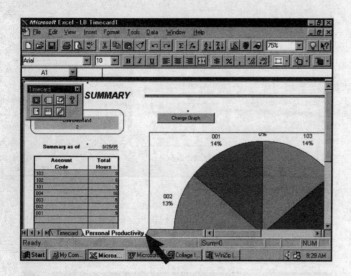

19 To view a summary of the hours you worked by time code and to see a graph of how the hours compare by category, click the Personal Productivity tab.

20 To print either the timecard or personal productivity worksheet, click on the tab you want to print and then click the **Print** button on the Standard toolbar.

Quote a Project or Product

Sales is a key component of success in any business. Let's face it—no matter how great your product or service is, you have to be able to let customers know about your products and services and convince the customer to give your products and services a try. Most sales transactions involve developing and presenting a quote to the customer and negotiating to seal the deal.

In working with the potential customer, presentation counts. Your quotations need to be detailed, clear, accurate, easy-to-read, and attractive. Excel's Sales Quote template provides a way to create accurate and professional quotations. The template enables you to enter specific information about products, services, pricing, and the customer.

The Sales Quote template provides a few features that make it perfect to use for multiple users on a network:

- It tracks the contents of each sales quote you generate in the Template Wizard database workbook for the template. Excel saves this database, called sqdb.xls, in the Library folder within the Excel folder.

- The template also enables you to assign a permanent sales quote number to the sales quote. A centralized numbering file on the network assigns a unique number to each file.

- Finally, you can enter all the employees and all the product and service information for the company in a centralized list file in the Library folder within the Excel folder, so you can choose an employee or product rather than typing in that information. This file is called Common.xls.

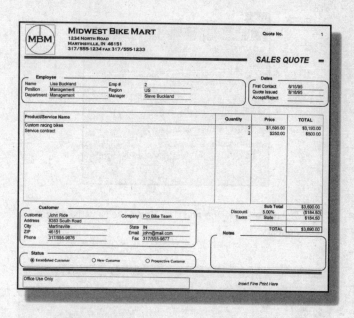

Simply click the **Product and Service Catalog** tab, enter the information and pricing for your products and services, and save and close the workbook.

You should start by customizing the Sales Quote template, adding your company name and the like. Preserve your changes by saving and renaming the customized template. The Do It Yourself steps explain how to work with Excel's Sales Quote template and use it to prepare a quote.

To install this template, open the **Control Panel**. Double-click **Add/Remove Programs**. On the Install/Uninstall tab, click **Microsoft Office** in the list of installed software. Insert the Office disk or CD in your drive and click **Add/Remove**. Follow the prompts on screen to add more Excel templates.

Begin Do It Yourself Customize and Use the Sales Quote Template

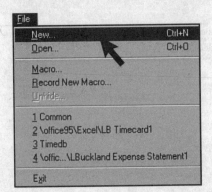

1 Open the **File** menu and click **New**. The New dialog box appears.

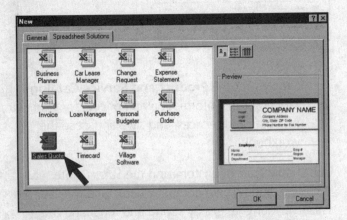

2 Click the **Spreadsheet Solutions** tab and then click the **Sales Quote** icon. The Preview area displays the template.

3 Click **OK** to open the template.

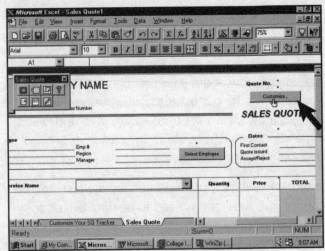

4 Click the **Customize** button on the template. The contents of the Customize Your SQ Tracker tab appear.

5 Enter your company information as described in "Bill a Customer with the Invoice," p. 392. Add a logo and choose a plate font.

6 In the Specify Default Sales Quote Information Here... section, change the tax amounts, as described in "Bill a Customer with the Invoice," p. 392.

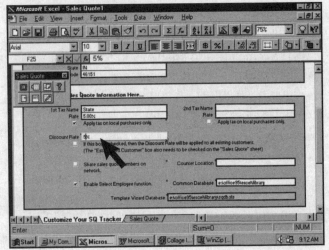

7 Specify a discount rate, if any, and enable the check box for it. Using the check boxes, specify whether to use a counter file on the network (enter a folder for the file), and whether to enable users to select employee information from the Common.xls list.

Do It Yourself Customize and Use the Sales Quote Template

8 Use the **Lock/Save Sheet** button to save and name the template as described in "Bill a Customer with the Invoice," p. 392. Close the customized template.

9 Open the **File** menu and click **New**. The New dialog box appears.

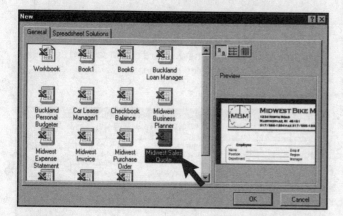

10 Click the icon for the custom Sales Quote template and click **OK**. A new, blank sales quote workbook appears.

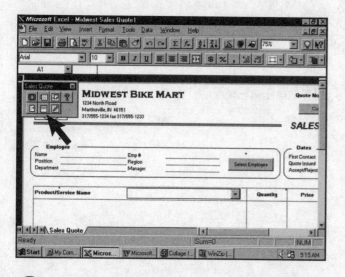

11 To number the sales quote, click the **Assign a Number** button on the Sales Quote toolbar. In the message box that asks if it's OK to permanently assign a number to the sales quote, click **OK**.

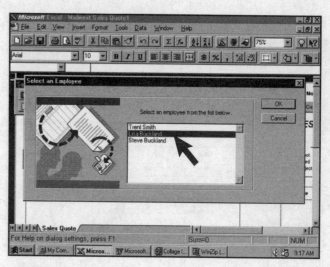

12 Enter your employee information in the Employee area. Or, if the select employee feature is enabled, click the **Select Employee** button and double-click your name in the Select an employee from the list below list that appears.

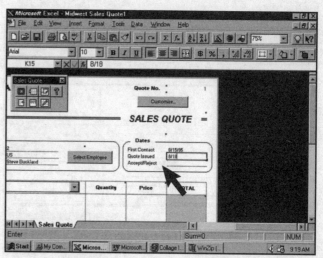

13 Enter the dates when you first contacted the customer and issued the quote.

(continues)

Do It Yourself   Customize and Use the Sales Quote Template   *(continued)*

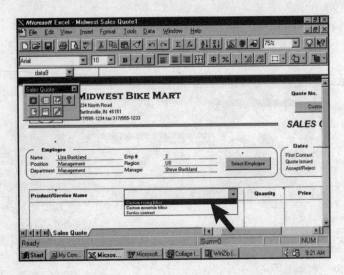

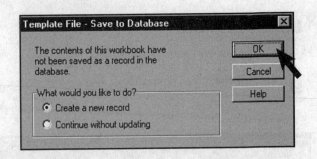

14 Enter the information for product or service you are selling on a separate line. Note that if you entered information about your products in the Product and Service Catalog sheet of the Common workbook, you can select each product or service from a drop-down list.

17 Leave the **Create a new record** option selected and click **OK**. The Save As dialog box appears.

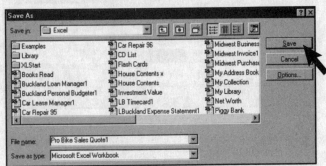

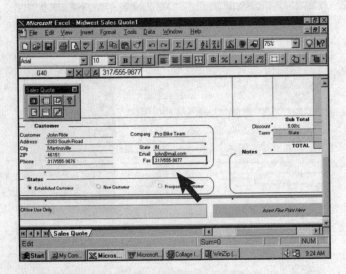

18 Navigate to the directory where you want to save the sales quote. Type a name in the File name text box, if needed, and click **Save**.

19 To print the sales quote, click the **Print** button on the Standard toolbar.

15 Scroll down and enter information about the customer, notes that apply, and fine print information (such as how long your company will honor the quote).

16 Click the **Save** tool on the Standard toolbar to save the sales quote. The Template File–Save to Database dialog box appears so you can specify whether to save the sales quote data to the sales quote tracking database.

Request Changes to a Project or Product

In a busy business, communication is often one of the first things to go out the window. Managers and employees rush around, with scarcely a moment to share details about the status or direction of a project. Using simple tools, however, you can clearly communicate expectations to others.

The Excel Change Request template is such a tool. You can use this template to request specific changes in a project or actions by others. You can use this template as a work order, communicating to others which projects they need to complete and when.

Like some of the other templates described in this section, the Change Request template tracks the contents of each request you generate in the Template Wizard database workbook for the template. Excel saves this database, called crdb.xls, in the Library folder within the Excel folder. The template also enables you to assign a permanent change request number to each request file. A centralized numbering file on the network assigns a unique number to each file.

You should start by customizing the Change Request template, adding your company name and the like. Preserve your changes by saving and renaming the customized template. Here's the rundown of the items you can customize:

- Add the company's name, address, and logo.

- Change the main title for the template. For example, for a bike repair shop, you may want to title these requests "Repair Work Order" instead.

- You can change the names of the fields you use to describe the project. For example, you can replace "Date Mfg" with "Req. Completion Date."

- You can change the title of any of the drop-down Field Lists and the items that appear on those lists.

- Specify whether or not to use a file on the network to number requests and enter a folder for the file.

The Do It Yourself steps explain how to work with Excel's Change Request template and use it to prepare a work request or order.

To install this template, open the **Control Panel**. Double-click **Add/Remove Programs**. On the Install/Uninstall tab, click **Microsoft Office** in the list of installed software. Insert the Office disk or CD in your drive and click **Add/Remove**. Follow the prompts on screen to add more Excel templates.

Begin Do It Yourself Customize and Use the Change Request Template

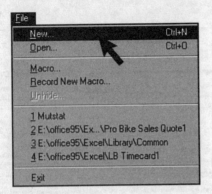

1 Open the **File** menu and click **New**. The New dialog box appears.

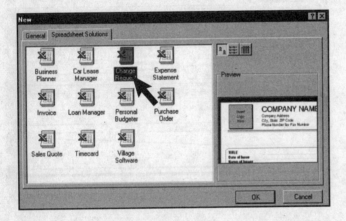

2 Click the **Spreadsheet Solutions** tab and then click the **Change Request** icon. The Preview area displays the template.

3 Click **OK** to open the template.

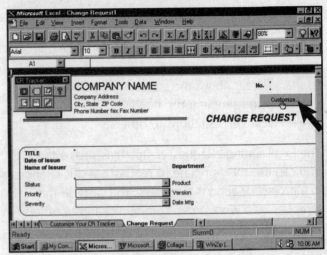

4 Click the **Customize** button on the template. The contents of the Customize Your CR Tracker tab appear.

5 Enter your company information as described in "Bill a Customer with the Invoice," p. 392. Add a logo and choose a plate font.

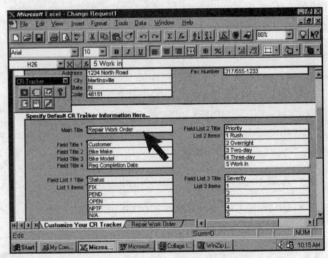

6 In the Specify Default CR Tracker Information Here... section, change the entries as described earlier.

7 Using the check box, specify whether to use a counter file on the network (enter a folder for the file).

8 Use the **Lock/Save Sheet** button to save and name the template as described in "Bill a Customer with the Invoice," p. 392. Close the customized template.

Do It Yourself Customize and Use the Change Request Template

9 Open the **File** menu and click **New**. The New dialog box appears.

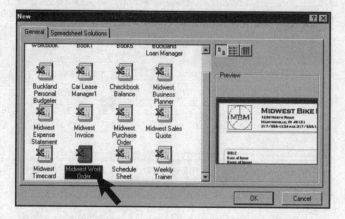

10 Click the icon for the custom Change Request template and click **OK**. A new, blank change request workbook appears.

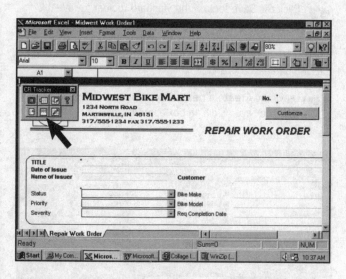

11 To number the change request, click the **Assign a Number** button on the CR Tracker toolbar. In the message box that asks if it's OK to permanently assign a number to the form, click **OK**.

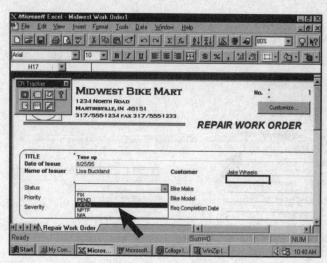

12 Enter information about the project, using the drop-down lists for the entries where they apply.

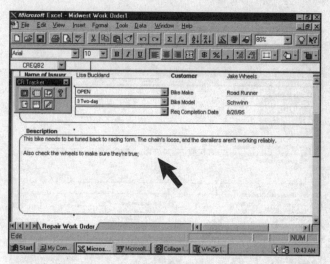

13 Scroll down to the Description area, click, and type a detailed description of the job.

(continues)

Do It Yourself Customize and Use the Change Request Template *(continued)*

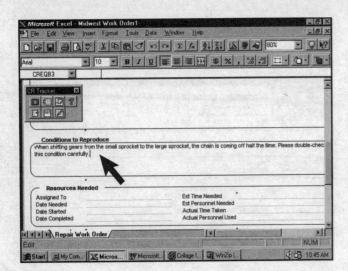

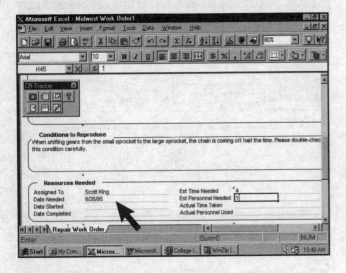

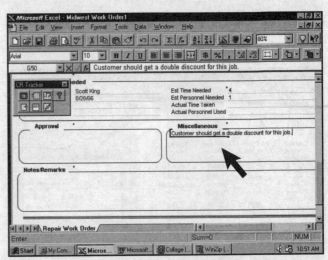

14 Scroll down to the Conditions to Reproduce area and note any particular problems that the person preparing the work needs to check.

15 Fill in the Resources Needed area. Make sure you only fill in the cells for estimated or anticipated needs. The person performing the work fills in the actual resources they used.

16 Enter any miscellaneous information, notes, or remarks that you want to pass along to the person performing the work. Also, the person performing the work can make notes about observations made while completing the work.

17 Click the **Save** tool on the Standard toolbar to save the change request (or work order, in this case). The Template File–Save to Database dialog box appears so you can specify whether to save the change request data to the change request tracking database.

18 Leave the **Create a new record** option selected and click **OK**. The Save As dialog box appears.

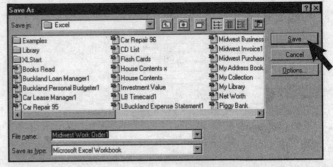

19 Navigate to the directory where you want to save the change request or work order. Type a name in the File name text box, if needed, and click **Save**.

20 To print the change request or work order, click the **Print** button on the Standard toolbar.

DO IT YOURSELF

Use Excel with Other Applications

Spreadsheets are popular applications, but word processors are the most popular. And the Microsoft Office suite of software applications gives you Word (word processing), Excel (spreadsheet), PowerPoint (presentation graphics), and more.

Chances are, if you're using Excel, you may be using one of the other Office applications. That's great! It's never a bad idea to use the right tool for the right job. But what if the job requires more than one tool? In cases like that, you can just relax and count on OLE (Object Linking and Embedding), a capability built into Windows and the Office applications. With OLE, you can use information and features from one application in a document you create in another application.

This section in *The Big Basics Book of Excel for Windows 95* reveals how you can combine the tools of various Office applications, among other features. The tasks here show you how to do the following tasks.

What You Will Find in This Section

Copy Worksheets Between Excel Files

"Why reinvent the wheel?" This question applies not only to everyday situations, but also to the Excel worksheets you create. Once you take the time to enter all the formulas and apply just the formatting you want, why perform these tasks again? To leverage the effort you've invested into a particular worksheet, copy the worksheet to other workbooks to reuse it.

For example, if you created the address book worksheet described in "Keep Your Address Book," p. 336, you can copy it to a new workbook file to provide to a coworker or co-scout leader who needs the same contact list.

The Do It Yourself steps in this task explain how to copy a favorite worksheet from one workbook file to an existing workbook or a new workbook Excel creates automatically. Read on to get the scoop.

If you refer to a task earlier in this book, you can get a refresher about copying worksheets in the same file. See "Move and Copy Worksheets Within a Workbook," p. 92.

Begin Do It Yourself Copy a Worksheet to Another Workbook

1 Open the workbook you want to copy the worksheet to (if it's an existing workbook). Or, to copy the worksheet to a new workbook, simply go to the next step.

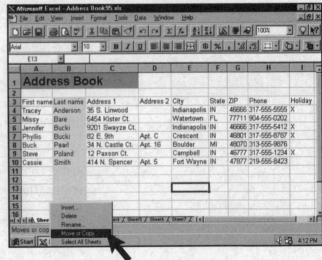

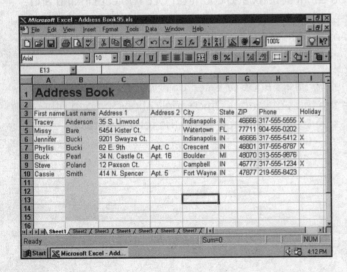

2 Open the workbook file that holds the worksheet you want to copy.

3 Right-click on the tab for the worksheet you want to copy and click **Move or Copy** from the shortcut menu that appears. (Or, you can click the tab, click the **Edit** menu, and then click **Move or Copy Sheet**.) The Move or Copy dialog box appears.

Do It Yourself   Copy a Worksheet to Another Workbook

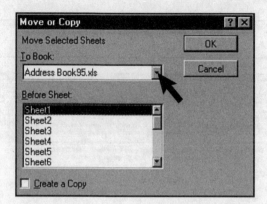

4 Click the arrow beside the To Book drop-down list to display its choices.

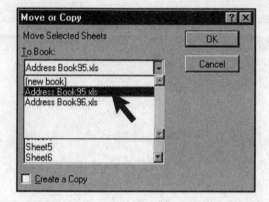

5 In the To Book drop-down list, click the name of the workbook file to which you want to copy the worksheet. Or, to create a new workbook to copy the sheet to, click **(new book)**.

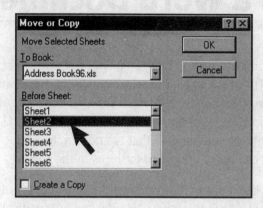

6 If you've chosen an existing workbook to copy the sheet to, click the name of the sheet you want to insert the copied sheet before in the Before Sheet list box.

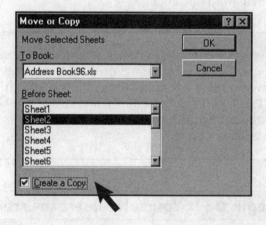

7 Click to add a check mark in the **Create a Copy** check box and click **OK**. Excel inserts a copy of the worksheet in the workbook you specified, before other sheets.

Insert an Excel Database in a Word Document

Computers often have an unwanted side effect. They turn us all into reluctant typists. However, if you're a *really* reluctant typist, typing a boatload of data into an Excel database once may be enough. The thought of repeating all that typing in a Word document can make you want to throw in the towel.

Well, don't sweat it. If you've entered a long list of data into an Excel worksheet, you can automatically insert that data into any Word document to keep your fingers from cramping up in rebellion. The Do It Yourself steps here explain how to recycle that Excel data in a Word document.

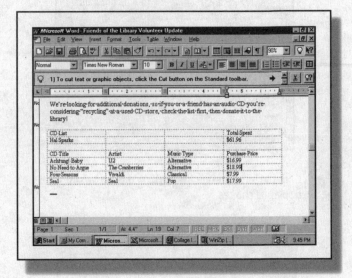

Several of the tasks in "Track Personal Information in Excel," which starts on p. 335, describe how to create databases (lists of information) in Excel. Refer to those tasks, and "Build a Database," p. 181, to learn how to create a database in Excel.

Begin Do It Yourself Insert an Excel Database into a Word Document

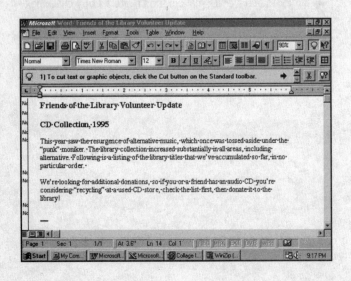

1 Create and save an Excel database. "Track Personal Information in Excel," which starts on p. 335, contains several ideas for Excel databases you can create.

2 Open a Word document and enter and format the text leading up to the area where you want to insert the Excel data. Or, simply click in a document where you want to insert the data.

Do It Yourself Insert an Excel Database into a Word Document

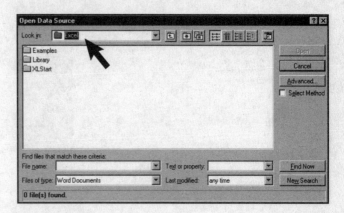

3 Open the **Insert** menu and click **Database**. Word displays its Database dialog box.

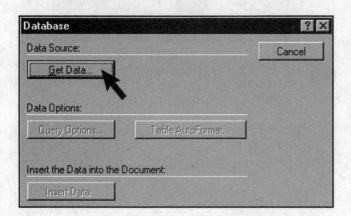

4 Click the **Get Data** button. The Open Data Source dialog box appears.

5 Using the Look in list and drop-down list, navigate to the folder that holds the Excel database to insert.

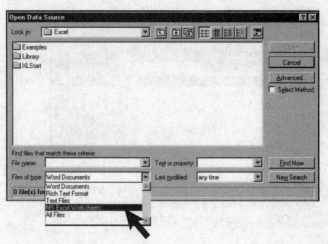

6 Make sure you select **MS Excel Worksheets** as the File of type choice.

(continues)

Do It Yourself Insert an Excel Database into a Word Document *(continued)*

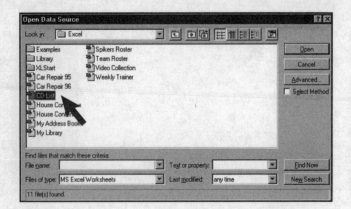

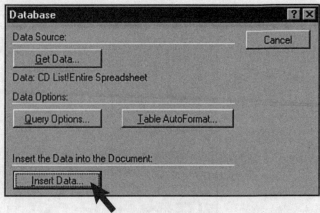

7 In the Look in list, click the name of the workbook that holds the database to insert and then click **Open**. The Microsoft Excel dialog box appears.

9 In the Database dialog box, click the **Insert Data** button. Excel displays the Insert Data dialog box.

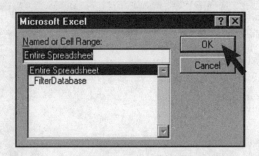

10 Click **OK** to insert all the records. Excel inserts the data as a table in Word.

8 In the Named or Cell Range list, click the name of the worksheet or range holding the database and then click **OK**. Excel displays the Database dialog box choices.

Insert a Picture in an Excel Worksheet

It's a multimedia world. No longer are simple words, numbers, or pictures enough to communicate your message. It very often takes more than a few clever calculations to make your point. Electronic images (also called graphic files or pictures) are widely available. You can buy neat artwork collections on floppy disk or CD-ROM, or download images from online services like CompuServe, Prodigy, and America Online or the Internet. And, the Windows 95 Paint accessory program is much easier to use than its predecessor, Paintbrush, which came with Windows 3.1x. If you're at all artistically inclined, you can use Paint to create an image to enhance your worksheet.

Excel enables you to automatically insert several types of images on an Excel worksheet, including:

Tagged Image Format (tif)

Encapsulated PostScript (eps)

Windows bitmap (bmp)

WordPerfect Graphics (wpg)

Macintosh PICT (pct)

JPEG Filters (jpg)

Windows Metafile (wmf)

PCX Files from Windows Paint (pcx)

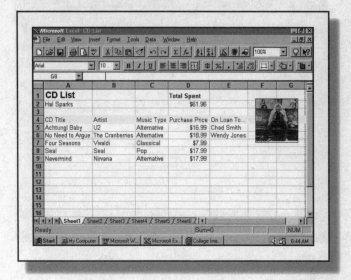

The Do It Yourself steps show you how easy it is to add an image to an Excel worksheet. The steps also tell you how to choose whether or not to display the images you've inserted. When you hide the display of an image, you can scroll around on the worksheet a bit more quickly, because Excel doesn't have to "redraw" the image on-screen as you scroll.

> You can create your own drawings, such as a team logo, right on an Excel worksheet. To do so, use the buttons on the Drawing toolbar, which you can display by right-clicking any toolbar and clicking **Drawing**.

Begin Do It Yourself Insert a Picture

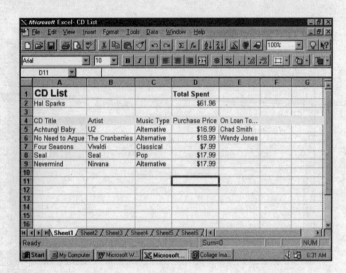

① Open the workbook and select the worksheet on which you want to insert the image.

② Open the **Insert** menu and click **Picture**. Excel displays the Picture dialog box. **All Graphics Files** is automatically selected as the Files of type choice, so you simply need to find and select a graphic file.

③ Navigate to the disk and folder that holds the picture to insert using the Look in drop-down list and list box.

④ In the Name list, click a picture file name. Excel displays a preview of the image to the right of the Name list.

⑤ Click **OK** to finish selecting the image and close the Picture dialog box. The picture appears on the worksheet, surrounded by black selection handles.

Do It Yourself   Insert a Picture

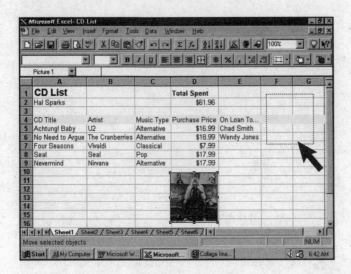

6 Drag the picture to the location you want on the worksheet and then use the selection handles to resize it, if needed.

Begin Do It Yourself   Hide and Display Pictures in the Workbook

1 With the workbook that contains the picture open, open the **Tools** menu and click **Options**. Excel displays the Options dialog box.

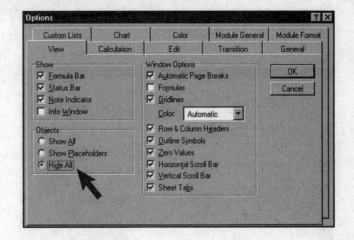

2 Click the **View** tab to bring it to the front and click the **Hide All** option button.

3 Click **OK** to close the dialog box. Excel removes all pictures (and other objects) from display.

(continues)

Do It Yourself Hide and Display Pictures in the Workbook *(continued)*

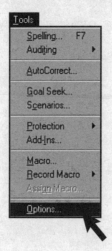

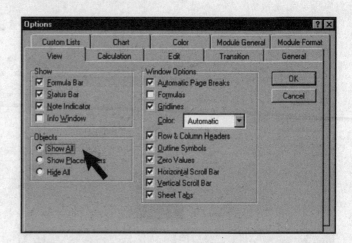

4 Open the **Tools** menu and click **Options**. Excel displays the Options dialog box.

5 On the View tab, click the **Show All** option button.

6 Click **OK** to finish redisplaying the picture.

Begin Do It Yourself Delete a Picture

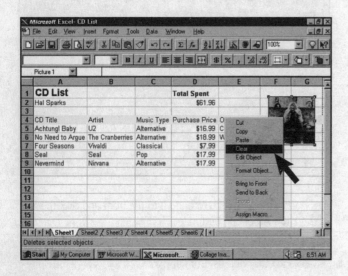

1 Right-click the picture you want to delete and choose **Clear** from the shortcut menu that appears. Excel removes the picture from the worksheet.

Link Data Between Excel Worksheets

In some ways, you can think of a range of cells as a photo negative. You can take that negative and make copies, or prints, to use in a variety of ways—one for the photo album, one for your wallet, one for Aunt Martha, and so on. But what if you decide to edit that photo a bit? Say you want to have it re-touched or printed in black and white? If you like it better with the changes, you have to throw out all the original prints and replace them with the new prints that you prefer.

That's how copying a range of cells in Excel used to be. Once you copied the data, it was a new, static "print" of the original information. If you made a change in the original data, you had to make that change manually in all the copies. No time saved there, and if you made a typo, that threw off one copy of the data.

Now, you can link copied information to the original data. When you link data, changes you make in the original data show up when you open a workbook that holds cells linked to the original data. In other words, Excel automatically updates the "print" of the data each time you open the workbook with the link.

You can link one or more cells between worksheets in a single workbook and between worksheets in different workbooks. When you click on a linked range, Excel displays a linking formula, including the name of the sheet holding the original data, in the Formula bar.

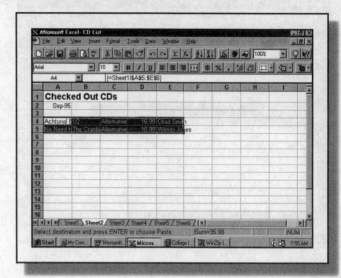

You also can link Excel data with a Word document. When you paste linked cells from Excel to Word, Word treats the linked data as a table, placing the contents of each cell from Excel into a single cell in the new table.

The Do It Yourself steps explain how to set up three kinds of links. Once you've gotten the hang of it, you'll use links often to make your workbooks self-updating. What a plus!

Linking data is much like moving and copying data. To review those basic techniques, see "Move and Copy Information," p. 56.

Begin Do It Yourself Link Data Between Sheets in the Same Workbook

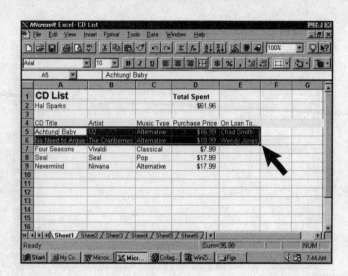

1 Select the worksheet holding the original information you want to link. Now drag to select the information to link.

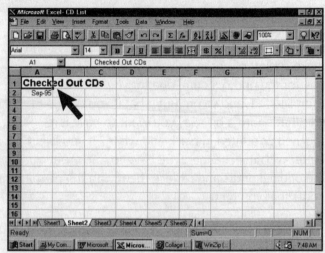

3 Click to select the tab for the worksheet to which you want to paste the linked cells.

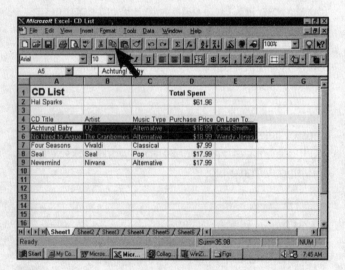

2 Click the **Copy** button on the Standard toolbar.

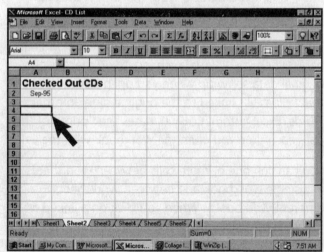

4 Click the cell that's in the upper left corner of the range to which you want to paste the linked information. Make sure the range to paste to is empty so you don't overwrite any entries.

Do It Yourself   Link Data Between Sheets in the Same Workbook

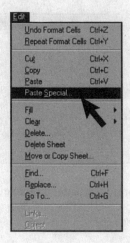

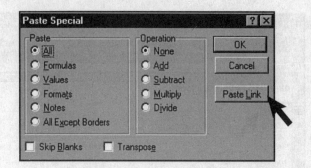

6 Click **Paste Link**. Excel pastes the information starting in the cell you specified and links the data to the information you copied originally.

5 Open the **Edit** menu and choose **Paste Special**. The Paste Special dialog box appears.

Begin Do It Yourself   Link Data Between Different Workbooks

1 Open or create the workbook to which you want to paste a link. Then open the workbook which contains the original information you want to link.

3 Click the **Copy** button on the Standard toolbar.

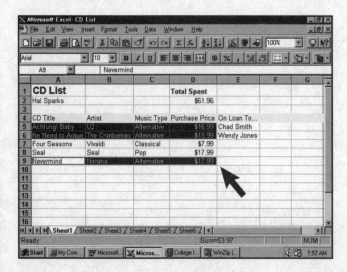

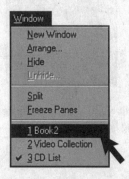

4 Open the **Window** menu and click the name of the workbook to which you want to link information.

2 Select the worksheet holding the original information you want to link and drag to select the information to link. You can select non-contiguous ranges, too!

5 If needed, click to select the tab for the worksheet to which you want to paste the linked cells.

(continues)

Do It Yourself Link Data Between Different Workbooks *(continued)*

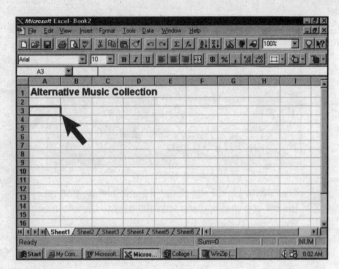

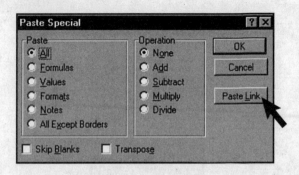

6 Click the cell that's in the upper left corner of the range to which you want to paste the linked information. Make sure the range to paste to is empty so you don't overwrite any entries.

8 Click **Paste Link**. Excel pastes the information starting in the cell you specified and links the data to the information you copied originally.

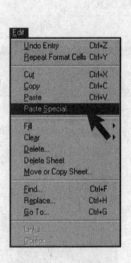

7 Open the **Edit** menu and choose **Paste Special**. The Paste Special dialog box appears.

Begin Do It Yourself   Link Cells in a Word Document

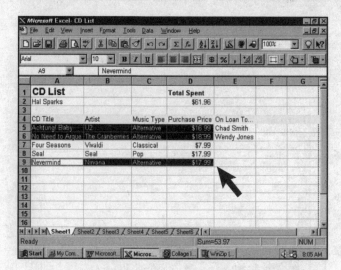

1 Select the worksheet holding the original information you want to link and drag to select the information to link.

2 Click the **Copy** button on the Standard toolbar.

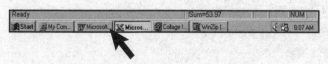

3 If the Word program isn't running, open it with the **Start** menu. Or, if Word is open, click the **Word** button on the taskbar to switch to Word.

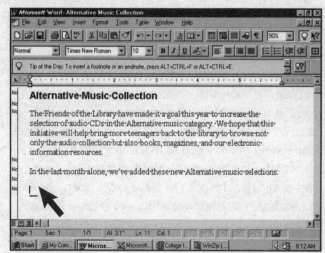

4 Open or create the document file into which you want to insert the linked information. Position the insertion point at the location where you want to insert the pasted table of Excel data.

5 Open the **Edit** menu and choose **Paste Special**. The Paste Special dialog box appears.

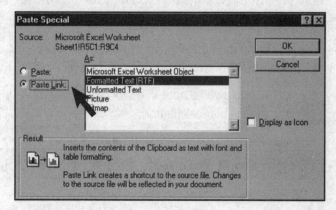

6 Click the **Paste Link** option and click **OK**. Word inserts a new table containing the information you specified and links the data to the information you copied originally.

Embed Objects in Excel

*E*mbedding an object in effect lets you add the features from another program into Excel. For example, if you embed a Paint object into Excel, you can use the tools that come with Paint to create or edit the picture. When you simply paste an object onto an Excel worksheet, you can't update the object. Embedding enables you to make changes to the object later, if you need to, right in the worksheet. This eliminates the need to leave Excel, open another application, edit and save a file, and repaste it into Excel.

You can embed both a new object that you create right in the worksheet, or an object based on an existing file that you can then edit if you want in the worksheet. The Do It Yourself Steps explain both techniques. Don't worry—embedding isn't as difficult as it sounds!

Here are just a few ways that you may use an embedded object in Excel:

- To create a unique Paint picture for the workbook that you may want to update later.

- To include a voice note in a worksheet explaining a particular calculation.

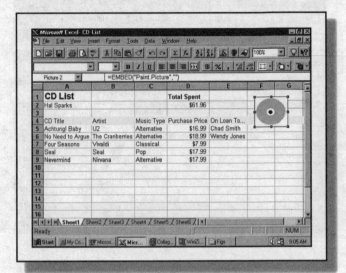

- To include a version of a neat PowerPoint slide you created on a worksheet.

- To insert a Word or WordPad object into the worksheet when you don't want to insert text in a cell because there's too much text. If you insert a Word or WordPad object instead, you can move, resize, and add more text into the object as needed without disturbing any of the worksheet cells.

Begin Do It Yourself Embed a New Object

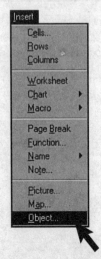

1 Select the worksheet where you want to embed the object.

2 Open the **Insert** menu and click **Object**. Excel displays the Object dialog box, with the Create New tab selected by default.

Do It Yourself Embed a New Object

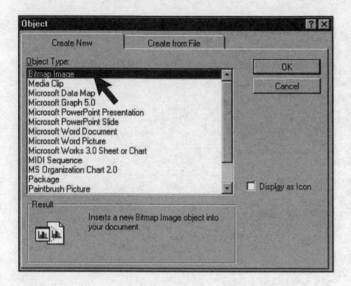

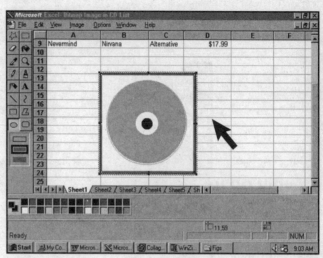

3 In the Object Type list, click to select the kind of object to insert. For example, choosing **Bitmap Image** opens Windows Paint so you can create a new Paint object.

4 Click **OK**. Excel inserts a blank frame (if the object is of a type that appears in a frame). It also displays the tools for the application, such as the Paint tools, so you can create the specified type of object.

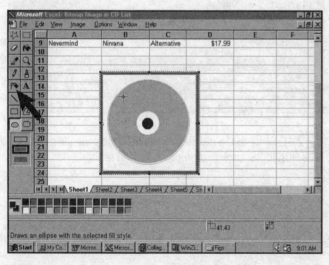

5 Use the tools to create the object.

6 To finish the object, click outside it on the worksheet. (For some objects, such as sounds you record, you need to exit the application used to create the object, instead.)

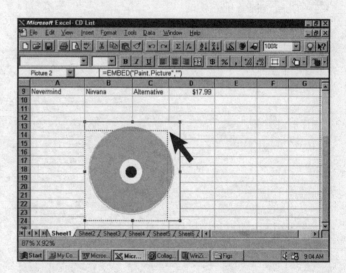

7 Move and resize the object on the worksheet, as needed.

Begin Do It Yourself Embed an Object Based on a File

1 Select the worksheet where you want to embed the object.

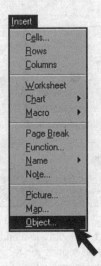

2 Open the **Insert** menu and click **Object**. Excel displays the Object dialog box.

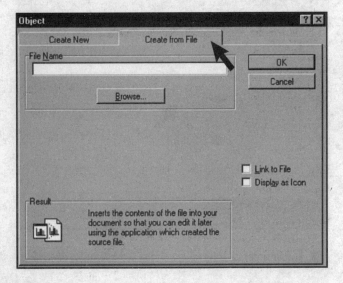

3 Click the **Create from File** tab to display its options.

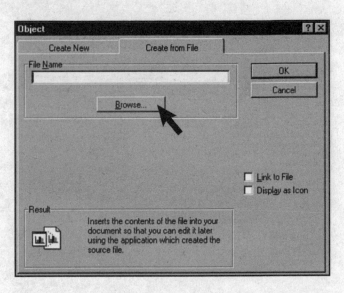

4 Click the **Browse** button. The Browse dialog box appears so you can select the file on which to base the object.

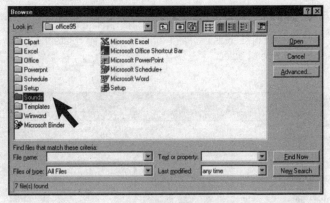

5 Navigate to the disk and folder that holds the file to insert using the Look in drop-down list and list box.

Do It Yourself   Embed an Object Based on a File

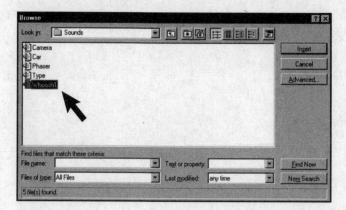
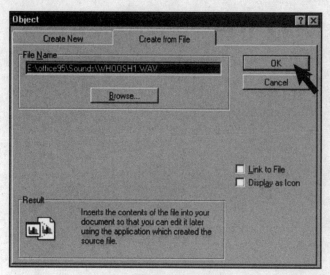

6 Click on the name of the file to use as the object and then click **Insert**. Excel inserts the selected file in the File Name text box of the Object dialog box.

7 Click **OK**. Excel inserts the object on the worksheet. Move and resize it as needed.

Begin Do It Yourself   Open an Embedded Object to Edit It

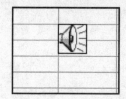

The first way to open an object for editing is to double-click on the object or the icon that represents it.

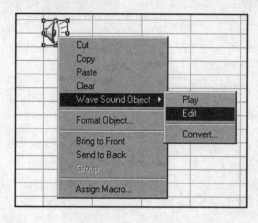

Alternatively, right-click the object, point to the object choice, and click **Edit**.

To finish editing, click outside the object (for objects in a frame), or close the application for the object (for objects that appear as icons by default).

PART 3

101 Quick Fixes

If you are having a problem with Excel, this part of the book is for you. This part contains 101 of the most common problems along with their solutions.

The problems are organized into the categories listed below. The easiest way to find your problem is to look in the Quick-Finder table, locate the category that you think matches your problem, and scan through the table to find the quick fix that you need. If you can't find a category that matches your need, try the Miscellaneous Problems category.

What You Will Find in This Part

101 QUICK FIXES

Questions and Answers

Quick-Finder Table

Calculation Problems

Charting Problems

(continues)

Charting Problems *Continued*

Editing Problems

File Problems

Problem	Quick Fix Number	Page
Imported Access table displays times as **1/0/00**	80	508
Dates need to be converted to the **1904 date system**	73	505
Access file doesn't convert from Excel	79	508
Access file doesn't open in Excel	79	508
Desired file **converter** was not installed with Excel	74	506
Dates are wrong in Excel for Macintosh	73	505
Default folder needs to be changed	76	507
Desired **file not available in Open dialog box**	78	507
Get **File is locked** error message when saving worksheet	81	509
Can't **find file**	78	507
Files always end up in the wrong **folder**	76	507
Imported Access table displays **incorrect times**	80	508
Get **Read-only** error message while saving	77	507
Desired file format is not in the **Save As Type** box	74	506
Values do not convert correctly	75	506

Formatting Problems

Problem	Quick Fix Number	Page
######## displays in cell	36	490
Excel changes **.05 to 5.00%**	44	493
1E+08 appears in the cell instead of 100000000	37	490
Can't **center text across columns**	40	492
Column width is too narrow	35	489
Excel **cuts off part of the entry**	35	489
Dates not formatted correctly	38	491
Excel changes **dates to a number**	38	491
Fonts do not display correctly	42	492
Can't change the **format of a cell**	41	492
Incorrect formatting after closing workbook	42	492
Leading zero does not display in zip code	39	491
Manual page breaks don't work correctly	43	493
Number is not formatted correctly	37	490
Cell is incorrectly formatted as a **percentage**	44	493
Number appears in **scientific notation**	37	490
Can't **see all of the contents** of the cell	35	489

(continues)

Formatting Problems   *Continued*

Installation Problems

Macro Problems

Menu and Toolbar Problems

(continues)

Printing Problems   *Continued*

Object Linking and Embedding Problems

System Problems

Num Lock is turned off	9	478
Numeric keypad does not work correctly	9	478
Mouse **pointer is hard to find**	13	480
Mouse **pointer moves too quickly**	11	479
Mouse **pointer speed** is set too fast	11	479
Mouse **pointer trails** are turned off	13	480
Keyboard **repeat rate** is set too high	10	478
The **screen resolution** is too high	6	475
Keys on my keyboard **stick**	10	478
It takes **too long to open files**	7	476
Worksheet is **too small to read**	6	475

Template Problems

Problem	Quick Fix Number	Page
Can't find **built-in template**	33	488
Accidentally changed the **default template**	34	488
Template wasn't **installed**	33	488
Template is **unavailable**	32	487
Can't find **user created template**	32	487

Installation Problems

These are the problems you may encounter with the Excel Setup program.

1 During Setup I got an error message that said Setup needs to modify a file on my floppy disk.

This error occurs when the first installation disk is write-protected. If you're like most people, the first thing you do when you get new software is to write-protect all of the disks. This is one of those rare cases where it may not be a good idea. Fortunately, the fix is easy. Just remove the disk and move the write-protect tab to the opposite position. Reinsert the disk and click the **OK** button. Setup now continues normally.

2 When I try to install Excel, it tells me that the disk set has already been used.

The first time you install Excel, it copies your name and company information to the first setup disk. The next time you try to install Excel from the same set of disks, the above error message appears. The message is basically meant to remind you of the licensing agreement. If you have a legitimate reason to install the software again, just click the **OK** button. Setup continues with the installation.

3 I got part way through installation and Setup told me that I didn't have enough disk space.

Excel can take up a lot of disk space. The Compact installation needs 8 MB of disk space, the Typical installation needs 18 MB, and the Custom installation can take up to 38 MB. There are a few different options you can choose from at this point. One thing you can do is to click on the **Exit Setup** button and try to free up some disk space. Or, you can remove backup files that you don't need from your hard drive. Another choice is to not install all of the Excel options. Follow these steps to change the setup options:

1. From the Setup dialog box, click the **Change Options** button.

2. Click the **Compact** button to install only the bare minimum to run Excel. Skip the remaining steps and continue with Setup. If you want to choose which options to install, click the **Custom** button.

3. Uncheck the options you don't need right now. Remember, you can always add or remove options later. You can also highlight an option and click the **Change Option** button to uncheck individual components of an option.

4. Continue to uncheck options until the required disk space is less than the available disk space (you can see the totals at the bottom of the dialog box). Click the **Continue** button to finish the installation.

5. A message box tells you when the installation is complete. Click the **OK** button.

4 During Setup I got an error message that said Setup did not complete successfully.

Be sure that you close all other applications before you run the Setup program. Any other applications that are running can interfere with the installation program (especially virus-checking applications). Close all open applications and run the Setup program again.

5 I can't copy the installation disks.

The installation disks use DMF formatting. DMF is a slick way to store 1.7 megabytes of data on a 1.44 megabyte floppy drive. This saves Microsoft money because the company doesn't have to distribute as many disks. Unfortunately, it also means that you cannot make backup copies of the disks. If it's any consolation, Microsoft replaces defective disks at no charge.

System Problems

System problems are the ones that have to do with Windows 95 in general. You will find common screen, memory, keyboard, and mouse problems here.

6 I'm getting eyestrain reading this worksheet because it's so small.

There is a fine line between maximizing the amount of information you can see on your screen and making the worksheet too hard to read. There are two possible causes for this problem. Either your screen resolution is too high or the magnification in Excel is too low. Changing the screen resolution affects all of your Windows applications, but changing the magnification only changes the size of your worksheet. If the toolbars and menus in Excel and other Windows applications are the right size, but your worksheet is too small, you can fix your problem with the *zoom control*. The zoom control enables you to change the magnification of your worksheet. Follow these steps to zoom in or out:

1. From the **View** menu, choose **Zoom**.

2. In the Magnification list of the Zoom dialog box, click on the desired magnification factor. 100% is normal size. Smaller percentages make the worksheet smaller, while larger percentages make it larger. If the desired magnification factor is not listed, click on **Custom** and type in the desired percentage.

3. Click **OK** to close the dialog box. If the worksheet is still too hard to read, repeat steps 1 through 3 until you are happy with the results.

If you have trouble seeing all of your applications, and everything in Windows seems to be too small, you may want to change the screen resolution. Follow these steps:

1. Minimize your applications and right-click on an empty space on your desktop. In the shortcut menu that appears, click on **Properties**.

2. Click on the **Settings** tab in the Display Properties dialog box.

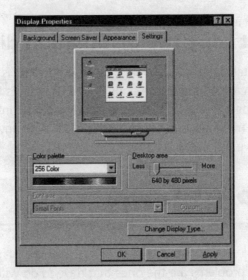

3. In the Desktop area section, slide the sliding scale to the left to decrease the screen resolution. Decreasing the resolution makes everything on the screen larger.

4. Click the **Apply** button. Depending on the type of video card you have, Windows reacts differently. Windows may tell you that it has to restart for the settings to take effect. Click **OK** and Windows restarts in the new resolution. If Windows doesn't tell you that it needs to restart, it tells you that it may take 15 seconds to resize the screen. Click **OK**. The screen resizes, and Windows asks you if you like the new resolution. Click **Yes** to keep the new resolution or **No** to take the resolution back to the original setting.

7 Excel seems to take longer to open files than it used to.

When your hard drive takes longer to open files, it usually means that it is *fragmented*. Fragmented means that your files are not placed on your hard drive in continuous sectors. In other words, part of your file is in one sector, the next sector has part of another file, and the rest of your file may be halfway across the disk. This happens naturally as you add data to the hard disk, but after awhile, it slows down performance. Fortunately, Windows 95 includes a utility to defragment your disk. Follow these steps:

1. From the **Start** menu, point to **Programs**, point to **Accessories**, point to **System Tools**, and click **Disk Defragmenter**.

2. The Select Drive dialog box appears, asking which drive you want to defragment. If you have more than one drive you can choose **All Hard Drives** from the drop-down list, or you can choose just one. Click **OK**.

3. The Disk Defragmenter dialog box opens. Click the **Start** button to begin defragmenting. Depending on the speed of your system, and how much of the disk was fragmented, it can take a couple of hours to defragment the disk. You can continue working in other applications while the Disk Defragmenter is running.

4. When the Defragmenter finishes, a dialog box pops up, asking if you want to defragment another drive. Click **Yes** if you want to, or **No** if you don't.

Your disk is now defragmented, and your files will not take as long to load. You should defragment your disk on a regular basis to keep performance at an optimum level.

8 When I try to start another application, I get a message that says there is insufficient memory.

While you may think that the problem is not enough RAM, the real problem is insufficient free space on your hard drive. Windows 95 uses virtual memory (using a portion of the hard drive as system memory), so you should be able to open applications until you run out of hard drive space. If your hard drive is almost full, you may not have enough space left to effectively use virtual memory. Try the following to free up disk space:

- Clean up your hard drive. Use My Computer or Explorer to copy files that you don't use anymore to floppy disks (or if you have a tape backup, use it). After you copy the files, delete them from your hard drive.

- When the Recycle Bin gets full, it can take a lot of disk space. Follow these steps to empty it:

    1. Double-click on the **Recycle Bin** icon.

    2. Check the list of files to be sure there isn't any that you wish to recover.

    3. From the **File** menu, choose **Empty Recycle Bin**.

    4. A dialog box pops up asking if you're sure you want to delete the files. Click **Yes** if you're sure.

    5. Close the Recycle Bin by clicking on its **Close** button.

If the above methods do not free up enough disk space, you may want to consider buying a new hard drive (the prices are pretty reasonable these days). If that's not an option for your budget, try using DriveSpace. DriveSpace is a program that is included in Windows 95. It takes all of the files on your disk and compresses them into smaller files. You can't use the smaller files while they are compressed, so DriveSpace automatically decompresses your files when you want to use them. Depending on the type of data on your drive, you could double the space available on your hard drive. In other words, if you have a 340 megabyte hard drive, you can put 680 megabytes of data on it. The penalty for this is that it may slow down your computer a little bit. If you have a pretty fast computer (486DX2-66 or above), you probably won't notice the difference. Follow these steps to compress your drive with DriveSpace:

1. From the **Start** menu, point to **Programs**, point to **Accessories**, point to **System Tools**, and then click **DriveSpace**.

2. In the DriveSpace dialog box, click on the drive that you want to compress and choose **Compress** from the **Drive** menu.

3. The Compress a Drive dialog box opens, showing you the details of the compression. Click **Start** to begin compressing the drive.

4. A dialog box opens, asking if you're sure you want to compress the drive. Click the **Compress Now** button to begin compression.

DriveSpace uses all of your computer's available resources while it is compressing your drive, so you won't be able to use your computer for awhile. Depending on your system, it may take several hours to finish.

9 I'm trying to enter numbers with the numeric keypad, but the active cell moves instead.

The numeric keypad on your keyboard serves a dual purpose. You can use it to type in numbers or to move the cursor around. To force the numeric keypad to enter numbers press the **Numlock** key (on most keyboards it's the key directly above the 7). Most keyboards also have a light that illuminates when the keypad is in numlock mode. When the light illuminates, you can use the numbers on the keypad to enter numbers.

10 When I type, the letter I press appears more than once.

You have a problem with the keyboard repeat rate or the repeat delay. The repeat rate is the speed that the characters repeat when you hold down a key. The repeat delay is how long you have to hold down a key before it repeats. Follow these steps to change the repeat rate or repeat delay:

1. From the **Start** menu, point to **Settings**, and click **Control Panel**.

2. Double-click on the **Keyboard** icon.

3. In the Keyboard Properties dialog box, click on the **Speed** tab.

4. Under Repeat delay and Repeat rate there are sliding scales. Move the sliders in the desired directions. Move the repeat delay slider to the left to increase the amount of time you hold the key down before the key repeats. Move the repeat rate slider to the left to slow down how fast the key repeats when you hold it down.

5. Click in the box labeled **Click here and hold down a key to test repeat rate** to check your settings. Hold down a key and see what happens. If the repeat rate or repeat delay is still not working correctly, repeat step 4 to fine-tune your settings.

6. When you are satisfied with the repeat rate and repeat delay, click the **OK** button.

11 It's hard to use the mouse because the pointer moves too quickly across the screen.

When the mouse settings are not set up correctly for your individual preference, it can make the mouse almost unusable. Fortunately, you can change the speed of your mouse pointer to make it easier to use. Follow the steps:

1. From the **Start** menu, point to **Settings**, and click **Control Panel**.

2. Double-click on the **Mouse** icon. In the Mouse Properties dialog box, click on the **Motion** tab.

3. Under Pointer speed there is a sliding scale. Move the slider to the left to slow down the speed of the pointer, or to the right to speed it up.

4. After you move the slider, click on the **Apply** button.

5. Try moving the mouse across the screen. Repeat steps 3 and 4 until you are comfortable with the speed.

6. Click **OK** to close the dialog box.

12 My mouse is set to right-handed, but I need it to be left-handed.

If you use your mouse with your left hand, it is easier to use it if you have it set for left-handed. This way the primary button is the one under your index finger. Just remember, when this book refers to the right mouse button, it really means the primary button (which is the left button on a left-handed mouse). Follow these steps to change the mouse button orientation to left-handed:

1. From the **Start** menu, highlight **Settings**, and click **Control Panel**.

2. Double-click the **Mouse** icon.

3. In the Mouse properties dialog box, click the **Buttons** tab and click on **Left-handed** option button.

4. Click **OK**. Now your mouse is set for a left-handed user.

13 I can't find the mouse pointer on my notebook computer.

The mouse pointer on a black and white LCD screen can be very difficult to see. You may want to try a feature called *pointer trails*. A pointer trail is a trail of pointers that follows the mouse pointer when you move it. Follow these steps to enable pointer trails:

1. From the **Start** menu, point to **Settings**, and click on **Control Panel**.

2. Double-click on the **Mouse** icon.

3. In the Mouse Properties dialog box, click on the **Motion** tab. In the Pointer trail section click on the **Show pointer trails** check box. You can also vary the length of the pointer trail by moving the slider below the check box.

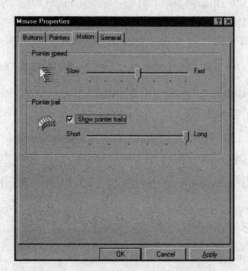

4. Now, move your mouse pointer around to see the pointer trails. If you like the way they look, click on **OK** to close the dialog box. If you don't like them, click on the check box again to remove the check mark and click **OK**.

Menu and Toolbar Problems

These are problems related to the toolbars and menus that you use with Excel.

14 The toolbar is no longer under the menu bar, but there's a box in the middle of the screen with all the buttons in it.

This box is called a *toolbox*. Some people prefer the buttons in a toolbox because you can move the toolbox anywhere on the screen. If you double-click on an empty space in the toolbar (not on a button) it turns into a *toolbox*. Double-click in the title bar of the toolbox to change it back into a toolbar.

15 There are no toolbars at the top of the screen.

Either you are in *full-screen mode*, or you did not select your toolbars for display. Full-screen mode is a method to maximize the viewing area of your worksheet. The only thing visible on your screen is the menu and row and column headings. To check if you are in full-screen mode, click on the **View** menu. If there is a check mark next to **Full Screen**, you are in full-screen mode. Click **Full Screen** to remove the check mark and return the screen to normal. If you aren't in full-screen mode, or the toolbars are still not visible, follow these steps:

1. Choose **Toolbars** from the **View** menu.
2. In the Toolbars dialog box, check the toolbars that you want to appear on the screen (the Standard and Formatting toolbars are the ones you usually display).
3. Click **OK** to close the dialog box and display your toolbars.

16 Someone changed the buttons on my toolbar. How can I get them back?

If you or someone else has changed the configuration of your toolbar, it's fairly easy to get it back to the way it used to be. Follow these steps:

1. Select **Toolbars** from the **View** menu.
2. In the Toolbars dialog box, click on the toolbar you wish to change in the **Toolbars** section and click the **Reset** button.
3. Click **OK** to close the dialog box. Your toolbar is as good as new.

17 My toolbars are in the wrong place on the screen.

Excel enables you to have great flexibility when it comes to the toolbars. You can move them practically anywhere on the screen. To move the toolbar back to a desired location, click on an empty space on the toolbar (not a button) and drag the toolbar to its new location. The toolbar stays in its new location every time you open Excel until you move it again.

18 I can't tell what the toolbar buttons are on my black and white screen.

By default, the toolbar buttons are set up to be displayed on a color monitor. If you don't have a color display on your computer, the buttons are very difficult to see. There is an easy way to fix this problem, however. Just follow these steps:

1. From the **View** menu, choose **Toolbars**.

2. At the bottom of the Toolbars dialog box, uncheck the **Color Toolbars** check box.

3. Click **OK**. The buttons are now easier to see.

19 The buttons on the toolbar are too small to see.

The toolbar is set up to be pretty small so that it doesn't take up much of your screen. This allows you the maximum space for editing your worksheets. Depending on the size of your monitor and the screen resolution you choose, the buttons can get pretty small. That's one of the reasons that the Excel toolbars have *ToolTips*. A ToolTip is a description of what the button does when you click on it. If you hold the mouse pointer over a button for a few seconds the ToolTip appears. If the ToolTip is not enough, you can make the buttons on the toolbar larger. Keep in mind that you will not have as many buttons on your toolbar if you increase the button size. Follow these steps to change the toolbar to large buttons:

1. Choose **Toolbars** from the **View** menu.

2. At the bottom of the Toolbars dialog box, check the **Large Buttons** check box.

3. Click **OK**. The toolbar buttons get bigger.

Editing Problems

If you are having trouble editing your worksheet, look in this section.

20 I selected some cells to paste, but the Paste command is grayed out.

Merely selecting the text does not make it available for pasting. You first have to cut or copy it to the Clipboard. If you want to move the contents of the selected cells, choose **Cut** from the **Edit** menu. If you want to copy the contents, choose **Copy** from the **Edit** menu. Now, move the insertion point to the cell to which you want to paste the copied data, click in the cell, and choose **Paste** from the **Edit** menu.

21 When I press Enter after entering data in a cell, the active cell moves down.

By default, Excel moves the active cell down one after you press Enter. If you want the active cell to remain where it is or to move in a different direction when you press Enter, follow these steps:

1. From the **Tools** menu, choose **Options**.

2. In the Options dialog box, click on the **Edit** tab.

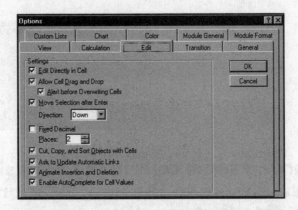

3. If you want the active cell to move in a different direction, choose the desired direction under **Move Selection after Enter**. To have the active cell remain where it is after you press Enter, uncheck the **Move Selection after Enter check box**.

4. Click **OK** to close the dialog box.

22 When I select the title at the top of the worksheet, nothing appears in the Formula bar. How can I edit the text?

You probably centered the title of your worksheet using the Center Across Columns command. The cell that contains the text is actually to the left of the text. The easiest way to find the cell that contains the text is to click on one of the cells where the text is. Now, use the left arrow on the keyboard and step through the cells one by one until the text appears in the Formula bar. You can now edit the text.

23 I want to delete an entire cell, but when I press the Delete key, only the contents are deleted.

When you use the Delete key to delete your data, you are only clearing the data from the cell, not removing the cell. If you want to completely remove the cell from the worksheet, follow these steps:

1. Select the cell you wish to delete.

2. From the **Edit** menu, click on **Delete** (or press **CTRL+minus sign**).

3. Excel opens the Delete dialog box, asking you what you want to do with the remaining cells. You can shift the cells below the deleted cell up to take its place, you can shift the cells to the right of the deleted cell left, or you can delete the entire row or column that the selected cell resides in. Click on the appropriate choice and click **OK**.

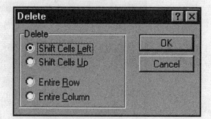

24 I moved some cells in my worksheet, but when I pasted them to the new location, they wrote over the data that was there.

When you paste data into cells, the data you paste into the cells automatically over-writes the data that was in the cells before. First, select **Undo** from the **Edit** menu. This returns the data that was in the cells before you pasted over them. Now, select an empty area on the worksheet to move your cells to and click on the **Paste** button on the toolbar (or choose **Paste** from the **Edit** menu).

25 Whenever I try to grab a selection to drag, I end up selecting another cell instead of dragging the selection.

When you use drag-and-drop to move a selection, it is important to point to the correct area of the selection. First select the range of cells you wish to move. Now, point to the box around the selection (your cursor changes to an arrow). While holding down the left mouse button, drag the selection to the desired location.

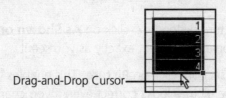

Drag-and-Drop Cursor

If you can't get the cursor to change to an arrow, you may have drag-and-drop editing turned off. Follow these steps to turn it back on:

1. From the **Tools** menu, choose **Options**.

2. In the Options dialog box, click on the **Edit** tab.

3. In the Settings area, check the **Allow Cell Drag-and-Drop** check box.

4. Click **OK** to close the dialog box.

Drag-and-drop is now available.

26 When I start typing text in a cell, Excel fills it in with another word.

Excel is trying to help you. If the first few characters you type in a cell match an entry in another cell in the column, Excel fills in the rest of the characters to match. To keep the filled-in entry, press Enter. If you keep typing, what you type replaces the filled-in entry. Press the Backspace key if you want to delete the characters that Excel filled in.

27 I want to copy some cells as a picture, but I can't find the Copy Picture option in the Edit menu.

When you copy an object as a picture, you can manipulate the object as a picture object. This is especially useful for adding Excel data to another application. Of course, if you can't find the command to copy the picture, it's not going to help you. You must hold down the **Shift** key when you click on the **Edit** menu for the **Copy Picture** command to be available. Follow these steps to copy cells or a chart as a picture:

1. Highlight the cells, or click the chart or drawing object that you want to copy as a picture.

2. While holding down the **Shift** key, choose **Copy Picture** from the **Edit** menu.

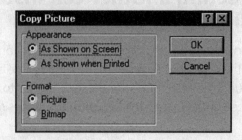

3. In the Copy Picture dialog box, click on **As Shown on Screen** in the Appearance section. This copies the object exactly as you see it.

4. In the **Format** section, click on **Picture**. This enables you to resize the picture and ensures that the picture looks correct even if you change your screen resolution.

5. Click **OK**.

6. Click where you want the picture to appear. It can be in another worksheet, or in an entirely different application.

7. If you are copying to another worksheet, hold down the **Shift** key and choose **Paste Picture** from the **Edit** menu. If you are copying into another application, use the **Paste Special** command from the **Edit** menu and click **OK** when the Paste Special dialog box opens.

28 I can't find the Remove Page Break option on the Insert menu. How can I remove the page break?

This can be a little tricky because the Remove Page Break option doesn't even appear in the Insert menu until you select the correct cell. To select a horizontal page break, select a cell directly below the page break. To select a vertical page break, select a cell directly to the right of the page break. To remove the page break, choose **Remove Page Break** from the **Insert** menu.

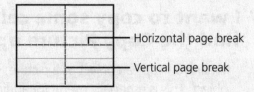

Horizontal page break

Vertical page break

29 When I try to edit a worksheet a co-worker gave me, I get an error message telling me that locked cells cannot be changed.

The worksheet your co-worker gave you is *protected*. That means that you cannot make any changes to the worksheet until you unprotect it. Follow these steps to fix the problem.

1. Click **OK** to close the error message box.

2. From the **Tools** menu, point to **Protection** and click on **Unprotect Sheet**.

3. If a dialog box opens asking you for a password, get the password from you co-worker and type it in the **Password** box.

4. Click **OK**.

You can make changes to the worksheet now.

30 When I use the arrow keys to move the active cell, the active cell disappears.

You have inadvertently turned on Scroll Lock. To turn it off, press the **Scroll Lock** button on your keyboard. The active cell moves normally now.

31 When I try to move a drawing object, the object just gets bigger instead of moving.

When you move an object it is important that you not click on a *sizing handle*. Sizing handles are the little squares that surround the object. When you click and drag on a sizing handle, the object grows or shrinks depending on where you drag it. To move the object, click on an area of the object that is not a sizing handle and drag the object to its new location.

Template Problems

These are the problems you may see when working with the templates that come with Excel.

32 I can't find a template I created when I open a new workbook.

When you open a new workbook, click on the **Spreadsheet Solutions** tab in the New dialog box to display a list of templates. If your template is not there, you probably saved it in a folder that Excel does not look for templates in. Make sure that you save your template in the Templates folder. If you didn't save it there, use My Computer or Explorer to move your newly created template into the Templates folder. Another possibility is that you accidentally saved your template as a workbook instead of a template. Make sure that you follow these steps when you create a template:

1. Open a new workbook and design your template.

2. Choose **Save As** from the **File** menu.

3. Select **Template** in the **Save As Type** box.

4. Type in the desired name for your template in the File name box and click **Save**.

33 I can't find one of the built-in templates when I open a new worksheet.

If you did not do a complete installation, not all of the templates are available. To use a built-in template that is not available, follow these steps to install the missing template:

1. From the **Start** menu, point to **Settings** and click on **Control Panel**.

2. Double-click on the **Add/Remove Programs** icon.

3. In the Add/Remove Programs Properties dialog box, click on the **Install/Uninstall** tab.

4. Click on **Microsoft Excel 7.0** and click on the **Add/Remove** button.

5. Windows tells you to insert the Excel disk 1. Insert the disk and click **OK**.

6. When the Setup dialog box opens, click the **Add/Remove** button.

7. In the Options dialog box, click on **Spreadsheet Templates**, and click the **Change Option** button.

8. In the Options dialog box, check the check boxes next to the templates you wish to install. If you want to install them all, click the **Select All** button.

9. Click **OK** and then click **Continue**.

10. Setup installs the necessary components and tells you when it is finished. Click **OK**.

34 I've changed some of the default settings for new worksheets. How can I get them back to the original settings?

Sometimes when you change things it seems like a good idea at the time, but now it doesn't look so good. Maybe you wanted all of your new worksheets to have a certain title at the top of the sheet, and now you no longer need that title. Whatever the case, Excel enables you to restore the original templates. Excel stores any changes that you made to the default templates in a file in the XLStart folder in your Excel folder. Follow these steps to remove the files that contain your custom settings:

1. Using My Computer or Explorer, open the **XLStart** folder in your Excel folder.

2. Delete the file called **Sheet.xlt** to restore the original settings for new worksheets. Delete the file called **Book.xlt** to restore the original settings for new workbooks.

The next time you open a new workbook or worksheet, it opens with Excel's default settings.

Formatting Problems

This section contains problems you may have with formatting. If the cells in your worksheet do not display properly, you can probably find the solution here. You can also find answers to problems with page breaks and fonts here.

35 If I type a long name in Excel, the end of it cuts off when I type something in the next column.

The name is still there; you just can't see it all because the column is not wide enough to show the full name. The easiest way to change the column width is with your mouse. Follow these steps:

1. Move your cursor to the right side of the gray lettered area at the top of the column (the column heading) until it turns into a vertical bar with arrows on each side.

2. Click and drag the edge of the column until it is the width you want. If you double-click on the right side, the column width changes to fit the largest value you have in that column.

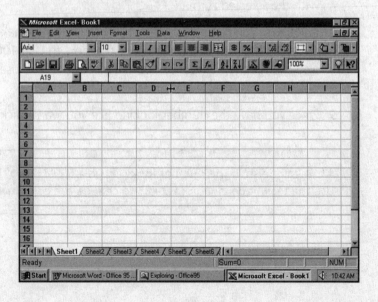

36 I see ####### in my cell instead of the answer to my calculation.

The result of your calculation is too wide to fit in the cell. Change the column width using the technique in the previous Quick Fix until it is wide enough to display the result.

37 1E+08 appears in the cell instead of 100000000. How can I get it back to 100000000?

You need to format the cells to display the number in the way you prefer. Follow these steps to change the number format:

1. Highlight the range of cells you want to format.

2. From the **Format** menu choose **Cells** and click on the **Number** tab.

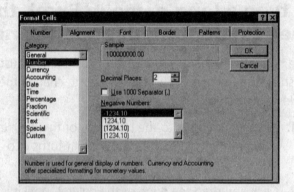

3. In the Format Cells dialog box, choose **Number** in the Category box. There is a sample at the top of the dialog box that shows you how your numbers will look with the selected format.

4. If you like, you can also use the 1000 separator to make your number look like 100,000,000. Just select the check box next to **Use 1000 Separator (,)**. You can also change the number of decimal places that you use in the **Decimal Places** box.

5. Once you have the number looking like you want, click **OK** to close the dialog box.

After you finish, if the number looks like #######, your column width is too small. Use the technique in Quick Fix #35 to change the column width.

38 Excel changed my date to a number.

Excel can usually figure out that you want the cell formatted as a date when you enter the date in the cell. However, if you already have the cell formatted in something other than date format, Excel changes it to the format you have specified. Don't worry, Excel changes the number back to the correct date when you change the formatting. Follow these steps to fix the problem:

1. Highlight the range of cells that you wish to change.

2. Select **Cells** from the **Format** menu and click on the **Number** tab.

3. In the Format Cells dialog box, select **Date** from the Category box and select the desired date format from the **Type** box.

4. Click **OK** to close the dialog box.

39 The leading zeros do not display in my zip code.

By default, Excel drops all leading zeros in your numbers. This works pretty well for most numbers, but zip codes look pretty funny with only four numbers (it will probably confuse the post office too). To display the leading zeros, you need to use the zip code format for the range of cells that contains your zip codes. Follow these steps to change the format:

1. Highlight the range of cells that contains the zip codes.

2. Choose the **Cells** option from the **Format** menu and click on the **Number** tab.

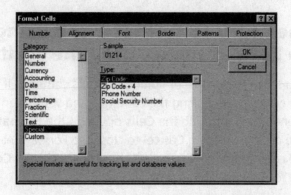

3. In the Format Cells dialog box, select **Special** in the Category box.

4. In the Type box, select **Zip Code** or **Zip Code + 4** (depending on which one you are using).

5. Click **OK** to close the dialog box.

40 The Center Across Columns command did not center my text properly.

The Center Across Columns command does not work properly if there is data in any of the cells you have selected to center across. To be sure there is no data in the cells, select the empty cells and press the **Delete** key. Now, type the desired text in the cell that is the farthest left in the range across which you are centering the text. Highlight the range of cells you want to center across (including the cell with the text in it) and click on the **Center Across Columns** button in the toolbar.

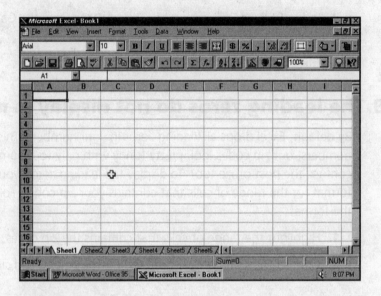

41 When I try to format a cell using the Cells option in the Format menu, only the Font tab is available.

You are in the middle of editing the cell's contents. If you just entered the contents of the cell (or were editing the contents, and you haven't pressed Enter yet, you can only change the font using the **Cells** option in the **Format** menu. To use the other formatting options, click on **Cancel** to close the Format Cells dialog box. Press **Enter** to accept the cell's contents. Now, select the cell and choose **Cells** from the **Format** menu. All of the formatting tabs are now available.

42 The formatting was correct the last time I opened my worksheet, but now it's all messed up.

The current printer is different than when you last opened your worksheet. The fonts and formatting that were acceptable for the other printer are not supported by the printer that is currently selected. Excel is showing you the best that the current printer can do. If you still have access to the other printer, follow these steps to change it:

1. From the **File** menu, choose **Print**.

2. In the Printer section of the Print dialog box, open the drop-down list of printers in the Name box.

3. Select the desired printer from the list and click the **Preview** button to see if the fonts are now correct.

4. Click the **Print** button to print the worksheet, or the **Close** button to return to your worksheet.

If you no longer have the original printer available, you have to choose fonts and formatting that are supported by your current printer.

43 The manual page breaks I set do not work correctly.

You have scaled the worksheet to be a certain number of pages wide by a certain number of pages long. When you scale your worksheet, Excel ignores manual page breaks. If you want to use your manual page breaks, follow these steps:

1. From the **File** menu, choose **Page Setup**.

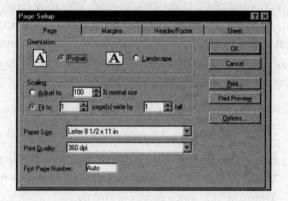

2. In the Page Setup dialog box, click on **Adjust to** in the Scaling box. You can also adjust the size if you wish.

3. Click **OK** to close the dialog box. Your manual page breaks now work correctly.

44 When I type .05 in a cell, Excel changes it to 5.00%.

You formatted the cell as a percentage. When you format cells as percentages, Excel automatically multiplies the numbers that you enter in the cells by 100 and adds a percent sign to them. If you don't want the cell formatted as a percentage, follow these steps to change the format:

1. Highlight the range of cells that you want to change.

2. Choose **Cells** from the **Format** menu.

3. Click on the **Number** tab in the Format Cells dialog box.

4. Choose the desired format from the **Category** box. If you want the number to appear as .05 you can use the **Number** or **General** category.

5. Click **OK** to apply the new formatting.

Calculation Problems

These problems involve creating and using formulas and functions in your worksheet.

45 Excel displays #NAME? in the cell when I enter a calculation.

There are two things that can cause this problem. First, make sure that you spelled the function correctly. If it isn't misspelled, you may have used a range name that doesn't exist. To check for valid range names, click on the arrow toward the left edge of the Formula bar to display a drop-down list of range names. If there are no names on the list, or the one you specified isn't there, you need to define the range you want to calculate. Follow these steps to define a range:

1. Highlight the range of cells you want to name.

2. Point to **Name** on the **Insert** menu and click on **Define**.

3. In the Define Name dialog box, type in a name for your range in the Names in Workbook box (make sure it's the same name that's in your function) and click **OK**. Your function now works correctly.

46 My calculation used to work fine, but now the result is #REF!.

More than likely, you deleted a cell that you needed in your calculation. Click on the cell that contains **#REF!**. Look up in the Formula bar and check the formula. The formula has **#REF!** where the deleted cell reference used to be (for example, =E10+#REF!). Edit the formula and replace the **#REF!** with the appropriate cell reference.

47 When I enter a formula, Excel displays #VALUE!.

Your formula contains a reference to a cell that is not the appropriate type for that calculation. A common cause for this error is trying to add a cell containing a number to a cell containing text (you may have accidentally included the column or row headings in your calculation). Click on the cell that contains your formula and ensure that one of the references in your formula does not contain text. Remove the reference to the cell containing text and press **Enter** to accept the change. Your formula should return the correct answer.

48 When I add a column of numbers, the result is incorrect.

You may have entered some of the entries in the range as text. Click on each cell in the column and look up in the Formula bar. If there is an apostrophe before your number, it is formatted as text. Excel won't use text in your calculations, so you need to remove the apostrophe to let Excel know you have a number in the cell.

49 When I try to add two cells, Excel displays B1+B2 instead of the answer.

You have forgotten to put an equal sign before your formula. You need to add this to let Excel know there is a formula in the cell. Edit the cell, insert the equal sign, and your calculation now works correctly.

50 Excel did not update the result of my calculation when I changed some cells in the range.

You probably have automatic calculation turned off. If you have a very large worksheet with many calculations, turning off automatic calculation can greatly improve the speed of Excel. To see the correct result press **F9**, and Excel recalculates the worksheet. If you want to turn automatic calculation back on, follow these steps:

1. Choose **Options** from the **Tools** menu and click on the **Calculation** tab.

2. Choose **Automatic** from the Calculation section of the Options dialog box.

3. Click **OK** to close the dialog box.

51 When I entered a formula I got an error message that said: Error in Formula.

There is an error in the formula you just entered. Excel tries to help you find the error by moving the cursor to the part of the formula that contains the error. If you're not sure what the problem is, click on the **Help** button in the error message dialog box. Excel gives you a list of common mistakes to look for, such as a wrong number of arguments in a function, invalid characters, missing operand (e.g., =2+3+), or an external reference without a workbook name (e.g., =!B2). These types of mistakes are frustrating to find because they usually involve a simple typing error. If you get tired of looking at the formula, remove the equal sign at the beginning of the formula and press **Enter**. This enables you to go on with something else and come back to the formula later. When you are ready to tackle the formula again, make sure you re-enter the equal sign.

52 When I entered a formula, Excel displayed the error message: Parentheses do not match.

Remember, when you use parentheses in a formula they must equal out. That is, for every open parenthesis there must be a closed parenthesis. Carefully check your formula to be sure you used the parentheses correctly. To have Excel help you find the missing parenthesis, click at the left edge of the formula in the Formula bar. Move the insertion point through the formula with the right arrow key. As you move through the formula, matching parentheses appear in bold. This may tip you off to where you need to add the missing parenthesis.

Charting Problems

This section deals with problems you may encounter while creating or editing a chart.

53 I created a bar chart, but I really wanted a pie chart.

It's easy to change the chart type after you create your chart. In fact you may change it several times to see which type you like the best. The easiest way to change the type is by using the Chart toolbox. Follow these steps to change the chart type:

1. Click in the chart to select it. The Chart toolbox opens (if you can't find the toolbox, it may have opened as a toolbar instead).

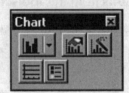

2. From the Chart toolbox, click on the **Chart Type** arrow.

3. Click on the desired chart type from the drop-down list to change your chart to that type.

54 When I add data to my worksheet, the chart does not show the new data.

When you add data to a range that is charted, you have to let Excel know you have added data to the range. The easiest way to do this is to run the ChartWizard again. Follow these steps to change the range using the ChartWizard:

1. Click on the chart to select it.

2. Click the **ChartWizard** button to start the ChartWizard.

3. Select the desired range to include the data you just added.

4. Click the **Finish** button. The chart now includes the new data.

55 Excel plotted my data backwards. The x-axis is where the y-axis should be.

Sometimes Excel chooses the axes differently than what you desire. The easiest way to change the axis orientation is to run the ChartWizard again. Follow these steps:

1. Click on the chart to select it.

2. Click the **ChartWizard** button to start the ChartWizard.

3. Click the **Next** button to use the same range.

4. Under Data Series in select the opposite option (for example, if it's set to **Columns**, select **Rows**).

5. Click **OK** to close the ChartWizard.

56 I changed some data in my worksheet, but my chart doesn't show the changes.

Excel is probably set for manual recalculation. You may have set calculation to manual if you are working on large worksheets that take a long time to calculate. Press the **F9** key to recalculate the worksheet; Excel updates your chart. If you want to change calculation back to automatic, follow these steps:

1. From the **Tools** menu, choose **Options**.

2. In the Options dialog box, click on the **Calculation** tab.

   3. In the Calculation area, click on **Automatic.**

   4. Click **OK** to close the dialog box.

57 When I delete a data point on my chart, Excel deletes the whole series.

There is no way to truly delete a data point on your chart. First, choose **Undo** from the **Edit** menu to get the series back. Now, you can either remove the data for the data point from the worksheet that your chart is made from, or you can hide the data point on your chart. Follow these steps to hide the data point:

   1. Double-click on the chart to edit it.

   2. Click on the data point that you want to hide.

   3. From the **Format** menu, choose **Selected Data Point**.

   4. Click the **Patterns** tab in the Format Data Point dialog box.

   5. If you are using a line chart, click on **None** in the Marker section. If you are using one of the other chart types, click on **None** in the Border and the Area sections.

   6. Click **OK** to close the dialog box. The data point is now hidden.

58 Now that I have my chart completed, the data is too hard to read. How can I make the chart bigger?

Excel makes it very easy to change the size of your chart. Single-click in the chart to activate it. You notice some little squares surrounding your chart. These are called *sizing handles*. Sizing handles enable you to easily change the size of an object. Just click on a sizing handle and drag it until your chart is the desired size. If you click a sizing handle on the edge, only that edge moves when you drag the handle. Clicking on a corner sizing handle enables you to change the size of two edges at once.

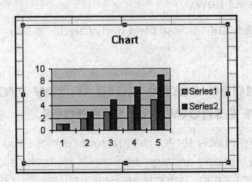

59 My chart doesn't have a legend.

To add a legend to your chart, double-click the chart (if it's embedded), or click on the sheet to activate your chart. In the Chart toolbox, click on the **Legend** button to display the legend. You probably need to rename the item in the legend to correctly describe your chart. To change the name of the series you need to edit the series. To do that follow these steps:

1. Double-click the desired series on the chart.

2. The Format Data Series dialog box opens. Click the **Name and Values** tab.

3. Type the desired name in the Name box.

4. Click **OK**. You see the name change in the legend.

5. Repeat steps 1 through 4 until you name all of the series.

60 I want my chart to have a logarithmic scale, but the scale is normal.

You can edit the scale on a chart after you create it. Follow these steps to edit the scale:

1. Double-click an embedded chart to edit it, or click the sheet tab if the chart is on a separate sheet.

2. Double-click on the axis that you wish to change to logarithmic scale.

3. The Format Axis dialog box opens. Click on the **Scale** tab.

4. Check the **Logarithmic Scale** check box and click **OK**.

61 I'm ready to scroll back to my data after editing an embedded chart, but the scroll bars are gone.

When you edit an embedded chart, Excel removes the scroll bars. To get the scroll bars back, click in a cell outside of the chart. This returns the scroll bars to their original positions.

Macro Problems

These are a few basic problems that occur when recording and running macros. This section also deals with the problems of assigning shortcut keys to macros and recording new steps in an existing macro.

62 I made some mistakes when I recorded a macro. Now the mistakes repeat every time I run the macro.

It's easy to make some mistakes while you are recording a macro (especially if it is a fairly long macro). There are two things you can do here. You can either record the macro again (not recommended if the macro is long), or you can edit the macro. Excel stores macros in a sheet called **Module**. The module sheet is usually at the end of the workbook. Click through the sheet tabs until you see the one called **Module**. When you are in the Module sheet, you see a list of macros. Find the one that matches the name of your macro and edit the mistakes. See "Record and Run an Easy Macro," p. [13TBD], for more information on macros.

63 I stopped recording the macro before I was finished. Do I have to record it all over again?

Fortunately, Excel doesn't make you waste all the time you spent recording your macro. If you accidentally stop recording before you finish, or if you just want to add some commands to the macro, it's easy to record them. Follow these steps to add commands to a macro:

1. From the **Tools** menu, choose **Macro**.

2. In the Macro dialog box, select the name of the macro you wish to add to from the list under Macro Name/Reference and click the **Edit** button.

3. Excel takes you to the macro's Module page. Click your cursor at the point where you want to add new commands to the macro. From the **Tools** menu, point to **Record Macro** and click on **Mark Position for Recording**.

4. Switch back to the sheet where you want to record the new steps. Position the active cell where you want to begin adding new steps.

5. From the **Tools** menu, point to **Record Macro** and click on **Record at Mark**.

6. Perform the desired commands. Remember to record only the new commands that you are adding to the macro. When you finish click on the **Stop** button.

The next time you run the macro, the new commands run also.

64 The shortcut key I assigned to my macro doesn't work.

First, make sure that the workbook you created the macro in is open. Next, follow these steps to make sure the shortcut key is assigned:

1. Choose **Macro** from the **Tools** menu.

2. In the Macro dialog box, select the name of the macro from the list under Macro Name/Reference and click the **Options** button.

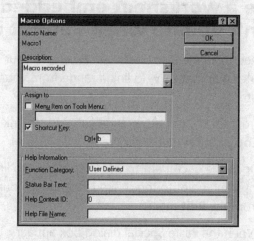

3. In the Assign to section, make sure that the **Shortcut Key** check box is checked and the appropriate shortcut key is defined. Remember CTRL+b is not the same as CTRL+SHIFT+B.

4. Click **OK**.

5. Repeat steps 1 through 4 for your other macros, checking that to make sure no other macro is assigned to the same shortcut key. If two macros have the same shortcut key, Excel runs the first macro assigned to the shortcut key.

6. Click **OK** to close the Macro dialog box.

65 After I recorded my macro, it ended up on a worksheet called Macro instead of Module.

You may also notice that the commands in the Macro sheet all start with an equal sign. You have inadvertently recorded your macro in the Excel 4.0 macro language. For compatibility, Excel enables you to record and run macros in the older Excel 4.0 macro language. If you want your macro be in Visual Basic, you have to record it again. Follow these steps to record a macro in Visual Basic:

1. From the **Tools** menu, point to **Record Macro** and click on **Record New Macro**.

2. Click the **Options** button in the Record New Macro dialog box.

3. In the Language section, click on **Visual Basic**.

4. Click **OK** to begin recording your macro.

Object Linking and Embedding Problems

These are the problems you may see when trying to share data between Excel and another application.

66 I have a worksheet embedded in a document, but it doesn't update when I edit it in Excel.

You need to create a link between Excel and your document. When you link an object, it updates automatically. To link a range from your worksheet to your document, follow these steps:

1. From Excel, select the range you wish to link to your document and click on the **Copy** button on the toolbar.

2. Open the document to which you want to link the Excel worksheet. Move the insertion point to the desired location in your document and choose **Paste Special** from the **Edit** menu.

3. When the Paste Special dialog box appears, choose **Microsoft Excel Worksheet Object** from the As box and click on **Paste Link**.

4. Click **OK**, and the selected range in your worksheet is linked to your document.

If you want to link the entire worksheet to your document, follow these steps:

1. Open the document and move the insertion point where you want to insert the Excel worksheet.

2. If you want to insert an entire worksheet that you already have made up, choose **Object** from the **Insert** menu and click on the **Create from File** tab.

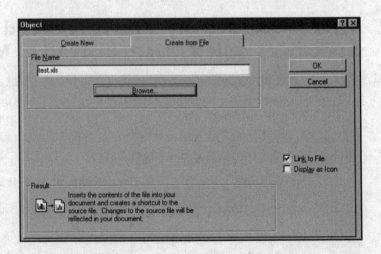

3. Enter the name and folder of your Excel file in the File Name box (if you don't remember where it is, click on the **Browse** button). Be sure to check the **Link to File** check box.

4. Click **OK**. This establishes the link between the two files. Any changes that you make to your worksheet in Excel are reflected in your document.

67 The link between Excel and my document used to work correctly, but now it doesn't.

Somehow the link is broken. This happens if you rename the Excel file or move it to a different directory. You can try to relink the files by doing the following:

1. Open the document that contains the link and choose **Links** from the **Edit** menu.

2. In the Links dialog box, click on the link you are having trouble with in the **Source File** box.

3. Click on the **Change Source** button and choose the name and folder where your worksheet is located.

4. Click the **Open** button.

5. Click the **Update Now** button to update the link. If the link is still not updated, you have to delete the Excel worksheet from your document and insert it again using the techniques in the previous Quick Fix.

68 After I copied a worksheet into PowerPoint, the data did not line up.

When you pasted the Excel data into PowerPoint you probably used the **Paste** command from the **Edit** menu. This will not work correctly because the Paste command tells PowerPoint that you are pasting text only. You need to let PowerPoint know that you are pasting Excel data. To do that, follow these steps:

1. Highlight the range of data in Excel and click on the **Copy** button in the toolbar.

2. Switch to PowerPoint, click where you want to insert your Excel data, and choose **Paste Special** from the **Edit** menu to bring up the Paste Special dialog box.

3. Click on **Microsoft Excel Worksheet Object** in the As box (it should already be highlighted) and click **OK**. Your worksheet is inserted as an object. If you need to edit the data, double-click in the middle of the Excel object.

69 When I double-click on a linked object, I get an error message telling me it cannot edit.

Whenever you double-click a linked object the *source* application (the application in which you created the object) opens to enable you to edit the object. If the source application doesn't open when you double-click the object, check the following:

- If the source application is open, close any open dialog boxes.

- Close all other open applications to make sure you have enough memory to open the source application.

- If you are on a network, check that someone else doesn't have the linked object open.

70 A co-worker gave me a worksheet with an embedded object, but I don't have the source application to edit the object.

If you don't have the application on your computer to edit the object, you may be able to convert the file into a format you can edit. Follow these steps to convert the object:

1. Click on the object to activate it.

2. Click on the **Edit** menu. At the bottom of the menu is an option for *file type* Object (for example, **Bitmap Image Object**). Point to this option and click **Convert**.

3. In the Convert dialog box, click on the desired format to which you want to convert the object.

4. Click **OK**.

If you are unable to find a format to convert to, you have to give the file back to your coworker to edit.

71 When I double-click an Excel object I embedded in another application, Excel doesn't open.

Excel is ignoring your request to open from another application (how rude!). This happens when the options have been set to ignore other applications. Follow these steps to change the options:

1. Open Excel and choose **Options** from the **Tools** menu.

2. In the Options dialog box, click on the **General** tab.

3. Uncheck the **Ignore Other Applications** check box.

4. Click **OK** to close the dialog box.

72 When I embed an object into Excel, the object appears as an icon.

This happens because you have Display as Icon checked when you embed the object. If you have a large object that you don't want to display all the time in your worksheet, it is useful to have the option to display it as an icon. When you double-click the icon, the source application opens to display the object. If you want to display the object instead of the icon, follow these steps:

1. Click on the icon to activate it.

2. Click on the **Edit** menu. At the bottom of the menu is an option for *file type* Object (for example, **Document Object**). Point to this option and click **Convert**.

3. In the Convert dialog box, uncheck the **Display as Icon** check box.

4. Click **OK** to close the dialog box. The object now appears in your worksheet.

File Problems

This section contains problems with creating and saving files. It also deals with obstacles you may encounter with read-only files, protected files, and file conversions.

73 I gave my Excel for Windows file to a friend using Excel for Macintosh, and now all the dates appear as four years later than they should be.

Excel for Windows uses the 1900 date system. If you enter January 1, 1900 a 1 is stored in memory. Excel for Macintosh uses the 1904 date system. That means when you enter January 2, 1904, Excel for Macintosh stores a 1 in its memory. Ordinarily, Excel is smart enough to convert the dates for you when switching between file formats, but if your friend is using Excel for Macintosh version 1.5 or earlier, you must take care of the conversion yourself. To do this, follow these steps:

1. Select **Options** from the **Tools** menu.

2. In the Options dialog box, click on the **Calculation** tab and check the **1904 Date System** check box.

3. Click **OK** to close the dialog box.

Unfortunately, Excel only fixes dates you enter after you have changed the date format. You have to reenter all the dates you already have in your worksheet to use them in your friend's program. In the future, be sure to change the date system before you start entering dates if you plan on sharing your worksheet with a friend.

74 I want to save my worksheet in a different format, but the format is not listed in the Save As Type box.

Check to be sure that the format you want to use is included with Excel. To check, click on **Answer Wizard** in the **Help** menu. In the first box, type in **file converters** and click the **Search** button. In the lower box under Tell Me About, click **File format converters supplied with Microsoft Excel** and click the **Display** button. If the converter you need is supplied with Excel, but it isn't listed in the Save As Type box, you probably didn't install it when you performed the installation. Follow these steps to install it now:

1. Close all open applications.

2. From the **Start** menu, point to **Settings** and click on **Control Panel**.

3. Double-click the **Add/Remove Programs** icon.

4. In the Add/Remove Programs Properties dialog box, click on the **Install/Uninstall** tab.

5. Click on **Microsoft Excel 7.0** and click on the **Add/Remove** button.

6. Windows tells you to insert the Excel disk 1. Insert the disk and click **OK**.

7. When the Setup dialog box opens, click the **Add/Remove** button.

8. In the Options box, click on **File and Graphics Converters,** and click the **Change Option** button.

9. In the Options box, click on **Spreadsheet Converters** and click the **Change Option** button.

10. In the Options box, check the check boxes next to the converters you wish to install. If you want to install them all, click the **Select All** button.

11. Click **OK**, click **OK** again, and then click **Continue**.

12. Setup installs the necessary components and tells you when it is finished. Click **OK**.

75 When I convert a worksheet from another program, some of the values are not the same.

Excel calculates some functions and operators differently than other spreadsheet programs. Luckily, you can change the way that Excel calculates these values. Follow these steps to fix the problem:

1. Choose **Options** from the **Tools** menu.

2. In the Options dialog box, click on the **Transition** tab.

3. In the Sheet Options area, check the **Transition Formula Evaluation** check box.

4. Click **OK** to close the dialog box.

5. Convert your file again. The values are now the same.

76 When I save my files, they always end up in the Excel folder. How can I change the default folder for my files?

By default, Excel saves the files you are working on in the Excel folder. This makes it very hard to find your files later because the Excel folder contains so many files. Therefore, it is a good idea to store your files in a different location. You can change the default location for your files by following these steps:

1. Choose **Options** from the **Tools** menu and click the **General** tab.

2. Type in the desired drive and folder in the Default File Location box.

3. Click **OK** to close the Options dialog box. The next time you save a file, Excel stores it in the folder you specified.

77 When I try to save a worksheet, I get a message telling me that the file is read-only.

You saved this document with the Read-Only Recommended option. Read-only means that you can look at the worksheet, but you can't save any changes that you make to the worksheet. If you need to keep changes, choose **Save As** from the **File** menu and save the worksheet under a different name or in another folder.

78 I can't find the file I want to open in the Open dialog box.

You probably saved the file in another folder than the one Excel uses for the default. The easiest way to find your file is to use the built-in file finder in the Open dialog box. Follow these steps:

1. From the **File** menu, choose **Open**.

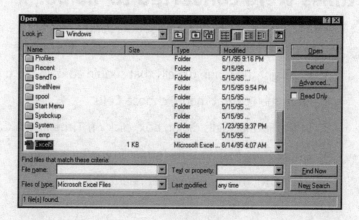

2. If you remember the file's name, type it in the File name box in the Open dialog box. If you don't remember the name, leave it blank.

3. If you want Excel to search all of the folders on the drive, click on the **Command and Settings** button and click on **Search Subfolders**. Excel searches the drive and lists all of the files that it finds.

4. Click on the file you wish to open and click on the **Open** button.

79 I want to open a Microsoft Access file in Excel, but I can't find Access in the Files of type box in the Open dialog box.

Excel does not have a built-in converter for Microsoft Access. Fortunately, Access does have a built-in converter for Excel. Follow these steps to convert an Access table to Excel:

1. Start Access and open the database that contains the table or query you wish to convert. Click on the **Tables** or **Queries** tab and select the name of table or query to export.

2. From the **File** menu, choose **Save As/Export**.

3. In the Save As dialog box, choose **To an external File or Database** option and click **OK**.

4. In the Save *filename* In dialog box, choose **Microsoft Excel** from the Save as Type drop-down list.

5. Choose a name and a folder for your exported table or query and click **Export**.

6. Open Excel and click on **Open** from the **File** menu.

7. Select the file that you just exported from Access and click **Open**.

80 After I exported a Microsoft Access table, all of the times were converted to 1/0/00.

Microsoft Access and Excel format dates and times differently. Luckily, there is an easy way to convert them back to the time format. Follow these steps:

1. Highlight the range of cells that should contain the times.

2. From the **Format** menu, choose **Cells**.

3. In the Format Cells dialog box, click on **Time** in the Category box.

4. Choose the desired time format in the Type box.

5. Click **OK**. Your times now appear correctly.

81 When I try to save my worksheet, Excel tells me that the file is locked.

This must be your unlucky day. It's pretty hard to get this error because circumstances must be exactly right (actually wrong) to get this error. First, you have to be working in a Shared List (a Shared List is a worksheet that has been set up to allow multiple users over a network to work on a worksheet at the same time). Second, you must have this particular worksheet open in a Quick View window (Quick View is a Windows 95 feature that enables you to take a quick glance at a file without opening it). Third, you have to try to save the worksheet. It may seem like the planets and stars are lined up against you, but the fix for this is easy. Simply switch back to the Quick View window and click on the **Close** button. Now, when you save your worksheet, you won't have any problems. In the future, you may want to stay away from those black cats.

Printing Problems

If you are having problems with printing your Excel file, look in this section.

82 The whole worksheet prints when I try to print an embedded chart.

To print a chart that is embedded in your worksheet, double-click the chart and choose **Print** from the **File** menu. Check that **Selected Chart** is highlighted in the Print What section of the Print dialog box. Click **OK**, and your chart prints.

83 All the pages are numbered 1 when I print a report from Report Manager.

Even though it seems obvious, you have to let Report Manager know that you want to number the pages continuously. To do this, follow these steps:

1. Choose **Report Manager** from the **View** menu.

2. In the Report Manager dialog box, choose the desired report from the **Reports** box and click the **Edit** button.

3. At the bottom of the Edit Report dialog box, check the **Use Continuous Page Numbers** check box and click **OK**.

4. Click on the **Print** button in the Print Report dialog box to print out your report using continuous page numbers.

84 When I select multiple print areas, only one prints.

You need to let Excel know that you are selecting more than one print area. To do this you have to type a comma between the ranges when you are entering them in. Follow these steps to print multiple print areas:

1. From the **File** menu, choose **Page Setup**.

2. In the Page Setup dialog box, click on the **Sheet** tab and click in the **Print Area** box.

3. Click in the title bar of the Page Setup dialog box and drag it out of the way, so you can see the worksheet.

4. Click in one corner of the first area and drag a box around the desired print area.

5. You see a range designated in the **Print Area** box. Type a comma at the end of the range.

6. Repeat steps 4 and 5 until you select all of the desired print areas.

7. Click **OK** to close the dialog box.

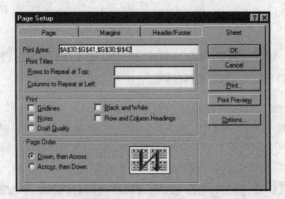

85 When I print my worksheet, the column and row headings print on the first page but not on the rest of the pages.

It is difficult to read a report if the column and row headings are not included on all of the pages. You have to keep turning back to page 1 to see what the headings are. If you are printing a multiple page worksheet and you want the column and row headings to be on all the pages, follow these steps:

1. From the **File** menu, choose **Page Setup**.

2. In the Page Setup dialog box, click on the **Sheet** tab.

3. Click in the **Print Area** box and click on the title bar of the dialog box and drag it out of the way. Click in the upper left corner of your desired print area and drag a box around the area you wish to print.

4. Under **Print Titles** click in the **Rows to Repeat at Top** box. Select the row(s) in your worksheet that contains the column headings.

5. If the number of columns spans across more than one page you may also want to include row headings on the subsequent pages. Click in the **Columns to Repeat at Left** box and select the column(s) in your worksheet that contains the row headings.

6. Click the **Print Preview** button to see what the printed worksheet will look like.

7. Click the **Print** button to print the worksheet, or the **Close** button to return to your work.

86 When I print my worksheet the gridlines do not print.

By default, the lines that define the cells on your screen, the *gridlines*, do not print. The gridlines are only there to show you where each cell starts and stops. If you want to include the gridlines in your printout, follow these steps:

1. From the **File** menu, choose **Page Setup**.

2. In the Page Setup dialog box, click on the **Sheet** tab. (See the previous Quick Fix #84 for a picture of the Page Setup dialog box.)

3. In the Print box, check the **Gridlines** check box.

4. Click the **Print** button to print your worksheet. The gridlines print along with your data.

87 When I print a chart on my laser printer, only half of it prints.

Your laser printer does not have enough internal memory to print a full page graphic. The best way to fix this problem is to add memory to your printer (consult your printer documentation for information). If you don't have the time or the money to upgrade the memory, you can either reduce the size of the chart or lower the resolution. See Quick Fix #58 to change the size of the chart. Follow these steps to change the resolution:

1. From the **File** menu, choose **Page Setup**.

2. In the Page Setup dialog box, click the **Options** button.

3. Click on the **Graphics** tab.

4. Open the drop-down list in the Resolution box, select a lower resolution, and click **OK**.

5. Click the **Print** button to print your chart.

If the entire chart still doesn't print, repeat steps 1 through 5 until the chart prints correctly. If you selected the lowest resolution, but the chart still doesn't print completely, you have to reduce the size of the chart.

88 When I print my worksheet, the embedded object doesn't print.

The object is not formatted to print. This is useful if you want an object in your worksheet for reference, but you don't want it to be printed. To format the object to print, follow these steps:

1. Click on the object to activate it.

2. From the **Format** menu, click on **Object**.

3. In the Format Object dialog box, click on the **Properties** tab.

4. Check the **Print Object** check box. The object now prints the next time you print your worksheet.

Miscellaneous Problems

If you can't find your problem in one of the other sections, look here. Problems with sorting, sheet protection, displays, hidden rows, and cell notes are examples of what you will find in this section.

89 I can't find the What's New screen when I open Excel.

The What's New screen gives a great overview of the new features in Excel. Follow these steps to open it again:

1. Choose **Answer Wizard** from the **Help** menu.

2. In the Help Topics dialog box, type in **What's New** in the first box and click the **Search** button.

3. From the list of topics under **Tell Me About**, select **What's New in...Microsoft Excel 95**.

4. Click the **Display** button to open the What's New screen.

90 The column headings are sorted with my data.

There are two ways to fix this problem. The easiest way is to select the range of cells you want to sort (but don't include the headings) and click on the **Sort Ascending** or **Sort Descending** button.

Sort Ascending button   Sort Descending button

Another way is to do the following:

1. Select **Sort** from the **Data** menu.

2. In the **My List Has** section of the Sort dialog box, click on **Header Row**.

3. Click **OK** to close the dialog box and sort the data.

91 When I sort a list, Excel only sorts part of the list.

If you click the mouse somewhere in your list and click on one of the Sort buttons, Excel figures out that you want to sort the entire list. If you decide to highlight the list before you sort, you need to make sure that you highlight the entire list. Otherwise, Excel only sorts the range of cells that you select. To keep the guesswork out of the sorting process, it is safer to highlight the range of cells that you wish to sort. Now, press the **Sort Ascending** or **Sort Descending** button on the toolbar to sort the list.

92 When I sort data, the sort order is different than it was in previous versions of Excel.

Windows 95 and Windows NT use a different order for sorting certain characters than Windows 3.x does (don't ask me why Microsoft suddenly decided to sort differently). Obviously, A still comes before B, but some characters do not end up where they used to. The following table is a summary of how special characters are sorted (ascending):

Excel 95	Previous versions of Excel		Excel 95	Previous versions of Excel
-	!		,	,
!	#		-	-
#	$		?	?
$	%		@	=
%	&		\	?
&	(		^	@
(	)		_	\
)	*		+	^
*	+		=	_

As you can see, the order is not that much different, but it is confusing if you're used to seeing the list sorted in a previous version of Excel. Another thing to keep in mind is that Windows 95 and Windows NT sort capital and lowercase letters differently. If you are performing a case sensitive search, an ascending search in a previous version of Excel results with the capital letters above the lowercase letters. Excel 95 has the lowercase letters above the capital letters.

93 When I try to protect my worksheet the Protect Sheet option is grayed out.

You are working on a new workbook that you haven't saved yet. Save the workbook by clicking on the **Save** button. Once you save the file, follow these steps to protect your worksheet:

1. From the **Tools** menu, point to **Protection**, and click on **Protect Sheet**.

2. In the Protect Sheet dialog box, type in a password in the Password box if you like.

3. Click **OK**, and Excel protects your worksheet.

94 I can't find the worksheet tabs at the bottom of my workbook.

Somehow the option to display the worksheet tabs has been turned off. Maybe you or someone else turned it off to display more of your worksheet at once. Follow these steps to turn them back on:

1. From the **Tools** menu, choose **Options**.

2. Click on the **View** tab in the Options dialog box.

3. Under **Window Options,** check the **Sheet Tabs** check box.

4. Click **OK** to close the dialog box.

95 The row and column headings do not appear on the screen.

You have inadvertently turned off the row and column headings option. Follow these steps to turn them back on:

1. Choose **Options** from the **Tools** menu.

2. In the Options dialog box, click on the **View** tab.

3. Under Window Options, select the **Row & Column Headers** check box.

4. Click **OK** to close the dialog box. Excel restores your column and row headings.

96 During spell check, I accidentally added an incorrectly spelled word to the custom dictionary. How can I remove it?

This is a real problem because every time you run the spell checker it no longer alerts you if you misspelled this word. Fortunately, it's easy to edit the custom dictionary.

The custom dictionary is simply a file with a list of words in it. To remove the incorrectly spelled word, all you need to do is edit the file. Follow these steps to edit the custom dictionary using Notepad:

1. From the **Start** menu, point to **Programs**, point to **Accessories**, and click on **Notepad**.

2. In Notepad, click on **Open** from the **File** menu.

3. Open the drop-down list in the Files of type box and choose **All Files (*.*)**. The custom dictionary does not have a TXT extension, but this option allows it to display in the box.

4. Double-click on the folder that contains your custom dictionary to open the folder. The dictionary usually resides in the C:\WINDOWS\MSAPPS\PROOF folder.

5. Click on your custom dictionary. It is usually called CUSTOM.DIC (the .DIC may not display in the window).

6. Click on the **Open** button to open the dictionary.

7. You see a single column of words that make up your custom dictionary. Find the incorrectly spelled word and delete it.

8. Choose **Save** from the **File** menu to save the changes you just made.

9. Click on the **Close** button to close Notepad.

97 One of my columns is missing. They are labeled A, B, D, E, and so on.

Your column is hidden. Hidden columns (or rows) are very useful for adding data to your worksheet that you don't want to print, or you don't need to see all of the time. When you hide a column (or row), all you do is change the column width (or row height) to zero. The easiest way to unhide the column (or row) is to follow these steps:

1. Highlight the columns (or rows) that surround the hidden column (or row).

2. From the **Format** menu, point to **Column** (or **Row**) and click on **Unhide**.

98 I just added a note to a cell, but it doesn't display when I move the mouse pointer over the cell.

Ordinarily your notes appear right under the cell when you hold the mouse pointer over the cell. Make sure that you leave the pointer on the cell for a few seconds. If the notes still do not appear, you have them turned off. Follow these steps to view the notes:

1. From the **Tools** menu, choose **Options**.

2. In the Options dialog box, click on the **View** tab.

3. In the **Show** area, check the **Note Indicator** check box.

4. Click **OK** to close the dialog box.

You notice that there is a little red square in the upper right corner of the cells that contain notes. Hold your mouse pointer over the cell to display the note.

99 I have a note in my cell, but I can't edit it.

In some older versions of Excel, you double-clicked on a cell to edit the note. In Excel for Windows 95, double-clicking a cell enables you to edit the cell's contents. If you want to edit the note, follow these steps:

1. Click on the cell that contains the note you want to edit.

2. Choose **Note** from the **Insert** menu.

3. Edit the note in the Text Note box in the Cell Note dialog box.

4. Click **OK** to close the dialog box.

100 I just upgraded from Lotus 1-2-3. Why doesn't the slash key bring up help for 1-2-3 users?

Excel has a neat utility to help previous users of Lotus 1-2-3, but you have to have it turned on. Follow these steps:

1. From the **Tools** menu, choose **Options**.

2. Click on the **Transition** tab in the Options dialog box.

3. In the **Settings** area click on the **Lotus 1-2-3 Help** option. If you want to use the same keys as Lotus 1-2-3 to move around in the worksheet, check the **Transition Navigation Keys** check box.

4. Click **OK** to close the dialog box.

Now, when you press the slash key, the Help for Lotus 1-2-3 dialog box opens.

101 All of the records in my database do not appear.

You probably have a *filter* active. A filter enables you to display records that meet a certain criteria. For example, if you have a database of customer addresses, you can set a filter to only display the customers in Indiana (for more information on setting filters, look in "Find, Replace, Sort, and Filter Information," p. 73). To see all of the records, point to **Filter** in the **Data** menu, and click on **Show All**.

PART 4

Handy Reference

This part includes some reference material you'll find helpful when you "can't remember." It identifies all the screen parts of the opening Excel screen and includes common mouse pointer shapes you'll see while using Excel as well as shortcuts for selecting cells and moving around a worksheet. Last, it includes some examples of Excel functions you'll commonly use.

Parts of the Excel Screen

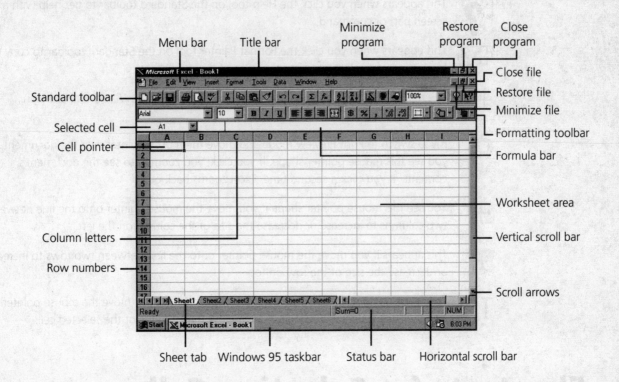

Labels around the screen:
- Menu bar
- Title bar
- Minimize program
- Restore program
- Close program
- Standard toolbar
- Selected cell
- Cell pointer
- Column letters
- Row numbers
- Close file
- Restore file
- Minimize file
- Formatting toolbar
- Formula bar
- Worksheet area
- Vertical scroll bar
- Scroll arrows
- Sheet tab
- Windows 95 taskbar
- Status bar
- Horizontal scroll bar

Common Mouse Pointer Shapes

The table in this section contains common mouse pointer shapes you'll see while working in Excel. Next to each shape in this table, you see a brief explanation of what the shape means or what you may be doing in Excel if you see the shape. If appropriate, the table indicates the action you need to take if you see a particular shape.

 Please wait while Excel processes.

 This mouse pointer shape appears when you move the mouse pointer into the menu bar, onto a menu command, onto a tool on a toolbar, or to the edge of a selected cell or range you can drag to move.

 This appears when you move the mouse pointer over the worksheet portion of the Excel screen.

 This means you are copying a cell's contents by dragging.

This mouse pointer shape means you are moving a cell's contents by dragging.

 This appears when you click the Help tool on the Standard toolbar to get help with a screen part or command.

 This appears when you click the Format Painter tool on the Standard toolbar to copy the formatting of a selection to another area of the worksheet.

 The mouse pointer changes to this when you click the ChartWizard tool to begin creating a chart.

 If you switch to Print Preview mode and move the mouse pointer over the document, you see this mouse pointer shape. If you click, you zoom in to see the document's contents. If you click a second time, Excel zooms back out.

 You see this mouse pointer shape if you move the mouse pointer onto the line between two columns to increase or decrease the size of the column on the left.

 This appears if you move the mouse pointer onto the line between two rows to increase or decrease the size of the row on top.

 This insertion point mouse pointer shape appears when you move the mouse pointer into the Formula bar. If you click, you can edit the contents of the selected cell.

Shortcuts for Selecting Cells

In this section, you find several tables that contain shortcuts for selecting cells. In the first table, you find shortcuts for selecting information using both the mouse and the keyboard. In the second table, you find shortcuts to change a selection. In the third table, you learn how End mode affects selecting cells. In the fourth table, you learn how to select cells with special characteristics. In the fifth table, you find shortcuts to select chart elements.

Selecting Cells

To Select This Item	Take This Action
A single cell	Click the cell, or press the arrow keys to move to the cell.
A range of cells	Click the first cell of the range and then drag to the last.
Non-adjacent cells or cell ranges	Select the first cell or range of cells and then hold down Ctrl and select the other cells or ranges.
A large range of cells	Click the first cell in the range and then hold down Shift and click the last cell in the range. You can scroll to make the last cell visible.
An entire row	Click the row heading, or press Shift+Spacebar.

To Select This Item	Take This Action
An entire column	Click the column heading, or press Ctrl+Spacebar.
Adjacent rows or columns	Drag across the row or column headings. Or select the first row or column and then hold down Shift and select the last row or column.
Non-adjacent rows or columns	Select the first row or column, and then hold down Ctrl and select the other rows or columns.
All cells of a worksheet	Click the button at the upper-left corner of the worksheet where the row and column headings intersect, or press Ctrl+A.

In general, when you want to change the current selection, hold down the Shift key and click the last cell you want to include in the new selection. The rectangular range between the active cell and the cell you click becomes the new selection.

Changing a Selection of Cells

Press the Following Keys	To Take This Action
Shift+arrow key	Extend or shrink the selection by one cell.
Ctrl+Shift+arrow key	Extend or shrink the selection to the edge of the current data region.
Shift+Home	Extend the selection to the beginning of the row.
Ctrl+Shift+Home	Extend the selection to the beginning of the worksheet.
Ctrl+Shift+End	Extend or shrink the selection to the last cell in the worksheet (lower-right corner).
Shift+Backspace	Collapse the selection to the active cell.
Shift+Page Down	Extend the selection down one screen.
Shift+Page Up	Extend the selection up one screen.
Ctrl+Shift+*	Select the current region.
Ctrl+Shift+Spacebar	With an object selected, select all objects on a sheet.

To work in END Mode, press the End key on your keyboard. You need to press End, as the first step, each time you want to take one of actions listed below.

Selecting Using END Mode

Press	To Take This Action
End, Shift+arrow key	Extend the selection to the end of the data block in the direction of the arrow.
End, Shift+Home	Extend the selection to the last cell in the worksheet (lower-right corner).
End, Shift+Enter	Extend the selection to the last cell in the current row (unavailable if you've selected the Transition Navigation Keys checkbox).

Select Cells with Special Characteristics Using Shortcut Keys

Press These Key Combinations	To Take This Action
Ctrl+Shift+?	Select all cells that contain notes.
Ctrl+/	Select the entire array to which the active cell belongs.
Ctrl+[	Select only cells that are directly referred to by formulas in the selection.
Ctrl+Shift+{	Select all cells that are directly or indirectly referred to by formulas in the selection.
Ctrl+]	Select only cells with formulas that refer directly to the active cell.
Ctrl+Shift+}	Select all cells with formulas that refer directly or indirectly to the active cell.

Some items, such as data series and data labels, are grouped together. First select the entire group and then select an individual item within the group.

Selecting Chart Items Using Shortcut Keys

Press These Keys	To Take This Action
Down arrow	Select the previous group of items.
Up arrow	Select the next group of items.
Right arrow	Select the next item within the group.
Left arrow	Select the previous item within the group.

Shortcuts for Moving Around a Worksheet

Use the following keyboard shortcuts to move in worksheets and workbooks.

Moving Around a Worksheet or Workbook

Press These Keys	To Take This Action
Any arrow key	Move one cell in a given direction.
Ctrl+ arrow key	Move, in the direction of the arrow key, to the edge of the current data region.
Tab	Move between unlocked cells in a protected worksheet.

Press These Keys	To Take This Action
Home	Move to the beginning of the row.
Ctrl+Home	Move to the beginning of the worksheet.
Ctrl+End	Move to the last cell in the worksheet (in the lower-right corner).
Page Down	Move one screen down.
Page Up	Move one screen up.
Alt+Page Down	Move one screen to the right.
Alt+Page Up	Move one screen to the left.
Ctrl+Page Down	Move to the next sheet in the workbook.
Ctrl+Page Up	Move to the previous sheet in the workbook.
Ctrl+F6	Move to the next workbook.
Ctrl+Shift+F6	Move to the previous workbook.
F6	Move to the next pane.
Shift+F6	Move to the previous pane.

To work in END Mode, press the End key on your keyboard. You need to press End, as the first step, each time you want to take one of actions listed below.

Moving Around a Worksheet or Workbook Using END Mode

Press These Keys	To Take This Action
End, arrow key	Move by one block of data within a row or column.
End, Home	Move to the last cell in the worksheet (in the lower-right corner).
End, Enter	Move to the last cell in the current row (unavailable if you've selected the Transition Navigation Keys checkbox).

Once you select cells, you can use the key combinations listed below to move within the selection.

Moving Around within a Selection

Press These Keys	To Take This Action
Enter	Move from top to bottom within the selection, or move to the right one cell if only one row is selected.
Shift+Enter	Move from bottom to top within the selection, or move to the left one cell if only one row is selected.
Tab	Move from left to right within the selection.
Shift+Tab	Move from right to left within the selection.
Ctrl+. (period)	Move clockwise to the next corner of the selection.
Ctrl+Alt+Right arrow	Move to the right between non-adjacent selections.
Ctrl+Alt+Left arrow	Move to the left between non-adjacent selections.

Commonly Used Functions

Part I covered several different functions available in Excel. In "Calculate a Total with the AutoSum Tool," page 152, you learned how to calculate a sum of a column of numbers using the AutoSum tool on the Standard toolbar. You also learned how to calculate an average and a net present value when you learned to use the Function Wizard. In "Use Database Functions to Analyze a Data List," page 189, you used database functions to count records in a data table, find the largest and smallest record, find a total and calculate an average.

As you may have noticed while using the Function Wizard, Excel sorts functions into categories, and there are hundreds of different functions available for you to use—far more than this book covers. This section presents you with the tools you need to understand how to set up a function for yourself and to explore all of the functions available to you.

Every function consists of the function name and at least one *argument*, which appears in parentheses after the function name. An argument is a parameter you want Excel to use when it calculates the function. To give you a taste of what's available, this section shows you the syntax for several common functions and explains the syntax.

Excel provides an excellent summary, in Help, of every function available to you, the purpose of the function, proper syntax for that function, and, often, examples of the function. You can find this information by following these steps:

1. Open the **Help** menu and choose **Microsoft Excel Help Topics**.

2. In the dialog box that appears, click the **Index** tab.

3. In the first text box, type **functions**. You see a list of topics related to "functions."

4. Double-click the worksheet function index. You see the Help window appear (see the next figure).

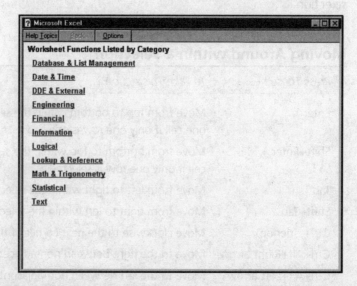

5. From the list in the window, click on the category in which you are interested. Excel displays a list of the functions in that category and their purpose (see the following figure).

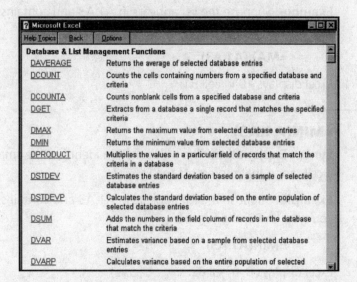

6. Click a function to see the syntax of the function and an explanation of the arguments of the function (see the next figure).

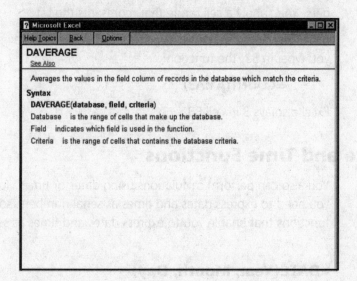

Statistical Functions

We're going to start with three functions for which you learned the database counterparts in "Use Database Functions to Analyze a Data List," p. 189: MAX, MIN, and COUNT. You also learned, in "Use the AutoCalculate Feature," p. 151, that you can use the AutoCalculate feature to make "quick" answers to these functions appear in Excel's status bar. These three functions fall into the Statistical category.

=MAX(Cell Range)

Syntax Explanation. The MAX function identifies the largest value in a list. You supply a cell range that represents the list.

Example. Suppose the list appears in A1:A3 and contains the numbers 8, 9, and 10. If you type, in B1, the function:

> **=MAX(A1:A3)**

Excel displays 10 in cell B1.

=MIN(A1:A3)

Syntax Explanation. The MIN function identifies the smallest value in a list. You supply a cell range that represents the list.

Example. Suppose the list appears in A1:A3 and contains the numbers 8, 9, and 10. If you type, in B2, the function:

> **=MIN(A1:A3)**

Excel displays 8 in cell B2.

=COUNT(Cell Range)

Syntax Explanation. The COUNT function counts the cells in a list that contain numbers. You supply a cell range that represents the list.

Example. Suppose the list appears in A1:A3 and contains the numbers 8, 9, and 10. If you type, in B3, the function:

> **=COUNT(A1:A3)**

Excel displays 3 in cell B3.

Date and Time Functions

You also can perform calculations using dates or times. To perform most calculations, you need to express dates and times as serial numbers, so we'll show you the two Excel functions that enable you to express dates and times as serial numbers.

=DATE(Year, Month, Day)

Syntax Explanation. The DATE function tells Excel to use the serial number to represent a year, month, and day that you supply. Once you convert a date to a serial number, Excel can perform math on dates. For example, Excel can calculate the number of days between two dates.

Example. Suppose you type the following functions in A1 and A2 respectively:

> =DATE(1995,9,4)
>
> =DATE(1995,10,14)

In Cell A3, you type the formula **=A2-A1**. Excel displays, in cell A3, 40.

=TIME(Hour, Minute, Second)

Syntax Explanation. The TIME function tells Excel to use the serial number to represent an hour, minute, and second that you supply. Once you convert a time to a serial number, Excel can perform math on times. For example, Excel can calculate the amount of time between two times.

Example. Suppose you type the following functions in A1 and A2 respectively:

> =TIME(23,0,0)
>
> =TIME(10,46,0)

In Cell A3, you type the formula **=A1-A2**. Excel displays, in cell A3, 12:14 p.m.

Text Functions

Text functions are useful. For example, you may want to convert all the text you typed in a certain range to uppercase.

=UPPER(text)

Syntax Explanation. The UPPER function converts text to uppercase. You can type the text in the argument (enclosed in parentheses), or you can use a cell reference in the argument that contains text.

Example. Suppose A1 contains the word **Hello**. You set up the following UPPER function in B1:

> =UPPER(A1)

Excel displays, in B1, the word HELLO.

Or suppose you want to place the word **Hello** in cell C1. Use the following UPPER function in C1:

> =UPPER("hello")

Logical Functions

IF(Test comparison,True Value, False Value)

Syntax Explanation. You use an IF function to determine if certain conditions are true or false. In an IF statement, you supply a condition you want Excel to test, an answer you want Excel to display if the result of the test is true, and an answer you want Excel to display if the result of the test is false.

Example. Suppose A1 contains the number 30. You set up the following IF statement in B1:

=IF(A1>45,TRUE,FALSE)

Because 30 is less than 45, Excel displays, in cell B1, FALSE.

Index

D

X-Y-Z

Complete and Return this Card
for a *FREE* Computer Book Catalog

Thank you for purchasing this book! You have purchased a superior computer book written expressly for your needs. To continue to provide the kind of up-to-date, pertinent coverage you've come to expect from us, we need to hear from you. Please take a minute to complete and return this self-addressed, postage-paid form. In return, we'll send you a free catalog of all our computer books on topics ranging from word processing to programming and the internet.

Mr. ☐   Mrs. ☐   Ms. ☐   Dr. ☐

Name (first) [ ] (M.I.) ☐   (last) [ ]

Address [ ]

City [ ]   State [ ]   Zip [ ] [ ]

Phone [ ]   Fax [ ] [ ]

Company Name [ ]

E-mail address [ ]

1. Please check at least (3) influencing factors for purchasing this book.

Front or back cover information on book .... ☐
Special approach to the content .... ☐
Completeness of content .... ☐
Author's reputation .... ☐
Publisher's reputation .... ☐
Book cover design or layout .... ☐
Index or table of contents of book .... ☐
Price of book .... ☐
Special effects, graphics, illustrations .... ☐
Other (Please specify): _____ ☐

2. How did you first learn about this book?

Saw in Macmillan Computer Publishing catalog .... ☐
Recommended by store personnel .... ☐
Saw the book on bookshelf at store .... ☐
Recommended by a friend .... ☐
Received advertisement in the mail .... ☐
Saw an advertisement in: _____ ☐
Read book review in: _____ ☐
Other (Please specify): _____ ☐

3. How many computer books have you purchased in the last six months?

This book only .... ☐   3 to 5 books .... ☐
2 books .... ☐   More than 5 .... ☐

4. Where did you purchase this book?

Bookstore .... ☐
Computer Store .... ☐
Consumer Electronics Store .... ☐
Department Store .... ☐
Office Club .... ☐
Warehouse Club .... ☐
Mail Order .... ☐
Direct from Publisher .... ☐
Internet site .... ☐
Other (Please specify): _____ ☐

5. How long have you been using a computer?

☐ Less than 6 months   ☐ 6 months to a year
☐ 1 to 3 years   ☐ More than 3 years

6. What is your level of experience with personal computers and with the subject of this book?

	With PCs	With subject of book
New	☐	☐
Casual	☐	☐
Accomplished	☐	☐
Expert	☐	☐

Source Code ISBN: 0-7897-0459-5

7. Which of the following best describes your job title?

Administrative Assistant .... ☐
Coordinator .... ☐
Manager/Supervisor .... ☐
Director .... ☐
Vice President .... ☐
President/CEO/COO .... ☐
Lawyer/Doctor/Medical Professional .... ☐
Teacher/Educator/Trainer .... ☐
Engineer/Technician .... ☐
Consultant .... ☐
Not employed/Student/Retired .... ☐
Other (Please specify): _____ ☐

8. Which of the following best describes the area of the company your job title falls under?

Accounting .... ☐
Engineering .... ☐
Manufacturing .... ☐
Operations .... ☐
Marketing .... ☐
Sales .... ☐
Other (Please specify): _____ ☐

Comments: _____
_____
_____
_____

9. What is your age?

Under 20 .... ☐
21-29 .... ☐
30-39 .... ☐
40-49 .... ☐
50-59 .... ☐
60-over .... ☐

10. Are you:

Male .... ☐
Female .... ☐

11. Which computer publications do you read regularly? (Please list)

_____
_____
_____
_____
_____
_____
_____
_____

Fold here and scotch-tape to mail.

BUSINESS REPLY MAIL
FIRST-CLASS MAIL PERMIT NO. 9918 INDIANAPOLIS IN

POSTAGE WILL BE PAID BY THE ADDRESSEE

ATTN MARKETING
MACMILLAN COMPUTER PUBLISHING
MACMILLAN PUBLISHING USA
201 W 103RD ST
INDIANAPOLIS IN 46290-9042

NO POSTAGE
NECESSARY
IF MAILED
IN THE
UNITED STATES